Musée cantonal des
Beaux-Arts de Lausanne
Guide to the Collection

Bernard Fibicher
Catherine Lepdor
Camille Lévêque-Claudet
Laurence Schmidlin
Nicole Schweizer
Camille de Alencastro

MUSÉE CANTONAL
DES BEAUX-ARTS
LAUSANNE

Scheidegger & Spiess

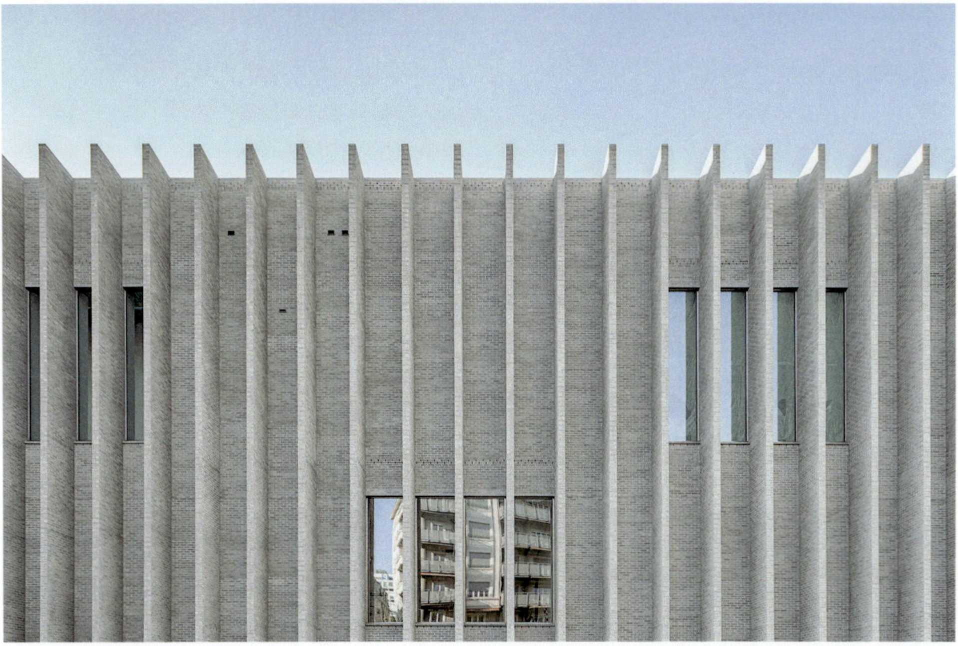

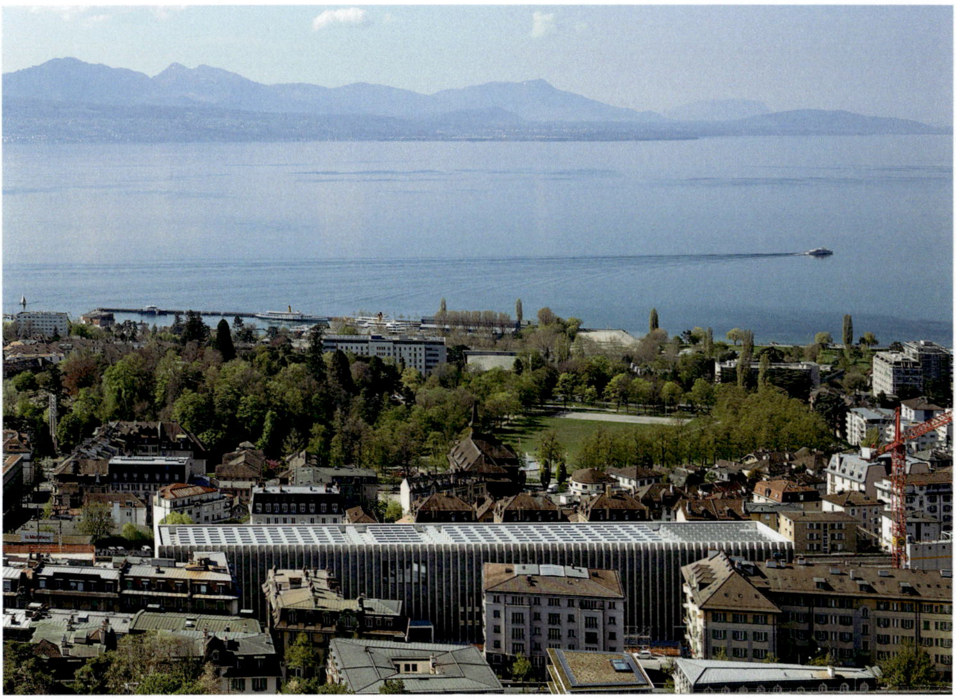

Table of contents

The Musée cantonal des Beaux-Arts de Lausanne and Its Collection

All public art collections have a core collection that reflects their community's earliest efforts to bring together a set of works to please the eye and enlighten the mind. In Lausanne, this was a small group of seventeenth-century Italian paintings collected by the neo-classical landscape painter Louis Ducros, together with several hundred of his own drawings and watercolours that he had brought back to his native Vaud after a career in Italy [n. 7, 8, 14]. Having lived in Rome, where private galleries and the Vatican treasures were open to the public, he tried – but failed – to interest the local community in purchasing the works to create a fledgling art collection for teaching purposes. However, a civic subscription was launched after his death to avoid breaking up the collection. In 1816, it was bought by the Canton of Vaud, reflecting the young state's ambition to establish the fine arts as a pillar of its new independence from the domination of Bern and joining the Swiss Confederation in 1803.

The works in the Ducros collection were first shown in the canton's small general museum, established in 1818, just a stone's throw from Lausanne Cathedral, where they were used as models for a drawing school in the same building. The head of the drawing school, the painter Marc-Louis Arlaud – another Vaud native – was the first to develop a more ambitious vision for the collection. He had studied with Jacques-Louis David in Paris, where the Louvre's royal collections were now open to the general public, and he was also inspired by the example of Geneva, where the Musée Rath opened in 1826, to donate a large sum of money to build new premises for the drawing school and a museum dedicated to the fine arts. Co-financed by the City of Lausanne and the Canton of Vaud, the Musée Arlaud was inaugurated in 1841 on Place de la Riponne [fig. 1]. Arlaud gifted the new museum his own paintings and his collection of works from the French and Dutch Schools, and commissioned casts of antique sculptures.

In the latter half of the nineteenth century, successive curators made a number of significant acquisitions. Private individuals pleased with the new museum supported the venture by donating or bequeathing artworks. The municipal authorities gifted it a major Renaissance work, François Dubois's *Le Massacre de la*

Saint-Barthélemy [n. 3]. In an age when regional and national identities were undergoing consolidation, the collection resolutely focused on contemporary artists from French-speaking Switzerland, purchasing and commissioning major paintings by François Diday [n. 19] and Alexandre Calame [n. 20], both Genevan artists working to build a Swiss School of landscape painting. It also acquired paintings by Benjamin Vautier and Frédéric Rouge, François Bocion's views of Lake Geneva, and Eugène Burnand's monumental canvases depicting idyllic rural scenes, as well as history and religious paintings promoting Burnand's view of Protestantism [n. 31, 59, 60]. Public subscriptions were launched in 1890 to acquire Albert Anker's *La reine Berthe et les fileuses*, and in 1899 for Charles Gleyre's *Le Déluge* [n. 25]. Though the collections were still dominated by Swiss landscapes and works glorifying the nation's past, over the years they gradually expanded in profile to reflect a broader view of art. Most Swiss artists travelled abroad to study and build a solid customer base for their art, studying and showing their work in major cities such as Paris, Düsseldorf and Munich. As elsewhere in Europe, academicism was dominant in history painting, just as realism was in genre and landscape painting. Charles Gleyre, a Vaud native who had found fame in Paris, was the perfect example of the sort of history painter whose work the Lausanne Museum wanted for its walls. His compatriots commissioned two monumental canvases illustrating glorious scenes from the struggle for freedom in the national historiography: *L'Exécution du major Davel*, 1850, and *Les Romains passant sous le joug*, 1858 [n. 22]. The 1908 purchase of 368 works from Gleyre's studio considerably increased his presence in the Museum's collection [n. 17, 23, 26].

The Canton of Vaud celebrated the centenary of its independence in 1903. Its capital Lausanne was now home to nearly fifty thousand people. The time had come to modernise: the Museum's much-extended collection had outgrown the Musée Arlaud, which by now was rather dilapidated. The collection was given a boost by the State's ambition to encourage higher education and the arts: the authorities had decided back in 1872 to grant the canton's university, library and museums of fine art, history and science the sum of 1.5 million francs presented to the canton by the Russian patron Gabriel de Rumine to finance a public building. The Palais de Rumine was a huge neo-Florentine building with a broad remit, typical of an age which, since London's Universal Exhibition of 1851, had sought to break down barriers between education, science and the arts [fig. 2]. The Musée des Beaux-Arts, which opened to the public in 1906, filled five exhibition rooms on the second floor in the north wing and featured all the works in the collection, displayed in several rows. Three large sky-lit rooms leading off each other were devoted to painting, showcasing the works of the Museum's founder Marc-Louis Arlaud, old masters from Switzerland and elsewhere, and the modern Swiss School [fig. 3]; one side room showed sculptures, while a hall divided into cabinets held the drawing collection.

At the Palais de Rumine, visitor numbers rose from 20,000 to 50,000 a year. With the new rooms at their disposal, the Museum's directors were free to promote and develop the collection, which still focused on contemporary Swiss and Vaud artists. They purchased works by living painters, who are still collected to the present day, such as Ferdinand Hodler [n. 40, 62, 65], Ernest Biéler [n. 30, 67, 68] and Eugène Grasset [n. 53, 56]. They took a particular interest in two Swiss artists based in Paris, acquiring several hundred of their works. These were Théophile-Alexandre Steinlen, whose art championed various social struggles [n. 46, 47, 77, 78], and Félix Vallotton, renowned for his bold experiments with form and colour, who was eventually to become the Museum's most emblematic artist [n. 37, 51, 52, 54, 63, 64, 79, 81, 82]. The acquisitions budget was modest, but major works came into the collection through gifts, bequests and long-term loans from the Swiss Confederation, the Gottfried Keller Foundation and the Société vaudoise des beaux-arts (Arts Visuels Vaud since 2016) [n. 10, 13, 21, 24, 31, 59, 67, 79, 173, 184]. The lack of space soon became a pressing issue. As early as 1924, having been promised the Lausanne doctor Henri-Auguste Widmer's prestigious collection, the director called for the Museum to be moved to its own premises.

The arrival of the over three hundred paintings, sculptures and drawings from the Widmer collection in 1936 and 1939 had a major impact. They considerably extended the Museum's chronological coverage, from Egyptian art to post-impressionism, broadening the range of a collection dominated by recent Swiss art. Having even greater significance was the bequest of works by major contemporary French and European masters, which drove a more ambitious acquisitions policy that has remained in place to the present day. Visitors could now admire works by Gustave Courbet [n. 27], Edgar Degas [n. 48, 49], Auguste Renoir, Paul Cézanne [n. 41], Henri Matisse [n. 42], Albert Marquet [n. 72], Maurice Utrillo and Maurice de Vlaminck. Widmer also collected works by his friend Édouard Vuillard [n. 50], Pierre Bonnard, Maurice Denis and Ker-Xavier Roussel, sparking the Museum's focus on the Nabi group. Another of Widmer's friends, Giovanni Giacometti, also joined the collection, while the doctor's passion for contemporary sculpture led him to acquire casts by Edgar Degas [n. 44], Constantin Meunier [n. 45], Auguste Rodin, Aristide Maillol, Albert Bartholomé, Carl Milles and Émile-Antoine Bourdelle [n. 57].

The Museum hosted its first temporary exhibition in 1938, heralding a new stage in which short-term displays gradually took precedence over the permanent collection. This led to a lengthy discrepancy between exhibitions that introduced audiences to the bold works of the Swiss and international avant-garde, such as *Du futurisme à nos jours* (1947) and *Rythmes et couleurs* (1952) on the one hand, and a somewhat timid acquisitions policy on the other. The Museum remained keen to represent the art of previous centuries, acquiring, for example, a fine set of works by the neoclassical painter Jacques Sablet [n. 10], and figurative art in general, taking an early interest in interior scenes by Marius Borgeaud [n. 83, 84]. As a result, it lost out on acquiring works reflecting the development of abstract art, then available at little cost. Not until the late 1930s did it begin to build collections around Alice Bailly [n. 73, 75, 76] and Gustave Buchet [n. 74, 86, 87], Vaud-born artists working in Paris in close dialogue with cubism and futurism. In the 1950s, the Museum began focusing on Charles Blanc-Gatti's musicalist works [n. 88], Maria Helena Vieira da Silva's abstract landscapes [n. 103] and Charles Rollier's art informel paintings. The Museum's major artistic commitment at this period, however, was to two marginal figures in the world of art rather than to the avant-garde. In 1956, some four hundred works by the visionary poet and artist Louis Soutter joined the collection, forming the basis for an exceptional special collection that now stands at over six hundred items [n. 93–97]. In the late 1960s, the self-taught artist Aloïse, whose work is typified by its complex iconography, likewise joined the collection, which now holds over three hundred of her drawings [n. 99–102].

In the early 1960s, Lausanne's population reached 100,000. The city benefited from the postwar boom, expanding and becoming urbanised. 1962 saw the launch of the International Tapestry Biennial at the Museum, making Lausanne the world leader in contemporary textile art for some thirty years. In 1964, the city welcomed twelve million visitors to the Swiss National Exhibition, a hymn to modernity with the slogan 'Believe and Create'. The art scene was enlivened by the arrival of new galleries such as the Galerie Alice Pauli in 1962 and the Galerie Rivolta in 1971, diversifying an art market long dominated by the Galerie Paul Vallotton. Social activism rose to new heights after the events of May 1968, with groups of young artists making their mark and street happenings by the movement Lôzane bouge. At the Museum, the three exhibitions run by the Salon international de galeries-pilotes (1963, 1966, 1970) were part of this broad protest movement. They also reflected an urge to break free from conservative provincialism. The Salon gave the Museum a new role in 'discovering' art as it was created, which had hitherto been the preserve of the art market. The original initiative, which drove the establishment of the Basel art fair in 1970, brought together a total of forty-nine galleries on three occasions who came to Lausanne to promote their new talents [fig. 4]. As New York and Paris vied with each other to be acknowledged as the world's leading art centre, the rooms at the Palais de Rumine were displaying geometric abstraction, constructivist, minimal, environmental, conceptual, kinetic art, pop art, new realism and land art. Young Swiss artists such as Olivier Mosset [n. 151, 161], René Bauermeister [n. 117] and Janos Urban [n. 118] were influenced by these exhibitions, taking their work in a more experimental direction. While the event placed Lausanne on the international art map, local scepticism and inadequate funding meant the Museum was unable to acquire even reasonably priced works that would have given its collection a new lease of life by opening it up to the international, and particularly American, scene. Some of the galleries present at the events generously gifted works by Marcel Broodthaers [n. 115] and Tadeusz Kantor [n. 124], while others were bequeathed by patrons [n. 121], maintaining a trace of the Museum's bold vision and prompting the later acquisition of works by artists who had taken part in the Salons [n. 113, 116, 119, 120].

One long-standing weak point in the collection was its holdings in video art, which has now become one of the Museum's main strengths. The Museum was in close contact with pioneering artists from French-speaking Switzerland working in the new medium from the early 1970s. It followed the careers and showed the works of the 'musketeers of the invisible', Jean Otth, Janos Urban, René Bauermeister, Muriel Olesen and Gérald Minkoff, and the IMPACT group, which brought all the leading international figures in the new art form to Lausanne in 1974. Although it took a while for their works to enter the Museum's collection in any significant quantity, this was still achieved earlier than in Bern, Basel or Zurich [n. 129]. Video art was not significantly represented in the collection until the 1990s when the Museum acquired videos and installations by renowned artists such as VALIE EXPORT [n. 130], Nam June Paik [n. 131], Joan Jonas [n. 132], Ana Mendieta [n. 142], Silvie and Chérif Defraoui [n. 155, 181], Kimsooja [n. 179], Francis Alÿs [n. 187], Harun Farocki [n. 188], and new talents such as Emmanuelle Antille [n. 175], Pauline Boudry / Renate Lorenz [n. 194], and Anne-Julie Raccoursier [n. 192].

In the latter half of the twentieth century, a number of other visual arts venues opened in Lausanne, including the Musée des arts décoratifs (1967), the Collection de l'Art Brut (1976), the Musée de l'Élysée (1980), which has specialised since 1985 in photography, and the Fondation de l'Hermitage (1984). The Museum's own collections developed in two directions, consolidating its major holdings in modern and contemporary art and exploring contemporary art. This has helped hone its specific profile, offering visitors a unique experience that cannot be found elsewhere. The Museum has also worked on developing a closer correlation between its exhibition and acquisitions programmes. In the 1980s, for instance, the focus on the resurgence of expressive figurativism and politically committed art led to exhibitions such as *Berlin. La rage de peindre* in 1982 and *New York Now* in 1983 and, parallel to that, the purchase of neo-expressionist works, particularly by German-speaking artists such as Arnulf Rainer [n. 122, 135], Rolf Iseli [n. 136], Luciano Castelli [n. 137], Miriam Cahn [n. 146], Leiko Ikemura [n. 177, 180], Martin Disler [n. 148], Günter Brus [n. 144] and Stephan Balkenhol [n. 157]. The last decade of the century saw major retrospectives of the Swiss artists Félix Vallotton, René Auberjonois, Giovanni Giacometti, Louis

Ducros, Ernest Biéler, Jean Otth, Louise Breslau, Louis Soutter, Olivier Mosset, Eugène Burnand, Alice Bailly, Charles Gleyre, Théophile-Alexandre Steinlen, Eugène Grasset and Aloïse [fig. 6], whose works were then acquired for the collections. The same was true of international artists [fig. 8, 9]: works by Aristide Maillol and Édouard Vuillard were acquired following exhibitions on the Nabi circle, while living artists joining the collection for the first time included Bruce Nauman [n. 156, 166, 170], Christian Boltanski [n. 163], Balthus, Bill Viola [n. 141], Sophie Calle, Thomas Huber [n. 160], Albert Oehlen [n. 143], Tom Burr [n. 193], Alfredo Jaar [n. 169], Esther Shalev-Gerz [n. 176], Nalini Malani [n. 182], Renée Green [n. 164; fig. 5], Kader Attia [n. 207] and Yael Bartana [n. 208]. A similar approach was taken to seeking out new home-grown talents, working in Switzerland or elsewhere by way of studio and gallery visits and the Museum played the role of a local Kunsthalle by hosting solo and group exhibitions, such as *Regard sur le présent*, held annually from 1982 to 1990, and *Accrochage [Vaud],* (2003–16). These also led to acquisitions of works by John M Armleder [n. 152], Jean-Luc Manz [n. 162], Alain Huck [n. 184], Robert Ireland [n. 183], Fabrice Gygi [n. 173], Philippe Decrauzat [n. 185], Didier Rittener [n. 186], Denis Savary, Valérie Favre [n. 202], Julian Charrière [n. 206; fig. 7], Claudia Comte [n. 200], Francis Baudevin [n. 197], and David Hominal [n. 195], some funded in part by the Commission cantonale des activités culturelles.

Once the canton had recovered from the financial crisis of the 1990s, the project to build a new Museum was relaunched – just one of the signs of Vaud's much-vaunted economic miracle. The project was backed by the State, the City of Lausanne, the Association des Amis du Musée, artists from the region and a group of collectors who promised to gift or loan major works of art. All participants were firmly convinced of the need for a new permanent space for the collections that would showcase two centuries' worth of efforts to promote and preserve the canton's artistic heritage and works from the local and international art scene collected by art lovers who, together, had built a truly remarkable body of art. The shared ambition to raise the artistic profile of a canton that was now home to 800,000 people and whose dynamic cultural scene was attracting attention far and wide bore fruit in 2019 with the inauguration of new stand-alone premises for the Museum, built by the Barcelona-based architects Barozzi Veiga near Lausanne station, easily accessed from across Europe's rail network [fig. 10–12].

The current Museum houses the Fondation Félix Vallotton and the Fondation Toms Pauli. It will be joined at the PLATEFORME 10 arts hub by two of the canton's other visual arts institutions, the Musée de l'Élysée, which specialises in photography, and mudac, the Museum of Contemporary Design and Applied Arts.

The hugely ambitious project has been an invaueable boon to the fine arts in the canton. The 2006 law on gifts in lieu of inheritance tax has borne fruit in the donation of works from Jacqueline Porret-Forel and Jean-Claude Givel art collections. Foundations such as the Foundation Gottfried Keller, the Walter A. Bechtler Stiftung and the Fondation Balthus Klossowski de Rola have also loaned or gifted major works. Private individuals, too, have been extraordinarily generous, including Alice Pauli, Alain and Suzanne Dubois, Mireille and James Lévy, Marcel Bahro, Betty and Hartmut Raguse-Stauffer, Paul and Tina Stohler, Françoise Marquet and a number of artists and anonymous donors. Their outstanding support has brought gifts and loans into the collections to strengthen its holdings in modern art, post-1945 schools such as abstract expressionism, the Paris School and arte povera, represented by Balthus [n. 91], Jean Dubuffet [n. 107–110], Alberto Giacometti, Zao Wou-Ki [n. 106], Pierre Soulages [n. 105, 154], Jannis Kounellis [n. 123] and Giuseppe Penone [n. 128, 205, 212], and contemporary art from Switzerland and elsewhere by artists including Franz Gertsch [n. 158], Thomas Hirschhorn [n. 171], Alex Katz [n. 126], Robert Motherwell [n. 139], Louise Nevelson [n. 153], William Kentridge [n. 210], Anish Kapoor [n. 189] and Anselm Kiefer [n. 211].

Annie Le Brun's 2018 book *Ce qui n'a pas de prix* describes 'entering a museum like jumping into the sea, in quest of a brand-new horizon'. Readers are invited to dive into the waves with the help of this guide, which features roughly two hundred works from a collection that has continued to grow out of the collective efforts of art lovers in and around Lausanne for two centuries.

Catherine Lepdor

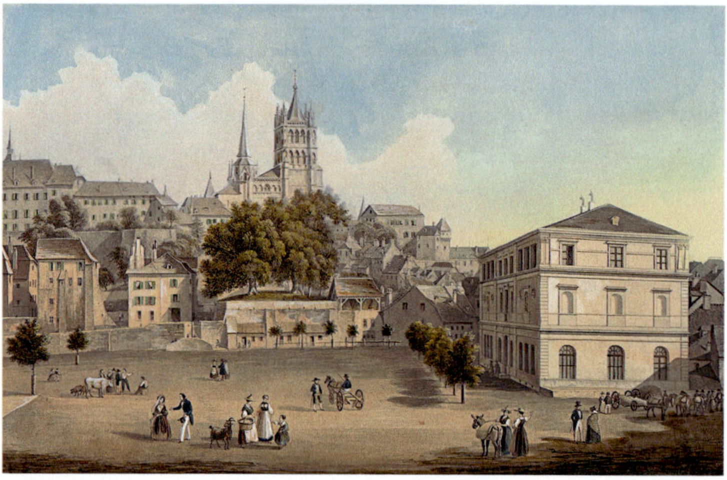

1. Friedrich von Martens, *La place de la Riponne avec, à droite, le musée Arlaud* (*Place de la Riponne with the Musée Arlaud on the Right*), c. 1845.

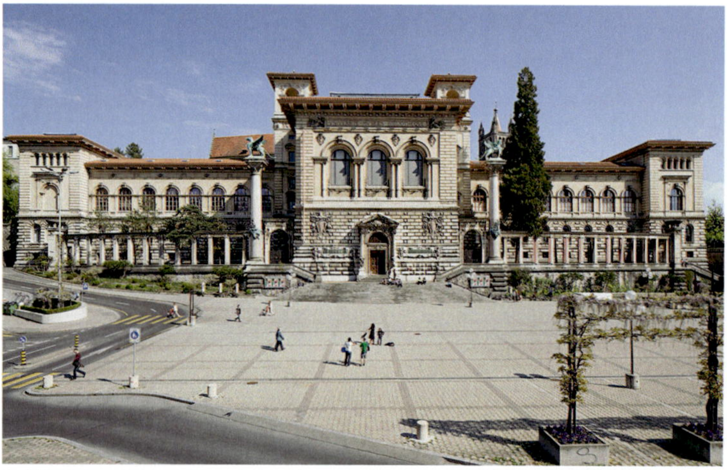

2. The Musée cantonal des Beaux-Arts at the Palais de Rumine.

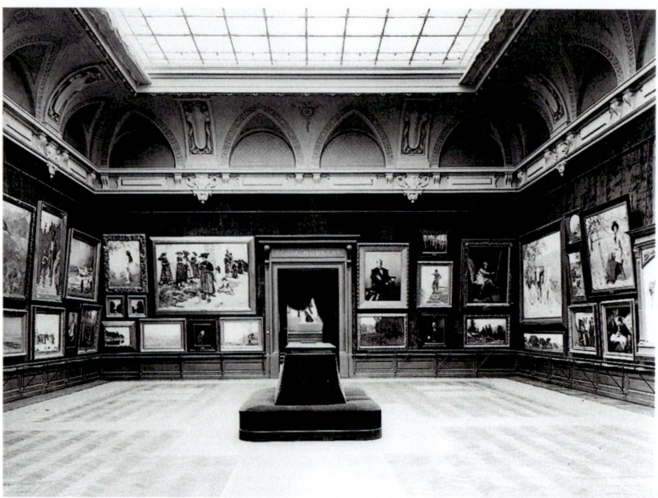

3. Palais de Rumine. The Modern Paintings Gallery, 1906.

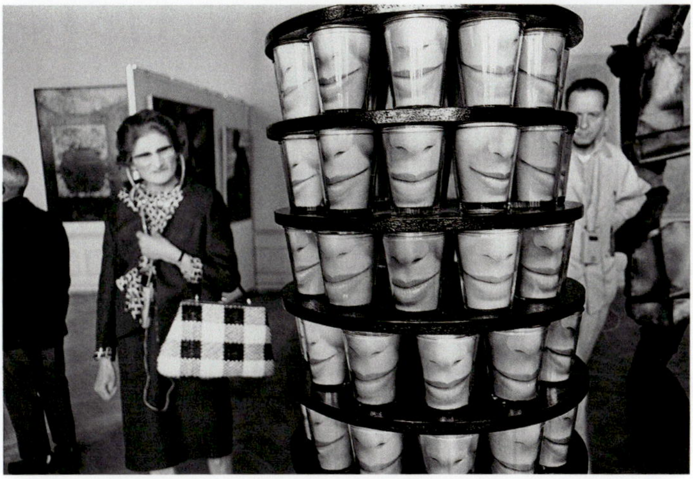

4. Palais de Rumine. *2ᵉ Salon international de galeries-pilotes*, 1966.

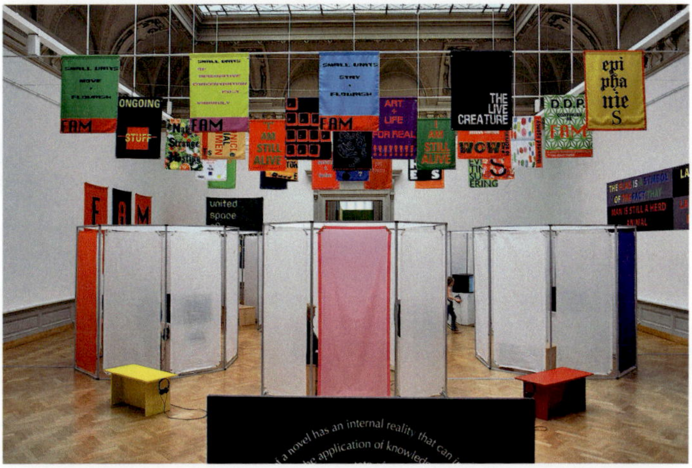

5. Palais de Rumine. *Renée Green. Ongoing Becomings*, 2009.

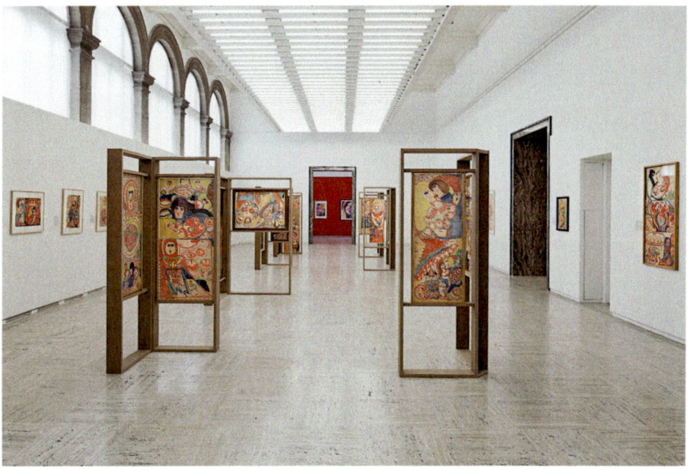

6. Palais de Rumine. *Aloïse. Le ricochet solaire*, 2012.

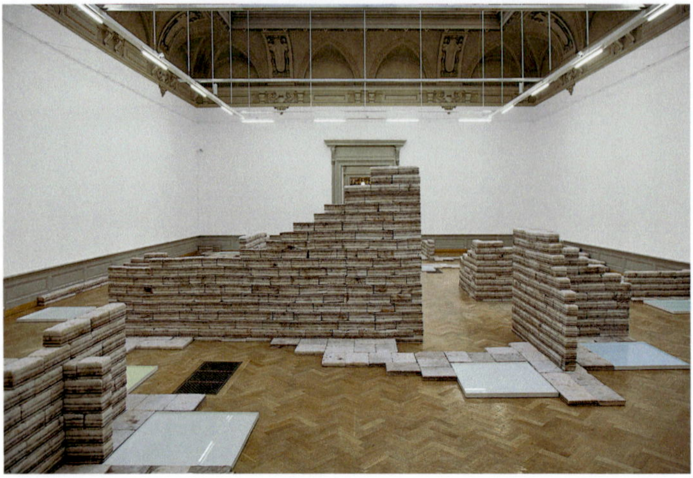

7. Palais de Rumine. *Julian Charrière. Future Fossil Spaces*, 2014.

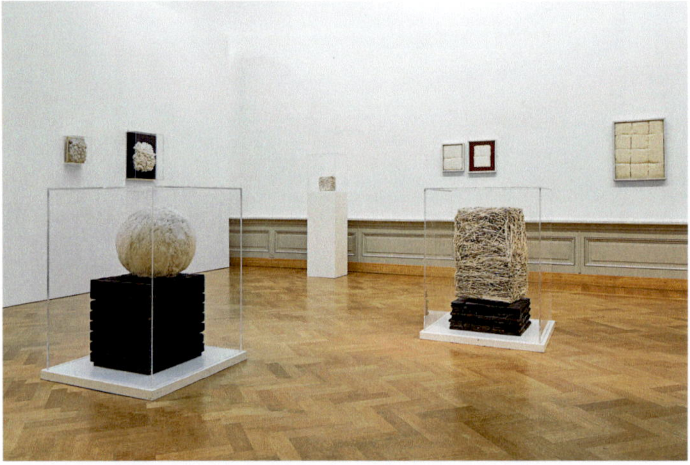

8. Palais de Rumine. *Achrome. Piero Manzoni, la peinture sans couleur*, 2016.

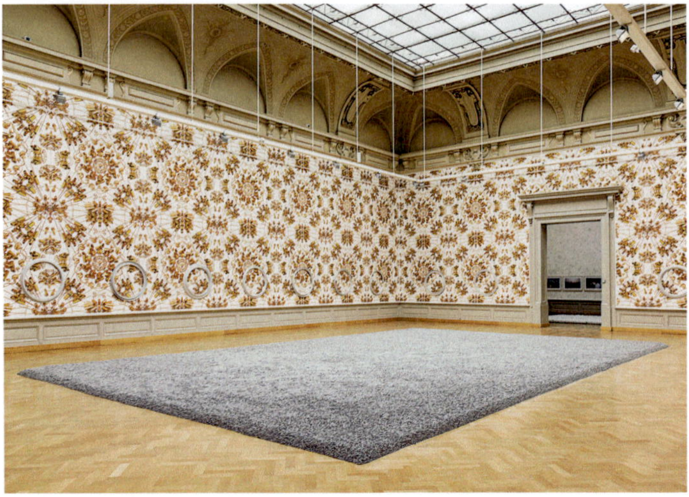

9. Palais de Rumine. *Ai Weiwei. D'ailleurs c'est toujours les autres*, 2017.

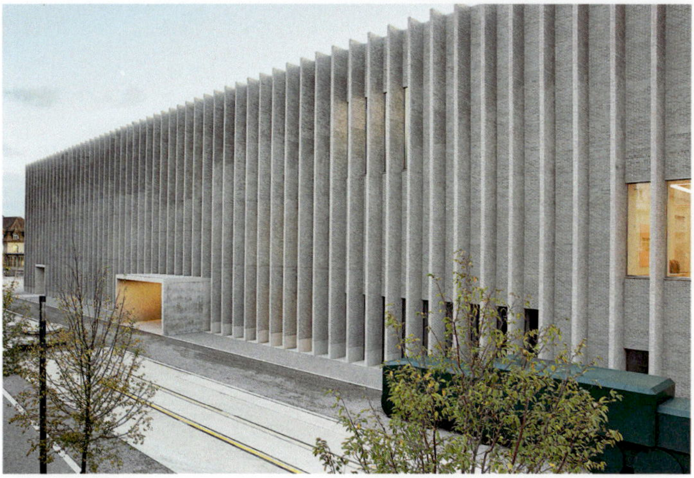

10. The Musée cantonal des Beaux-Arts at PLATEFORME 10.

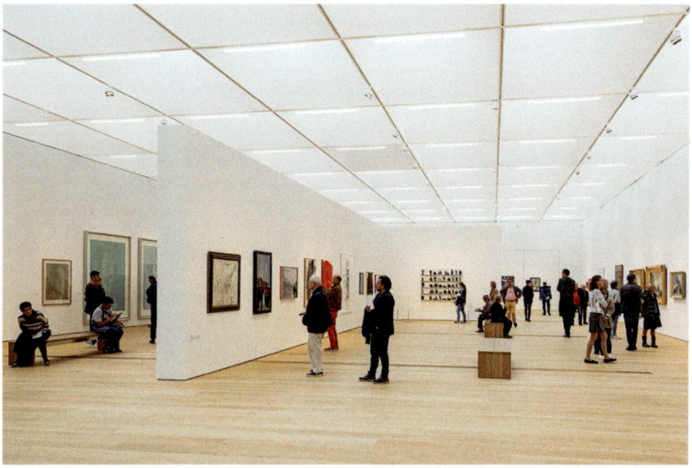

11. PLATEFORME 10. *Atlas. Cartographie du don*, 2019.

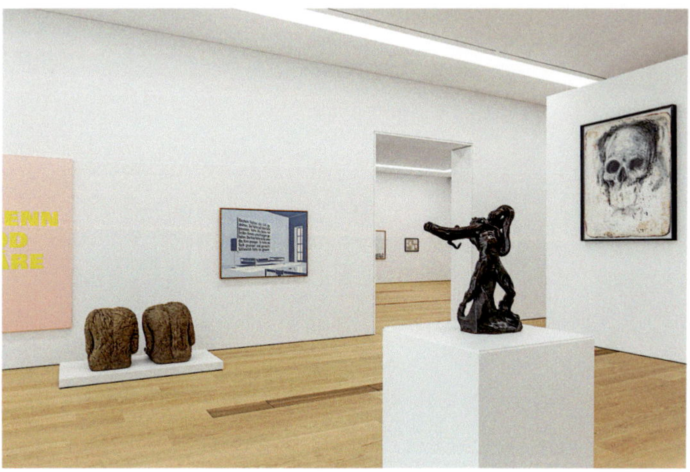

12. PLATEFORME 10. *Atlas. Cartographie du don*, 2019.

Works in Focus

1

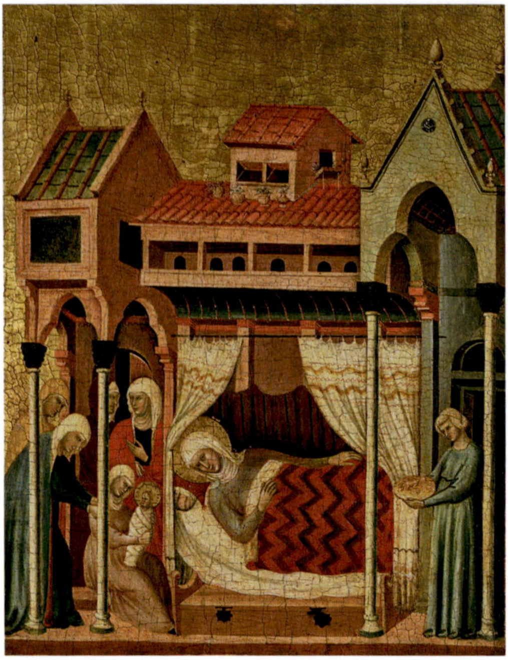

2

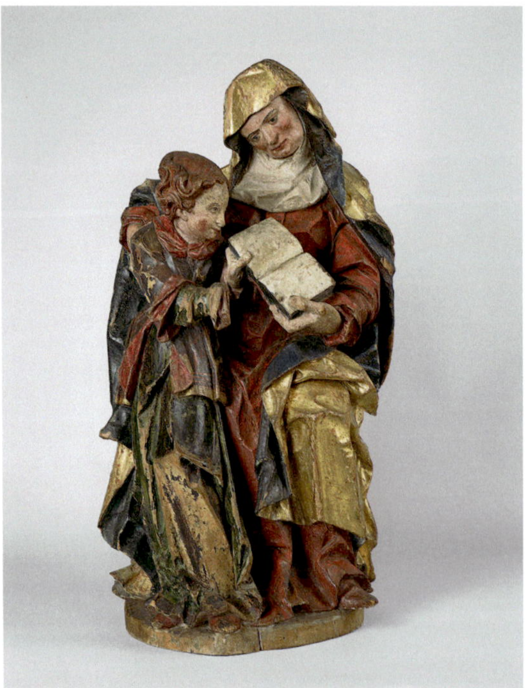

Francesco da Rimini, Naissance de la Vierge, c. 1320–30
Unknown artist, Sainte Anne enseignant la Vierge, c. 1550–80

1

Francesco da Rimini (documented in Rimini between 1313 and 1348)
Naissance de la Vierge (*The Birth of the Virgin*), c. 1320–30
Tempera on wood, 46 × 37 cm
Gift of the executors of Francesc Cambó, 1950. Inv. 1951-063

This representation of the birth of the Virgin bathes in the universality of the divine presence manifested by the gold ground. At the centre, we see Saint Anne in her bed, looking out at the viewer; on the left, five veiled servants, one of them holding Mary in her swaddling clothes; on the right, a young girl brings food. The realistic details (fabrics, tiles, pots of flowers) give a contemporary twist to the episode narrated in the Biblical apocrypha. The perspective 'signifies': the size of the figures is proportional to their importance. The architecture, which combines the profane and religious registers, presents a complex analysis of space, a century before the invention of central perspective.

This remarkable panel was originally part of an altarpiece whose central panel, representing the *Virgin and Child with Saint Claire and Saint Francis*, is now held at the Fondazione Giorgio Cini in Venice, while its three other panels and two side wings (the *Annunciation*, *Presentation in the Temple* and *Death of the Virgin*) are at the Museu Nacional d'Art de Catalunya in Barcelona. It bears witness to a key moment in painting in medieval Emilia Romagna: the creative explosion provoked by Giotto's presence in Rimini, where he had been summoned by the Malatestas in about 1300 to decorate the apse of the church of Saint Francis. There have been numerous hypotheses about the identity of the painter of this altarpiece. Because of the manifest influence of Giotto, he was at first referred to as a 'Friend of Giotto' and then, when the parts of the Franciscan triptych were reassembled, as the 'Master of the Cini Madonna'. Today, the ensemble is attributed to Francesco da Rimini.

Acquired in 1929 by the Catalan politician Francesc Cambó, this *Birth of the Virgin* was gifted to the Museum in recognition of the hospitality extended to his collection by the institution during the Second World War. [CL]

2

Unknown artist (western Switzerland)
Sainte Anne enseignant la Vierge (*Saint Anne Teaching the Virgin to Read*), c. 1550–80
Polychromed wood, 77 × 40 × 27 cm
Henri-Auguste Widmer bequest, 1939. Inv. 215

Anne and Joachim, Mary's parents, are not mentioned in the Bible but do appear in the Apocrypha. The cult of Saint Anne developed in the West during the period of the Crusades, when relics were brought back from the Orient, where she had been venerated since the sixth century. In the second half of the sixteenth century, this veneration was revived, particularly as a result of the Counter-Reformation. Anne meeting Joachim at the Golden Gate or teaching Mary Holy Scripture were among the scenes most frequently commissioned from painters and sculptors. The education of the Virgin continued to be illustrated by artists up to the nineteenth century, when it was used to promote the instruction of young women.

In this early-Baroque group in wood, used as a decorative attachment or as part of an altarpiece, Saint Anne is shown teaching Mary. The mother has a protective arm round her daughter and both are holding open the book, proffering it to the worshippers and encouraging them to read in turn. This is also an allusion to the intercessory role of the saints.

For all its numerous Late Gothic stylistic features, notably the rounded faces, the stiffness of the postures and the deep, dark folds of the drapery, this work does also herald the Baroque: the volumes are more substantial and the figures therefore more present, while here and there the drapery allows a glimpse of the body, even if this is still hidden by the abundant broken folds that reflect the light. We can also observe the timid beginnings of a dialogue between the bodies and their clothing.

This piece, which is exceptional in that it has kept much of its original polychrome, was one of the highlights of the ensemble put together by Henri-Auguste Widmer in the early twentieth century. This doctor from Lausanne owned one of the very few private collections of medieval sculpture in French-speaking Switzerland. [CLC]

3

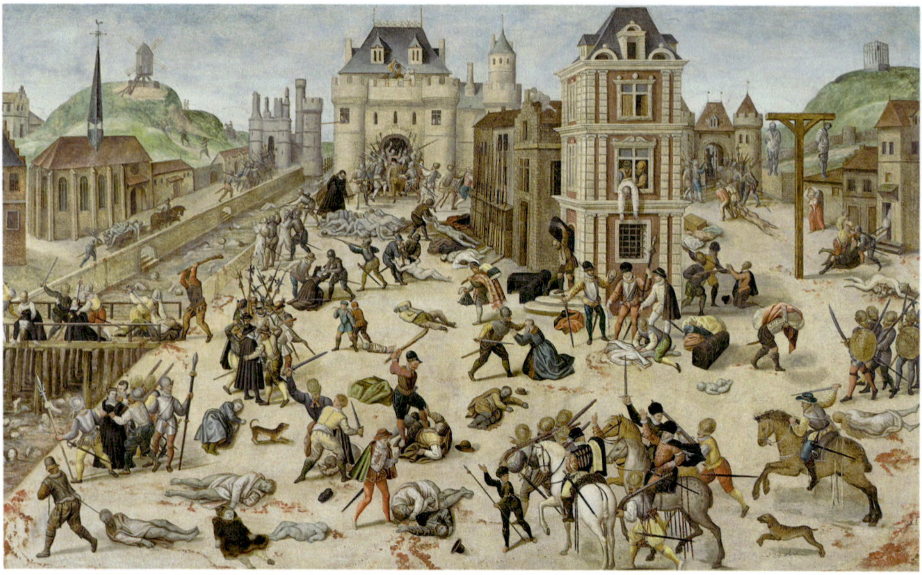

4

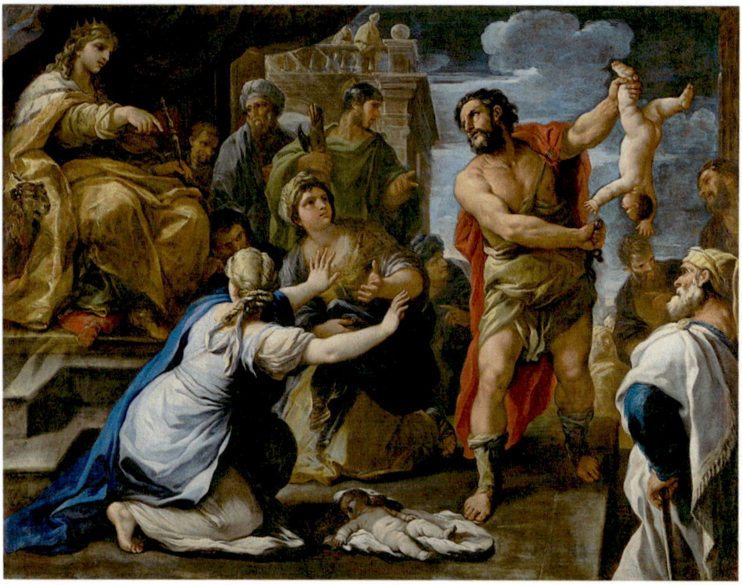

François Dubois, Le massacre de la Saint-Barthélemy, c. 1572–84
Luca Giordano, Le jugement de Salomon, c. 1670–85

3

François Dubois (Amiens, 1529–Geneva, 1584)
Le massacre de la Saint-Barthélemy (*The Saint Bartholomew's Day Massacre*), c. 1572–84
Oil on walnut wood, 93.5 × 154.1 cm
Gift of the Municipalité de Lausanne, 1862. Inv. 729

This painting represents the massacre of the Protestants that was triggered on 24 August 1572 in Paris and continued for several days: The Saint Bartholomew's Day Massacre. In a striking view of Paris, it sums up the main events in this bloody episode during France's Wars of Religion.

The topography has been manipulated in order to show the main locations of the tragedy. On the left, we recognise the church of the Grands-Augustins convent (no longer extant), where the knell that set off the killing was sounded, as well as the Seine and the Pont des Meuniers; centre back, the Louvre and, standing in front of it, Catherine de Médicis, the widow in black, seen as the main instigator of the massacre. To the right and in front of the Louvre is the townhouse of Anne de Laval, where Admiral de Coligny, leader of the Protestants, was killed: we see him being defenestrated, decapitated and castrated. Gathering around his corpse are the leaders of the Catholic party, the dukes of Guise and Aumale and the Chevalier d'Angoulême. On the right, in the background, is the Porte Saint-Honoré and the Montfaucon gibbet, where the admiral's body was hung by the feet. Featuring over 150 figures, this work is a veritable catalogue of civil-war cruelty, with a pregnant woman disembowelled, children dragging an infant by a rope, a man skewered on a roaster's spit, corpses stripped and piled up, and houses being pillaged.

This painting is exceptional, not only for the quality of its execution, but also because contemporary representations of the Saint Bartholomew's Day Massacre are extremely rare. Inscribed on the first step of the perron outside the townhouse where the Admiral de Coligny was murdered are the words: 'franciscus Sylvius Ambianus pinx[it]'. This was the signature that the painter François Dubois placed on his sole surviving work, and its positioning here speaks volumes about the convictions of this Protestant from Amiens who took refuge in Geneva after the massacre. [CL]

4

Luca Giordano (Naples, 1634–1705)
Le jugement de Salomon (*The Judgement of Solomon*), c. 1670–85
Oil on canvas, 182.2 × 242.5 cm
Gift of Georges Mörikofer, 1922. Inv. 1223

This painting illustrates an episode in the Old Testament. Two prostitutes, who had given birth at the same moment, both claim to be the mother of the same child after the other had been smothered at birth. Asked to judge, Solomon ordered: 'Cut the child in two and give one half to the first woman and the other to the second.' When one of the women renounces her half so that the child can live, the king of Israel recognises her as the true mother.

In keeping with tradition, the work represents the high point of the drama. In the half-light, a young monarch is sitting on a throne, looking down on the scene, the light illuminating his hand drawing attention to the order he has just made. To the right, a soldier holds up the living child with his other hand on the hilt of his sword. One of the mothers holds her hands out in horror, turning to the sovereign to beseech him to prevent the mortal blow. Around them, courtiers observe the scene.

Everything here serves the dramatic effect of the action. The composition is tight-knit, ordered by two diagonals that intersect at the point where the contrast of the chiaroscuro is at its strongest. The powerful figure of the soldier seems to pierce the space. The eloquent gestures heighten the theatricality of the scene. Giordano creates striking effects of colour and light. The violently lit whites and blues of the foreground contrast with the gold-hued semi-penumbra of the background, punctuated by the reds of the cushion under Salomon's foot rest and the soldier's cloak.

The influence of Veronese on the composition and colours place this painting after the Giordano's Venetian sojourn, and the lighting and quotations, which show a close link with the mature work of Mattia Preti, allow us to date this *Jugement de Salomon* to around 1670–85, when Giordano was working in and around Naples. [CLC]

5

6

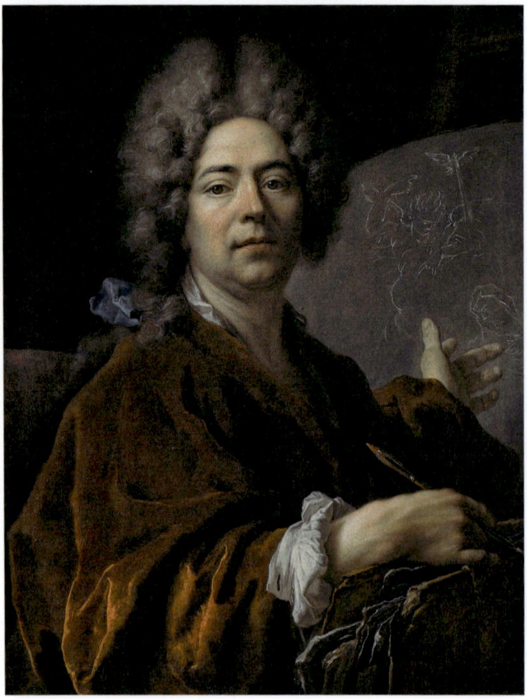

Hyacinthe Rigaud, Marie d'Orléans, duchesse de Nemours, 1705
Nicolas de Largillierre, Autoportrait, 1711

5

Hyacinthe Rigaud (Perpignan, 1659–Paris, 1743)
Marie d'Orléans, duchesse de Nemours (*Marie d'Orléans, Duchess of Nemours*), 1705
Oil on canvas, 147.5×115 cm
Gift of Germaine Sevastopoulo, 1955. Inv. 1955-003

With his contemporary Nicolas de Largillierre, Hyacinthe Rigaud dominated the market for formal portraits in France during the first decades of the eighteenth century. He established his reputation with his famous portrait of the king in his coronation clothes, *Louis XIV en costume de sacre* (*Portrait of Louis XIV, in Coronation Robes*, 1701, Paris, Musée du Louvre). The prolific production that followed demonstrated his skill at capturing conventional poses, the intense richness of his colours and the virtuosity with which he rendered the shimmer of drapery. These skills won him patrons among the nobility and high bourgeoisie in France and around Europe.

This portrait shows the Duchess of Nemours in three-quarters profile, her face turned towards the viewer. A widow for over forty years, now nearly eighty years old, she still wears the black of mourning, a fashion inaugurated at the court by Anne de Bretagne in 1498. With one hand, she holds the panels of the mourning veil knotted around her neck and, with the other, she touches a crown in the background placed on a crimson cushion. The red hues employed in her surroundings warmly frame the model, while at the centre the light flesh tones of her face and hands stand out against the dark mass of her dress. Set off by the clever lighting effect, the aristocrat, one of the richest heiresses in the kingdom, clearly displays her rank: the fleurs-de-lis adorning the crown placed nearby point to her status as a princess of the blood, born of the two royal houses of France.

Saint-Simon wrote in his *Mémoires* that Marie de Nemours 'had infinite wit with an eloquent, lively tongue, which she never held back'. By giving the elderly woman a mocking expression, Rigaud marvellously captures the doughty temperament that was evident in the fight she took up in 1674 to claim the inheritance of the county of Neuchâtel, for which she even opposed the Sun King. In 1694, with the support of the Neuchâtelois themselves, she was recognised as their legitimate sovereign. [CL]

6

Nicolas de Largillierre (Paris, 1656–1746)
Autoportrait (*Self-Portrait*), 1711
Oil on canvas, 80.5×63.2 cm
Gift of Arlaud, 1841. Inv. 735

This painting is a copy by Largillierre of his 1711 *Autoportrait* (*Self-Portrait*), now in the Château de Versailles. The artist depicts himself with the tools of his trade: in his right hand is a holder for two pieces of chalk, one red, one white, and a portfolio crammed with drawings. His left hand is gesturing to a canvas featuring a white chalk sketch for an Annunciation on a grey wash ground. The sweeping gesture towards a religious work of art seems to lay claim to the status of a history painter. It could, however, also be considered that highlighting the difference between the extraordinary detail of the self-portrait in the foreground and the unfinished work in the background is a way of hinting at the superiority of portraiture: it was his skill as a portraitist that earned him a place at the Royal Academy of Painting and Sculpture in Paris in 1686.

The ambivalent message, the position of the body that generates depth of field, the theatricality of the left hand's gesture, the smooth, soft texture, particularly suited to rendering the sitter's complexion, the warmth of the colours, the sumptuous, sensuous rust-red velvet coat, and the fluidity of the movement from foreground to middle and background all locate the work firmly within the Rococo tradition. It could hardly be more different from Nicolas Poussin's well-known *Autoportrait* (*Self-Portrait*) of 1650 (Paris, Musée du Louvre), though the two works are very similar in terms of iconography: it responds to Poussin's iconic classical work with the dignity worthy of an artist who, alongside Hyacinthe Rigaud, was one of France's two greatest portraitists of the period. Largillierre, who studied portraiture in England, surpassed Rigaud in capturing the psychology of his sitters; another key difference was that he preferred working for bourgeois clients rather than the French court, often claiming their expectations were more realistic and they paid more promptly! [CL]

7

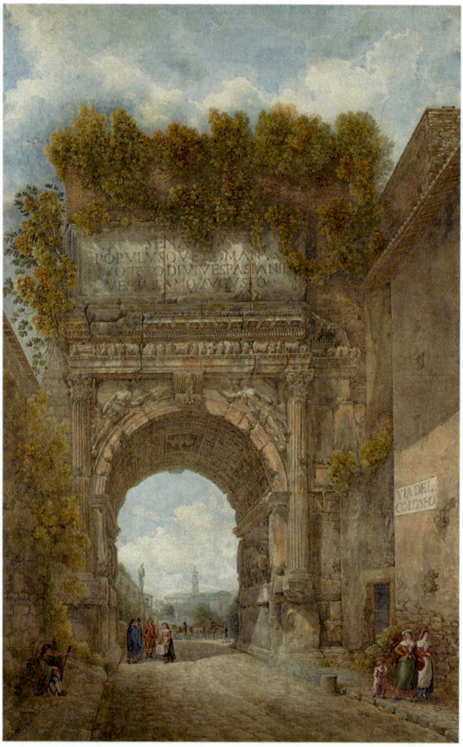

8

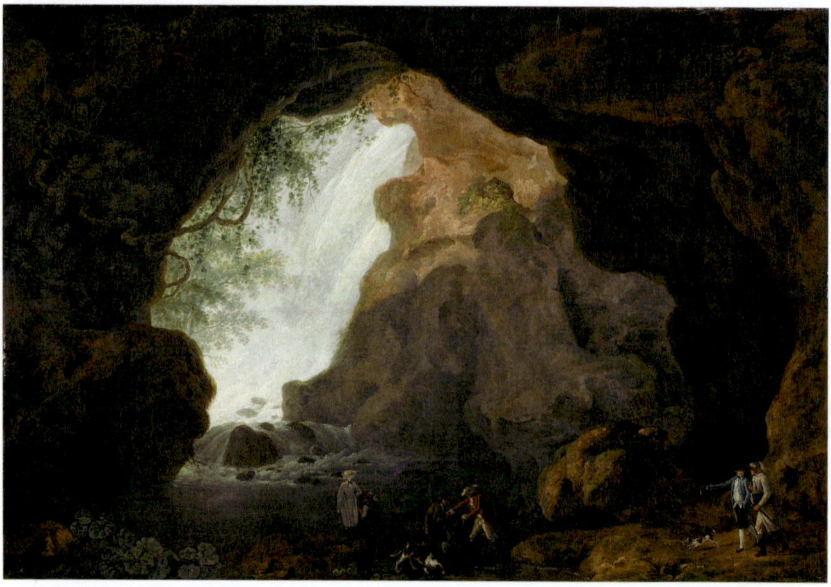

Louis Ducros, L’arc de Titus, between 1782 and 1787
Louis Ducros, Groupe de touristes visitant la grotte de Neptune à Tivoli, c. 1782

7

Louis Ducros (Moudon, 1748–Lausanne, 1810)
L'arc de Titus (*The Arch of Titus*), between 1782 and 1787
Pen and Indian ink, watercolour and gouache highlights on papers glued together and backed with canvas, 103 x 67 cm. Acquisition, 1816. Inv. 816

The Vaud-born artist Louis Ducros began his career by studying at the private academy in Geneva run by the artist Nicolas-Henri-Joseph de Fassin, a native of Liège in Belgium. He then honed his skills by copying Dutch paintings and working on watercolours from life. He arrived in Rome in 1776 at the age of twenty-eight, eventually spending almost all of his thirty years in Italy in the city. Since he was unable to take on major commissions for religious art, reserved for Catholic painters, he quickly realised that tourists would be his only customers, meaning he had little choice but to specialise in landscapes. In 1779, he set up a partnership with the engraver Giovanni Volpato to publish a series of views of Rome and its surroundings, featuring twenty-four engravings with watercolour details.

In the 1780s, Ducros consolidated his reputation as a specialist of topographical views of the remains of ancient Rome, the modern city's buildings and gardens, and natural curiosities and picturesque sites in the surrounding countryside. He soon attracted renowned customers including the Swedish King Gustav III, Pope Pius VI, and the British collector Sir Richard Colt Hoare.

This Arch of Titus, built towards the end of the first century AD, showcases Ducros's exceptional talent and explains his successful career. The format, unusual for watercolour before Joseph Mallord William Turner took it up twenty years later, consists of several sheets of paper mounted on a canvas on a stretcher that was then framed behind glass. Ducros's works were seen as the equal of oil paintings. Alongside the innovative procedure, the piece shows impressive virtuoso mastery of technique in the minute rendering of the monument, imaginative use of vigorous nature swallowing up the traces of history, and appealing presence of common folk creating a link with the present day. [CL]

8

Louis Ducros (Moudon, 1748–Lausanne, 1810)
Groupe de touristes visitant la grotte de Neptune à Tivoli (*Group of Tourists Visiting Neptune's Grotto at Tivoli*), c. 1782
Oil on canvas, 90 × 132.2 cm
Acquisition, 2016. Inv. 2016-055

When Ducros began making a name for himself in Rome in 1785 with his large-format views of the city and the surrounding countryside, it was because his unusually large watercolours enabled him to find a niche in a landscape market then dominated by Jacob Philipp Hackert. In the early 1780s, however, the Swiss artist had yet to abandon oils. Two ambitious paintings now kept at the Pavlovsk Palace in Saint Petersburg exemplify his work in this medium. Confirmation of Ducros' growing renown, they show the future tsar of Russia, Grand Duke Paul, and his wife Maria Feodorovna in the Roman Forum and at Tivoli, and they were painted on the occasion of the couple's stay in Rome during an incognito Grand Tour of Western Europe that they undertook in 1781–2.

All the evidence is that the work in Lausanne is connected to this Russian episode and records an excursion by Grand Duke Paul's retinue. In the foreground, three aristocrats are accompanied by local guides and a scholarly figure holding a portfolio. The man wearing a blue jacket has been identified as the famous art collector Prince Nikolay Yusupov.

The scene takes place in Tivoli, a site renowned for its waterfalls and archaeological ruins. From Claude Lorrain to Hubert Robert, many an artist represented this destination prized by tourists. Ducros innovates here with his tight framing, focusing on the entrance of Neptune's Grotto. In the foreground are steep black rocks; in the background, through the opening of a vault, is a waterfall brightly lit by the sun and foliage with sunlight shining through it. Ducros, a distinguished landscape painter, sometimes enlisted other artists for his figures. It may be that the figures who enliven this painting were painted by his fellow countryman, Jacques Sablet, his collaborator and co-tenant at the Strada della Croce in 1782. [CL]

9

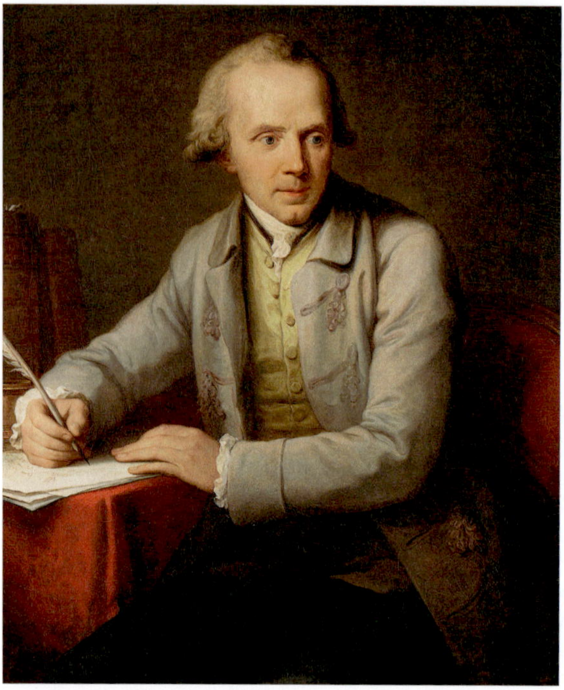

10

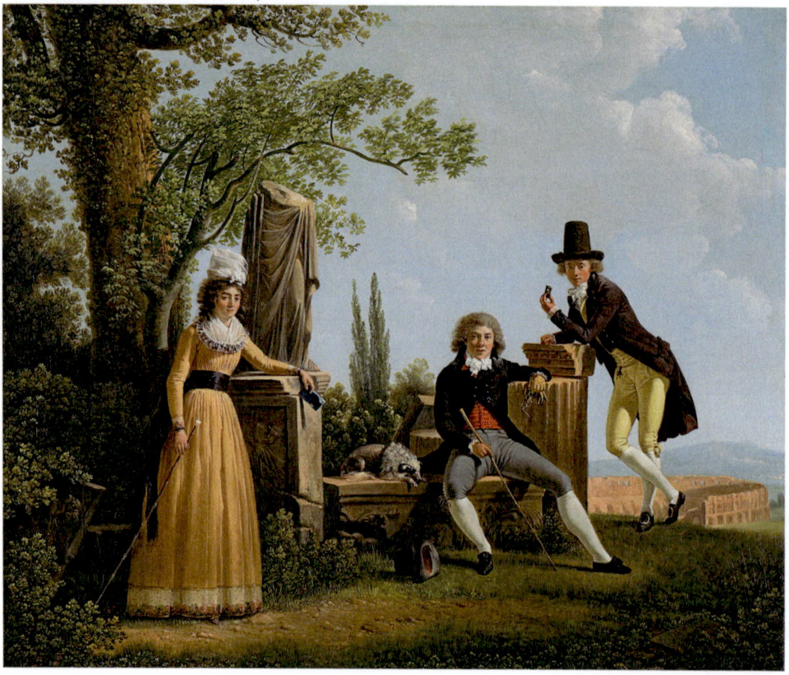

Angelika Kauffmann, Portrait du docteur Auguste Tissot, 1783
Jacques Sablet, Portrait de famille avec le Colisée, 1791

9

Angelika Kauffmann (Chur, 1741–Rome, 1807)
Portrait du docteur Auguste Tissot (*Portrait of Doctor Auguste Tissot*), 1783
Oil on canvas, 94.6 × 79.7 cm
Acquisition with support from numerous sources, 1928. Inv. 763

Doctor Auguste Tissot, a native of the Canton of Vaud, admired by his patient Voltaire and a regular correspondent of Jean-Jacques Rousseau, rose to fame in 1752 for his exemplary conduct with his patients during a smallpox epidemic, earning him the epithet 'the poor man's doctor'. He published a number of medical treatises including *L'inoculation justifiée* (*A Justification of Inoculation*) (1754), *L'onanisme* (*Onanism*) (1758) and *Avis au peuple sur sa santé* (*Advice To the Population On Health*) (1761), which were read across Europe. He refused numerous prestigious invitations, preferring to stay in Lausanne, save for some short travels and four semesters teaching at the University of Pavia from 1781–3. It was during his time there that he sat for a portrait by the Swiss artist Angelika Kauffmann.

When Angelika Kauffmann first visited Italy in the early 1760s, she was influenced by artists such as Pompeo Batoni, the precursor of neo-classicism, and soon earned a reputation as a skilled portraitist. Back in Italy twenty years later after a long period in London, where she was one of two female founder members of the Royal Academy, she worked in Venice, then Naples, before eventually settling in Rome.

This *Portrait du docteur Auguste Tissot* draws largely on the same pose and décor as her 1764 portrait of Johann Joachim Winckelmann (Zurich, Kunsthaus), while reflecting a softer, rounder approach typical of her work in the 1780s. The composition avoids the language of attributes, preferring a more intimate approach: the doctor is shown lost in thought, and the ray of light falling across his forehead and onto the page where his pen is poised hints at his status as a man of the Enlightenment. This portrait already expresses the same pre-Romantic sensibility. [CL]

10

Jacques Sablet (Morges, 1749–Paris, 1803)
Portrait de famille avec le Colisée (*Family Portrait with the Colosseum*), 1791
Oil on canvas, 60 × 72 cm
On deposit from the Gottfried Keller Foundation, Federal Office of Culture, Bern, 1932. Inv. 738

The impression of a snapshot on canvas is typical of the conversation piece, a kind of informal group portrait, usually set outside, which was fashionable in England from the second half of the eighteenth century. Sablet took up this genre in Rome in the early 1790s, scaling it down and making it more affordable so as to offer clients looking for greater simplicity a welcome alternative to the solemnity of the ceremonial portrait.

This family portrait expresses the taste for antiquity and love of nature found at this time. Sablet places his figures on the Palatine, with a steep view down to Rome's famous Colosseum. The three young people and their dog stand nonchalantly in the picturesque setting of the Farnese Gardens, with their numerous ruins. Their garments exemplify the fashion of the day, which afforded the body a new freedom. The young woman is wearing a muslin toque and a belted *en fourreau* dress, and holds a notebook and a walking stick. Her companions wear simplified clothing, their low-cut frock coats revealing embroidered waistcoats, breeches and stockings. Their hair is free and only lightly powdered. One sports the yellow gloves of the dandy, the other has a Claude glass (a blackened mirror that could be used to encompass and unify the hues of a given landscape).

In this instance Sablet demonstrates the remarkable skill in notating light that would earn him the nickname of 'painter of the sun'. Thanks to the artifice of a very low horizon, the figures look almost as if they have been cut out against the light blue sky subtly modulated by clouds. The palette is light and refined and the colours play effectively on the opposition of white and black, complemented by several isolated zones of bright colour. The sun shines through the foliage. The modelling of the flesh is gentle, careful to capture the humanity of the models. [CL]

11

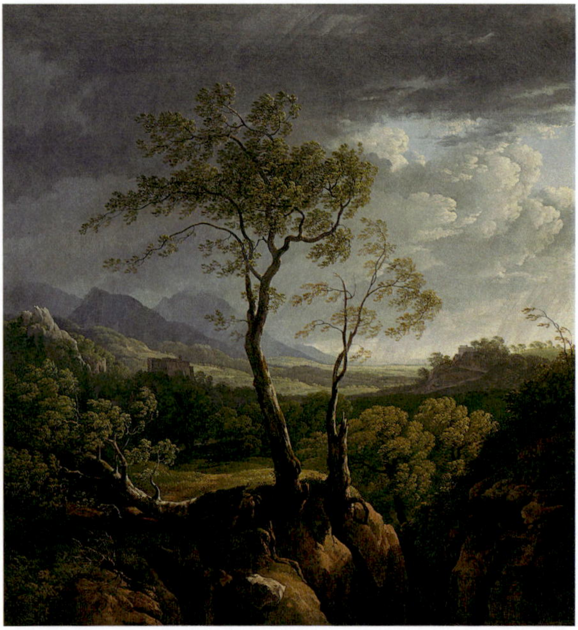

12

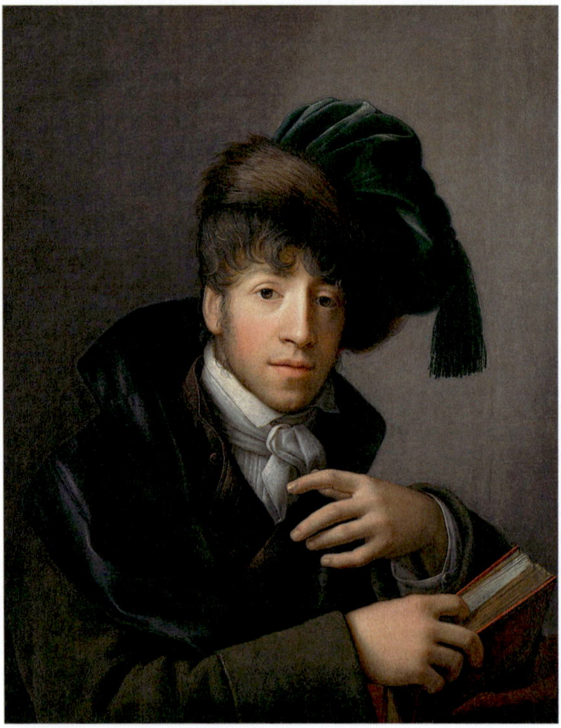

Hendrik Voogd, Campagne romaine sous un ciel d'orage, c. 1800
Johann Friedrich August Tischbein, Portrait de Nicolas Châtelain, c. 1800–10

11

Hendrik Voogd (Amsterdam, 1768–Rome, 1839)
Campagne romaine sous un ciel d'orage (*Roman Countryside under a Stormy Sky*), c. 1800
Oil on canvas, 118.5 × 112.8 cm
Acquired with an exceptional credit from the État de Vaud and the support of the Association des Amis du Musée and the Loterie Romande, 1999. Inv. 1999-004

Born in Amsterdam and trained at the city's municipal art school, Hendrik Voogd spent all his career in Rome, where he settled at the age of twenty. There he frequented the landscape painters Johann Christian Reinhart from Germany and Joseph Anton Koch from Austria, as well as the Frenchman Nicolas-Didier Boguet. Like them, he found his clientele among international aristocrats passing through Rome on the Grand Tour. The appeal of his at times monumental canvases derives from their balanced composition in parallel planes, the great clarity of their forms, and their cool, luminous palette, which earned him the nickname of 'the Dutch Claude' (Claude Lorrain was indeed one of his main models). It was not long before his landscapes showing the Roman countryside were fetching high prices. The artist further consolidated his reputation by disseminating his work in the form of lithographs.

Around 1800, Voogd's essentially neoclassical art began a discreet but palpable evolution, which explains today's interest in his work. This *Campagne romaine sous un ciel d'orage* shows his receptiveness to this movement, the spirit of which was spreading throughout Europe. Landscape painting, which hitherto had conveyed a clear and harmonious vision of the universe, now acquired new kinds of content; it expressed individual feelings and reflected the great upheavals of this period roiled by the wars entrained by the French Revolution. It is this loss of bearings, and the worries shared by a disoriented generation, that this painting evokes through the motifs of the gathering storm and the tall trees exposed to the wind or uprooted, poised on the edge of a gulf. The sky of Arcadia has darkened. Gathering black clouds hide the sky and begin to cover the foreground in a darkness heavy with menace. [CL]

12

Johann Friedrich August Tischbein (Maastricht, 1750–Heidelberg, 1812)
Portrait de Nicolas Châtelain (*Portrait of Nicolas Châtelain*), c. 1800–10
Oil on paper mounted on canvas, 68.6 × 55 cm
Joséphine Chavannes bequest, 1918. Inv. 1155

Nicolas Châtelain and Johann Friedrich August Tischbein – the model and his painter – both belonged to grand dynasties. Châtelain, the son of a pastor, came from a rich family of booksellers in Rotterdam who had been forced to take refuge in the Pays de Vaud by the Prussian invasion of 1787. A great traveller, he stayed in Italy in the 1790s and made a name for himself with his novels and literary pastiches. Tischbein, known as the 'Leipziger Tischbein', belonged to a German family that produced three generations of famous painters. Having trained in Paris and Rome, he turned his back on the ceremonial portrait in favour of a 'sentimental' neoclassicism influenced by Élisabeth Vigée Le Brun (France) and Thomas Gainsborough and George Romney (England). He was the most sought-after portraitist in Germany in the late eighteenth century.

Tischbein painted two earlier portraits of Châtelain (Munich, Neue Pinakothek) in 1791 and 1794, probably in Rotterdam. They show the sitter at full height and actual size, posing, in one as an elegant young man in a garden and in the other in an interior wearing a Renaissance costume. The Museum's portrait was made after 1800, when Tischbein was director of the Kunstakademie in Leipzig. In this bust-length work, Châtelain poses as a man of letters, his finger marking his page in the book that he has just closed, in front of a neutral ground. He is entering his thirties and looks out at the viewer with a melancholy gaze. The black, shiny material of his coat lapel and the white muslin of his shirt and cravat form a frame for his pale face, with its slightly reddened cheeks and handsome sensual lips. His hair done in the 'Titus-style', Châtelain wears an 'à la Turque' headpiece lined with fur, which brings out the delicacy of his features in this portrait that is halfway between neoclassical severity and Romantic gentleness. [CL]

13

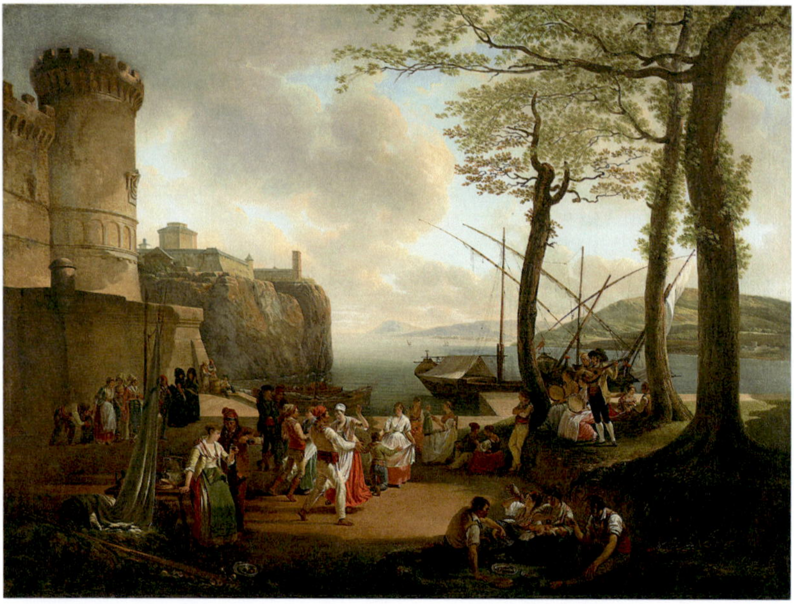

14

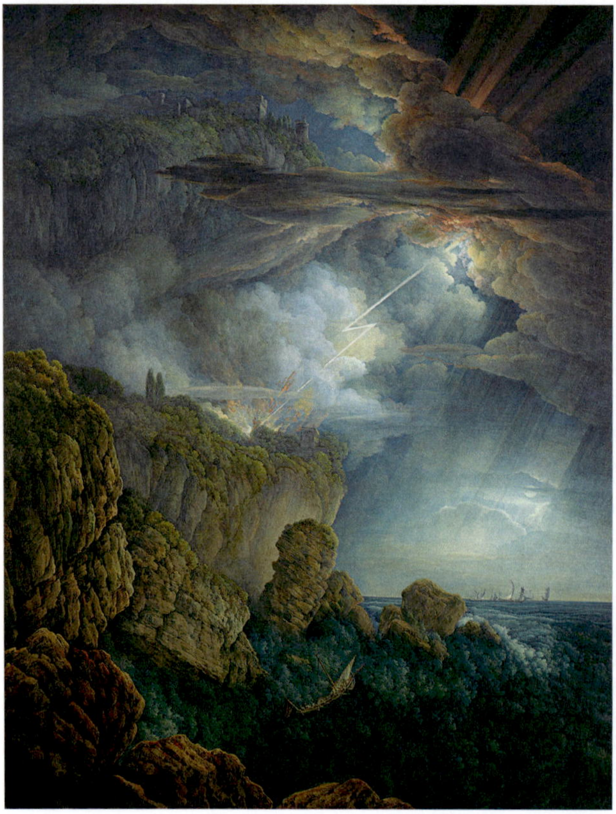

Jacques Sablet, La tarentelle, 1799
Louis Ducros, Orage nocturne à Cefalù, c. 1800–5

13

Jacques Sablet (Morges, 1749–Paris, 1803)
La tarentelle (*Tarentella*), 1799
Oil on canvas, 155 × 212 cm
On deposit from the Gottfried Keller Foundation, Federal Office of Culture, Bern, 2016. Inv. 2016-067

Forced to flee Rome due to repercussions from the French Revolution, Jacques Sablet arrived in Paris in January 1794. There he was accepted into the Société populaire et républicaine des arts and regularly exhibited exotic scenes that were extremely well received by the audiences. At the Salon of Year V (1796) he enjoyed great success with *Le colin-maillard* (*Blind Man's Bluff*, c. 1790, held at this Museum), a *fête galante* transposed into an Italian garden.

This *Tarentelle*, or *Bord de mer au crépuscule avec paysans napolitains dansant la Tarantella* (*Seaside at Dusk with Neapolitan Peasants Dancing the Tarentella*) is one of the most ambitious and accomplished works from the artist's late period. It is a variant on the *Danse à Naples* he painted in Rome in 1784, which was acquired by King Gustav III of Sweden (Drottningholm Palace, near Stockholm). Here, Sablet has placed his scene by the sea, between Rome and Naples, at the foot of the fortress of Gaeta. Some thirty figures have gathered for the tarantella, the popular Neapolitan dance accompanied by guitar and Basque tambourines for the rhythm. This work sees the Swiss painter playing the card that had made his reputation in Paris, that of the contemporary genre scene with picturesque costumes, bathed in the handsome light that earned him the nickname 'painter of the sun'.

When *La tarentelle* was exhibited at the Salon of the Year VII (1799), critics praised its composition, its colours and the naturalness of the poses: 'This picture skilfully paints nature and the sun shining with all its light; the daylight is pure, the hues of the shadows very well judged; the landscape is piquant and filled with diverse details; the group of musicians is the most felicitously arranged of all.'

A great admirer of Sablet, who advised him on his acquisitions, Cardinal Joseph Fesch, the uncle of Napoleon Bonaparte and one of the greatest collectors of the day, acquired *La tarentelle* after the artist's death for what at the time was the astronomical sum of six thousand francs. [CL]

14

Louis Ducros (Moudon, 1748–Lausanne, 1810)
Orage nocturne à Cefalù (*Night Storm at Cefalù*), c. 1800–5
Watercolour, gouache and oil on papers glued together and backed with canvas, 96 × 74 cm
Acquisition, 1816. Inv. 812

After nearly twenty years in Rome, during which he achieved great renown, Louis Ducros was forced to leave the city in 1793, due to measures taken by the Papal States against French residents, who were suspected of propagating revolutionary ideas. Ducros travelled to the Abruzzi, then lived in Naples for several years, before being cast out again as a Jacobin. After a short stay in Malta, he returned to his home country of Switzerland in 1807, where he lived in Lausanne until his death in 1810.

Orage nocturne à Cefalù is among his masterpieces. The circumstances in which it was painted remain unknown as does any evidence of the artist visiting Sicily at this time. The landscape is divided into four juxtaposed realms: at the bottom, the raging sea driving a boat onto reefs on which it will be smashed; next, a steep cliff on which a building is being shattered by lightning; after that, a castle, standing either in what is an imaginary heaven or on another promontory; and finally, the dark mass of a stratus veiling a red sun. This strong, tiered composition, dramatized by powerful diagonals that streak its surface, dazzles by the extraordinary mastery of watercolour seen in the transparency of the sky and also in the effects of opacity obtained by adding gouache, oil and lacquer. The palette is extensive, moving from the warm ochres of the rocks to the cold touches of Prussian blue in the sky and sea.

After its bright, luminous neoclassical origins, Ducros's art becomes tenebrous and pre-Romantic here, evoking the worlds of Johann Heinrich Füssli and John Martin. Behind this lies the influence of the artist's own misfortunes combined with the taste of his British patrons for the sublime and Gothic novels, as well as a new 'meteorological' sensibility in which the themes of the storm at sea and volcanic eruption transpose a sense of insecurity in an age of revolutionary wars. [CL]

15

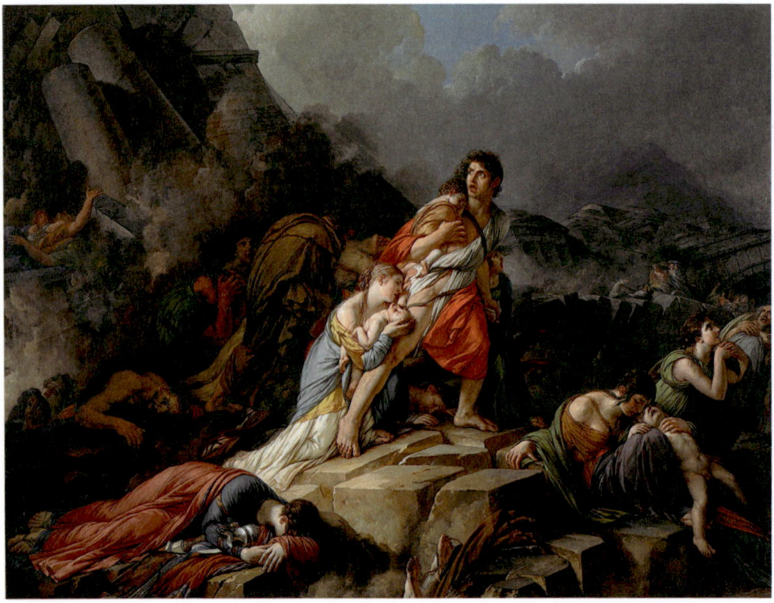

16

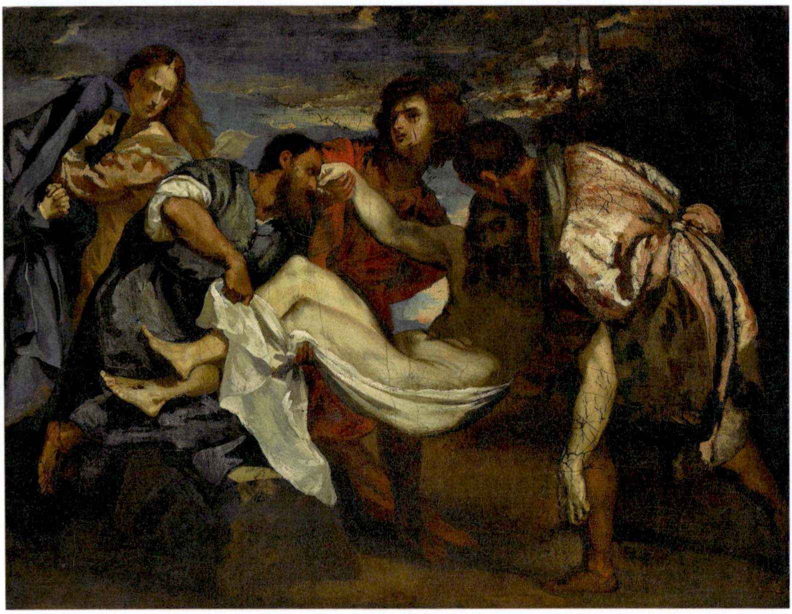

Jean-Pierre Saint-Ours, Le tremblement de terre, 1806
Théodore Géricault, La mise au tombeau, c. 1810–12

15

Jean-Pierre Saint-Ours (Geneva, 1752–1809)
Le tremblement de terre (*The Earthquake*), 1806
Oil on canvas, 143.5 × 186.5 cm
Gift of the artist's family, 1871. Inv. 1132

Trained in Paris in the studio of Joseph-Marie Vien, Saint-Ours set up in Rome in 1780. In 1792 he returned to Geneva to fight for his ideas of social justice and democracy in his homeland, which was in great political turmoil at the time. Up to 1806, he devoted a good number of drawings and five paintings to earthquakes. The subject was inspired by the catastrophe that destroyed the Sicilian town of Messina in 1783, causing tens of thousands of deaths. This tragedy revived memories of the Lisbon earthquake in 1755, which had inspired the Enlightenment philosophers to formulate ideas about human destiny emancipated from the notion of catastrophe as a divine punishment. Beyond this fascination with natural disasters, which was very much of his time, Saint-Ours, in choosing this theme, also sought to convey the destabilising effects of a period roiled by revolutionary upheaval.

Visual means here work to strengthen the feeling of insecurity that is the main point of the scene. The lighting underscores the isolation of the family taking refuge on a last islet of safety, surrounded by corpses, ruins, chariots and ash clouds. The powerful movement of flight suggested by the diagonal running across the composition seems to be stopped by the postures of the kneeling mother and the man looking to the rear. The handling shows the neoclassical rejection of the impulsive modelling and shimmering highlights typical of rococo painting. Saint-Ours uses firm contours that emphasise purity of line, and areas of bold colour that contrast with the dark hues. The primary colours (blue, red and yellow) and the white are used exclusively for the central group and symbolise life; they struggle against the blacks surrounding them. The farewell to a certain kind of civilisation and the shifting ground on which the future is to be built – that is what this work excels at conveying. [CL]

16

Théodore Géricault (Rouen, 1791–Paris, 1824), after Titian
La mise au tombeau (*The Entombment of Christ*), c. 1810–12
Oil on canvas, 46.1 × 60.9 cm
Gift of Max Bangerter, 1966. Inv. 1966-035

Although Théodore Géricault was no admirer of his art teachers Carle Vernet and Pierre-Narcisse Guérin, feeling his creativity stifled in their studios, he nonetheless followed the traditional path of copying old masters, as was then common practice in art academies. What set him apart from his peers was his highly individual choice of paintings and sculptures to copy and his free interpretation of the originals.

At the Musée Napoléon, later the Musée du Louvre, Géricault studied works from Antiquity and masterpieces by Rembrandt, Peter Paul Rubens, the French school and the Italian masters. The works that caught his eye all shared a powerful use of colour, like Titian's *Entombment of Christ* of c. 1520 (Paris, Musée du Louvre). In giving his own interpretation of the Venetian master's painting in his own, much smaller copy, he experimented with the relationship between shades of colour, testing how to apply paint in various textures and mastering the art of composition. He built the painting on colour rather than on lines, replacing Titian's warm hues with colder ones. He studied the effects of thick paint and broad brushstrokes. In tightening the focus, monumentalising the figures and heightening the contrasts of light and shadow, he sought to imbue the scene with drama.

More than a simple copy, this is a remarkable reworking of the Italian master's oeuvre, already showing the vigorous brushwork, sensitive, tactile paint, and powerful framing typical of Géricault's Romantic masterpieces and showcasing his genius for colour.

Géricault rarely parted with his copies, indicating how important he saw them for his development as an artist. This painting hung in his bedroom until he died. [CLC]

17

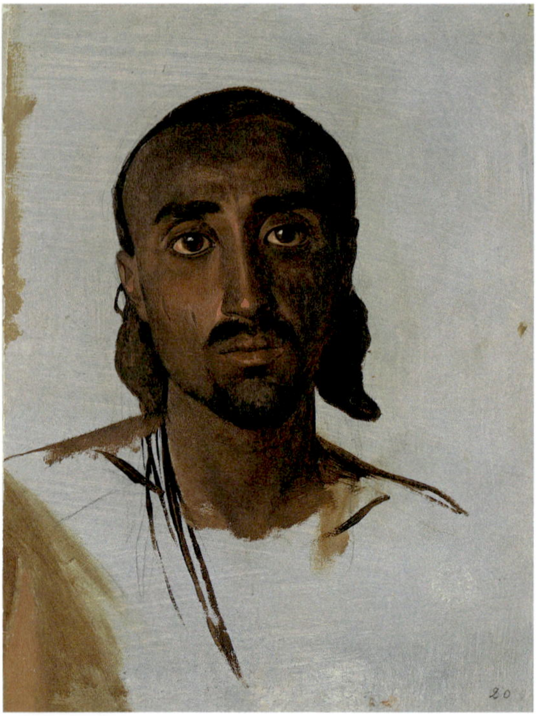

18

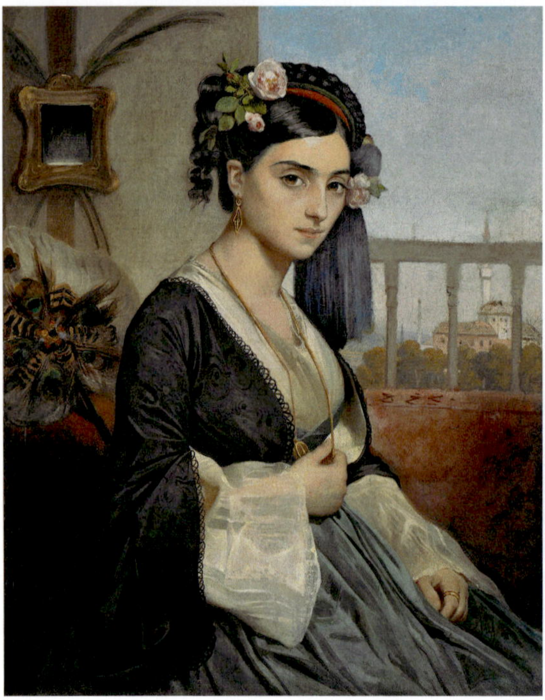

Charles Gleyre, Étude d'un Nubien, between 1835 and 1837
Charles Gleyre, Femme turque (Dudo Narikos), 1840

17

Charles Gleyre (Chevilly, 1806–Paris, 1874)
Étude d'un Nubien (*Study of a Nubian*), between 1835 and 1837
Graphite and oil on paper, 28.2×22.1 cm
Acquisition, 1908. Inv. 1027

Charles Gleyre had been in Rome for five years when, in spring 1834, he had the opportunity to live the dream that obsessed all Romantics: to travel to the Orient, to discover the monuments of Ancient Egypt and meet its famously 'exotic' people. His Italian career had ground to a halt and he was living precariously, so he leapt at the chance of working as a draughtsman and documentarian for John Lowell Jr., an industrialist from Boston. Their journey took them from Italy to Greece and on to Asia Minor, then finally to Egypt and Sudan. The artist produced over 150 drawings and watercolours, among them many measured archaeological drawings. The adventure made a lasting impression, and also gave him a special status among artists of his generation, few of whom had travelled beyond the Sixth Cataract on the Nile, from Alexandria all the way to the 'land of the Blacks'.

This study belongs to a set of a dozen paintings, probably executed in Sennar, a province of southern Nubia. Painted in oils, these tightly framed portraits from real life show faces of men and women from different ethnic groups. Gleyre carefully set about capturing individual features, creating an unmatched gallery at a time when the condescending attention of Europeans who travelled to Africa focused only on the picturesqueness of the costumes and strangeness of the rites. His work on light brings out the details of the skin, hair and finery against the grey ground of the prepared paper, placing us in the presence of human beings whose grave expressions seem to interrogate our perception of alterity.

At the time he made this portrait, Gleyre was living immersed with the local population. In November 1835 he parted company with his American patron in Khartoum. Weakened by dysentery, ophthalmia and fever, he completed the last stage of his oriental journey in complete solitude, before returning to France via Lebanon in spring 1838. [CL]

18

Charles Gleyre (Chevilly, 1806–Paris, 1874)
Femme turque (Dudo Narikos) (*Turkish Woman [Dudo Narikos]*), 1840
Oil on canvas, 41×33 cm
Gift of Mathilde Gleyre, 1911. Inv. 1347

On his return to Paris in 1838 after a lengthy journey in the Mediterranean in the pay of the American John Lowell Jr., Charles Gleyre decided to build his clientele by working in the fashionable Orientalist genre. He hoped to make use of the studies he had produced as a record of his travels, as Eugène Delacroix had done with his sketchbooks after visiting Morocco in 1832. However, Gleyre was forced to hand over all his work to his employer and his watercolours and drawings were sent to Boston. Only in 1839 did he manage to get them back so that he could build up a repertoire of exotic motifs. This took him most of the year 1840.

Femme turque is typical of the work Gleyre intended to produce based on his Oriental material. It is a version in oils of a watercolour painted six years earlier in Smyrna, where Gleyre and Lowell had spent part of autumn 1834. Like his fellow Swiss artist Jean-Étienne Liotard a century earlier, Gleyre collected a series of portraits of local personalities, including the sisters Annetta and Dudo Narikos. A comparison with the original watercolour (Boston, Museum of Fine Arts) shows Gleyre's extra touches to attract clients in Paris. He kept the luxuriant splendour of the sitter's costume and the roses and blue lace adornment in her hair. In the original, Dudo stood out against a plain wall; in this version, he has added a terrace, blue sky, the Aegean Sea, and a white minaret. A mirror and peacock feather fan, both typical features of Orientalist painting, also make their appearance. The painting owes its charm to one aspect that remains unchanged from the watercolour: the sitter's calm, reserved, graceful gaze. [CL]

19

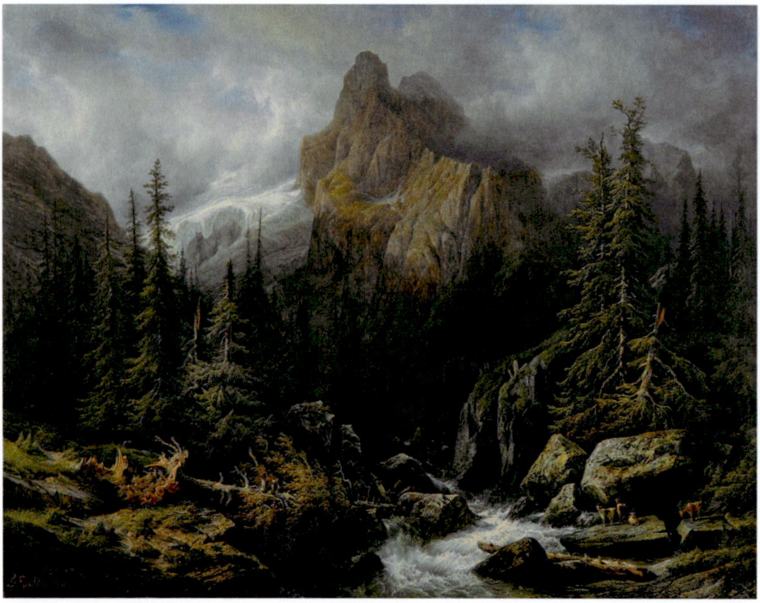

20

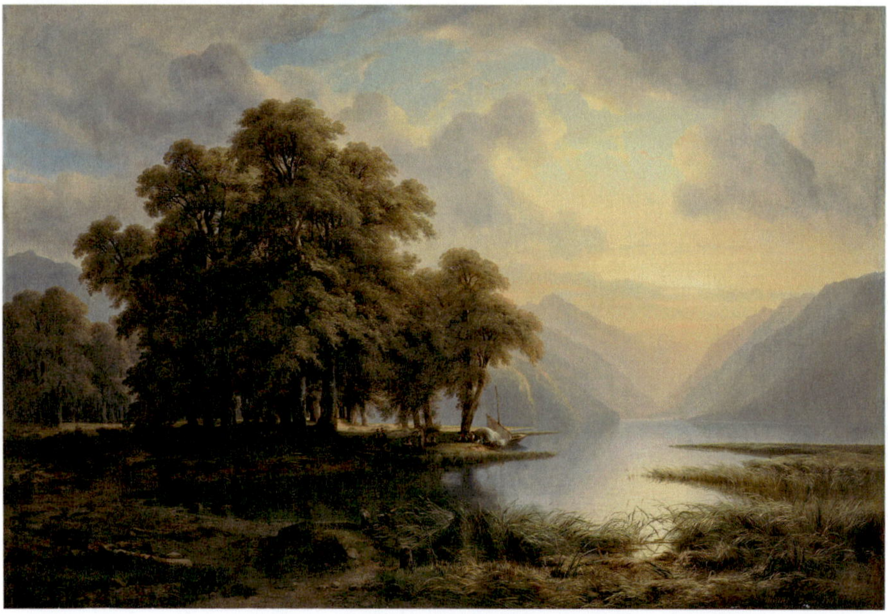

François Diday, Le glacier du Rosenlaui, 1841
Alexandre Calame, Le lac de Brienz, 1843

19

François Diday (Geneva, 1802–1877)
Le glacier du Rosenlaui (*The Rosenlaui Glacier*), 1841
Oil on canvas, 200 × 259 cm
Acquisition, 1842. Inv. 1079

François Diday studied fine art in Geneva and then in Antoine-Jean Gros' studio in Paris. He showed his work regularly at the Paris Salon, where he presented this monumental *Vue du glacier de Rosenland, dans le Canton de berne, en Suisse* (*View of the Rosenland Glacier in the Canton of Bern, Switzerland*), in 1841. The subject was designed to delight the Parisian judges, who had asked foreign entrants to showcase the specific characteristics of their national schools, particularly landscape features. The painting proved highly popular with visitors and sparked something of an Alpine tourism boom.

Diday and his pupil Alexandre Calame came to embody a new departure in Swiss landscape painting in the first half of the nineteenth century. From the late 1820s on, they set out to conquer the highest peaks, developing a style that perfectly married realism and romanticism. Starting with studies drawn from life, they returned to the studio to design large-format canvases that could almost have been stage backdrops. The paintings combine topographical description and sublime emotions, carefully orchestrating an image of grandiose nature in which man is conspicuous by his absence: vertiginous mountains, glowering clouds, trees bent double or ripped up by the roots, their branches torn off, thundering mountain torrents, and rocks with chamois goats perched precariously on them.

King Louis-Philippe purchased Diday's *Soir dans la vallée, Oberland bernois* (*Evening in the Valley in the Bern Oberland*, now destroyed) at the 1840 Salon. The Canton of Vaud followed suit the following year, reserving this *Glacier du Rosenlaui* for its Museum. [CLC]

20

Alexandre Calame (Vevey, 1810–Menton, 1864)
Le lac de Brienz (*Lake Brienz*), 1843
Oil on canvas, 98 × 146 cm
Commissioned from the artist, 1843. Inv. 589

Alexandre Calame's talent was first spotted in 1829 by the banker Jacques-Amédée Diodati, who paid for him to study with François Diday, the master of Alpine landscapes in and around Geneva. Calame first started looking for subjects in the surrounding hills, then from 1835 on in the Bernese Oberland, famous for its spectacular mountain peaks. He explored central Switzerland, finding artistic inspiration in mid-altitude settings and painting many views of Lakes Lucerne and Brienz. The mountain summits form the backdrop to views with a long depth of field. The calm, light-filled, almost timeless panoramas offered a welcome change from Diday's use of the sublime and pathos and were much appreciated by art lovers.

This view of Lake Brienz is typical of how Calame was influenced by seventeenth-century Dutch landscape painting. In 1838, he travelled to Holland to study the work of Meindert Hobbema and Jacob van Ruisdael, having discovered the Dutch school from Genevan collectors who preferred its painstaking realism and predilection for local views to the academic, idealised works of the Italian school. Calame learned from the technical mastery of the Dutch school, particularly in rendering the clear waters of the lake and the shimmer of foliage. The clear, warm, calm atmosphere of Lake Brienz radiates emotion. The play of light is extremely subtle, filtering through the thicket of trees on the left to create a foil for the elements in the foreground and middle ground, highlighted by the rays of light on the right-hand side.

Calame's fame was assured when he came to paint this view of Lake Brienz. He had enjoyed his first major international success at the Paris Salon in 1839 with *Storm at Handeck*, purchased by the Musée d'art et d'histoire in Geneva, and his collectors included members of the Russian imperial family and King Louis-Philippe of France. [CLC]

21

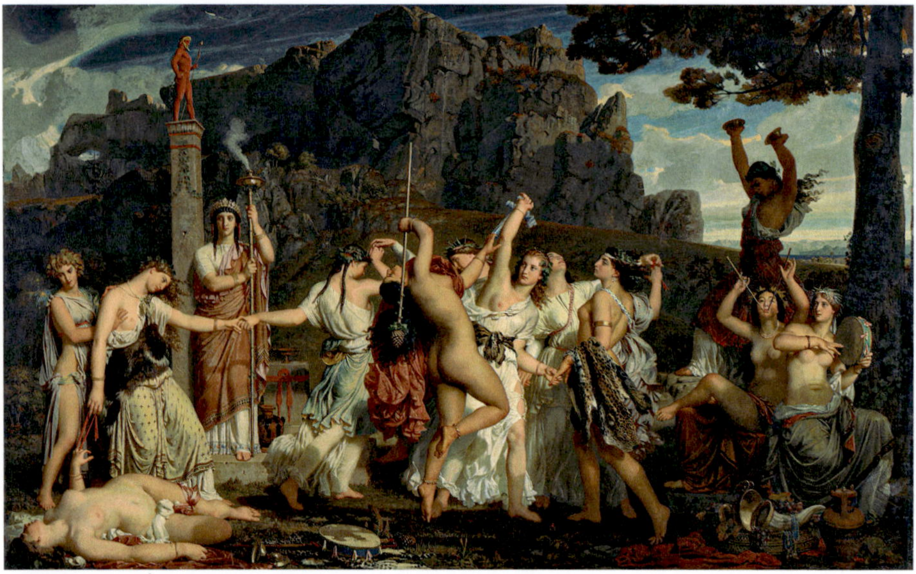

22

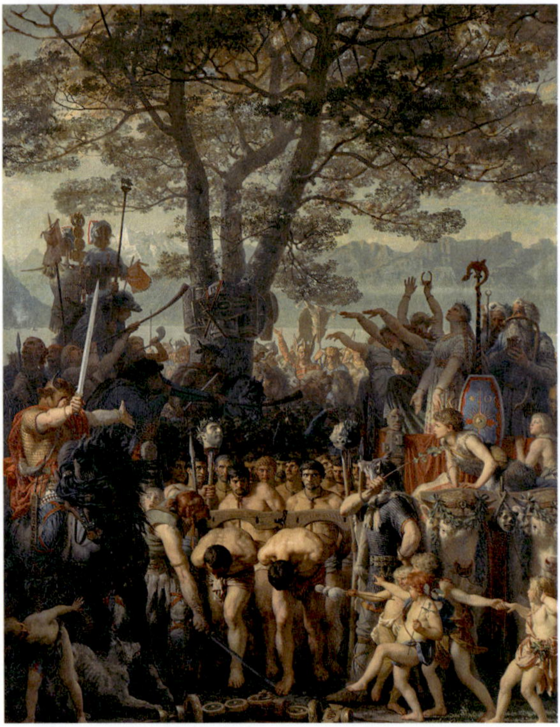

Charles Gleyre, La danse des bacchantes, 1849
Charles Gleyre, Les Romains passant sous le joug, 1858

21

Charles Gleyre (Chevilly, 1806–Paris, 1874)
La danse des bacchantes (*The Dance of the Bacchantes*), 1849
Oil on canvas, 147 × 243 cm
Acquisition with a special credit from the État de Vaud and the support of the Gottfried Keller Foundation, Gonset Holding S.A., Fondation Ernst Göhner, Association des Amis du Musée, ATAG Ernst & Young, 1995. Inv. 1995-093

An exclusively female affair, the bacchanal takes place under the implacable gaze of a hieratic priestess who is the guardian of the altar supporting the astonishing statue of a scarlet Bacchus. Where Titian's *Bacchanal of the Andrians* (1523–6, Madrid, Museo del Prado), from which Gleyre took his figure of a bacchante exhausted by the Dionysian ceremony, overflows with life, the flesh here is petrified by a chill wind. There is no wild eroticism with the Swiss master, just partially denuded bodies bestowing a delicately sensual note on the scene; no frantic savagery, but instead a severe ritual. Gleyre renews the iconography by turning the bacchanal into a cultic and mystic moment. But if his Antiquity is meditative, it is not so dreamlike as to overlook even the slightest archaeological detail, which he revisits in the light of contemporary research, particularly with regard to polychrome sculpture.

Before the rocky mass of a mountain around which we observe two patches of sky, one threatening and the other serene, the artist unfolds his composition in a subtle low relief. The centre is occupied by a tight group of six dancers. To the left, two bacchantes have left the circle, exhausted with drunkenness, one of them held up by a servant. To the right, three musicians set the rhythm of the dance with the sound of a tambourine, aulos and crotalums. The composition forms an ellipse punctuated by the pronounced verticals of a column, the shaft of an incense burner, a brandished thyrsus and the raised arms of the musician. The transition from one figure to another is achieved fluently by the joining of hands and ribbons held between them. On the far right, a still life with vase, basket of grapes, golden dish and red fabric serve as a pendant to the bacchante lying on the ground. [CL]

22

Charles Gleyre (Chevilly, 1806–Paris, 1874)
Les Romains passant sous le joug (*Romans Passing under the Yoke*) or *La bataille du Léman* (*The Battle of Lake Geneva*), 1858
Oil on canvas, 230.5 × 181.4 cm
Commissioned by the État de Vaud, 1850. Inv. 1392

Charles Gleyre's republican convictions explain his enthusiastic acceptance of a commission from the radical new government in his native Canton of Vaud. He was asked to paint a companion piece to *Major Davel* (1850, also in the Museum), a monumental history painting that he had recently completed to general acclaim. After depicting the beheading of Jean Daniel Abraham Davel, the hero of the 1723 uprising of the Vaud people against the regime in Bern, he chose another instance of people struggling for independence. *Les Romains passant sous le joug* refers to the defeat in 107 BC of the Consul Lucius Cassius and his Roman legion by the Helvetians under their chief Divico. The Celts fighting against the invader replace Davel, the solitary hero, and thus a high deed of classical Antiquity, recounted by Julius Caesar in *The Gallic Wars*, replaces a revolt in modern Swiss history. The work was to become an icon for Switzerland as the young country sought after 1848 to generate unity through myths promoting a sense of national identity.

The painting took Gleyre eight years to complete. He read widely on Celtic material culture and worked on numerous preparatory sketches. Though the scene is now known to have taken place near Agen in southern France, he located it on the shores of Lake Geneva. The scene shows the humiliation of the Roman army. The reference to the battle of the Caudine Forks overlays the claim to a rural, agrarian identity, as the artist shows the Romans forced by the Helvetians to put on yokes usually worn by oxen. The incredibly packed, complex composition is structured around an age-old oak. The upper part features a landscape, while the lower half is full of action. On the left, the Helvetian army is led by Divico, brandishing his sword; on the right is a cart for the druids and priestesses who are singing the victory chant to the heavens, while in the centre, the prisoners are being flogged by warriors as children point and laugh. [CL]

23

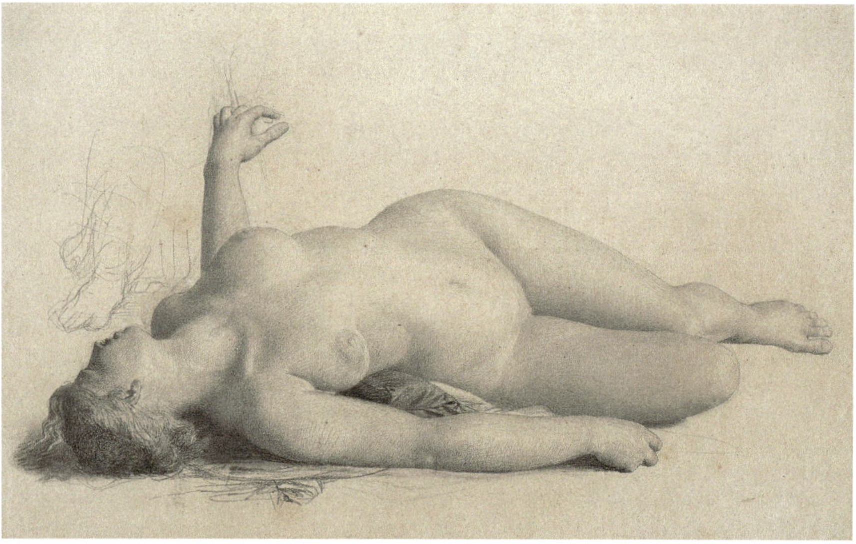

24

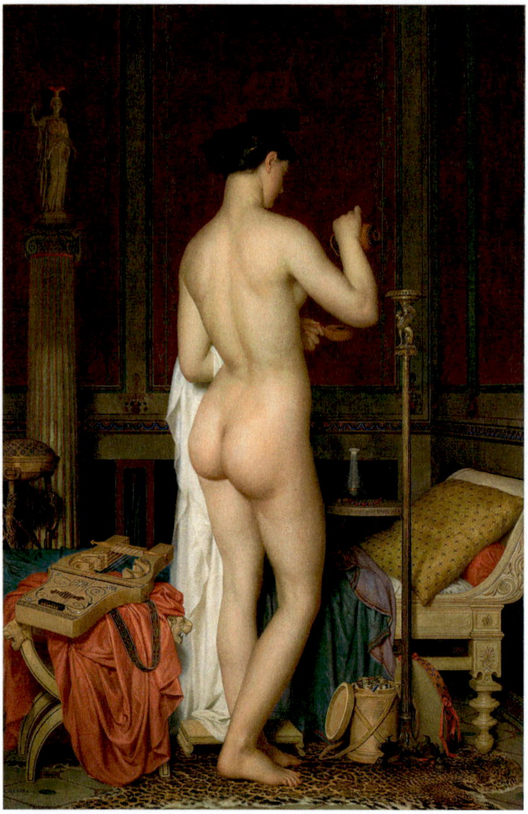

Charles Gleyre, Étude pour La danse des bacchantes, c. 1848–9
Charles Gleyre, Le coucher de Sapho, 1867

23

Charles Gleyre (Chevilly, 1806–Paris, 1874)
Étude pour La danse des bacchantes (*Study for the Dance of the Bacchantes*), c. 1848–9
Black pencil on paper, 27.7 × 44.5 cm
Acquisition, 1908. Inv. 1096

Charles Gleyre never had relationships with women. He refused any physical contact with women, while at the same time displaying an obsession with the naked female form expressed in his history paintings. His first major canvas, *Les Brigands Romains* (*The Roman Bandits*, 1831, Paris, Musée du Louvre) depicts a rape carried out in broad daylight. He did not return to such crude modern subjects after his Romantic period, though the female body remained a constant feature. This underlying obsession may have driven his choice of episodes from classical Antiquity and Greek mythology from the late 1840s on. These works present a broad repertoire of lascivious poses whose sensuality is heightened by the chilly detachment of academic painting.

Detailed studies from nature were at the heart of Gleyre's aesthetic, encouraging constant encounters with women called on to exhibit their bodies 'for art's sake'. A form of voyeurism? Undeniably, if that means erotic tension arising from the continually renewed practice of meticulously studying the object of desire from a safe distance in the clear knowledge that only the artist's pen or brush will ever caress it.

This preparatory work for *La danse des bacchantes* (1849, see n. 21) is a study of the figure on the far left of the painting, depicting a woman overcome by drunkenness, lying naked on the floor. The highly detailed study is typical of Gleyre's drawing, with a strong light from the front pushing the darker shades to the sides to accentuate the body's contours. Did Gustave Courbet see the finished painting or admire this masterful study in which the woman's belly, breasts and thighs are shamelessly offered up to the viewer's gaze? His *Femme au Perroquet* (*Woman with a Parrot*, 1866, New York, Metropolitan Museum of Art) seems to quote this work almost literally, simply adding a bird fluttering down to perch on the woman's raised arm. [CL]

24

Charles Gleyre (Chevilly, 1806–Paris, 1874)
Le coucher de Sapho (Jeune fille dans un intérieur pompéien) (*Sappho Preparing for Bed: Young Woman in a Pompeii Interior*), 1867
Oil on canvas, 108 × 72 cm
On deposit from the Gottfried Keller Foundation, Federal Office of Culture, Bern, 1909. Inv. 1332

In the latter half of the nineteenth century, artists drew on depictions of daily life in ancient Greece and Rome to reconcile the neoclassical and Romantic traditions. The New Greeks – young artists who had studied in Gleyre's studio, such as Jean-Léon Gérôme and Jean-Louis Hamon – left high deeds and heroic scenes behind, preferring sentimental, intimate moments shown in large formats. The scenes they imagined drew on the excavations in Pompeii and Greece, where everyday objects were being discovered, letting artists depict the lives of ordinary people of the past in more detail.

Gleyre joined this new tradition with his painting of a young woman filling an oil lamp while preparing for bed. Like a modern Pygmalion, he breathed life into an antique marble statue – a Callipygian Venus he had sketched in Naples in 1834 – and placed her in a bedchamber painted in tones of red and black that he had seen in Pompeii. Around her unclothed body he placed a set of 'antique' accessories that focus the viewer's attention on her nakedness, including a glass bottle, a basket holding parchments, a lyre and tambourine, and a leopard-skin bedside rug. A lion carved into a wooden chair seems to be about to bite her calf, a caustic reference to the bourgeois visitors to art salons who feast their eyes on the naked female form.

While Gleyre certainly sought to depict an intimate scene from Antiquity, the title is not his: it was only given to the work after his death. His contemporaries thought the woman preparing for bed was Sappho, reflecting the new-found interest in the muse of Mytilene, for instance in the poetry of Charles Baudelaire (*Lesbos*, 1857) and Paul Verlaine (*Sappho*, 1867). Gleyre was a keen amateur archaeologist and would never have committed such a terrible anachronism as to put a Greek poetess who lived in the seventh century BC in a decor inspired by Pompeii, an Italian city destroyed by the eruption of Vesuvius in August 79 AD! [CL]

25

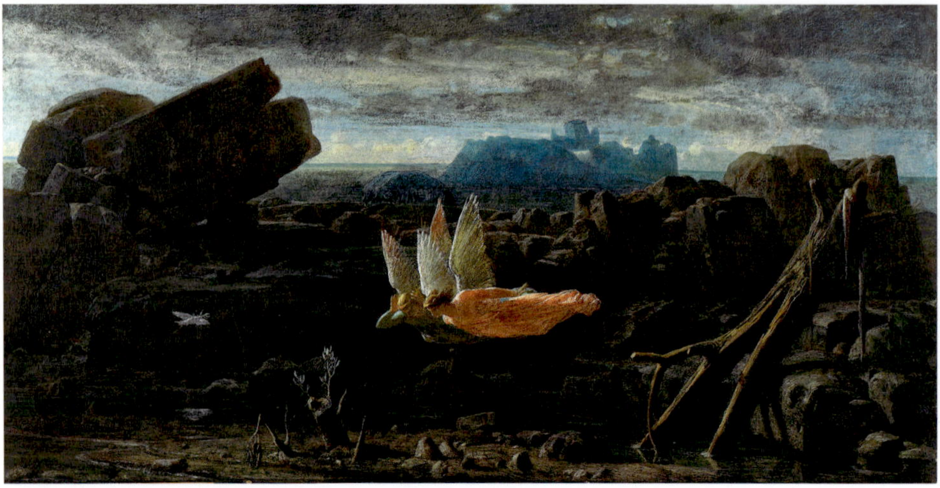

26

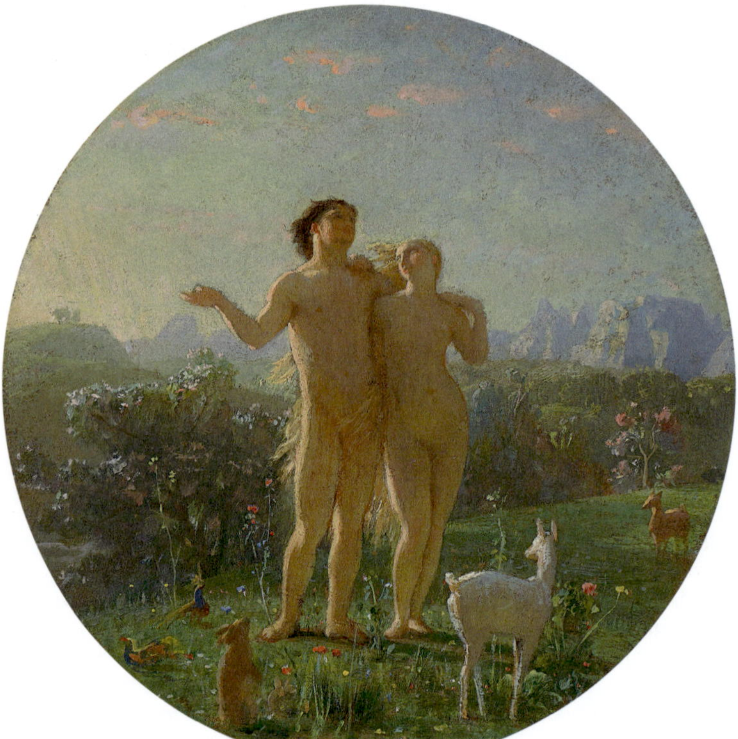

Charles Gleyre, Le Déluge, 1856
Charles Gleyre, Esquisse pour Le paradis terrestre or Le matin, between 1869 and 1874

25

Charles Gleyre (Chevilly, 1806–Paris, 1874)
Le Déluge (*The Flood*), 1856
Oil and pastel on canvas, 99.5 × 197 cm
Acquired by public subscription, 1899.
Inv. 1243

Charles Gleyre's approach to depicting the Biblical myth of the flood and the rebirth of the human race is innovative. Unlike earlier artists, he focuses not on the moment of the flood itself, or the fate of the few to survive the cataclysm ordered by God to punish the sins of the sons of Adam. There are no bodies floating on the waters, no survivors clinging to trees, or animals leaving the ark. Instead, he has chosen a broad landscape bathed in dim light, scattered with strangely shaped rocks, with the intense light of a new dawn in the background. The work reflects his love of expanses of desert after his travels in the Orient in the 1830s.

The painting shows the new face of the earth after the waters have receded. The ark is shown perched on Mount Ararat in the distance, waiting for the dove hovering in the foreground. On the right is a dead snake draped over a tree trunk, symbolising the defeat of evil. The centre of the composition is dominated by two splendid angels, frozen in mid-flight at the sight of life bursting anew from the olive branch. The supernatural light haloing the angels was achieved by a brand new technique, applying touches of pastel to the surface of the oil paint.

Gleyre's principal source of inspiration for the angels seems not to have been Pierre-Paul Prud'hon's *La Justice et la Vengeance divine poursuivant le Crime* (*Justice and Divine Vengeance Pursuing Crime*, 1808, Paris, Musée du Louvre), as has sometimes been suggested, but rather the naïve frescoes of Italian primitive painters. How should the presence of the angels be read, given the Bible does not mention them in its account of the flood? Gleyre may have drawn on the non-canonical *Book of Enoch*, which suggests the real cause of the flood was angels falling in love with humans – a superb metaphor for art itself! [CL]

26

Charles Gleyre (Chevilly, 1806–Paris, 1874)
Esquisse pour Le paradis terrestre (*Sketch for the Earthly Paradise*) or *Le matin* (*Morning*), between 1869 and 1874
Oil on wood, 24 cm (diam.)
Acquisition, 1908. Inv. 1366

On his return from Egypt in the mid-1830s, Charles Gleyre began contemplating a complex series featuring several paintings of hours of the day, the stages of life, and the decline and renaissance of peoples, summing up his own considerations on the history of humanity. Three major works form part of the project, which was never completed. These were *Le Soir* or *Les Illusions perdues* (*Evening*, or *Lost Illusions*, Paris, Musée du Louvre), evoking the collapse of civilisations, which was much admired at the 1843 Paris Salon, *Le Déluge* (*The Flood*, 1856, see facing page), in which a dove flies over the devastated earth, bringing hope of rebirth, and this *Paradis terrestre*, on which he was working when he died in 1874.

Despite the title it has been given by posterity, *Le paradis terrestre* is more than just an episode from the Bible. The tondo, a sketch for a planned monumental work, does refer to Adam and Eve to symbolise the birth of humanity. However, Gleyre draws on Ovid for the description of the *locus amoenus* and Jean-Jacques Rousseau for the tender sentimentality of the couple's pose. Eve is an almost literal copy of Sandro Botticelli's *Birth of Venus* (c. 1484–5, Florence, Uffizi Gallery). A rabbit, kid goats, and female pheasants are clustered around the couple, shown walking with their backs to the rising sun. The fruit of the forbidden tree is merely hinted at by a flowering apple tree lost in the beautiful bucolic setting. In the foreground is a meadow scattered with poppies and buttercups; a river flows through the middle ground, while in the background are snowy mountain caps reminiscent of the foothills of the Jura, where the artist was born and spent his earliest years.

Gleyre rediscovered the pleasure of painting in colour in *Le paradis terrestre*. The work also reflects his hope in a future golden age, shared by many nineteenth-century artists from Ingres to Pierre Puvis de Chavannes. [CL]

27

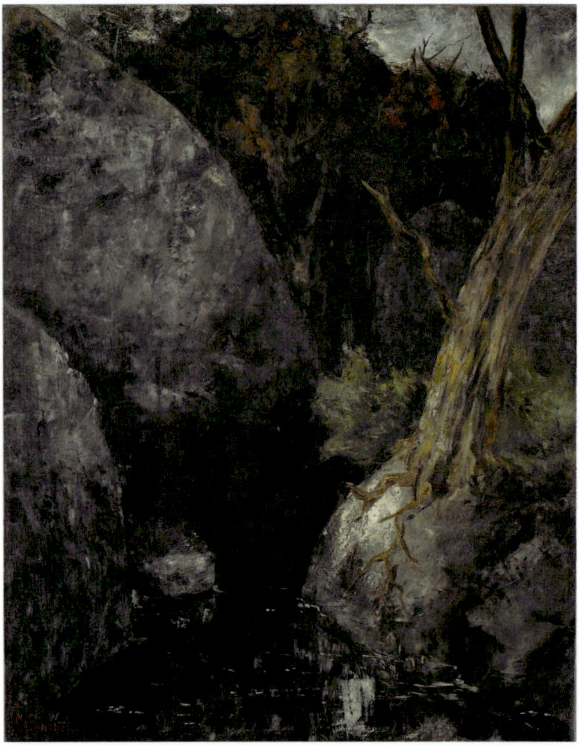

28

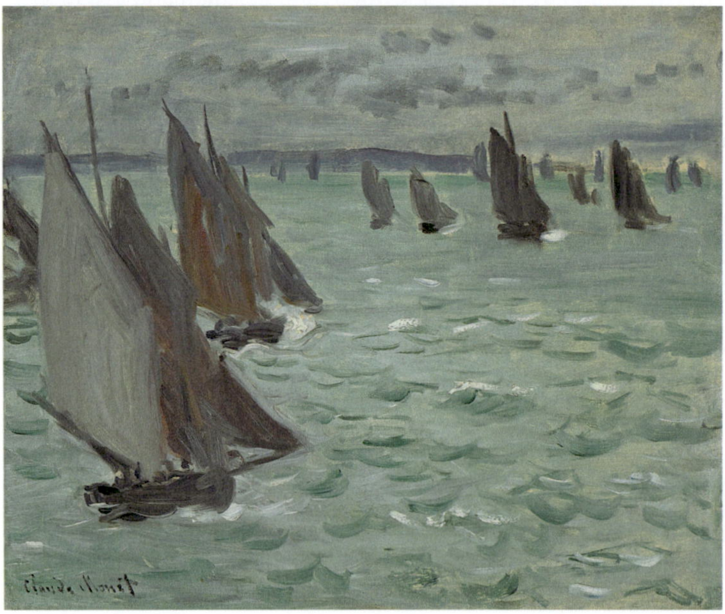

Gustave Courbet, Le vieil arbre dans la gorge, 1871
Claude Monet, Voiliers en mer, 1868

27

Gustave Courbet (Ornans, 1819–La Tour-de-Peilz, 1877)
Le vieil arbre dans la gorge (*The Old Tree in the Gorge*), 1871
Oil on canvas, 92 × 73 cm
Henri-Auguste Widmer bequest, 1939. Inv. 324

From the early 1840s on, Gustave Courbet's paintings expressed both the vagaries of collective history and his own inner torment. His landscapes and still lifes in particular have hidden depths behind their seemingly banal realism. In the final years of his life, his paintings of trout that had been caught but were not yet dead and worm-eaten red apples reflected both the failed dreams of the Paris Commune and the tragic turn his own life had taken.

He faced a precarious situation in 1871. A committed socialist and democrat, he took part in the Paris Commune alongside his fellow revolutionaries inspired by Proudhon. He was arrested in June that year and sentenced to prison for inciting the destruction of the Vendôme column. In 1873 he was required to pay the cost of rebuilding the monument and had little choice but to go into exile in Switzerland.

This old tree in a gorge, probably painted in his home region of Franche-Comté in eastern France or from memory, echoes the torment of the times, just as Honoré Daumier and Jean-François Millet's storm-tossed trees had done earlier in the century. A stream crawls along sluggishly in the depths of the dark, narrow gorge. A knotty tree clings to the rock on the edge of the black water, where it has survived many storms. Silvery light falls through the almost nocturnal landscape onto its withered roots. It is tempting to draw a parallel between the old tree and Courbet himself, as years earlier he had painted himself as an oak in the prime of life (*Le Chêne de Flagey*, 1864, Ornans, Musée Courbet). The gorge, long a refreshing Arcadia, is now no more than a narrow ravine lit by the dying glimmers of a stormy day. The use of dark hues roughly applied with a palette knife heightens the scene's dramatic impact. [CLC]

28

Claude Monet (Paris, 1840–Giverny, 1926)
Voiliers en mer (*Sailing Boats at Sea*), 1868
Oil on canvas, 50 × 61 cm
Edwige Guyot bequest, 2006. Inv. 2006-001

After several years in Paris, Claude Monet returned to Le Havre for a few months in the summer of 1862. He went painting along the Normandy coast with Johan Barthold Jongkind, studying the rugged cliffs and constantly shifting play of light and waves on the sea. In May 1864, he and his fellow painter Frédéric Bazille moved into the Saint-Siméon farm in Honfleur, on the other side of the Seine estuary, a spot popular with landscape painters including Camille Corot, Charles-François Daubigny and Gustave Courbet.

Monet spent every summer season working on numerous studies between Honfleur and Le Havre, starting his paintings out in the open. He also worked up his sketches in the studio, building on the tradition of the heroic landscape that dated back to the seventeenth century. The seashore and the open water beyond it were his favourite subjects.

Late in 1868, Monet was living in Étretat when he painted three canvases depicting fishing boats setting out to sea. He was at pains to capture the fleeting shimmer of light on the waves, studying the effect of wind as it ruffled the water, scudded the clouds across the sky, and swelled the sails. The swift brushstrokes mimic the boats skating across the waves. The horizon is very high, reflecting the influence of Japanese prints on Monet's 1860s seascapes, while the broad strokes in hues of blue-grey and brown are comparable to Édouard Manet's works of the same period. Monet builds shapes through colour rather than lines and contours. The swift dabs of the brush give the impression of spontaneity. The creative process is both free and utterly controlled: a number of preparatory pencil sketches for this painting feature detailed studies of the various boats. [CLC]

29

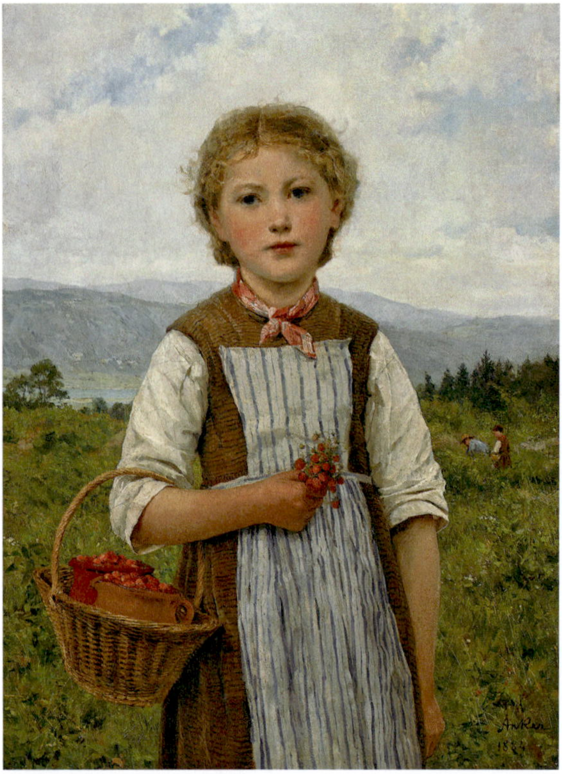

30

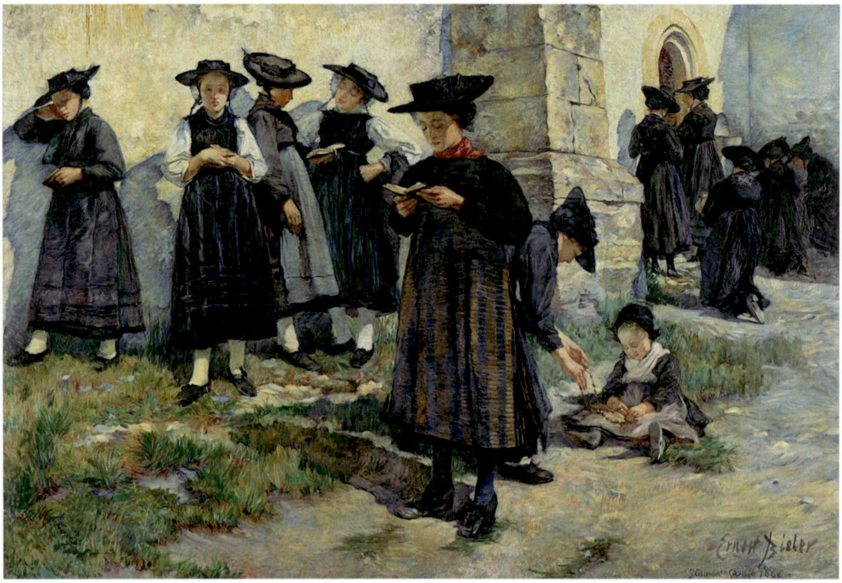

Albert Anker, La Mariette aux fraises, 1884
Ernest Biéler, Devant l'église de Saint-Germain à Savièse, 1886

29

Albert Anker (Anet, 1831–1910)
La Mariette aux fraises (*Mariette with Strawberries*), 1884
Oil on canvas, 81×60 cm
Gift of Bertha Bovon, in memory of her sister Elisa Spühler, 1939. Inv. 691

After a youth spent between Anet, Neuchâtel and Bern, Albert Anker put his two languages (French and German) to use in conquering the art markets in both Paris and German-speaking Switzerland. From autumn to spring, he lived in the French capital and exhibited at the Salon; in the summer, he withdrew to his country house in the Bernese Seeland. Here is where he painted this portrait typical of the world we still associate him with today: peaceful village life, the worlds of childhood and of old age, and the social and educational activities that are the bedrock of the democratic spirit.

Listed by the painter in his sales catalogue as 'young girl with strawberries (chaperon)', the canvas became popular under the title *La Mariette aux fraises* (*Das Erdbeeri-Mareili*), which it shared with a novella by the Bernese writer Jeremias Gotthelf published in 1852. Anker himself later illustrated this book, although none of his drawings resemble this painting.

Anker chose a ten year-old girl from his village, Rosa Zesiger, to pose as his strawberry picker. She wears a blouse, a dress and an apron cut from crude, locally produced cloth. The kerchief knotted around her neck, typical of the textiles produced by the mills in eastern Switzerland, enlivens the ensemble with a dash of rouge, echoed by the strawberries, the girl's mouth and the clothes of another little girl in the background. The enamelled pots common in all Bernese kitchens in the nineteenth century, together with the landscape, which includes Lake Biel and the Jura mountains, ensure the scene's realism and consummately Helvetian character. At the same time, the young girl's dreamy, wandering gaze conveys the tedium of the hours she has spent posing for this portrait, which strives for an effect of immediacy. They confirm the impression that this figure standing out against a flowery meadow has almost been collaged onto its background. [CL]

30

Ernest Biéler (Rolle, 1863–Lausanne, 1948)
Devant l'église de Saint-Germain à Savièse (*Outside the Church of Saint-Germain in Savièse*), 1886
Oil on canvas, 204×302 cm
Acquisition, 1886. Inv. 556

Born in the Canton of Vaud, Ernest Biéler moved to Paris in the early 1880s but continued to live in Switzerland from time to time. He discovered the village of Savièse in the Valais in the summer of 1884 and was charmed by the customs of its people, attached as they still were to the traditional way of life, but also by the brilliant light and limpid air. He returned in the autumn and made several sketches for *Devant l'église de Saint-Germain*. The following summer he had a large stretcher delivered to him for this ambitious work. The painting, which he completed in his Parisian studio, was seen by a counsellor of state from Vaud, Eugène Ruffy, who acquired it for the Museum. Biéler was allowed to keep it for a while, however, so that he could present it at the Salon of 1887 in Paris.

For many painters in the late nineteenth century, rural life and religious practices stood for a stable world that was in fact disappearing, as populations left the countryside for the city and religious belief waned. During the industrial age these traditions came to represent reassuring values and Biéler – like Jean-François Millet and Jules Breton before him – offers a universalising vision of them in this work. Rather than a precisely located village or a particular Catholic rite, the artist shows simple, timeless activities: a banal church with its sturdy stone pier and its arched doorway; women gathering silently in the warmth of a fine summer day. Dressed in their dark blue Sunday dress, some are following the Mass from outside while others are reading their missals or looking after their children.

By its composition and handling, the work was bound to arouse the interest of avant-garde circles: the figures made monumental by the close framing, the way the folds of the clothes reflect the intense light and the bluish shadows applied in broad touches to the walls, all show that the artist had learned from the impressionists. [CL]

31

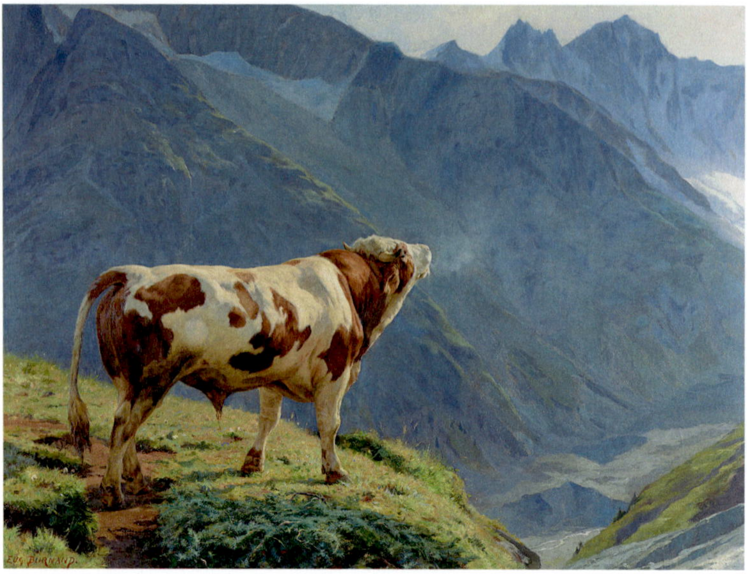

32

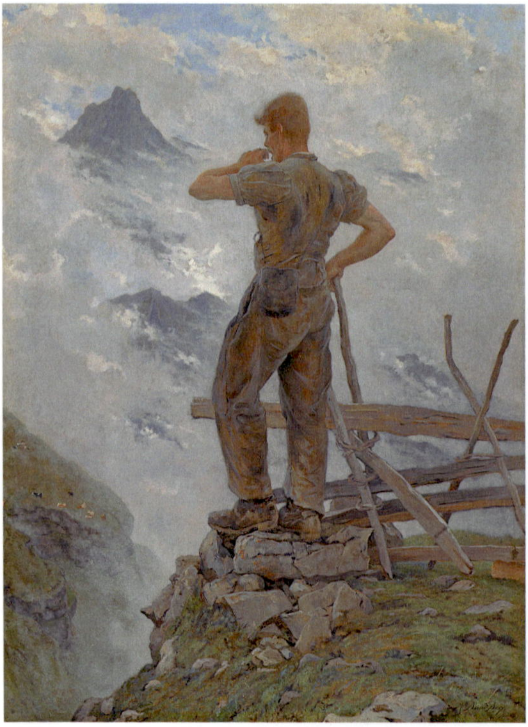

Eugène Burnand, Taureau dans les Alpes, 1884
Auguste Baud-Bovy, Lioba! Berger de l'Oberland bernois rappelant son troupeau, 1886

31

Eugène Burnand (Moudon, 1850–Paris, 1921)
Taureau dans les Alpes (*Bull in the Alps*), 1884
Oil on canvas, 200 × 270 cm
Acquired by subscription with a special credit from the Conseil d'État vaudois, and the support of individual patrons and the Société vaudoise des beaux-arts, 1884. Inv. 535

Eugène Burnand, from the Canton of Vaud, moved to Paris in 1872 and studied with Jean-Léon Gérôme. By the early 1880s he was working within the broad naturalist trend spreading throughout Europe, specialising in rural genre scenes with peasants and animals executed in formats that were usually the preserve of history painting.

While in Switzerland during the summer of 1884, over a period of two months, the artist painted this *Taureau dans les Alpes*, a monumental work that he considered his manifesto. Following in the footsteps of his predecessors in the Dutch school, and in competition with Rudolf Koller from Zurich, his take on the bovine portrait resulted in a resonant image capable of speaking to the identity of his fellow countrymen while also positioning him in France as one of the great proponents of modern realism.

The painting is based on studies of a Valais landscape observed from Arolla, and sketches made in the family home at Seppey, in the Canton of Vaud, of a severed bull's head. The artwork is spectacular, the colours are bold, the rendering virtuosic. A fine Simmental bull, its tawny coat blotched with white, overlooks the valley from the heights of its pastureland, steam escaping from its muzzle indicating the coolness of the morning air at high altitude. The carpet of grass dotted with flowers shines in the sun and sets a summery tone. The atmospheric treatment of the mountains covered in snow dirtied by the thaw conveys their distance and the depth of the Val d'Hérens. The French landscape painter Jules Breton lauded Burnand for revitalising the Helvetian school: 'This is Switzerland, you will be the one to reveal this country.'

Before its presentation at the Salon of 1885 in Paris, this *Taureau dans les Alpes* was previewed in Lausanne in November 1884, and was immediately purchased by subscription for the Museum. [CL]

32

Auguste Baud-Bovy (Geneva, 1848–Davos, 1899)
Lioba! Berger de l'Oberland bernois rappelant son troupeau (*Lioba! A Shepherd in the Bernese Oberland Calling back His Flock*), 1886
Oil on canvas, 130 × 98 cm
Acquisition, 1900. Inv. 1058

In 1882, Auguste Baud-Bovy left Geneva for Paris to be with his Communard friends and the artists of the French-Swiss colony. During his time there he became fascinated by the palette of Camille Corot and gave up the dark, thick paint he had previously used in his portraits. In 1888 he returned to Switzerland and settled in Aeschi, a small village in the Bernese Oberland.

Lioba! heralds this return to the homeland impelled by nostalgia for a life surrounded by nature. The painting is part of a series of six large-format canvases illustrating the 'Heroic actions of the shepherd' executed between 1886 and 1890. It was inspired by sketches made in the summer of 1885 at the place called the Bundalp, in the Kiental Valley. The work was executed with thinly applied paint in shades of light greys and soft greens warmed by ochres mixed with red. The emphasis is on the noble assurance of the solitary shepherd whose imposing figure, standing *contrapposto* like a Donatello sculpture, dominates the valley and the tiny herd of cows.

Painted almost seventy years after *Der Wanderer über dem Nebelmeer* (*Wanderer Above the Mist*) by Caspar David Friedrich (c. 1817, Hamburg, Kunsthalle), this canvas offers a surprising reformulation of that work, with which it shares its vertical format and the figure of a man seen from behind standing on the summit of a rocky promontory with his right hand resting on his hip, facing mountains on the horizon and clouds rising from the plain. However, the works evince differing relations to landscape: whereas the icon of German Romanticism confronted a city-dweller with the immensity of virgin nature, and invited reflection on the insignificance of the human episode in the history of the earth, Baud-Bovy's summer genre scene celebrates the harmonious relationship between the primitive civilisation of the shepherds and the high mountain valleys. The title of the painting, which refers to the traditional cry for calling in the herds and to the echo sent back by the mountains, underscores this osmosis [CL]

33

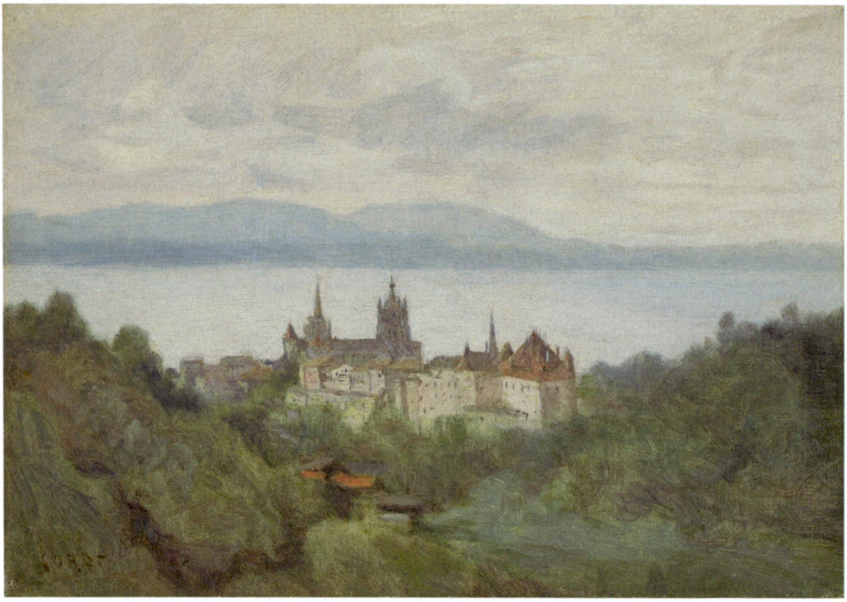

34

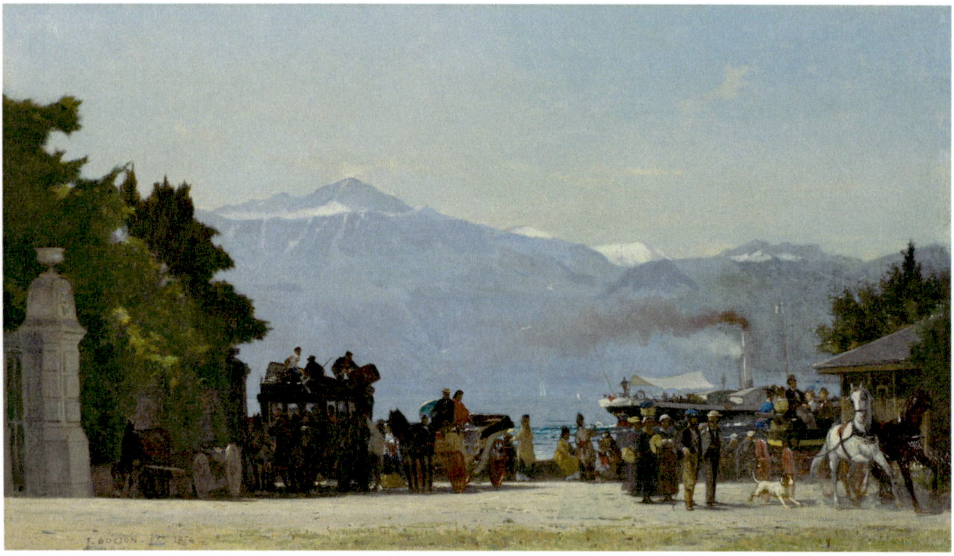

Jean-Baptiste Camille Corot, Lausanne et le lac Léman, 1842
François Bocion, À Ouchy en 1874, 1874

33

Jean-Baptiste Camille Corot (Paris, 1796–1875)
Lausanne et le lac Léman (*Lausanne and Lake Geneva*), 1842
Oil on canvas, 25 × 36 cm
Gift of Alfred Strölin, 1955. Inv. 1955-016

While Jean-Baptiste Camille Corot's three visits to Italy are the best-known of his travels outside France, he actually visited Switzerland more often. His mother was from Freiburg and he was a frequent visitor there, becoming friends with many local artists. One such was Barthélemy Menn, who showed his paintings in exhibitions in Geneva. Corot and Menn together visited the château in Gruyères, which belonged to the Bovy family, and Corot helped decorate the Salon with four landscapes in roundels (1853–7).

Corot stopped in Lausanne on his way to Rome in October 1825, painting his first view of the city from a spot overlooking Lake Geneva in the Flon valley, not far from the Hermitage property (now in a private collection). This had become a popular spot for travelling artists to stop and paint in the late eighteenth century. Corot returned to the same spot for two new paintings in the 1840s, including this view of Lausanne and Lake Geneva.

His viewpoint in this painting is noticeably more distant than in the 1825 version, with a broader framing of the scene to include more of the natural setting. An abundance of foliage fills the lower third of the canvas to frame the town, whose rooftops stand out against the calm waters of the lake. In the distance, the Alpine peaks merge into the clouds. The profile of the cathedral has changed slightly, since the lantern-tower was struck by lightning and rebuilt in 1827. The foreground foliage is sketched in with swift, overlapping dabs of the paintbrush in a rich palette of greens. The lake, mountains, and sky in the background all come together in one hazy blend of silvery greens and blue-greys, with lengthy brushstrokes that underline the horizontal composition. The red roofs provide a splash of brighter colour in the centre of the painting. [CLC]

34

François Bocion (Lausanne, 1828–1890)
À Ouchy en 1874 (*Ouchy, 1874*), 1874
Oil on canvas, 34 × 61 cm
Acquisition, 1941. Inv. 246

François Bocion was one of the first Vaud-born artists to choose to return to work in the canton after studying in Paris, where, like many others, he dreamed of an illustrious career as a history painter. His art is rooted in direct observation of nature, very unlike the tormented Romantic vision typical of the previous generation. His concern to capture daily events in the modern world as he saw it made him an outstanding chronicler of his age. This composition shows a stagecoach, several horse-drawn coaches, and a steam boat, all reflecting the increasing mobility of nineteenth-century society. The scene is bustling with activity, with locals hard at work and the new breed of tourists busy making the most of their leisure time. The travellers have just arrived by boat and are catching the stagecoach to the centre of Lausanne.

1874 marked the death of Charles Gleyre, Bocion's teacher in Paris, and the first impressionist exhibition, held in the same city. Bocion has often been compared to the impressionists for his practice of painting outdoors from life and his talent for capturing variations in atmosphere, but he is also a master of carefully staged scenes characteristic of painting practiced in the studio. This painting is one such example, with the light cleverly planned to place the middle ground on the left in shadow.

Bocion's interest in realist depictions of modern life is also reminiscent of Gustave Courbet, who was in exile in La Tour-de-Peilz from July 1873. Bocion and Courbet both loved painting Lake Geneva at all times of day. It is not known whether the two men ever painted together from life, but they may well have known each other: when Courbet died in 1877, Bocion was asked to draw up the inventory of his studio. [YG]

35

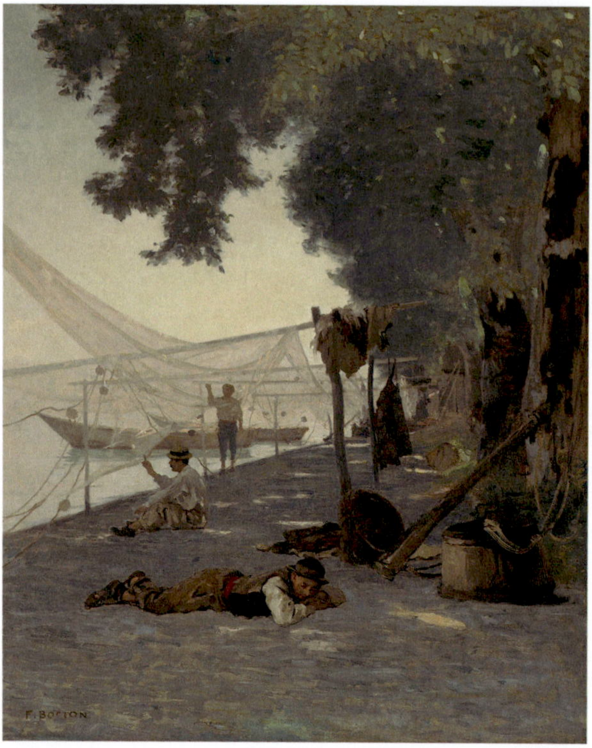

36

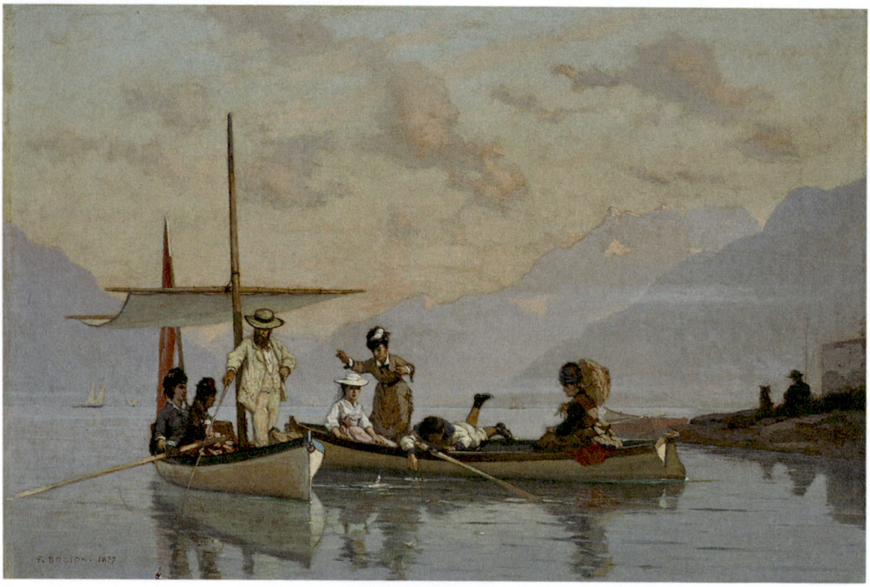

François Bocion, Filets et pêcheurs, c. 1877
François Bocion, Bocion et sa famille à la pêche, 1877

35

François Bocion (Lausanne, 1828–1890)
Filets et pêcheurs (*Nets and Fishermen*), c. 1877
Oil on canvas, 61 × 50 cm
Acquisition, 1913. Inv. 247

François Bocion's painting depicts an everyday fishing scene, a common theme in his work from the 1860s on. A young fisherman just back from an outing on the lake has fallen asleep on the jetty in the warm summer sun. Two more fishermen are seen repairing their nets in the background. As a careful study of the painting shows, nineteenth-century fishing nets were still made of natural fibres and were hung out to dry on open-air stands so that the owners could spot any tears in need of repair. The man in the middle ground is busy repairing his net with a shuttle or needle.

While many naturalist artists recorded the daily lives of lake and sea fishermen at this time, from Jules Breton in Brittany to Peder Severin Krøyer in Denmark, François Bocion's work stands out from that of other regional artists for its impressionist sensibility, seeking to capture a specific atmosphere rather than simply documenting working practices. The tight focus lends the shaded jetty considerable appeal, while the semi-transparent nets veil the deeper background of the lake, the mountains, and the sky. Tall trees frame the composition to the right and the upper edge, drawing the viewer's focus in to the quayside, speckled with light filtering through the foliage.

Three variants on the same motif, now in the Musée d'art et d'histoire in Geneva, the Kunst Museum Winterthur / Reinhart am Stadtgarten, and the Musée Jenisch Vevey, date the scene and identify it as the French shore of Lake Geneva, probably somewhere near Tourronde, where Bocion was a regular visitor. [CdA]

36

François Bocion (Lausanne, 1828–1890)
Bocion et sa famille à la pêche (*Bocion and His Family Out Fishing*), 1877
Oil on wood, 32 × 48.5 cm
Acquisition, 1939. Inv. 250

The leisure activity depicted in this work was still rare in the 1870s: such boating was the preserve of a circle of initiates, otherwise the only sailors to venture out onto Lake Geneva were fishermen, tug boatmen and other transporters. The relative closeness of the mountains shows the scene to be set near Vevey, the home region of François Bocion's family on his mother's side, where he spent part of his youth. Indeed, his early schooling took place not far away, in Montreux, where he no doubt picked up his grandfather's passion for sailing on the lake. By having the water reach all the way to the lower edge of the painting, with no hint of terra firma, Bocion makes the viewer feel close to the boats, as if sitting in another vessel. The low horizon produces an effect of space, amplified by the oar and by the spit of land on the right, while the hazy blue of the mountains adds depth to the scene. The skilfully rendered reflections in the water, the luminosity, and especially the handling of the female figures strongly outlined in black, bring to mind Édouard Manet.

Standing in the boat on the left, we recognise Bocion, all in white, his pose recalling the one struck by Louis XIV in the famous portrait by Hyacinthe Rigaud (1701, Paris, Musée du Louvre), complete with royal cane and ceremonial canopy. In the other boat, a woman sheltering under a parasol could well be the artist's wife, Anna-Barbara Furrer, a native of Zurich. The composition, which thus shows the painter and his family occupying two boats, turns out to be more ambitious than its modest dimensions might suggest. It is unusual in that it stands at the juncture of genre painting, landscape and self-portrait. [CL]

37

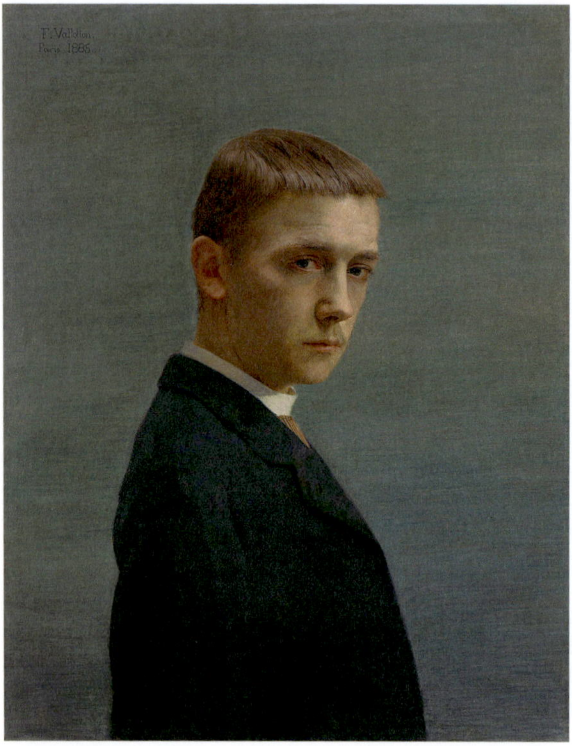

38

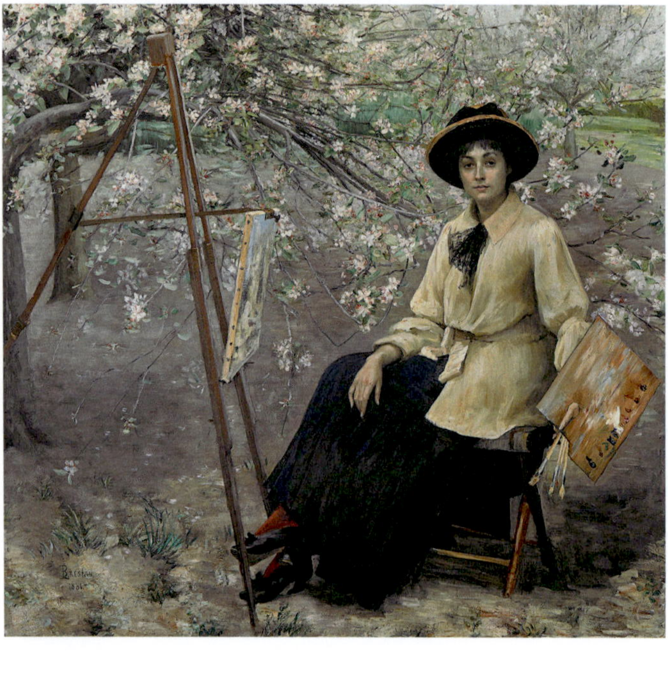

Félix Vallotton, Autoportrait à l'âge de vingt ans, 1885
Louise Breslau, Portrait de Mlle Julie Feurgard, 1886

37

Félix Vallotton (Lausanne, 1865–Paris, 1925)
Autoportrait à l'âge de vingt ans (*Self-Portrait at the Age of Twenty*), 1885
Oil on canvas, 70 × 55.2 cm
Acquisition, 1896. Inv. 620

Félix Vallotton arrived in Paris from his native Lausanne at the age of sixteen and attended courses at the Académie Julian. He soon began looking for guidance from the incisive objectivity of the great historic realists: Cranach the Elder, Albrecht Dürer and Hans Holbein to the north, and Nicolas Poussin and Jean-Auguste-Dominique Ingres in France. Probity and honesty were his watchwords: not only as an inheritance from the Protestant ethics that had shaped his youth, but also as a programme for the years ahead, when he emerged as a virulent critic of social oppression and bourgeois hypocrisy. The portrait, a genre he practised regularly in his early days, gave him a chance to show his rejection of idealisation by taking a candid approach to his models, whether members of his family or his own reflection in the mirror.

Vallotton had his first exhibition at the age of twenty, at the Salon des artistes français in 1885, which is when he began keeping his list of works. Writing about this self-portrait in 1886, he noted: 'It was not made for the public, but for me. Artists may find a few qualities in it, but the bourgeoisie will undoubtedly find it unpleasant and I don't give a damn!'

Vallotton's portrayal of himself is certainly uncompromising. Wearing an oversized dark jacket and a formal white collar that makes him look like a clergyman, he stands in profile, his pale face turned towards the viewer, bags under his reddened eyes, modest fluff on his upper lip. The painting is a statement that refuses to portray the usual attributes of a painter, conveying its message through the cold, calm gaze of the artist severely studying his subject, and through the great expanse of blue in the background, which observed closely, turns out to be subtly modulated by horizontal lines. Vallotton has depicted himself in front of Lake Geneva, which he frequently looked out upon as a child, and which he left in order to go and make his name in the French capital. [CL]

38

Louise Breslau (Munich, 1856–Neuilly-sur-Seine, 1927)
Portrait de Mlle Julie Feurgard (*Portrait of Mlle Julie Feurgard*) or *Sous les pommiers* (*Under the Apple Trees*), 1886
Oil on canvas, 171.5 × 186.5 cm
Acquisition, 1889. Inv. 1082

Louise Breslau from Zurich was already more than two years into an existential and artistic crisis when she painted this portrait in 1886. She had moved to Paris in 1876 and attended the women's ateliers at the Académie Julian, where her teachers spotted her talent. Influenced by Edgar Degas and after 1880 by the naturalism of Jules Breton, she had already produced several remarkable portraits, including *Chez soi* (*At Home*, 1885, Rouen, Musée des beaux-arts), but was dragged down by doubt: 'If I cannot give a new and certain proof of my value, I am lost', she wrote in January 1885.

Breslau then travelled to the countryside, with the purpose of meeting the challenge of producing her first monumental outdoor work. In Sannois, in the garden of a studio comrade, she made studies for the painting that she would exhibit at the Paris Salon in 1886. The press immediately classified her among the disciples of impressionism: 'Do you want outdoor work? Here it is by Miss Breslau: the portrait of an artistic companion of hers sitting in a garden, which, as you can imagine, is going to colour her green and, consequently, make her horrid, pictorially speaking.' In reality, this work, which shows exceptional vigour, records the changing effects of the light and the painter is unafraid to dull her model's face under the shadow of her hat.

The artist was represented by this painting at the 1889 Exposition Universelle in Paris, where the jury awarded her a gold medal. It was acquired by the Museum that same year. With this life-size representation of a woman painting outdoors and staring boldly at the viewer, Breslau was continuing her fight for the recognition of women painters at a time when the doors of the Académie des beaux-arts in Paris still remained closed to them. [CL]

39

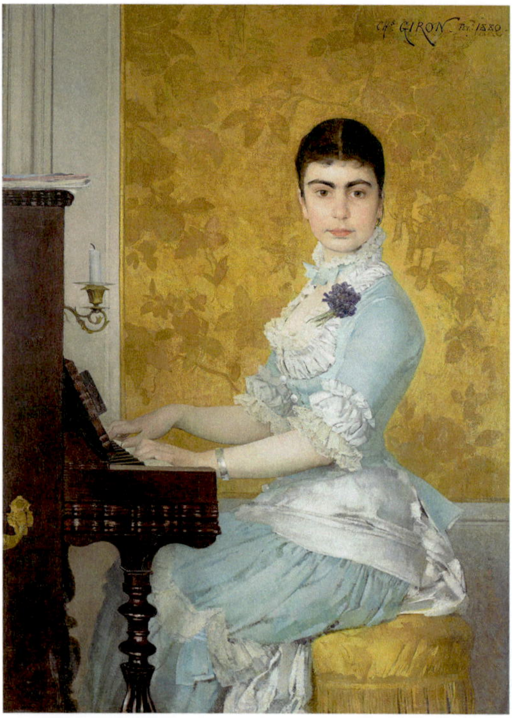

40

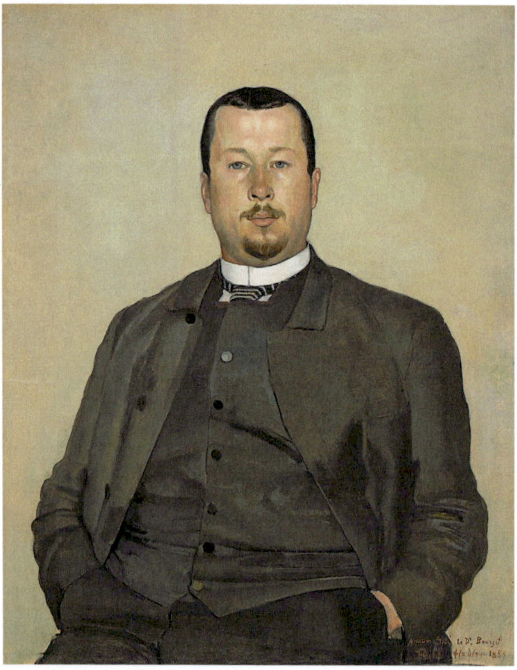

Charles Giron, Jeune femme au piano, 1880
Ferdinand Hodler, Portrait du Dr Louis Bourget, 1889

39

Charles Giron (Geneva, 1850–Genthod, 1914)
Jeune femme au piano (*Young Woman at the Piano*) or *Portrait de Mlle Maguie D.* (*Portrait of Mlle Maguie D.*), 1880
Oil on canvas, 124 × 90 cm
Acquisition, 2017. Inv. 2017-015

For the Swiss, Charles Giron's most emblematic work is undoubtedly *Le berceau de la Confédération* (*The Cradle of the Confederation*, 1901), a gigantic Alpine landscape which decorates a room in the Parliament in Bern; for the French, the name Giron evokes *La Parisienne* (1883, Paris, Petit Palais), a large society portrait showing the quintessence of Belle Époque feminine grace. Together, these two paintings sum up the contrasting career of this Genevan painter who lived and exhibited in Paris from 1876, and did not move back to Switzerland permanently until 1896.

In the 1880s, Giron shared his time between summer stays in the Swiss mountains, where he devoted his time to genre and landscape painting, and Paris, where his portraiture found clients among the upper bourgeoisie and aristocracy. Basking in the prestige garnered abroad, he returned fairly regularly to Geneva and received commissions there, including this painting for which his sitter was Jeanne-Marguerite Dominicé, a twenty-year-old daughter of the local bourgeoisie. Maguie, as she was nicknamed, is shown sitting up straight on a pouf, her hands graciously resting on the keyboard of an upright piano.

The fashion for 'musical' portraits was started by James Abbott McNeill Whistler in the 1860s with his *Symphonies in White* series. In these pieces a limited palette was like a visual chord setting off the faces of melancholic women. Here, Giron proposes an arpeggio chord in yellow, black, blue and white. Against the muted, austere note of a floral tapestry evoking the golden grounds of proto-Renaissance Italian painters, he sets up the firework display of a turquoise silk dress with purple violets pinned to the bodice. This contrast is repeated in the disparity between the apparent docility of the model – who lends herself to the conventional social exercise of playing the piano – and the wild power of her face with its thick eyebrows, boldly fixing the viewer with a strange and disconcertingly placid gaze. [CL]

40

Ferdinand Hodler (Bern, 1853–Geneva, 1918)
Portrait du Dr Louis Bourget (*Portrait of Dr. Louis Bourget*), 1889
Oil on canvas, 83 × 67 cm
Gift of Louis Bourget, 1910. Inv. 713

Hodler's particular interest in the portrait towards the end of the 1880s is reflected in the idea of a course on the subject that he offered to teach at the University of Geneva (which declined it). From a practice inspired by the use of chiaroscuro in the sixteenth and seventeenth centuries, in which the flesh tones of faces stood out against dark grounds, he had moved towards a lighter palette and concentration on the gaze, which led him to prefer frontal poses. While his first models were working class men (artisans or day labourers) or members of his close circle, he was now becoming established as one of the most sought-after portrait painters for the Swiss bourgeoisie and political elites.

Here, the plump figure of Louis Bourget stands out against a light green ground subtly enlivened by red tones. The surgical precision of the outline makes manifest the importance of drawing. The man, in his early thirties, faces us frontally although his body is at a slight angle. His colourful flesh contrasts with the whiteness of his stiff collar, brightened by a tie with a *régate* knot, and the dark mass of his three-piece suit. His posture relaxed, with his hands in his pockets and his gaze calmly levelled at the artist, Bourget embodies self-assurance.

Doctor Louis Bourget was a *privat-docent* at the University of Geneva in 1887. He would also be the author of poems and the illustrator of books expressing his passion for ornithology. Close to Hodler in his youth, he offered the artist his advice when his partner, Valentine Godé-Darel, fell ill in 1912. He very likely commissioned this portrait to help Hodler with his financial difficulties. The work was completed in 1889 and the doctor offered it to the Museum in 1910, after he had sent it back to Hodler to be signed, on which occasion the artist added an affectionate dedication: 'To my Friend, Dr. Bourget'. [CL]

41

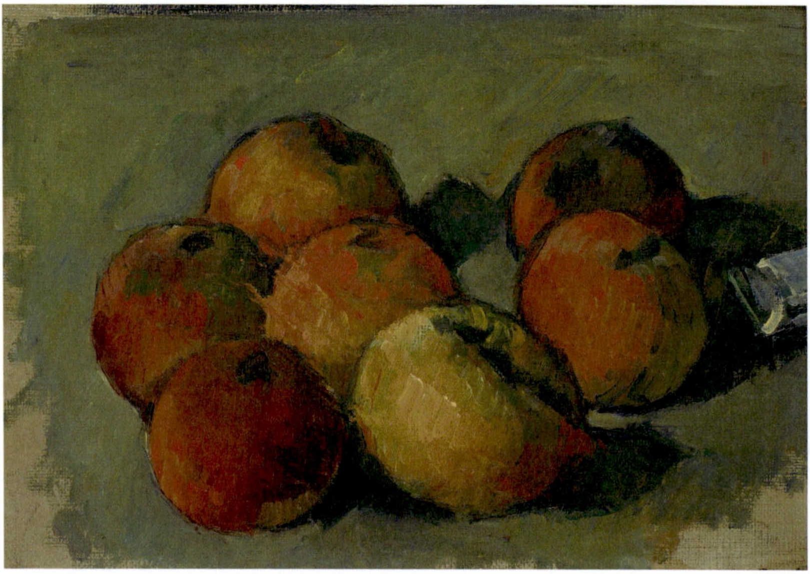

42

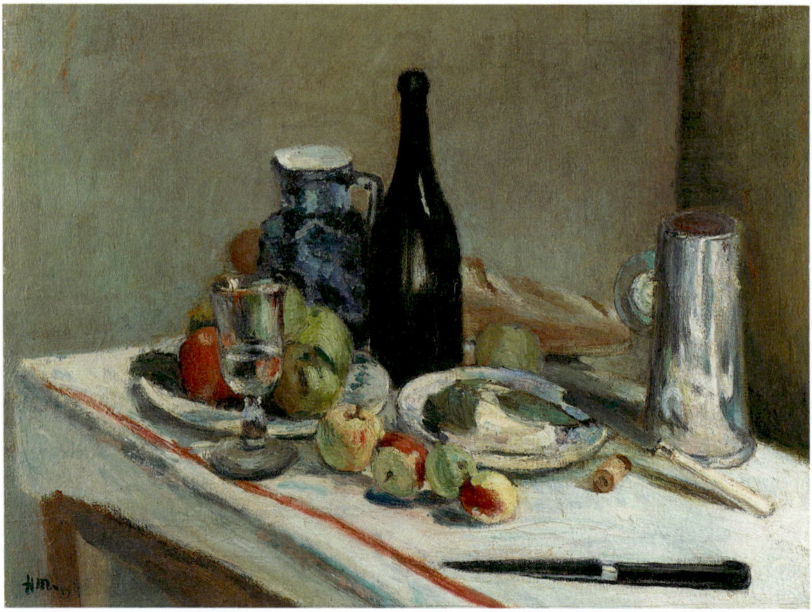

Paul Cézanne, Nature morte aux sept pommes et tube de couleur, 1878–9
Henri Matisse, Nature morte au couteau noir, 1896

41

Paul Cézanne (Aix-en-Provence, 1839–1906)
Nature morte aux sept pommes et tube de couleur (*Still Life with Seven Apples and Tube of Paint*), 1878–9
Oil on canvas, 17.2 × 24 cm
Henri-Auguste Widmer bequest, 1936.
Inv. 311

Paul Cézanne started using apples as the subject of his still lifes in the 1870s. Whether piled up in a fruit bowl, artfully spread over a tablecloth or, as here, shown on a table top, they became a familiar theme in his work. Indeed, this humble fruit served the artist as a medium for reassessing the fundamentals of academic painting and even conquering the French capital: his aim, he once said, was to 'astonish Paris with an apple'.

Nature morte aux sept pommes et tube de couleur is one of those small canvases in which Cézanne concentrates on the fruit, analysing its colours and its appearance from every angle. Such works were like studies with which he practised his scales before going on to more ambitious compositions. A step towards cubism, this work was painted after Cézanne had emerged from his impressionist period but still shows what he had learnt about the analysis of light and cast shadow from the outdoor painting of Camille Pissarro. However, here concern with atmospheric effects gives way to formal and plastic considerations: the painter focuses on the arrangement of the objects, on the relations between them, on the handling of space and effects of light.

Cézanne, who criticized impressionism for its overly impulsive handling, produced a strongly structured composition. His brushstrokes are constructive, dense, precise and methodical. The apples, seven spheres isolated by a black outline, are given volume here by means of quick, slanting touches, simply by the modulation of colour, which makes them seem to swell from within. The white tube of paint breaks the warm harmony of the dominant complementary colours; the red of the apples and the ochre-green of the background. Cut off by the framing, this tube raises the question of what lies outside the painting. It is also, and above all, an anti-illusionist statement: these apples are in oil! [CL]

42

Henri Matisse (Le Cateau-Cambrésis, 1869–Nice, 1954)
Nature morte au couteau noir (*Still Life with a Black Knife*), 1896
Oil on canvas, 59 × 81 cm
Henri-Auguste Widmer bequest, 1939.
Inv. 370

Henri Matisse spent hours at the Louvre copying the old masters as his teacher at the School of Fine Arts in Paris, Gustave Moreau, had advised him to do. His early still lifes reflect the influence of Jean Siméon Chardin, an artist he admired greatly. This *Nature morte au couteau noir* contains several virtuoso displays of skill, such as the reflections in the glass and pewter pot, revealing Matisse's interest in seventeenth-century Dutch still life painting.

The tableware and food are grouped together in one compact space. The curves of the fruit and tableware counterbalance the diagonal of the table leading down to the bottom right-hand corner. The painting's main axes, based on ninety-degree angles, are laid out in black, with the knife lying parallel to the table's lower edge and the bottle standing proudly in the centre. Slanting lines are highlighted in the white of the tablecloth and the second knife at the edge of the table. These form the backdrop for the painting's main colours in shades of red, yellow, green and blue.

Matisse clearly enjoyed painting the various textures: the fabric of the white tablecloth, the ceramic plates, the blue earthenware pitcher, the pewter pot, the glass bottle and the metal knife blades. The light, shining in from one side, reflects on their surfaces, creating a sense of chromatic harmony.

Nature morte au couteau noir presents a major milestone on Matisse's journey from tonal values to pure colour in the years from 1895 to 1900. Using heavy brushstrokes from a palette of thick paints, Matisse gave colour wings. This painting's reds, greens and yellows, though as yet discreet, herald the breakthrough of pure colour in Matisse's work in the years to come. [BF]

43

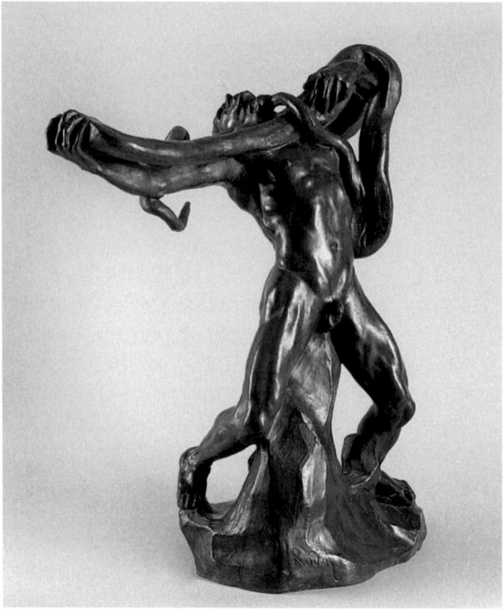

44

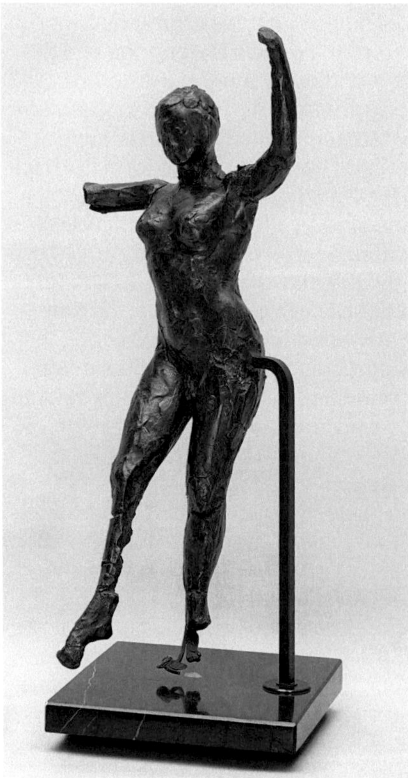

Auguste Rodin, L’homme au serpent, 1887
Edgar Degas, Danseuse s’avançant, les bras levés, jambe droite en avant (deuxième étude), c. 1885–90

43

Auguste Rodin (Paris, 1840–Meudon, 1917)
L'homme au serpent (*Man with Serpent*), 1887
Bronze, 69.5 × 55 × 29 cm
Anonymous gift, 2015. Inv. 2015-028

This sculpture may have been inspired by Dante's description of the damned fighting with snakes, as here, in Canto XXV of the *Inferno*: 'As we watched, a six-foot-long snake slithered up and began to wrap itself around one of them. It twisted up his body.'

The work is striking by virtue of its impeccable rendering of the male anatomy, the dramatic expression of a man battling against an animal, and the powerful yet sensitive modelling of a body thrown backwards, making it a noteworthy example of Michelangelo's influence. Antiquity, too, is evoked in the manifest reference to the Hellenistic sculptural group, the Laocoon. Above all, the subject is inseparable from the two-hundred figures and groups modelled by Rodin over the years for his *Porte de l'Enfer* (*Gates of Hell*), commissioned by the French State in 1880. Although this was never finished, it did constitute a rich repertoire for the artist's new creations. *L'homme au serpent* can be set beside *L'homme qui tombe* (*Falling Man*, c. 1883), a figure attached to the lintel in the bronze version of the *Gates of Hell* that was cast after the sculptor's death.

The plaster version of *L'homme au serpent* (*Man with Serpent*, c. 1882–3, Williamstown, Clark Art Institute) was spotted by the collector Antony Roux in Rodin's studio in 1885. This fervent admirer was in the habit of demanding that he be the exclusive owner of his acquisitions. On 28 January 1887, he wrote to the master: 'You asked me for two thousand francs for the man with the snake, moulded and cast in bronze. I agree [on the condition that] I should remain the only owner of this group of the man struggling against the snake. You retain the right to use the man figure, but with modifications in the pose and without the serpent.' Rodin accepted, which is why there is only one example of this bronze cast by François Rudier, making it quite an exceptional work. [CL]

44

Edgar Degas (Paris, 1834–1917)
Danseuse s'avançant, les bras levés, jambe droite en avant (deuxième étude) (*Dancer Stepping Forward, her Arms Raised, Right Leg Forward [second study]*), c. 1885–90
Bronze, lost wax cast, 65 × 25.5 × 22 cm
Henri-Auguste Widmer bequest, 1936. Inv. 58

Ballet dancers training, resting or performing on stage were a major motif in Edgar Degas' oeuvre from the early 1870s to his death. He often visited the Paris opera to study them and was later allowed into the wings at the ballet. However, he took his studies furthest in his own studio, safe from prying eyes, making his models dance, taking up dance poses himself, and analysing the mysteries of movement in the photographs of Eadweard Muybridge (*Animal Locomotion*, 1884–6) and his own, taken with his Eastman Kodak.

Though many of his drawings and pastels were inspired by dance, he emphatically pointed out in 1897: 'You will only obtain the truth by modelling, which places a constraint on the artist that forces him not to neglect anything of importance'. When he died, found in his studio were 150 wax and bronze sculptures, including many female dancers in a variety of poses. Later cast in bronze, they reflect his tireless quest to translate the body in motion into three-dimensional sculptures. One of them was this airy *Danseuse s'avançant*, the entire weight of whose body is held on one pointed toe.

Degas only ever exhibited one sculpture in his lifetime, the *Petite danseuse de 14 ans*, at the sixth impressionist exhibition in 1881. For that piece, he felt the need to colour the wax, add real human hair tied back with a pink satin ribbon, and clothe her in ballet shoes and a tulle tutu. Then, underscoring its status as a work of art in its own right, he placed it in a glass cage. Its realism caused a scandal: it was judged to be almost simian in appearance. Degas' nude dancers would have been an even greater shock for fin-de-siècle bourgeois morals. They are mature women with animalistic bodies forged by nature, adopting choreographed poses forged by culture. [CL]

45

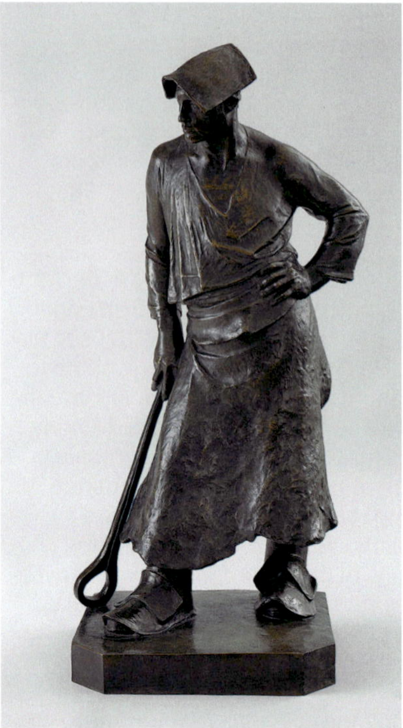

46

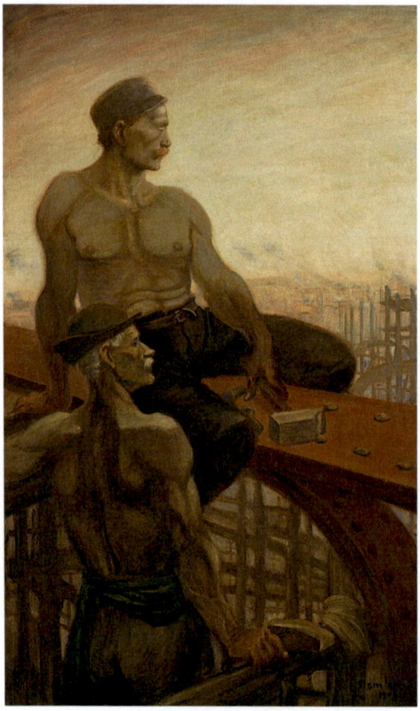

Constantin Meunier, Le marteleur, 1886
Théophile-Alexandre Steinlen, L’aurore, 1903

45

Constantin Meunier (Etterbeek, 1831–Ixelles, 1905)
Le marteleur (*The Drop Forger*), 1886
Bronze, 117.5 × 60 × 43.5 cm
Henri-Auguste Widmer bequest, 1936. Inv. 74

Following his academic training, Meunier attended classes given by the Belgian sculptor Louis Jéhotte, an admirer of Greek art, before taking up painting, a medium that he considered less bogged down in academicism and more open to the great movement of renovation sweeping through the arts. He did not come back to sculpture until 1884, inspired by his vision of the 'plastic grandeur of the industrial worker'.

Le marteleur is contemporaneous with the Walloon uprising of 1886, a wave of ferociously repressed workers' strikes. Meunier's realist approach to his subject brings out the difficulty of the man's work, demanding both strength and dexterity, all in the suffocating heat of the furnaces and beset by the dangers of handling molten metal. The drop forger's body, gesture and posture when at rest recall what the artist observed at the Cockerill foundry in Seraing, as does the man's characteristic outfit with visor, big leather apron, shoe protectors and pincers. By combining this realism with a *contrapposto* posture – left hand resting on the hip, right foot forward – straight out of the classical repertoire, Meunier elevates his steelworker to the status of a hero of modern times.

The full-scale plaster version of *Le marteleur* was exhibited at the Salon des artistes français, Paris, in 1886. This work, of which the Museum has a two-thirds-life-size cast, won the artist his first critical acclaim. It was praised by the art critic Octave Mirbeau, who acclaimed it as a modern answer to the traditional allegories in which women draped in the antique style contemplate the attributes of labour. 'Meunier actually met this powerful, superb worker in the Borinage, and he made him as he saw him, and as he is.' Placed in the tradition of a Jean-François Millet or Charles de Groux, Meunier was henceforth seen as one of the major representatives of socially-engaged art in Belgium. [CL]

46

Théophile-Alexandre Steinlen (Lausanne, 1859–Paris, 1923)
L'aurore (*Aurora*), 1903
Oil on canvas, 182 × 111.1 cm
Acquisition, 1903. Inv. 47

A major exhibition and sale of 101 works by Théophile-Alexandre Steinlen opened in Paris in 1903. In the catalogue, the writer Anatole France emphasised the singularity of the event. Although the artist was 'too famous for any thought of introducing him here', he had nevertheless prepared a surprise for visitors already enthusiastic about his drawings and stamps: a presentation of his paintings. The artist was showing the forty-odd pictures produced that same year and, for the first time, 'large figures' signalling a new artistic ambition.

L'aurore is notable for its tall, narrow format. The canvas shows two workers sitting atop a structure, contemplating the sunrise. Perched on its piers, they are about to assemble the metal parts using red-hot rivets whose heads will then be flattened with a hammer. The building under construction recalls recent Parisian projects such as the Eiffel Tower and Sacré-Cœur. With this work, Steinlen was adding to his chronicle of the world of work – that 'apocalypse of misery' that, in France's words, moved him deeply. The warm palette, in shades of browns and oranges, recalls Honoré Daumier. The symbolic dimension of this work, indicated by its title, points to the hope of a better future. It is expressed in the heroic rendering of the men's bodies, which draws from the emphatic modelling of the naturalist sculptors, from Jules Dalou, and also from Constantin Meunier, another poet of the proletarian condition. The older carpenter is positioned in the lower half of the picture with his back to us, in the shadow, whereas his younger comrade, catching the light and staring into the distance, stands for the new generation and the struggle it must take up.

L'aurore was sufficiently important to Steinlen for him to put a smaller version of the work on the cover of his exhibition catalogue. When the Museum in Lausanne, his home town, acquired the work, it did so at his own express request: according to the keeper there at the time, he would have been disgruntled if Lausanne had purchased his *Chats* and *Midinettes*. [CL]

47

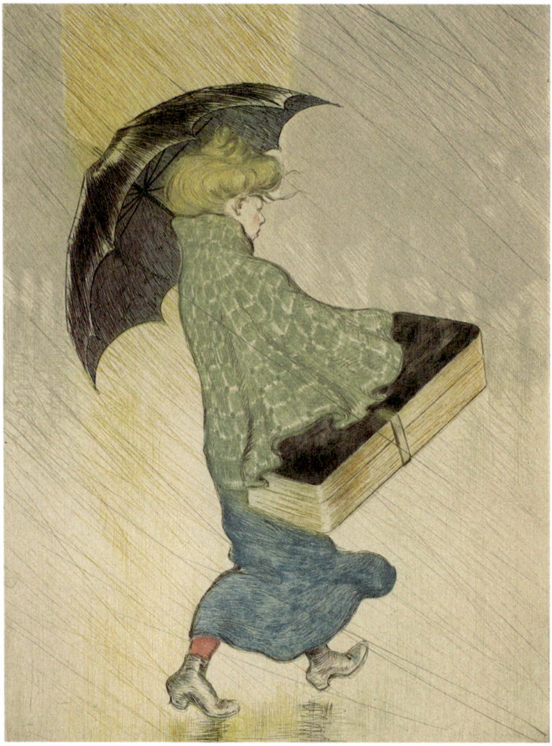

48

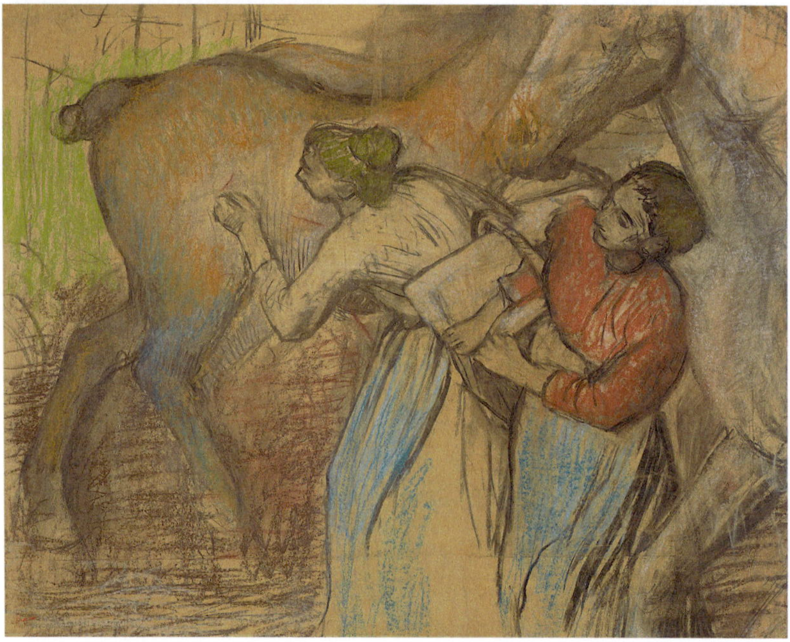

Théophile-Alexandre Steinlen, Trottin sous la pluie, 1898
Edgar Degas, Blanchisseuses et chevaux, c. 1904

47

Théophile-Alexandre Steinlen
(Lausanne, 1859–Paris, 1923)
Trottin sous la pluie (*Delivery Girl in the Rain*), 1898
Coloured etching and drypoint on zinc on paper, 36×27 cm, ed. I/12 trial proofs
Paul and Tina Stohler Donation, 2018.
Inv. 2018-046

The four thousand or so works in Théophile-Alexandre Steinlen's print oeuvre made use of all the mechanical and photomechanical reproduction techniques available to him at the time. His compositions were almost all intended for journals, song sheets and newspaper covers. Alongside his illustrative work, which was his main source of income, he also produced his own work for the print market. These works were printed in short runs on better paper with more careful inking.

The thirty-two prints of *Trottin sous la pluie* are an example of the latter. This trial proof belonged to the great print collector Alfred II Beurdeley. It dates from 1898, the year Steinlen produced his very first etchings, doubtless on the advice of Eugène Delâtre, a famous printer who did much to promote the technique. Steinlen produced 150 such engravings experimenting with copper and zinc, drypoint and etching, soft varnish and aquatint. He also used colour, as was becoming fashionable in the 1890s, much to the disgust of purists who preferred the tradition of printing in gradations of black.

Steinlen spoke of how after first arriving in Paris, he was charmed by 'the world of the streets', sketching 'workers and delivery girls, washerwomen and paupers'. This work depicts a girl working for a milliner or seamstress delivering an order. The artist excels at capturing the movement of the typically Parisian figure, struggling along with her heavy parcel, buffeted by the wind and driving rain. For an early experiment in etching, it is a dazzling virtuoso display, particularly in the discreet bustle in the background: a thronging crowd, almost entirely hidden by the fog and drizzle, passes in front of a shop window that casts yellow glints on the flooded tarmac. [CL]

48

Edgar Degas (Paris, 1834–1917)
Blanchisseuses et chevaux (*Laundrywomen and Horses*), c. 1904
Pastel, charcoal and stumping on tracing paper glued onto cardboard, 84.2×107.4 cm
Henri-Auguste Widmer bequest, 1936.
Inv. 333

Two laundrywomen are on the way to deliver linen to a client. But why do they have to squeeze between two horses in a muddy courtyard? Why does one of them seem to be currying a croup as she passes? This incongruous situation is not so much the fruit of the artist's narrative imagination as proof that Degas, now seventy years old, was less concerned with capturing reality than with exploring formal questions. At the very end of the 1850s he began filling his notebooks with sketches of real horses. This predilection for equids has been explained by his many stays in the Orne, a French department known for its stud farms and racecourses. As for the laundrywomen, Degas had observed and drawn their postures in the late 1870s. Also at this time, he developed the habit of reprising elements from the past and working through variations on a given motif, or collaging two subjects that had originally been observed separately.

This pastel and charcoal made c. 1904 recalls an oil on canvas from 1879, *Blanchisseuses portant du linge* (*Laundress Carrying Linen*, private collection) as well as several drawings in charcoal. Rather than a narrative, what guided Degas here was the concern to achieve dynamic equilibrium in his composition and the sculptural elegance of the forms. The energetic, ample and repeated touches in charcoal give this work a monumentality reminiscent of the Parthenon friezes. The smooth surface of the tracing paper, crisscrossed with lines, hatchings, zigzags and eddies of pastel is conducive to the very free use of colour characteristic of the artist's late manner.

The combination of two very different motifs, the modification of the format during the creative process, achieved here not by the usual addition of a strip of paper but by unfolding the lower part of the sheet, as well as the work's considerable size, make this pastel exceptional. [CLC]

49

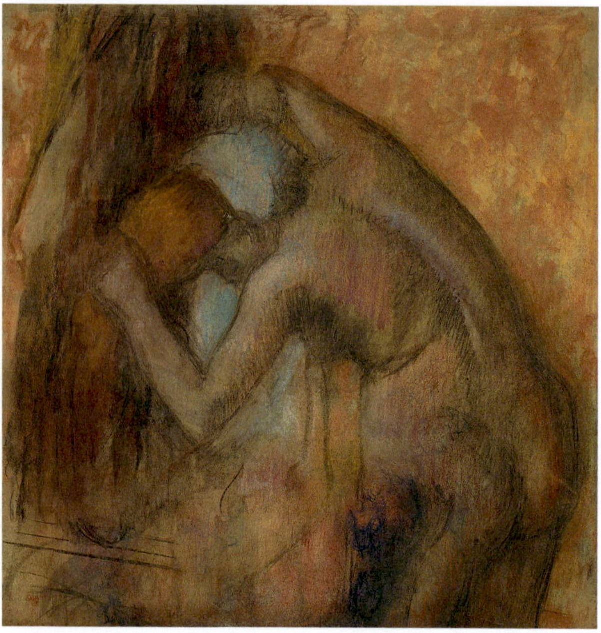

50

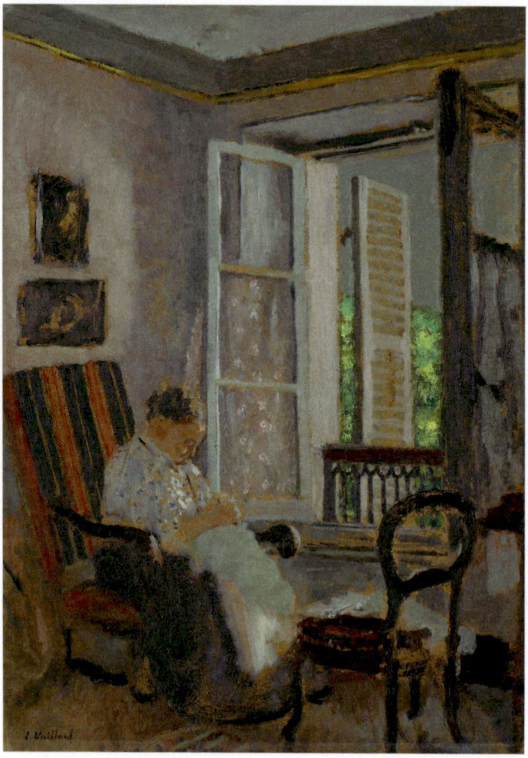

Edgar Degas, Femme s'essuyant la nuque, c. 1903
Édouard Vuillard, Madame Vuillard cousant, rue Truffaut, c. 1900

49

Edgar Degas (Paris, 1834–1917)
Femme s'essuyant la nuque (*Woman Drying Her Neck*), c. 1903
Charcoal and pastel on tracing paper, 76.7×76.1 cm
Henri-Auguste Widmer bequest, 1939. Inv. 1032

Degas produced some two hundred pastels on the theme of women washing, placing the emphasis on the action itself: the figure is presented in close up with little room for her surroundings. Here, we see a naked woman rubbing her neck. Standing and leaning forward, with her head down, she is pulling her long hair to one side in order to allow the short, energetic rubbing movements of her right hand.

As Degas constructed his drawing, he continually added and superposed the colours, merging the application of a new pastel with the previous one. To soften the texture and make it more velvety or more effectively mix the shades, he rubbed the pastel with his fingertips or with paper. He also made strong, abrupt movements that left behind thick lumps of pastel on the paper. But whereas other works by Degas on this subject play on cold hues and develop complementary combinations of oranges and greens, or reds and purples, the colours in *Femme s'essuyant la nuque* are warm, apart from the icy blue of the towel. The space is filled with an orange-red that extends and diffuses the pinks of the flesh and the ginger of the hair.

At the same time, Degas used charcoal not only to define the composition but also to dialogue with the pastel. Vigorously applied, in repeated, overlaid strokes that clarify the forms and bestow on them a certain monumentality, the black charcoal melds with the zones of luminous pastel colour. In a complex network of hatchings and vertical and horizontal striations, the two mediums together construct the figure's carnal density.

Degas' late pastels were still in his studio when he died. Their discovery in 1918 revealed an unexpected degree of artistic freedom in his work. [CLC]

50

Édouard Vuillard (Cuiseaux, 1868–La Baule, 1940)
Madame Vuillard cousant, rue Truffaut (*Madame Vuillard Sewing, Rue Truffaut*), c. 1900
Oil on cardboard, 50×37 cm
Henri-Auguste Widmer bequest, 1936. Inv. 401

Painted on a small piece of cardboard, this work dates from towards the end of Édouard Vuillard's Nabi period and shows the living room of the apartment-cum-studio he rented from 1899 to 1904 at 28 Rue Truffaut in Paris. The painter's mother is shown sitting in a Louis XIII armchair upholstered with a fabric of broad brown and red stripes. Busy sewing (or dozing?), she is enjoying the warmth of the ray of sunlight entering the room through the window whose shutters and panes have been opened wide. Pictorially, the result is a sophisticated interplay between the areas lit by the sun, done in a fresh palette of whites, greens and yellows, and the shadowy areas, rendered in warm greys, browns and reds.

The paint is thin and matt, the brushwork swift and notational: small, juxtaposed touches allow the colour of the cardboard underneath to show through, while a dry brush has been used to draw in the paint. The fabrics (dress, lace curtains at the windows) contain the most vigorous contrasts: transparent and speckled with white where they are touched by the light, opaque and grey when in shadow.

'No artist has known so well how to capture the soul of an interior', said the critic Julius Meier-Graefe of Vuillard in 1904. Indeed, at the turn of the twentieth century, Vuillard, with his fellow Nabis, helped elevate the interior to the rank of a genre in its own right. His brushwork dissolves figures and objects in a rendering of form by colour that manifests a very personal sense of colours and close values, with a noted predilection for grey. Vuillard transposes his subject into a decorative mode, but just as clearly articulates the contours of space and suggests the temporal dimension by his evocation of an action. In this regard, his work heralds the decorative interiors of Henri Matisse, but also the still lifes of the cubists. [CL]

51

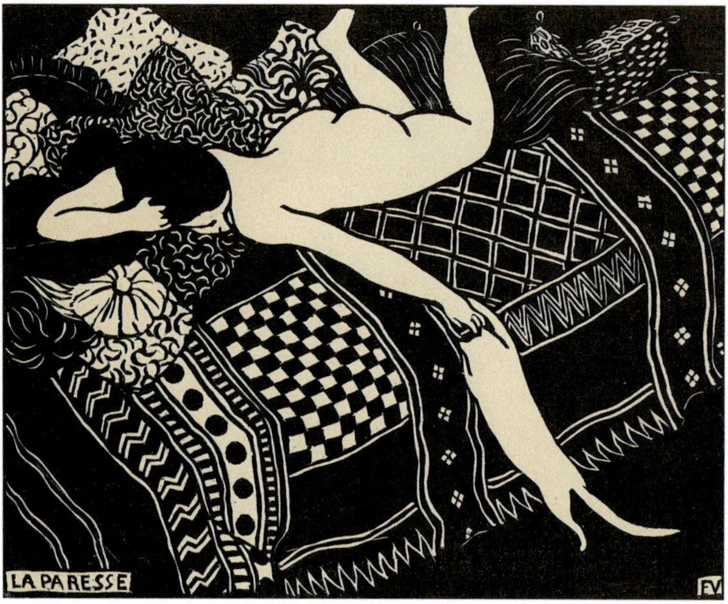

52

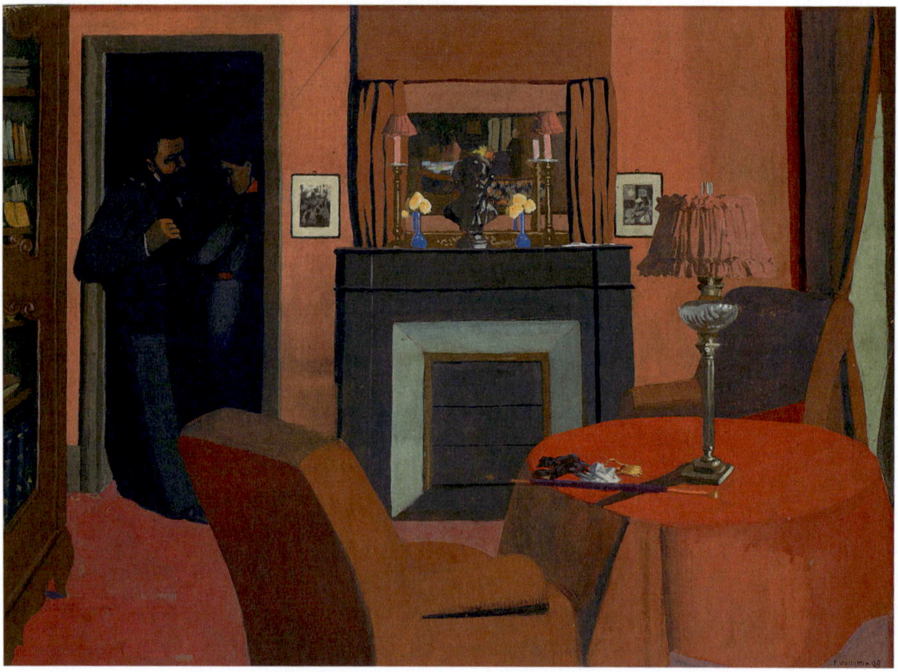

Félix Vallotton, La paresse, 1896
Félix Vallotton, La chambre rouge, 1898

51

Félix Vallotton (Lausanne, 1865–Paris, 1925)
La paresse (*Idleness*), 1896
Woodcut on paper, 17.7 × 22.2 cm, proof n. 18 in an edition of approx. 180
Acquisition, 1903. Inv. 1188

By 1900, Vallotton was renowned in Paris as one of the major protagonists in the revival of printmaking. He had begun making drypoint works and etchings in 1887, but his reputation was really established a few years later, when he became the main illustrator for *La Revue blanche*. He triumphed in particular with his woodcuts, a practice that he began in 1891 and continued with some regularity until 1899, when he devoted himself to painting.

There are several factors behind Vallotton's success. First, his choice of the woodcut, a medium that had been abandoned by artists after its hour of glory in the Renaissance. A great admirer of Albrecht Dürer, he thoroughly explored the potential of the medium: working with a vertical grain wood, he used a knife to gouge out broad, clearly defined surfaces, thus dispensing with effects of gradation. He also made the radical choice of black-and-white: at a time when his Nabi friends were producing multi-coloured posters and colourful prints, Vallotton opted for the contrast between deep black and the white of the paper. This approach served a synthetic graphic language influenced by Japanese prints. Depth was flattened, with everything brought to the picture plane, and expressivity was entrusted to line, to Vallotton's supple arabesques delimiting zones of black, a precise line animating them with decorative motifs.

La paresse shows Vallotton's art at its most accomplished. From the darkness he summons the naked body of a woman lying on her belly: a model, or a prostitute awaiting a client? Her feet in the air, she is lolling on a sofa covered with geometrically patterned fabric and teasing a cat that is rearing up on its hind legs. United by the whiteness of their bodies, the two partners in play embody the nonchalant freedom of those who, like artists, refuse to be tamed and to conform to the demands of bourgeois morality. [CL]

52

Félix Vallotton (Lausanne, 1865–Paris, 1925)
La chambre rouge (*The Red Room*), 1898
Tempera on cardboard, 50 × 68.5 cm
Acquisition, 1983. Inv. 1983-067

Félix Vallotton attained recognition in the 1890s with his woodcuts, and in particular with his *Intimités* (*Intimacies*) series, ten scenes from the private life (*intimité*) of a modern couple. For a shared exhibition with the Nabis to be put on at the Durand-Ruel gallery in 1899, the Swiss artist presented a new series of *Intimités*, but this time they were paintings. With their uncompromising colours, clinical delineation of forms and strangely disquieting themes, these six *Intérieurs avec figures* represent the quintessence of Vallotton's art at the turn of the century.

La chambre rouge is the first work in the series, and gives the key. While descriptive, the title could also refer to the novel by August Strindberg (1879), a mordant attack on the hypocrisy of bourgeois life. Here, Vallotton – himself about to take the marital vows – denounces adultery, the flip side of the sacrosanct institution of marriage.

The painting is a close-up of a theatre set whose vermilion colour symbolises the violence of male desire. In the shadow of a doorway, a man is trying to force himself on a grief-stricken woman. Each object is like a clue to the crime, starting with the curtains, which suggest an open vulva. On the table, gloves nestling beside a handkerchief used to dry tears, a purse indicating some financial transaction, and a parasol pointing to the guilty party. On the mantelpiece is a curious altarpiece formed by the bust of Vallotton himself set between two bright yellow bouquets, themselves flanked by modern lamps and then Japanese prints. Behind the bust – 'behind its back' – is a mirror protected by red curtains and reflecting, but not inverting, a work by Édouard Vuillard. And not just any work: this is *Grand intérieur aux six personnages* (*Large Interior with Six figures*, 1897, Zurich, Kunsthaus), in which the family circle accuses two adulterers, the painter Ker-Xavier Roussel and Germaine Rousseau, wife of the artist Paul Ranson. Finally, the bookcase on the left ironically alludes to the declared function of literature, which, like painting, is said to raise man above the animal. [CL]

53

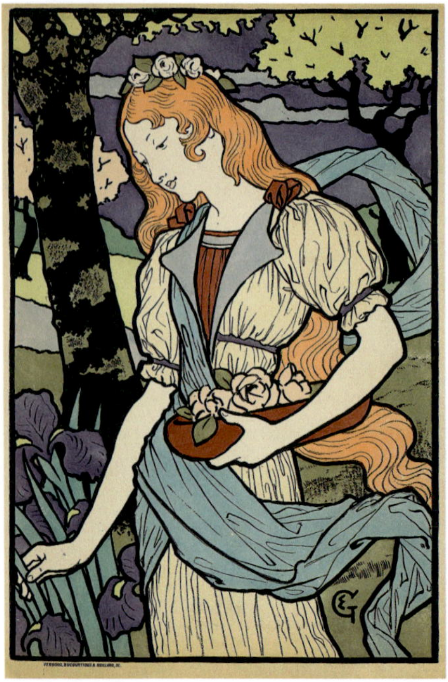

54

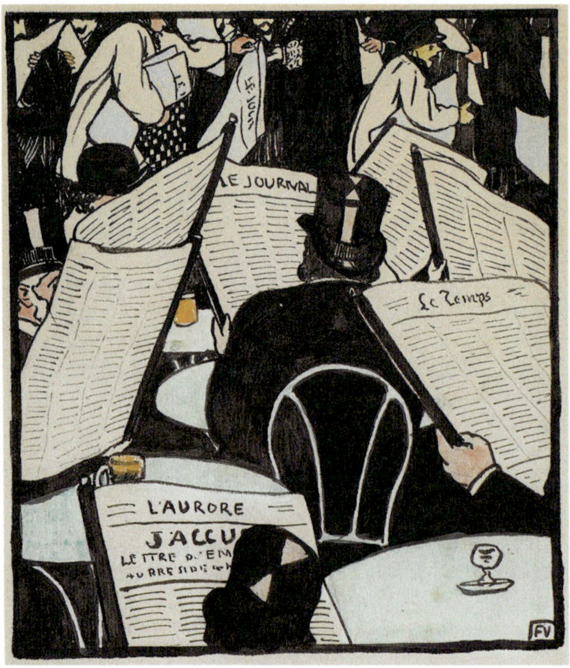

Eugène Grasset, Affiche pour une exposition d'art décoratif français, 1893
Félix Vallotton, L'âge du papier, 1898

53

Eugène Grasset (Lausanne, 1845–Sceaux, 1917)
Affiche pour une exposition d'art décoratif français à la Grafton Gallery de Londres (*Poster for an Exhibition of French Decorative Art at the Grafton Gallery, London*), 1893
Chromolithograph on paper, 66.4 × 45 cm.
Acquisition, 1909. Inv. 304

Eugène Grasset made his first forays into poster design in the mid-1880s and soon acquired an excellent reputation, working both commercially and for publishers as well as for art exhibitions and the theatre. His first compositions drew on the neo-medieval register and took a painterly approach, but from the early 1890s on, his formal language was influenced by Japanese prints and gained in limpidity and monumentality. The drawings were strongly outlined with even zones of colour producing great luminosity. However, Grasset's tone remained severe and he refused to produce the kind of loud, alluring images required by advertising. His timeless women have the solemnity of classical allegories.

In its extreme formal simplification and great tonal freshness, with broad expanses of colour delimited by black contours, this poster for an exhibition of French decorative art at the Grafton Gallery in London applied everything that Grasset had learnt from his practice of making stained glass. The young woman, her body draped, her long red hair untied, is shown at knee height and in half profile, slightly off-centre. Her expression pensive, she holds a basket of roses and is picking a flower from a bed of irises in the foreground, inspired by the prints of Hiroshige and Hokusai.

The neo-Botticellian look of the gardener and the correspondences the artist suggests between nature and the female temperament were widely echoed by his contemporaries. From symbolist descriptions of this work it is clear that the way it was received at the time was very different from our response today. In 1894, for example, the Swiss artist William Ritter spoke of the poster as follows: 'A vision that one never forgets, in which the anaemia and chlorosis of the decadents join with the deep, intense radiance of stained glass.' [CL]

54

Félix Vallotton (Lausanne, 1865–Paris, 1925)
L'âge du papier. Dessin pour Le Cri de Paris (*The Age of Paper. Drawing for Le Cri de Paris*), 1898
Indian ink and brush, watercolour highlights on paper, 19.5 × 17.2 cm
Acquisition, 2016. Inv. 2016-029

Félix Vallotton rose to fame in the 1890s with his woodblock engravings and his illustrations for the rapidly growing press industry. Having moved from Switzerland to Paris, he produced his first press illustrations in 1894 for the journals *Rire*, *Le Courrier français* and above all *La Revue blanche*, where he was the official illustrator until 1902.

Le Cri de Paris was a sixteen-page weekly printed in black. Vallotton completed over seventy illustrations for its cover. The journal was created in 1897 as an offshoot of *La Revue blanche* to satirise political corruption of all sorts. The magazine's greatest struggle was to obtain a retrial for Captain Alfred Dreyfus, whose fate was hotly debated in France for years, prompting intellectuals and artists to speak out publicly and contributing to the modern image of creators and thinkers as politically committed public individuals.

This drawing (subsequently heightened with watercolour by the artist himself) was featured on the cover of *Le Cri de Paris* on 23 January 1898, as an immediate response to Emile Zola's famous *J'accuse*. Zola's open letter, printed in *L'Aurore* ten days earlier, accused the French army of a crime against justice and of anti-Semitism in sending Dreyfus to prison for treason. *L'âge du papier* foregrounds the power of the press that Vallotton – drawing on that same power – translates as a host of newspapers including *L'Aurore*, *Le Temps*, *Le Journal* and *Le Soir*, being read in cafés and sold by newspaper boys in the street. The draughtsman's paper was literally turned into news. The very tight framing turns the infinitely proliferating print into a tidal wave of protest. *L'âge du papier* also proclaims the age of the press illustrator! [CL]

55

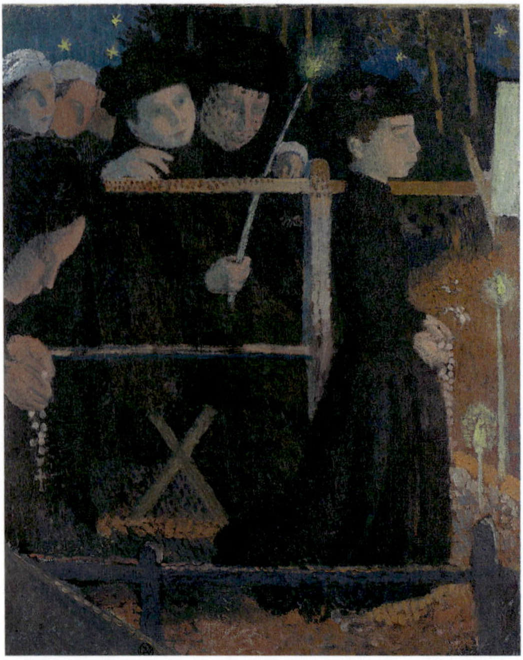

56

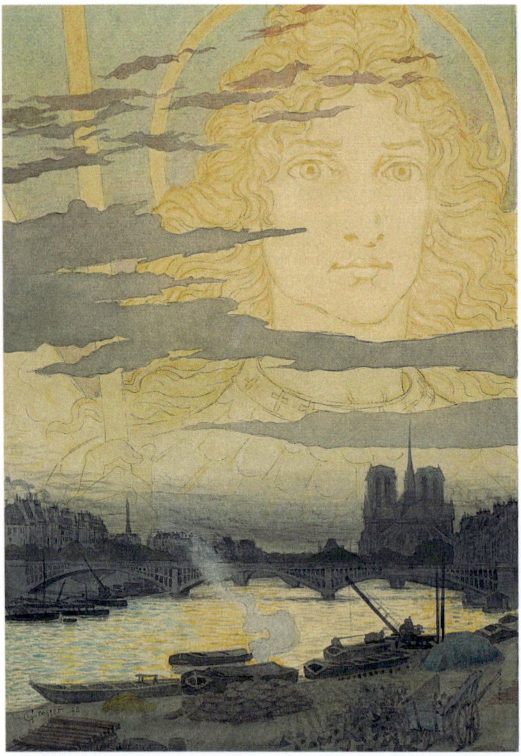

Maurice Denis, Le chapelet, c. 1890
Eugène Grasset, Apparition d'un visage nimbé dans le ciel au-dessus de Paris, 1898

55

Maurice Denis (Granville, 1870–Paris, 1943)
Le chapelet (*The Rosary*), c. 1890
Oil on canvas, 73 × 60 cm
Acquisition, 2018. Inv. 2018-151

From very early in his career, Maurice Denis saw a link between his artistic vocation and Catholic faith: 'Yes, I must be a Christian painter ...!' (*Diary*, 22 May 1885). This painting shows a procession marking the Feast of Our Lady of the Rosary on 7 October. Bathed in light from stars and candles, young women kneel as they count the rosary. On the left is the profile of Jeanne, an apprentice milliner with whom Denis was in love, who regularly features in paintings dating from around 1890, such as *Audi filia* (private collection), where she symbolises the religious calling, and various versions of the *Mystère catholique*, where she is depicted as the Virgin Mary.

In the summer of 1889, Denis visited an exhibition of impressionist and synthesist art at the Café Volpini in Paris, including the latest work by Paul Gauguin, who was just back from Pont-Aven. It was a revelation for Denis and his friends in the Nabi movement.

The hieratic, mystical, nocturnal *Chapelet* has much in common with *La vision après le sermon* (*Vision of the Sermon*, 1888, Edinburgh, Scottish National Gallery), a well-known symbolist painting by Gauguin: a religious scene in a natural landscape where reality and dream freely mingle, a close-up view cut off by the frame, a composition opening up on the left with the profile of an adolescent with her hands joined, a tight-knit frieze of young women at prayer, and the synthetism of the forms. In this work, Maurice Denis, inspired by the Italian primitives and Japanese prints as much as by Gauguin, took a decisive step away from naturalism. He abandons illusionism and depth of field in favour of an ornamental arrangement of the painted surface, fragmented here and there by powerful horizontal and vertical lines. The painter known as the 'Nabi of the beautiful icons' stands apart from his contemporaries by his delicate, almost pointillist touch in the rosaries and veils. His palette is also typical, the complexions of the young women reflecting his preference for delicate mother-of-pearl and pink hues. [CL]

56

Eugène Grasset (Lausanne, 1845–Sceaux, 1917)
Apparition d'un visage nimbé dans le ciel au-dessus de Paris (*Appearance of a Haloed Face in the Sky over Paris*), 1898
Pencil and watercolour on paper, 45.3 × 31.8 cm
Acquisition, 2018. Inv. 2018-023

This painting is one of a number of subjects imagined by Eugène Grasset that explains the interest idealists took in his work from the early 1890s on. Like them, he was sensitive to the sacred, to mystery and dreams, and also shared the symbolist and decadent taste for angels, figures from legend, female musicians, and for the heroic narratives of the middle ages.

Here, a haloed face is a vast, surreal apparition in the night sky over Paris. The timeless epiphany forms a striking contrast with the modern view of the city from the banks of the Seine by the Sully bridge, with the towers of Notre Dame in the distance. The contrast is taken up in the palette of colours, from the cadmium yellow of the ethereal face to the blue-black of the river snaking between the quays, and in the naturalist approach to the foreground and the decoratively stylised clouds striping the sky – one of Grasset's favourite motifs since his famous 1889 poster *Jeanne d'Arc*, for a play featuring Sarah Bernhardt.

The androgynous, youthful, strict-looking young woman staring out at us could indeed be Joan of Arc, wearing chain mail and holding a banner. Like Jean-Auguste-Dominique Ingres, whose *Jeanne d'Arc au sacre du roi Charles VII* (*Joan of Arc at the Coronation of King Charles VII*, 1854, Paris, Musée du Louvre) he no doubt had in mind, Grasset has given the figure a halo. The Church had begun the process of raising Joan of Arc to sainthood the year before, in 1897. Grasset often showed his devotion to the French heroine – his mother shared the same name with her. As well as the aforementioned poster, he told Joan of Arc's story in ten stained-glass windows designed for a contest for the cathedral of the Holy Cross in Orleans in 1893. In this work, he makes her appear like a new star whose light is destined to rouse the consciences of a sleeping city. [CL]

57

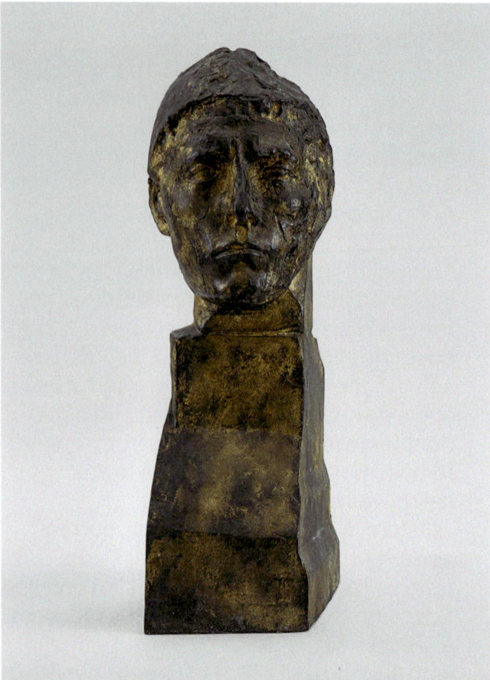

58

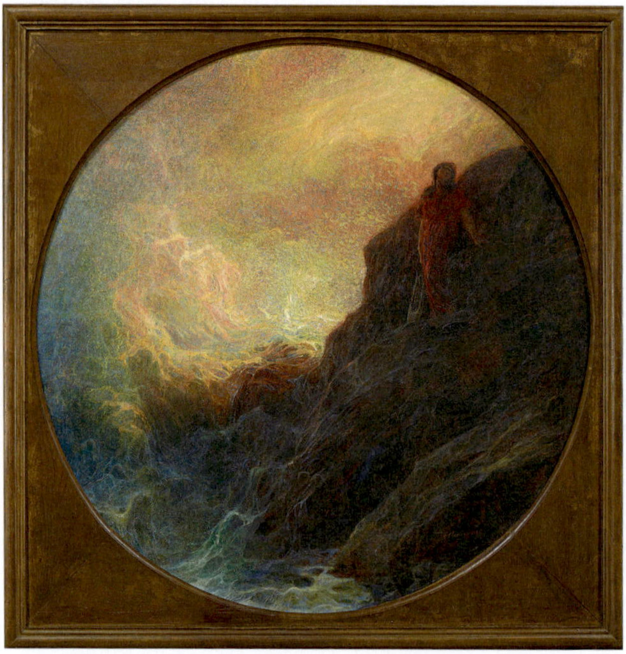

Émile-Antoine Bourdelle, Tête d’Apollon, between 1900 and 1909
Plinio Nomellini, Polifonia, 1905

57

Émile-Antoine Bourdelle (Montauban, 1861–Le Vésinet, 1929)
Tête d'Apollon (*Head of Apollo*), between 1900 and 1909
Partially gilded bronze, 67 × 23 × 30 cm
Henri-Auguste Widmer bequest, 1939. Inv. 50

Émile-Antoine Bourdelle, who was a keen student of Greek art, took inspiration from the works of Antiquity for many of his pieces. One such was this *Tête d'Apollon*, modelled in clay c. 1898, while he was still an assistant in Auguste Rodin's studio, and then set aside. Bourdelle returned to the work in 1900. After having sat in the studio for nearly two years, it bore the traces of the passage of time. The artist chose to foreground the cuts, cracks and chips to imbue the work with new meaning.

By accepting its imperfections, Bourdelle broke with both the classical taste for marble complexions and the romantic preference for virtuosity. He remodelled the head until 1909 on the basis of plaster casts. The rough, energetic modelling and vigour of the features, combined with the decision to maintain a record of changes to the work and to use a pared-down, simple form rather than sensuous formation, all indicate that he was taking a step back from Rodin's influence and seeking his own path. The piece offers a synthetic vision, constructing the work by means of simplification, and taking it in a more architectural direction. This new radicality may have been what prompted him to tell his students in May 1910, 'Here, we take the skin off the model and look inside', and 'When a sculpture is made like I tell you, what you obtain is not a resemblance, but a presence'.

The head stands on a faceted, asymmetrical base, also heralding a new page in art. The base is as important as the head, showcasing it with its rhythmical succession of planes. Other copies of the *Tête d'Apollon* are held at the Musée Bourdelle and Musée d'Orsay in Paris and the Nationalmuseum in Stockholm. [CLC]

58

Plinio Nomellini (Livorno, 1866–Florence, 1943)
Polifonia, 1905
Oil on canvas, 125 cm (diam.)
Acquisition, 2015. Inv. 2015-177

Plinio Nomellini learned to master the art of capturing light in paint when studying fine art in Florence with Giovanni Fattori, a member of the macchiaioli school. Under the influence of French impressionism, he worked with swift dabs of the brush. After meeting Giuseppe Pellizza da Volpedo in 1888, he developed his own unique divisionist technique, marrying comma-shaped dabs with dots of colour. The technique sets his work apart from other artists of his generation who, like him, were seeking to breathe fresh life into Italian art.

In the 1890s, Nomellini was close to the radical left in Genoa and was one of the most outspoken of Italy's political artists. As a keen reader of Gabriele d'Annunzio, however, he turned towards dreamlike symbolism in the early twentieth century, developing an allegorical vocabulary rich in references to Antiquity.

This work shows the Greek poetess Sappho, her lyre at her feet, preparing to throw herself from the Rock of Leucate. This was a popular theme in the nineteenth century, shared by artists from Théodore Chassériau to Gustave Moreau. Its title, *Polifonia*, highlights the link between music and painting and reflects Nomellini's urge to develop a language that spanned the arts. The swift, energetic dabs of the brush play the music of nature, the waves crashing on the rocks, and the howling of the swirling wind. The explosion of colours plays into the same phosphorescent, acid, electric polyphony. Seeking to render light ever more intensely, he thickened his paint and abandoned his familiar comma-shaped dabs in favour of layering coloured strands, adding sand to the paint to catch the light in many places. Such experiments influenced the new generation of futurists, who saw the painting at the Venice Biennale in 1905. [CLC]

59

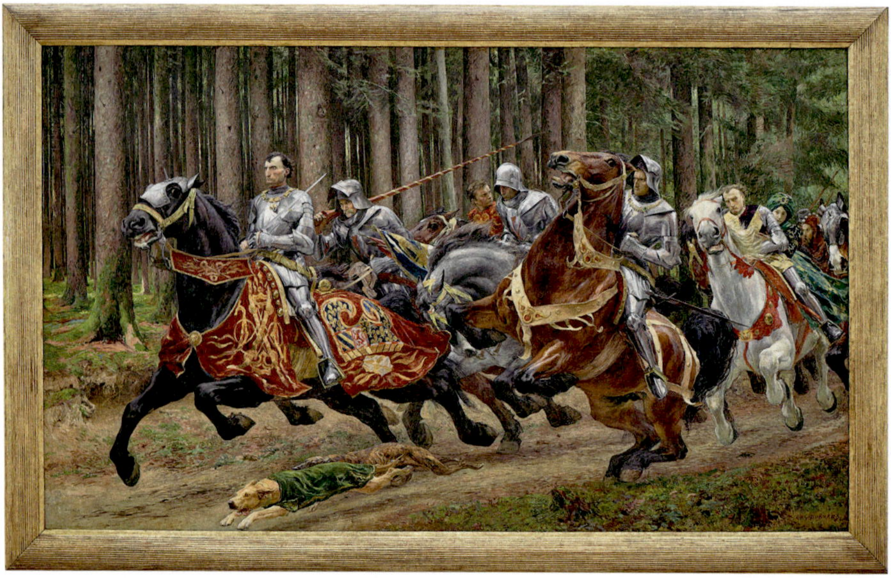

60

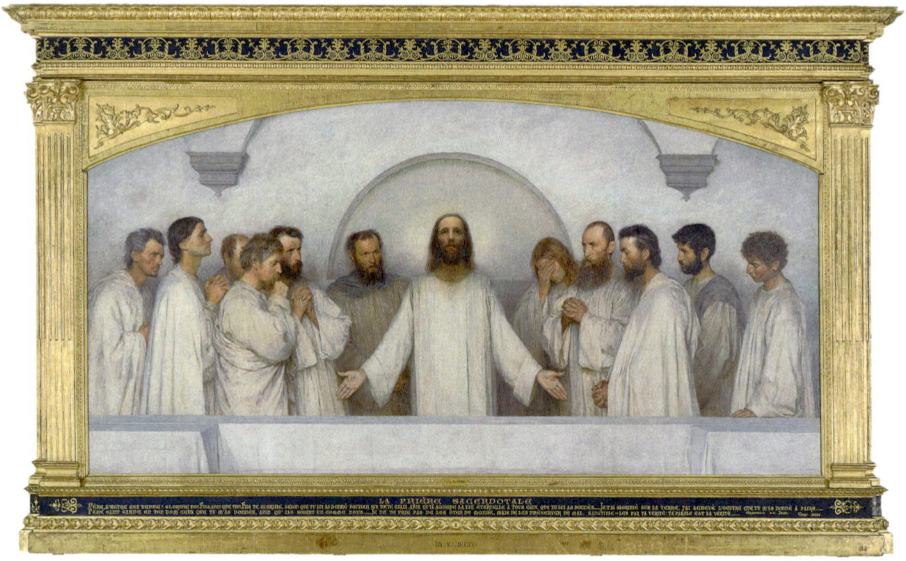

Eugène Burnand, La fuite de Charles le Téméraire, between 1894–5
Eugène Burnand, La prière sacerdotale, 1900–18

59

Eugène Burnand (Moudon, 1850–Paris, 1921)
La fuite de Charles le Téméraire (*The Flight of Charles the Bold*), between 1894–5
Oil on canvas, 320 × 540 cm
On deposit from the Swiss Confederation, Federal Office of Culture, Bern, 1896. Inv. 814

With this monumental canvas, Eugène Burnand set out to show his value as a history painter, having already succeeded in rural and animal paintings. The Swiss artist was a great admirer of Ernest Meissonier, the French painter of military history, and shared his concern for veracity. However, he also had in mind his fellow countrymen Charles Gleyre who, half a century earlier, had painted *Les Romains passant sous le joug* (1858, also held at the Museum, see n. 22), an icon of the Swiss struggle for independence, and Ferdinand Hodler, who in 1898 would inaugurate his edifying representation of the battles of Morat and Marignano in the Weapons Room at the Swiss National Museum in Zurich. Like Gleyre, he considered that only 'scenes with a strong dramatic or moral significance, in the heroic or legendary sense' were worthy of representation. Like Hodler, he chose the battle of Morat, that 1476 episode during the Burgundian Wars when the victorious Confederates confirmed their reputation for courage and the superiority of the militia system: 'Apart from the fact that everyone knows [Charles the Bold], his wild flight and the collapse of his grandeur have a moral and social meaning that goes beyond the immediate event and is capable of giving the artwork a general, typical and human character.'

In order to carry out his big naturalist project, Burnand, who was obsessed with exactitude and authenticity, read the historians. He went to museums to copy jewellery, fabrics and armour from the period and reconstituted a pine forest in front of his studio's glass room, making his models sitting wearing costumes sewn by his wife. An Italian peddler played the role of the Burgundian duke and the inhabitants of his village of Seppey provided the other figures. However, what is truly striking here, more so than this stunning and enchanting cavalcade, is the role Burnand attributes to nature, to this dark forest of Jorat, which absorbs a brief moment of terror in the density of its mystery and the eternity of its silence. [CL]

60

Eugène Burnand (Moudon, 1850–Paris, 1921)
La prière sacerdotale (*The Sacerdotal Prayer*), 1900–18
Oil on canvas, 190 × 370 cm
Gift of Jean-Jacques Mercier-de Molin, 1904. Inv. 201

When, at the turn of the twentieth century, Burnand dreamed of excelling at high art, it was religious art that he had in mind. Where Maurice Denis was the proponent of a new form of decorative art in the service of Catholicism, his Swiss peer championed a Protestant, naturalist art that could carry a contemporary spiritual message. The kind of painting he was thinking of was informed by a Reformation theology that emphasised the material reality of Christ's existence: 'Jesus lived historically, corporeally among men; he took on our human form ..., worked, ate, suffered, wept', he wrote, and his aesthetic bore out his words: he painted only what he saw, giving his Christ features that were not idealised but faithfully reproduced, the reality of a physical, living man.

However, the genesis of *La prière sacerdotale* shows just how ambiguous Burnand's credo could be. The artist may have loathed the iconography of popular piety and the fantastic visions of the symbolists, but he also presented himself as literally the victim of a hallucination when describing how his subject, an episode from the Gospel according to John, appeared to him: 'There really was something supernatural in this sudden burst that made the whole work appear to me in a clear vision.' As for the model, he claimed his choice was determined by 'God's providence', which placed a perfectly suited Florentine in his path.

The work, which uses a frieze-like composition positioning the disciples on either side of Jesus in a subtle play of bluish whites, was exhibited in England and Germany immediately after its completion. But the painter was still not satisfied. In 1904 he met an upholsterer in Neuchâtel and corrected the portrait accordingly: 'Now I have my Christ!' Shown that same year at the *Exposition nationale suisse des beaux-arts* in Lausanne, the painting was then given to the Museum, but the artist still took it back to his studio at Seppey several more times. It was his own son, Franz, who embodied the Saviour in the fifth and final version of the work in 1918. [CL]

61

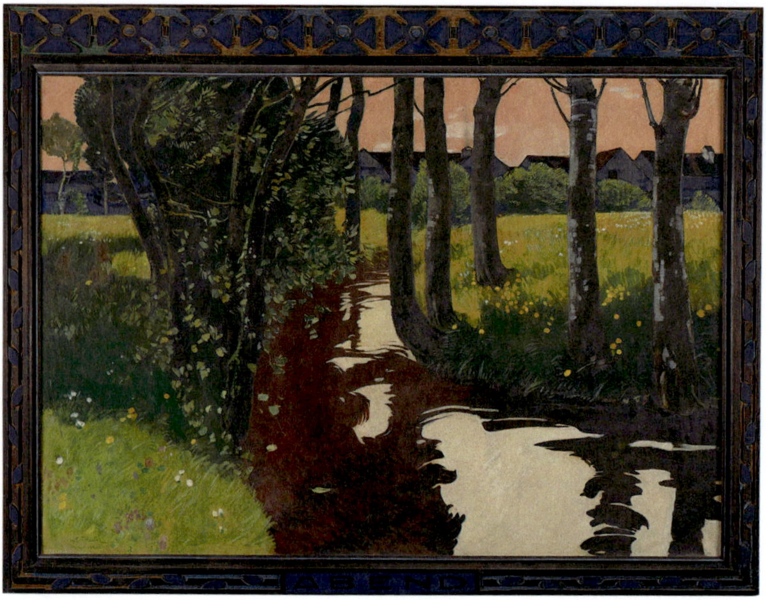

62

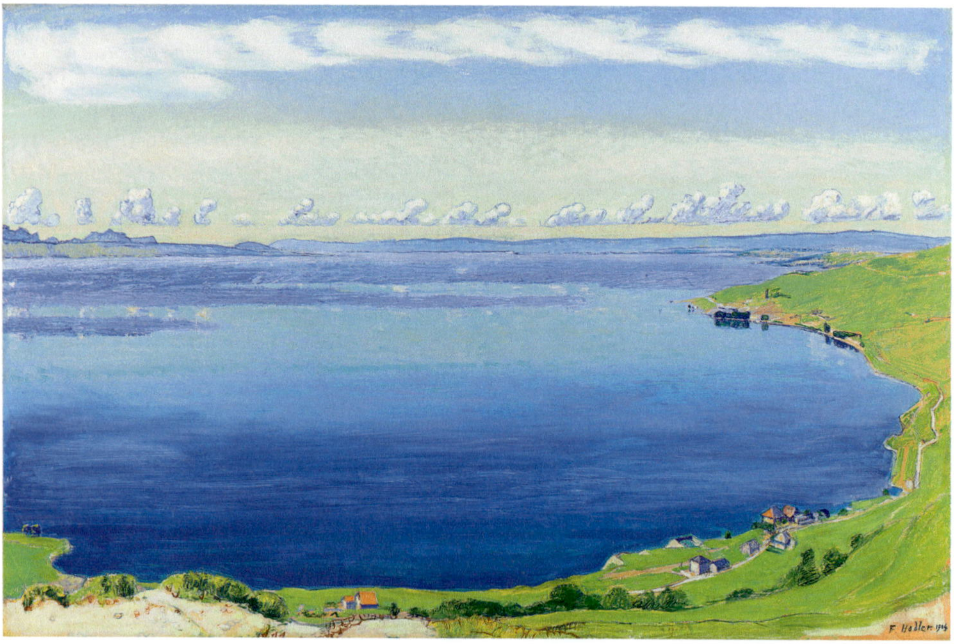

Hans Sandreuter, Abend, 1900
Ferdinand Hodler, Le lac Léman vu de Chexbres, 1904

61

Hans Sandreuter (Basel, 1850–Riehen, 1901)
Abend (*Evening*), 1900
Oil on canvas, 124×180 cm
Acquisition, 2016. Inv. 2016-047

Hans Sandreuter received academic training in Munich, having travelled there in 1873 on the recommendation of his compatriot Arnold Böcklin. He later followed Böcklin to Florence before returning to live in Basel in 1855. The influence of the great symbolist master was long evident in his allegorical compositions, while his most personal work, in the realm of pure landscape, came relatively late in his career. The large canvases painted from nature in the 1890s tended towards monumentalism and stylisation, yet retained the freshness and spontaneity of observation of the living subject, which makes them original.

Abend was painted in Riehen, in the countryside around Basel where Sandreuter had built a house in 1898, for which he also designed all its decoration. Finished not long before his death, this work with its premonitory title could be considered a 'landscape of the soul', the kind of painting that originated with Romanticism. The genre was at the heart of the symbolist imagination, where it informed poetry as well as painting and sculpture. In terms of portraiture, this meant that the soul was described as a landscape (a dark forest or stormy ocean), while in landscapes themselves nature became a mirror of the unconscious and receptacle of projections (conducive to reverie, suggesting mystery).

The horizon in this large-format painting is placed very high and the atmosphere is crepuscular, with the glow of the setting sun cooling the pink sky but still illuminating a flowering meadow, while projecting the shadows of the tall trees onto the surface of a winding river. A tension arises between the decorative stylisation, on the one hand, which heightens the parallel lines of the trunks and synthesises the planar forms of the shadows on the water, and, on the other hand, the naturalism, which focuses on the details and affirms the artist's temperament through its gesturality. The frame was carved by Sandreuter himself, who painted it in a blue colour reminiscent of his work in the applied arts. [CL]

62

Ferdinand Hodler (Bern, 1853–Geneva, 1918)
Le lac Léman vu de Chexbres (*Lake Geneva Seen from Chexbres*), 1904
Oil on canvas, 70.5×108.3 cm
Acquisition, 1904. Inv. 715

On the train journey into Lausanne from the German-speaking part of Switzerland, travellers reaching the heights of Chexbres enjoy spectacular panoramas as Lake Geneva and the Alps of Savoy heave into view. This superb vista made a lasting impression on Ferdinand Hodler who travelled frequently between his native Bern and Geneva, which became his home in 1872. A painter for whom emotion played a decisive role in his choice of subjects, he first represented this view in 1895 (*Le Léman vu de Chexbres, le soir* [*Lake Geneva Seen from Chexbres at Night*], Zurich, Kunsthaus).

Nearly ten years later, after his exhibition at the 1904 Secession in Vienna had solidified his reputation in Europe, he returned to Chexbres. In late April he took up residence at the Hôtel Bellevue and began work on a new series of landscapes. *Lac Léman vu de Chexbres* was the first, but all the works produced during his fortnight there adopt the same high viewpoint over the terraced vineyards of Lavaux, with the distinctive contours of the lake shore between the heights of Puidoux on the left and the village of Cully lower on the right, the chain of the Jura in the distance and a sky striated by clouds.

Here, too, the viewpoint is elevated. In this elongated canvas the colours are intense and the handling of the forms is synthetic and ornamental. The big blue mass of the lake, which asserts the main harmony, is contained within the contour of a broad, clearly drawn ellipse. The upper horizontal band contains the suggestion of a melody, with the staccato of the clouds reflected in the water. Hodler replaces the fleeting character of impressionist painting with a rhythmic organisation capable of revealing the timeless order of nature.

In 1894 the Museum was the first public institution to acquire a landscape by Hodler (*Au pied du Salève* [*At the Foot of Mount Salève*], 1888). *Lac Léman vu de Chexbres* entered the collection in 1904, the year it was painted. [CL]

63

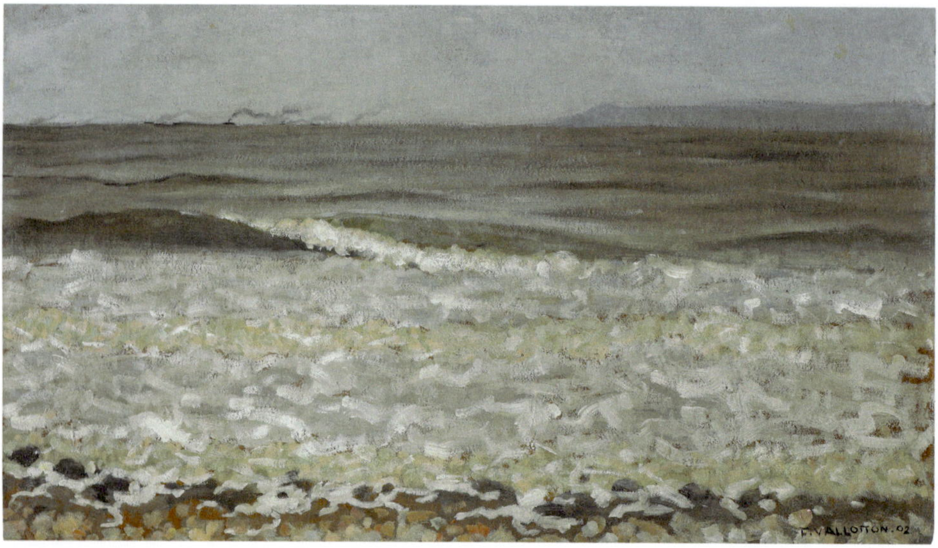

64

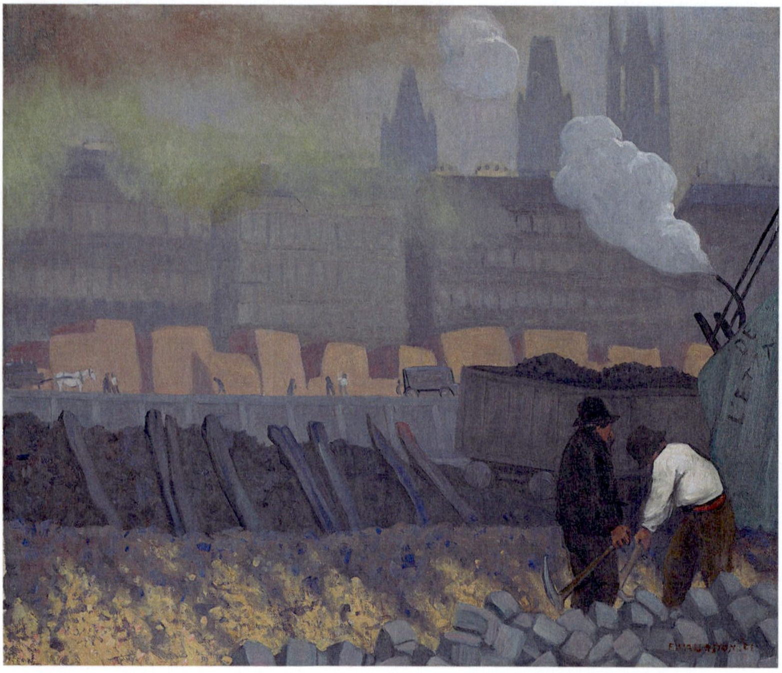

Félix Vallotton, Mer haute, Villerville, 1902
Félix Vallotton, Le port de Rouen, 1901

63

Félix Vallotton (Lausanne, 1865–Paris, 1925)
Mer haute, Villerville (*High Tide, Villerville*), 1902
Oil on cardboard, 34 × 59.5 cm
On deposit loan by the Dr. Marcel Bahro collection, 2015. Inv. 2015-030

Having risen to fame as an engraver, Félix Vallotton declared in 1898 that he now intended to devote himself wholly to painting. From the turn of the twentieth century, landscapes took on as much importance in his oeuvre as portraits and interiors. He had a productive year in 1900 with numerous views from the banks of the Seine and sketches of the mountains around Lake Geneva seen from Romanel. In 1901, he began spending his summers in and around Honfleur and Brittany.

Charles-François Daubigny and Eugène Boudin had earlier painted the narrow pebble beach at Villerville, a fishing village between Honfleur and Trouville in Normandy. Their works had focused on the storm-tossed clouds and dramatic play of light; Vallotton takes a low viewpoint looking up at the sea, breaking the landscape down into parallel horizontal bands. The radical approach builds on Caspar David Friedrich's *Der Mönch am Meer* (*Monk by the Sea*, 1808–10, Berlin, Alte Nationalgalerie), which reduces the landscape to three bands of colour, extending the perception of space to infinity by abolishing the margins. Vallotton uses a minimal, dark palette of greys with touches of ochre, yellow and dirty white. The sea could almost be a ribbon of lead. The curling wave that subtly stitches the upper and lower halves of the painting echoes Gustave Courbet's frontal views of waves. The sea spume has been handled with extraordinary artistic freedom. The sole vertical movement comes from the streams of black smoke pouring from the boats from the nearby port of Le Havre.

Mer haute, Villerville is one of a set of four paintings on the same subject, all dated 1902, but in a variety of media and formats. *Les galets, Villerville* (*Pebbles, Villerville*), also in the Museum's collection, shows a vertical view of the long beach. [BF]

64

Félix Vallotton (Lausanne, 1865–Paris, 1925)
Le port de Rouen (*The Port of Rouen*), 1901
Oil on canvas, 54 × 65.2 cm
Gift in lieu of inheritance tax, estate of Jean-Claude Givel, 2018. Inv. 2018-001

At the turn of the twentieth century, Rouen was one of France's busiest river ports and a popular destination for painters. Camille Pissarro visited its docks along the Seine for the first time in the autumn of 1883. Paul Gauguin painted its city centre streets and the surrounding countryside in 1884, while Claude Monet devoted a series of canvases to the façade of Rouen cathedral from 1892 to 1894.

Félix Vallotton was a frequent visitor to Normandy, but made only one painting of the region's main city. In 1901 his favourite subject was the seaside town of Honfleur, with its fishing boats and picturesque quays lined with brightly coloured houses. Rouen appears drab and grey in contrast. The elegant buildings on the right bank are barely visible in the dull grey atmosphere and the cathedral, little more than a ghostly shadow, is stripped of the steeple that gives it its slender silhouette, swallowed up by a sulphurous cloud. We are looking at a port without water, where the business of river transport is referenced only indirectly. On the right, cut off by the edge of the paintings, is a steam-powered crane used to load and unload barges, while in the middle ground, piles of goods waiting for transport glow pink in the sun. The artist's focus is on the workers levelling the earth on the left bank, one wearing a white shirt that almost seems to glow.

While Vallotton's views of work sites on the banks of the Seine in Paris painted the same year are characterised by powerful, energetic diagonals, here the work is built in horizontal bands. Certain stylistic features, such as broad swathes of colour, are reminiscent of Vallotton's Nabi period. The return of a sense of volume, most notably in the piles of goods, the whorls of smoke, and the golden shimmer of the earthworks, foreshadows the composite landscapes he was to work on after 1909. [CLC]

65

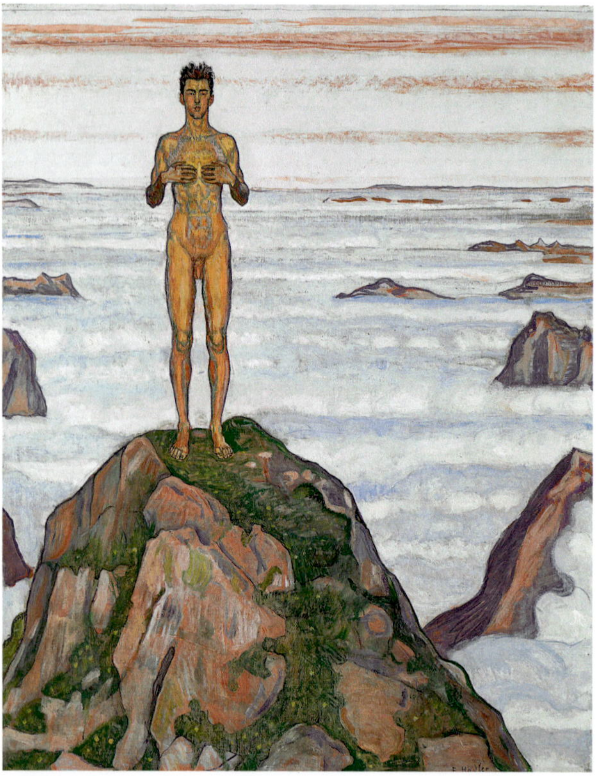

66

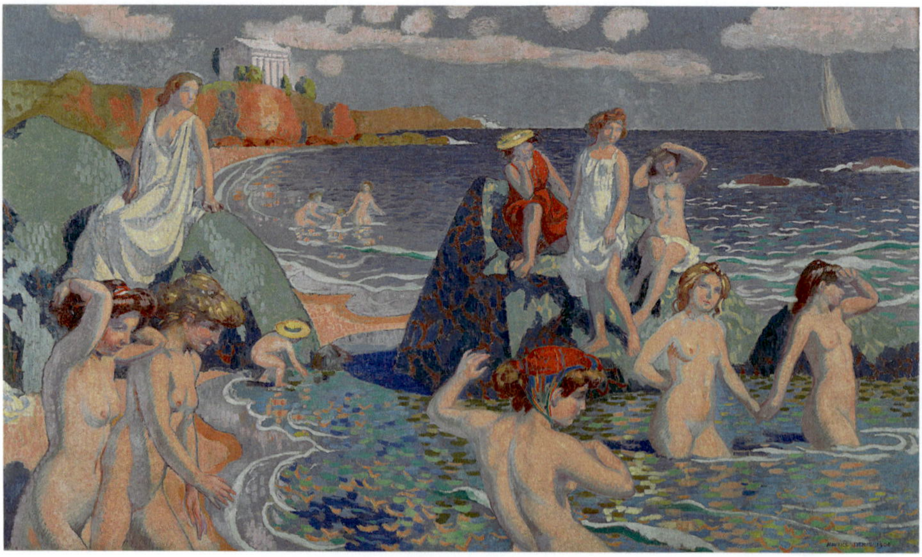

Ferdinand Hodler, Blick ins Unendliche, 1903/4
Maurice Denis, Baigneuses or Plage au petit temple, 1906

65

Ferdinand Hodler (Bern, 1853–Geneva, 1918)
Blick ins Unendliche (*Gaze into Infinity*), 1903/4
Oil on canvas, 100 × 80 cm
Acquisition, 1994. Inv. 1994-032

Ferdinand Hodler met Gustav Klimt and many other artists of the Viennese avant-garde, as well as their collectors, when visiting the Austro-Hungarian capital in early 1903. Aged fifty, the Swiss painter was now internationally known and he was invited back the following year as guest of honour at the Viennese Secession's nineteenth exhibition. He sent thirty-one works to this exhibition, which marked a turning point in his career. *Blick ins Unendliche*, numbered twenty-eight in the catalogue, was conceived within this stimulating context.

In the foreground of this painting we see a naked young man standing on the top of a rocky promontory. This vertical figure, derived from the traditional representation of stylites (hermits who lived at the top of columns), breaks up the parallel pattern formed by the stylised sea of clouds and sky. The colours are harmonised: cold blue for the air higher up and a warm pink for the rising sun tingeing the scene. The figure, whose model was the artist's fifteen-year-old son Hector, symbolises the artist's lofty, far-reaching vision. The hands crossed on his chest express the strength and interiority of a physical and mystical communion with cosmic forces. Here, Hodler imagines a veritable hymn to the beauty of youth, itself as eternal, pure and unspoilt as Alpine nature.

This painting was immediately acquired by the Austrian industrialist and art collector Carl Reininghaus after the exhibition in Vienna in 1904, but Hodler insisted that he must first be allowed to put 'a few finishing touches' to the work in his studio in Geneva. That was where it was given the form it has today. This picture marks an important stage in representations of the idea of paradise. The Garden of Eden theme was indeed much reformulated in the early twentieth century, as here, where it becomes a place in the upper mountains, out of the reach of modern civilisation. [CL]

66

Maurice Denis (Granville, 1870–Paris, 1943)
Baigneuses (*Bathers*) or *Plage au petit temple* (*Petit Temple Beach*), 1906
Oil on canvas, 114 × 196 cm
Acquired with the support of the Association des Amis du Musée, 1996. Inv. 1996-051

Displayed at the 1906 Salon de la Société nationale des beaux-arts and acquired in 1907 by the Belgian patron and painter Anna Boch, this large-format canvas is one of the most complex works in the series of beach paintings that Maurice Denis inaugurated in 1898 with *Baigneuses, Perros* (*On the Beach of Trestrignel*, New York, The Museum of Modern Art). It belongs to the artist's 'classical moment', the period that followed his discovery of the works of Raphael in Rome. This saw his colours become more luminous, acid and electric, his compositions more strict. A dazzling sun sears his views of Brittany, his chosen territory from his Nabi years onwards.

Baigneuses represents the Grands Sables site at Le Pouldu in the Finistère. Among Denis's paintings of beaches, this one depicts the ocean less as a maternal place that gave birth to civilisation than as the theatre of a spiritual union with nature, ritualised by the act of diving into the waves. Everything here is turned towards the ocean: the coast, wide open and ending with a Greek temple; the cohort of naked women and children contemplating, organised in triads; the boat launching out onto the waves.

The work is syncretic in its mixture of antique but also modern elements, including the presence of Marthe, the painter's wife, who modelled for the nude on the far left. On either side of the two figures placed along the median axis – heightened by the red of a dress and a bonnet – there is an alternation of naked and draped nudes, their plasticity close to that of Aristide Maillol's sculptures. Decorative in its rhythm and in the arabesques of the foam, using an almost pointillist touch, *Baigneuses* has the vivacity of Henri Matisse's fauve palette but with a calming effect. Its composition digests the tempered art of Paul Cézanne's *Grandes Baigneuses* (*The Large Bathers*, 1900–6, Philadelphia, Museum of Art). [CL]

67

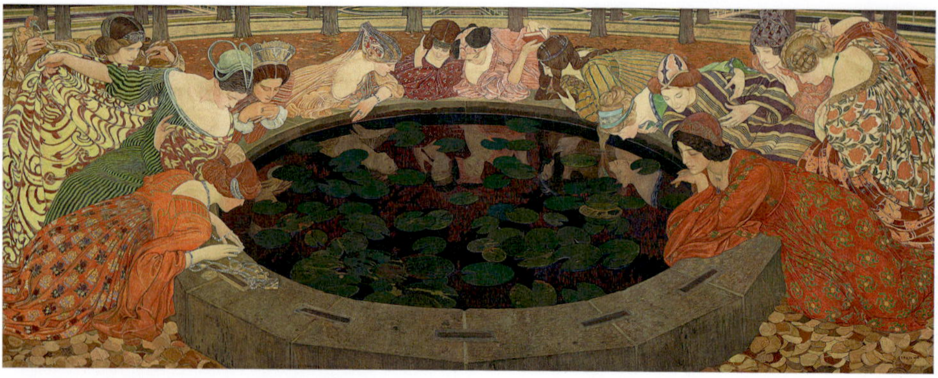

68

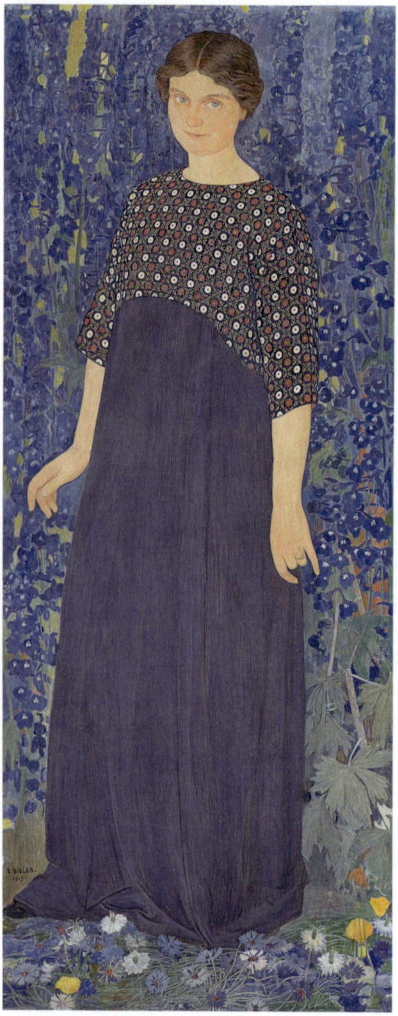

Ernest Biéler, L'eau mystérieuse, 1911
Ernest Biéler, Femme en bleu, 1913

67

Ernest Biéler (Rolle, 1863–Lausanne, 1948)
L'eau mystérieuse (*The Mysterious Water*), 1911
Tempera on paper mounted on canvas, 146.3 × 376.4 cm
On deposit from the Gottfried Keller Foundation, Federal Office of Culture, Bern, 1913. Inv. 555

Ernest Biéler worked tirelessly on *L'eau mystérieuse* from 1908 to 1911. From the outset, he conceived the painting as an art nouveau manifesto aiming to establish in Paris the supremacy of this graphic style and of the medium of egg tempera.

This work of monumental dimensions extended the series of symbolist panels inaugurated by the artist with *Les feuilles mortes* (*The Dead Leaves*) and *Les sources* (*The Spring*), respectively 1899 and 1900 (Bern, Kunstmuseum). It is painted on sheets of paper mounted on canvas and set within a large wooden frame made to the painter's instructions. Its long, narrow format recalls the Italian tradition of *cassone*, which had been revived by the English Pre-Raphaelite Edward Burne-Jones. The unified colour scheme – a harmony of yellows, browns and reds – leans towards the monochrome. The legato of the thirteen women fanning out in the foreground is countered by the staccato of the trees in the background. The steep, downward perspective heightens the impression that the elements have been squeezed onto a single plane. The basin occupies nearly half the painted surface.

The scene is set in an autumnal French-style garden. Young women are reflected in a dark pool dotted with the leaves of water lilies. Their sumptuous outfits combine historical and oriental features with the kind of contemporary fashion pioneered by Paul Poiret. Kneeling and frozen in theatrical poses, these princesses are absorbed in a melancholic fascination with their own reflections, tinged with worry at ageing and an awareness of the narrow limits of their existence. They have renounced material wealth, nature and culture, as symbolised by the three women emphatically turning away, respectively, from a necklace, a carnation and a book. This theme, revisiting Ovid's myth of Narcissus, reflects the taste for enchantment and the feminisation of heroes characteristic of symbolist and decadent circles at the turn to the twentieth century. [CL]

68

Ernest Biéler (Rolle, 1863–Lausanne, 1948)
Femme en bleu (*Woman in Blue*), 1913
Tempera on wood, 190 × 77 cm
Acquisition, 1981. Inv. 1981-086

Ernest Biéler's dire financial situation forced him to leave Paris in 1892. He returned to Switzerland, yet happiness eluded him, whether in Geneva, where he first settled, in Lausanne, where his Vaudois origins won him support in artistic circles, in Zurich, where friends provided him with portrait commissions, or finally in Savièse, in the Valais, where he had a studio built in 1901. The malaise reflected in this endless wandering was the sign of personal unhappiness. Now past the age of forty, the artist was still looking for a woman who would share his life. In 1909, he finally made up his mind to return to the French capital. There he met and married Michelle Vimont-Laronde, a young drawing teacher.

Femme en bleu, a life-size portrait painted four years later, brings to mind the English Pre-Raphaelites and Gustav Klimt. Michelle is depicted as someone with a strong character, as the intellectual who, in February 1911, put her name to a talented manifesto in favour of her husband's style, titled 'The Graphic Style in Painting'. The pale and delicate flesh tones of the face, arms and hand, and the glittering wedding ring, are set off by the mass of blue that constitutes the skirt and the floral surrounding, echoing the colour of the young woman's eyes. The dress she wears seems to champion the avant-garde fashion launched in Paris by the couturiers Paul Poiret and Madeleine Vionnet, one whose straight lines and supple materials emancipated the female body from the corset.

Biéler also connects his Parisian spouse with his homeland by surrounding her with certain flowers, such as larkspur, a perennial from the Alpine meadows. One wonders if the later storminess of their relationship, which would lead the couple to divorce in 1921, is also presaged here by this plant whose toxicity Swiss farmers blamed for poisoning their livestock. [CL]

69

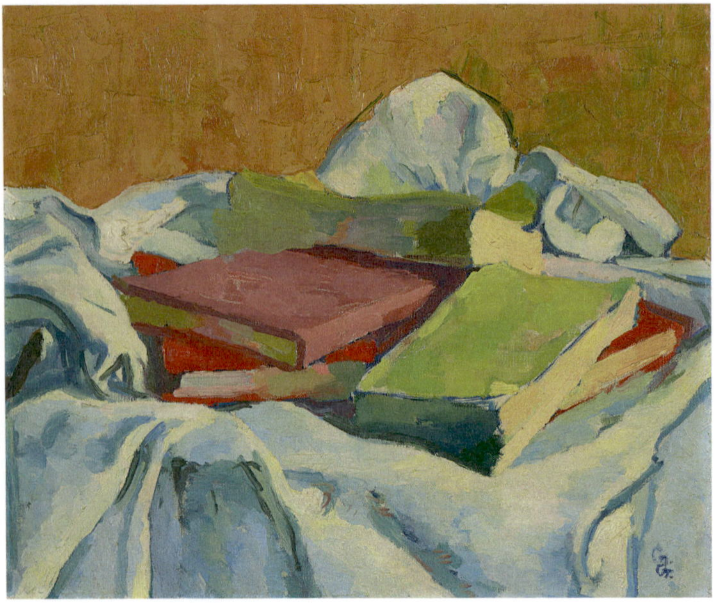

70

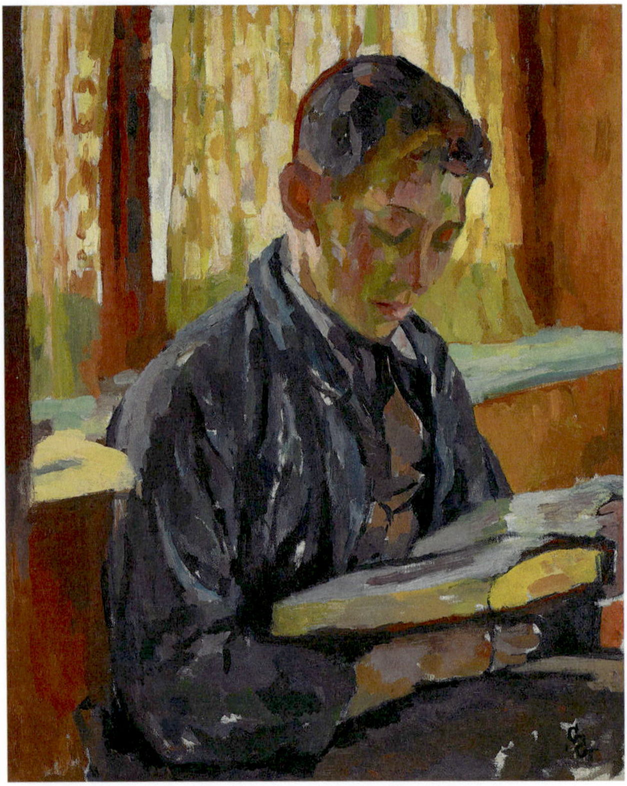

Giovanni Giacometti, Nature morte aux livres, c. 1907–8
Giovanni Giacometti, Alberto che legge, c. 1915

69

Giovanni Giacometti (Stampa, 1868–Glion-sur-Montreux, 1933)
Nature morte aux livres (*Still Life with Books*), c. 1907–8
Oil on canvas, 38.3 × 46.3 cm
Gift in lieu of inheritance tax, estate of Jean-Claude Givel, 2018. Inv. 2018-004

After studying applied arts in Munich, Giovanni Giacometti left for Paris in 1888 with his friend Cuno Amiet to further his artistic education. However, his painting remained largely uninfluenced by the modern art scene, and maintained pre-impressionist conventions. A brief visit to Italy in 1893 led to a paler palette of colours and more richly detailed hues. The key influence on his art came the following year when he met Giovanni Segantini and began drawing on the latter's Alpine themes and divisionist technique.

Even after Giacometti had settled permanently in Graubünden, he kept abreast of the French art scene. In mid-October 1907, he travelled to Paris for the Paul Cézanne retrospective at the Autumn Salon. He was dazzled by the experience, writing to Hedy Hahnloser-Bühler on 27 October that year, 'The journey to Paris was fully recompensed by the marvellous Cézanne exhibition. He is one of the purest artists ever to have existed ... One is completely bowled over by his great simplicity. To begin with one wonders in surprise, is that all? Yet taking a closer look, the simplest still life stirs in us the sensation of the infinite.'

This *Nature morte aux livres* seems to have been laid out to evoke an Alpine landscape. It is influenced by Cézanne in terms of its composition, with the cloth covering the table and the books arranged almost at random, like Cézanne's apples. Giacometti likewise draws on the master's constructive touch, both in the objects themselves and in the yellow-ochre background, and he has incorporated similar broad strokes of contrasting colours. Yet he goes further than Cézanne in capturing the play of light on the sharply contrasting green, purple and red of the books and the blue-green of the tablecloth. This energy is borrowed from Gauguin and Van Gogh, two other masters who had a decisive influence on Giacometti's art. [CLC]

70

Giovanni Giacometti (Stampa, 1868–Glion-sur-Montreux, 1933)
Alberto che legge (*Alberto Reading*), c. 1915
Oil on canvas, 46 × 38 cm
On deposit loan by the Dr. Marcel Bahro collection, 2011. Inv. 2011-016

This portrait shows the home in Stampa where Giovanni Giacometti spent the last four decades of his life. By the time Alberto, the first of his four children, was born in 1901, he had already returned to settle in his home region of Graubünden after studying abroad. His first meeting with the symbolist artist Giovanni Segantini in Maloja in 1894 convinced him that living at high altitude, surrounded by hostile, sublime nature, with a set daily routine, would not be an obstacle, but rather a boost to his ability to focus on what was important. His wife Annetta and children at home, the mountains of Val Bregaglia and the upper Engadine lakes nearby were material enough to give fresh impetus to his study of the play of light and colour. In 1909, he wrote, 'The painter only sees colours in nature; the colours do not lie inert alongside each other, they live, they quiver.'

Here, Alberto is shown from the waist up, lost in a book. He is seen against the light in front of a window whose curtain veils a bright landscape; his body and the skin of his face are typical of Giacometti's mature style. The artist's aim was now simply to capture his own visual sensations, recording the facts as he observed them and pinning down localised patches of colour in an intense, bold palette.

Giacometti spotted Alberto's talent very early on. When he sat for the portrait, Alberto had just completed his first oil painting, a still life with apples, and his first sculpture, a bust of his brother Diego. His father let him off his chores to nurture his talent, and the two of them drew together. The portrait reflects the father's strict yet affectionate view of a young man taking his first steps on the difficult path towards becoming an artist. [CL]

71

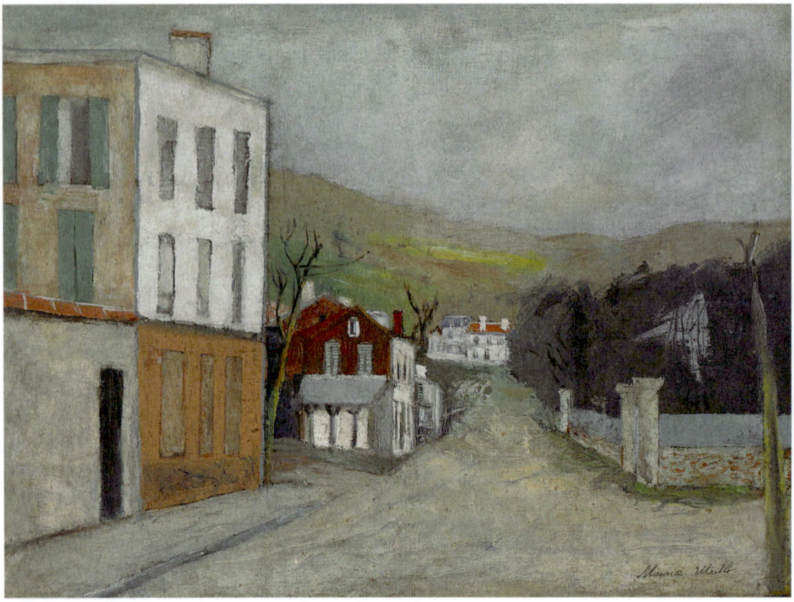

72

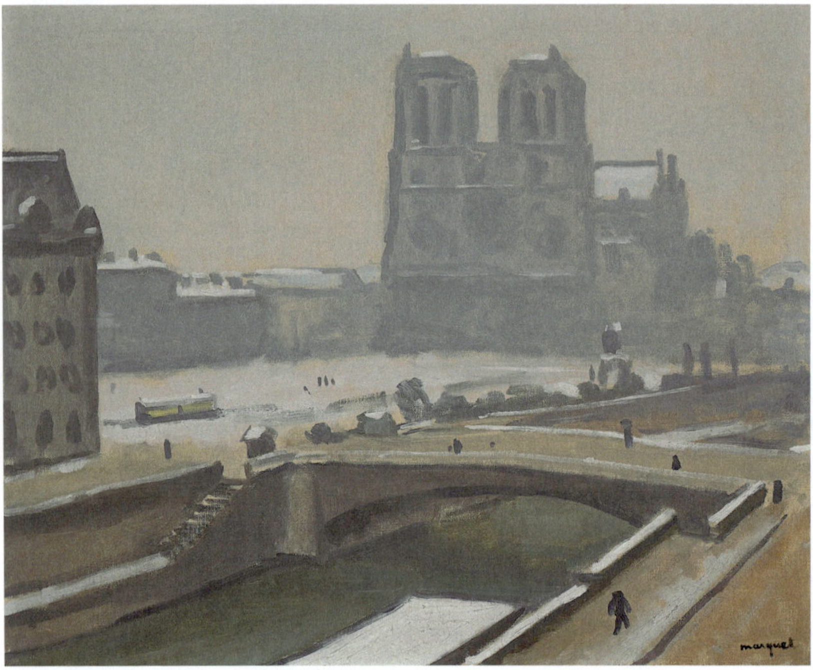

Maurice Utrillo, Paysage, Corse, 1913
Albert Marquet, Notre-Dame, temps de neige, c. 1914

71

Maurice Utrillo (Paris, 1883–Dax, 1955)
Paysage, Corse (*Landscape, Corsica*), 1913
Oil on canvas, 54 × 73 cm
On deposit loan by Max Bangerter, 1962.
Inv. 1962-020

As a teenager, Maurice Utrillo was encouraged to paint by his mother, Suzanne Valadon, a model and self-taught artist, who hoped that it would have a therapeutic effect in calming his violent mood swings and allay his precocious alcoholism. In any case, he proved to have real talent and in the 1920s began to enjoy great success with his views of deserted streets and colourful façades in Montmartre. Whereas predecessors such as Toulouse-Lautrec had shown the hubbub of the cafés and the bohemian life on the Butte, Utrillo's urban landscapes are striking in their austerity and the feeling of solitude that they exude.

After an early phase characterised by the application of thick impasto and dark colours, the 1910s marked the beginning of Utrillo's 'white period'. His palette grew lighter. Instead of the old green and blue ochre tones, the artist now preferred zinc white, which he applied with a palette knife, sometimes mixed with plaster. In those days he left Montmartre only for therapy with Doctor Revertégat in the Parisian suburb of Sannois. The only other movement that broke up his monotonous existence were a few trips with his mother and his father-in-law, André Utter. In autumn 1913 the three travelled to Corsica but the taciturn Utrillo refused to let the Isle of Beauty work its magic. Everywhere he went, he turned his back on the sea, preferring the streets of Corte and Belgodère. There he continued to look for stony colours, enlivened, as here, by one or two green or grey shutters. True, there is a greater contrast than in Paris, his whites now being set against more Mediterranean browns and ochres, but the sun of the South did not reinvigorate his colours, which remained muted.

In Corsica as in Paris, Utrillo avoided agitation, taking refuge in the pensive contemplation of anonymous, soulless architecture. Empty streets and closed shutters contribute once again to the expression of that deep melancholy that was part of his temperament. [CLC]

72

Albert Marquet (Bordeaux, 1875–Paris, 1947)
Notre-Dame, temps de neige (*Notre Dame under Snow*), c. 1914
Oil on canvas, 65 × 81 cm
Henri-Auguste Widmer bequest, 1936.
Inv. 326

By January 1908 Albert Marquet was living on the fifth floor at 19 Quai Saint-Michel. He approached the scene in Paris as a totality, as he had elsewhere, with a preference for steep downward perspectives. Like his neighbour, Henri Matisse, he captured multiple views of Notre Dame, constantly changing the angle.

The muted colours of *Notre-Dame, temps de neige*, contrasting with the expanses of white, show Marquet adopting a more limited palette after his fauve period. The painter now abandoned the distortions and pure colours – yellows, blues and vermilions – favoured by his comrades André Derain and Maurice de Vlaminck and concentrated instead on synthesis and a certain kind of harmony. In this case, the snow allows him to dispense with all depth and paint almost in black and white.

This urban view of the banks of the Seine is highly characteristic of the way in which Marquet constructed his canvases. A network of thick lines, like underscores, constitutes the armature of the landscape. Combined with these, broad brushstrokes and the occasional broad swathe of colour or unpainted canvas form essential elements of the composition. There are no superfluous details. A few swift touches animate the painting. The painter poetically captures the atmosphere of a Paris slowed down by bad weather. The barge frozen in a thick coat of snow echoes the dark mass of the cathedral. Only a handful of people, rendered by short black strokes, have ventured outside.

Marquet was a frequent traveller but returned to Paris regularly until 1931 to paint the Seine, the bridges and the Île de la Cité from the window of his apartment. He painted several canvases with this exact same composition, be it in snowy, such as here, sunny or rainy weather. [CLC]

73

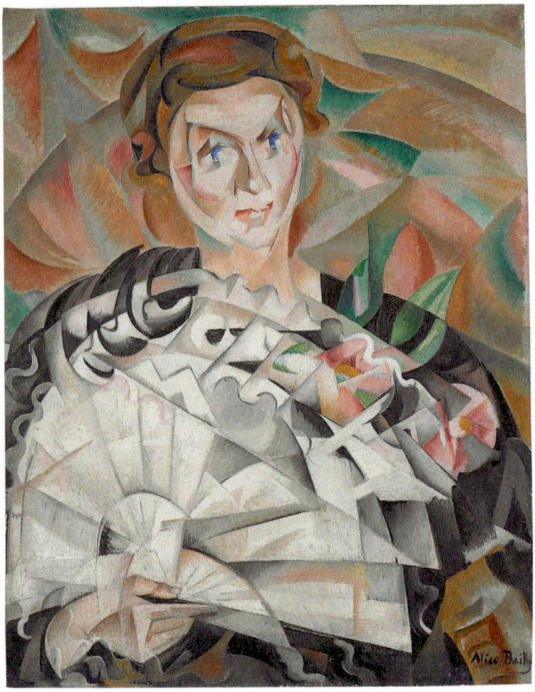

74

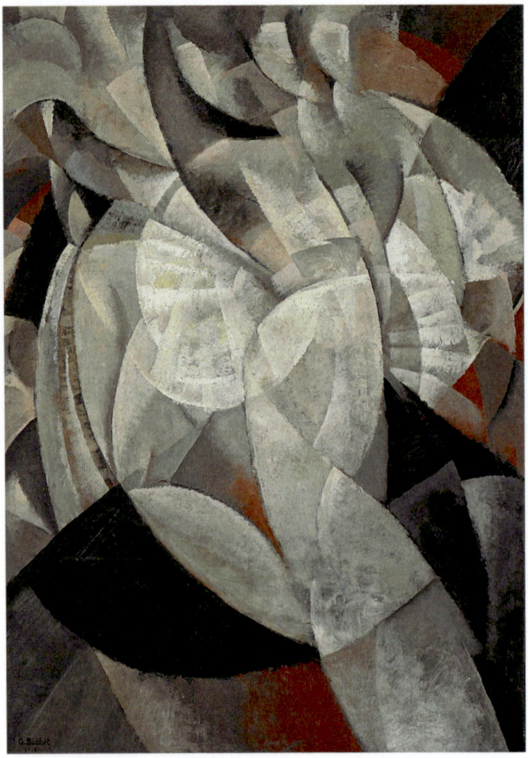

Alice Bailly, Jeu d'éventail or Femme à l'éventail, 1913
Gustave Buchet, Danseuse en mouvement, 1918

73

Alice Bailly (Geneva, 1872–Lausanne, 1938)
Jeu d'éventail (*Playing with a Fan*) or *Femme à l'éventail* (*Woman with a Fan*), 1913
Oil on canvas, 92 × 73 cm
Acquisition, 1997. Inv. 1997-093

Alice Bailly studied in Geneva before moving to Paris in 1906, where she became an admirer of fauvism. Her work already showed signs of the extremely bright colours that would later typify her oeuvre. In 1912, she encountered the futurist movement for the first time. She also began to embrace cubist abstraction after seeing the works on display at the Salon de la Section d'or and reading Albert Gleizes' and Jean Metzinger's manifesto on cubism. Together with Robert Delaunay's orphic cubism, these influenced her style towards the transcription of movement by bold lines and interpenetrating expanses and volumes, both served by an increasingly transparent use of colour.

In 1913, the year when she painted this *Jeu d'éventail*, Bailly's work caught Guillaume Apollinaire's eye at the Salon des Indépendants: 'Miss Alice Bailly has found an entirely new direction. Her subtle cubism is one of the interesting novelties of the Salon'. Convinced that this was the start of a glorious new career, Bailly produced an energetic burst of work in a wide range of genres, including the portrait, which she had not touched for several years.

The sitter for this portrait, which was probably painted in Geneva, was the artist's sister Louisa. It clearly calls to mind Auguste Renoir's *Femme à l'éventail* (*Girl with a Fan*, 1881, Saint Petersburg, Hermitage Museum), but the more immediate reference is to Jean Metzinger's *Femme à l'éventail* (*Woman with a Fan*, 1912, New York, Solomon R. Guggenheim Museum). However, Bailly's approach to the subject is unique in her focus on the shapes produced by the fan's rhythmical movement, stirring the air to such an extent that it blurs the sitter's entire surroundings. The scene could almost be set in the open air, as suggested by the warm palette and the green in the background, contrasting with the shades of grey, white and pink in the foreground. [CL]

74

Gustave Buchet (Etoy, 1888–Lausanne, 1963)
Danseuse en mouvement (*Dancer in Motion*), 1918
Oil on canvas, 148 × 107 cm
Acquisition, 1958. Inv. 1959-005

Trained at the École des beaux-arts in Geneva, Gustave Buchet first stayed in Paris in winter 1910. In 1915 he was in Geneva as cofounder of the Le Falot group, which defined itself in opposition to Ferdinand Hodler. During a second stay in Paris, in 1916-7, he was particularly interested in futurism, which chimed with his own concern for movement. Having returned to Switzerland, in 1918 he began to adopt the principle of 'continuity of space' whereby the figure and their surroundings interact and overlap.

In the 1910s, dance was at the heart of many aesthetic experiments focusing on the exploration of new ways of perceiving. Buchet based this canvas on the eminently dramatic element of the spiral. Influenced by the orphism of Robert and Sonia Delaunay, with its interest in rhythm, contrast and capturing the sensation of movement, Buchet structured his composition with coloured blocks delimited by curves and counter-curves. This assemblage of semi-circular forms animates the canvas, eddying in a dazzling white colour that perfectly renders the dancer's energetic movement through space. This space itself seems contaminated and subjected to the waves created by the movements of the body and thus breaks up into so many geometrical forms.

Exhibited alongside other futurist works in Geneva in 1918, *Danseuse en mouvement* met with an enthusiastic response from Alexander Archipenko but failed to convince either the public or the critics. In spring 1920 – he had just moved back to Paris for what would be a stay of twenty years – Buchet gave up futurism in favour of a flat, geometrical style of painting. The artist continued with his research in the slipstream of the avant-garde, but this time following the conservative mood of the *retour à l'ordre*, whereby rules and rigour became the watchwords, as exemplified by the purism of Le Corbusier and Amédée Ozenfant. [CLC]

75

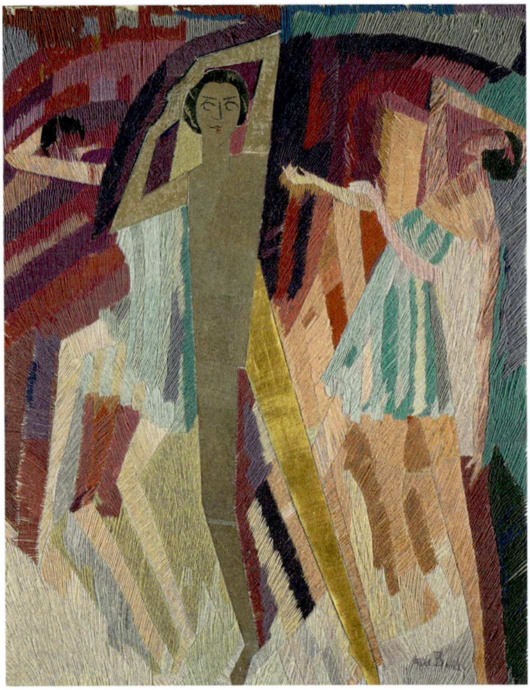

76

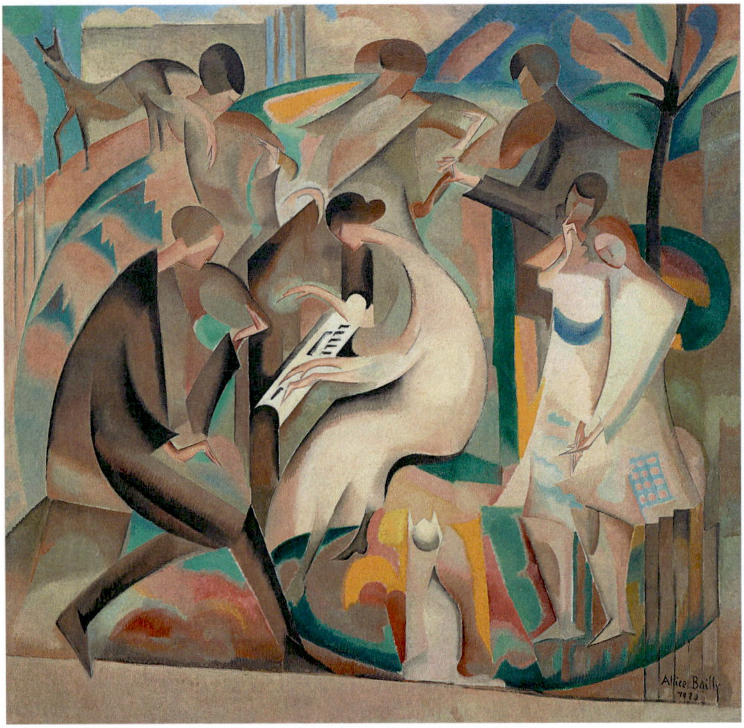

Alice Bailly, Les rythmiciennes, 1918–19
Alice Bailly, Le concert dans le jardin, 1920

75

Alice Bailly (Geneva, 1872–Lausanne, 1938)
Les rythmiciennes (*The Rhythmicians*), 1918–19
Wool, silk, glued paper and ink on canvas, 82 × 66.5 cm
Gift of the Comité de la Fondation Alice Bailly, 1957. Inv. 1957-006

Published in 1918 by Albert Rheinwald, the first monograph on Bailly insists on the originality of her most recent work: '[B]efore our eyes wool becomes a precious, expressive and living material on a par with oil, pastel, marble or gold.' Bailly refused to see any hierarchy between her oil paintings and her 'wool pictures': in her eyes, this innovative technique was simply an extension of the register of her means of expression. 'Let no one come and talk to me about applied art!' insisted Rheinwald, who had a sense of the risk taken by the artist in exhibiting her needle works, after having fought so hard to assert herself as the equal of men in the art world.

Bailly made her first wool pictures in Geneva in 1916. *Les rythmiciennes* shows a dance performance with dramatic lighting in the foreground. In the background, two dancers with short skirts and hair perform a set of expressive movements inspired by the choreography of the Genevan Émile Jaques-Dalcroze, the promoter of eurhythmics. Most of the surface is rendered in muted colour thread and pastel. The matt wool is used only for costumes and sets, and glossy silk for the bared parts of the legs and arms. For the main dancer, Bailly also used collage, with gold and silver paper for the leotard. Her face is outlined in black ink, with the line of her eyes and her nose imitating the stitch of the oversewing.

For this composition, Bailly took inspiration from a show by Lucienne Rouché, daughter of the director of the Opéra de Paris Jacques Rouché and wife of the painter Valdo Barbey. This work is yet another reflection of the artist's continuing interest in dance, which runs from her portrait of Jacqueline Marval at the Bal Van Dongen (1914, private collection) to her final large paintings for the foyer of the Théâtre municipal in Lausanne (1936). [CL]

76

Alice Bailly (Geneva, 1872–Lausanne, 1938)
Le concert dans le jardin (*Concert in the Garden*), 1920
Oil on canvas, 94.5 × 99.5 cm
Acquisition, 2017. Inv. 2017-030

As a Swiss citizen, Alice Bailly was forced to leave Paris during the First World War and struggled to make a living in Geneva. Most of her admirers were in German-speaking Switzerland. In Winterthur, where collectors interested in modern art had helped bring about the creation of a new museum in 1916, she met the patron Werner Reinhart, who would continue to support her for the rest of her life. She also met Arthur and Hedy Hahnloser, whose company she kept regularly from 1918 to 1920 and who invited her to stay at Villa Flora, where their rich collection of contemporary art was displayed.

Le concert dans le jardin is one of the works inspired by Bailly's visits to Villa Flora. There she saw open-air performances organised by the Hahnlosers, who shared her passion for music. Several sketches were made in Winterthur and the painting was executed in Paris, where the artist returned to live in 1920. A young man, two teenagers, a cat and a goat are gathered around a piano quartet. The model for one of the violinists was the collector Richard Bühler's sister-in-law. The figure of the pianist Maria de Senger comes from an earlier painting *La Sonate à Dukas* (1918, Collection Crédit Suisse Group).

Having assimilated the advances of fauvism, cubism and futurism, the early 1920s saw Bailly move towards a new kind of stylisation, while renouncing none of her chromatic vigour. On this nearly square canvas, the curves organising the eddying composition spread amply and supply around the piano keyboard, from which they seem to emanate. The speed of musical execution is conveyed by the multiplication of hands. The tubular, shaded forms and the complementary hues of green and orange interlock and fuse on a flat space that, as a portion of reality filtered by a heightened sensibility, expresses a belief in the power of universal dynamism. [CL]

77

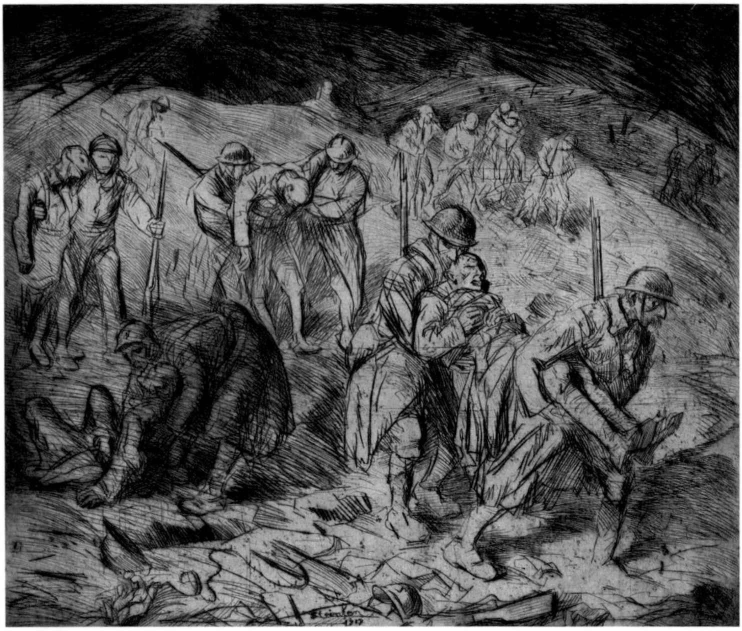

78

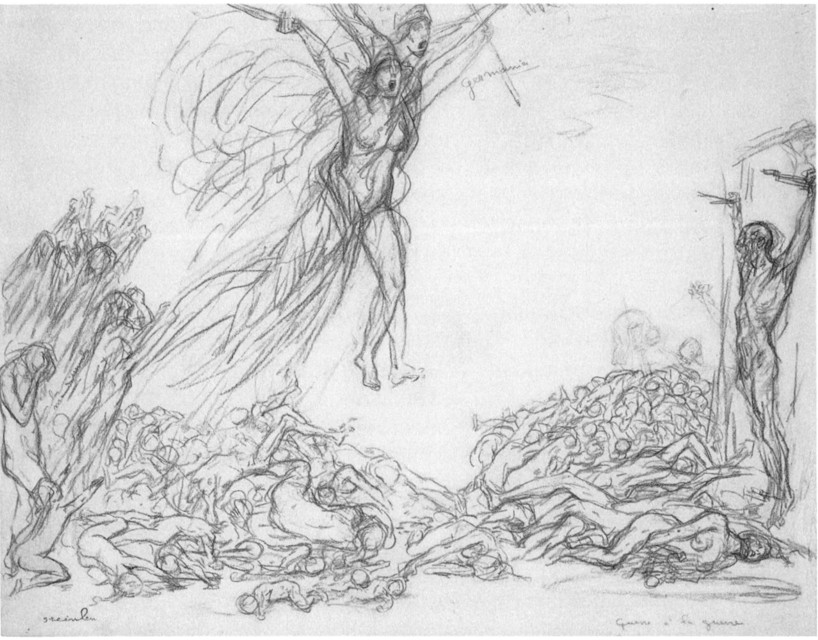

Théophile-Alexandre Steinlen, Les échappés de l’enfer II, 1917
Théophile-Alexandre Steinlen, Guerre à la guerre, between 1916 and 1920

77

Théophile-Alexandre Steinlen (Lausanne, 1859–Paris, 1923)
Les échappés de l'enfer II (*Survivors of Hell II*), 1917
Etching and black aquatint on paper, 49.3×59.7 cm, ed. 4/12
Former Jacques Christophe collection. Acquisition with the support of the Loterie Romande, the Association des Amis du Musée and Pierre Gonset, 2008.
Inv. 2008-060

Théophile-Alexandre Steinlen was fifty-five years old when Germany declared war on France on 3 August 1914, ushering in the twentieth century's litany of horrors. The worldwide conflict killed nearly ten million soldiers and almost as many civilians, destroyed entire cities, and laid waste to vast swathes of the European countryside. Steinlen reacted to the utter disaster of war with a vast body of work. Firmly convinced that it was his duty to reach as many people as possible, he produced more than two hundred prints.

Though Steinlen was an anti-militarist and a socialist, part of his work is devoted to the 'sacred union', the tendency to unite across political differences in the face of adversity. His lithographs, printed and distributed in large numbers, express his pity for soldiers and his solidarity with the civilian population left behind in Paris.

In parallel, Steinlen created sumptuous etchings in small editions. These denounced the violence of the fighting, the soldiers trapped by exploding shells, the rattle of machine guns and clouds of mustard gas. He requested to become an army artist in 1916 and described the darkness surrounding the men dug into the trenches, unable to move. At the time he was working on the *Échappés de l'enfer*, he had already travelled close to the front twice by his own means. The deeply moving scene doubtless also draws on photographs from the illustrated press. The artist takes up a nocturnal, Rembrandtesque tone to depict the survivors escaping the slaughter, carried on the backs of their fellow soldiers. The explicit reference in the foreground to traditional representations of the entombment of Christ lends universal relevance to the scene of broken bodies being taken from the battlefield. [CL]

78

Théophile-Alexandre Steinlen (Lausanne, 1859–Paris, 1923)
Guerre à la guerre (*War to War*), between 1916 and 1920
Blue, grey, and red pencil on paper, 48.1×63.2 cm
Paul and Tina Stohler Donation, 2018.
Inv. 2018-043

This drawing poignantly reworks two pieces of art that were a lifelong inspiration for Steinlen: the painting *La Liberté guidant le peuple* (*Liberty Leading the People*) by Eugène Delacroix (1830, Paris, Musée du Louvre) and the sculpture *La Marseillaise* by François Rude (1833–6, Paris, Arc de Triomphe). The two masterpieces of French Romanticism depict armed female allegories wearing Phrygian caps and leading the people to victory. Starting in the late 1890s, the two works inspired Steinlen to develop an iconographic repertoire of men and women struggling against capitalism.

Steinlen's deep-rooted anti-militarism was sorely tested by the outbreak of the First World War. He supported the troops and, after the atrocities committed during the invasions of Belgium and Serbia, developed an anti-German streak that was widely shared at the time. The woman leading the people to freedom in his works took on a new guise. In his 1915 etching *La Marseillaise*, she flies over Paris, guiding the crowds who are invading the streets, which are filled with fluttering flags. In the 1916 lithograph *La Poilue*, she is a threatening nude, her hair streaming in the wind, embodying resistance against invading forces.

In *Guerre à la guerre*, Steinlen returns to his radical pacifism. The aim is no longer to defeat the Germans, but to fight war itself, in which, as he wrote in 1916, 'millions of men ... die like miserable beasts'. Here, he depicts the victims of war as a heap of corpses, including children, disembowelled bodies, and a man crucified on a door. On the left, women plead with the Liberator, now transformed into Germania, to put an end to the dreadful crimes against the civilian population. Steinlen made numerous changes to the figure of the allegory, the virulence of his drawing rivalling Goya's series of etchings *Los desastres de la Guerra* (*Disasters of War*, 1810–15). [CL]

79

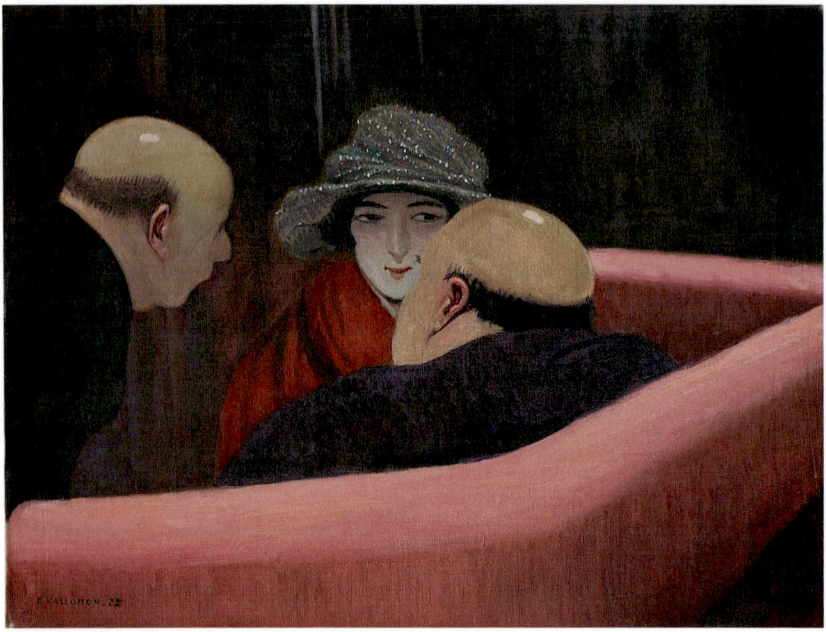

80

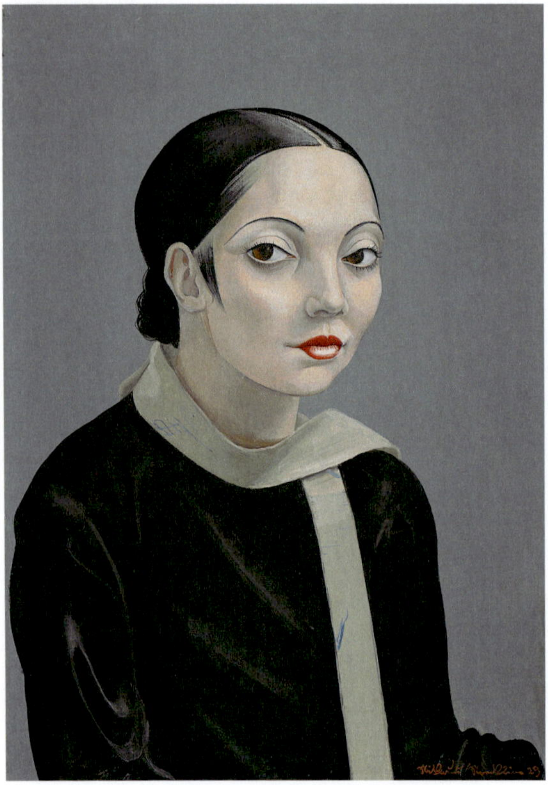

Félix Vallotton, La chaste Suzanne, 1922
Niklaus Stoecklin, Portrait de Tatjana Barbakoff, 1929

79

Félix Vallotton (Lausanne, 1865–Paris, 1925)
La chaste Suzanne (*The Chaste Susanna*), 1922
Oil on canvas, 54 × 73 cm
Acquisition in co-ownership with the Gottfried Keller Foundation, Federal Office of Culture, Bern, with a special credit from the État de Vaud and a gift from the Association des Amis du Musée, 1993. Inv. 1993-017

The act of seeing – from dazzlement to the risk of unhinging reason – is the guiding thread of the biblical story that Vallotton, now nearly sixty years old, ironically alludes to here. Because they 'see' Susanna, two Jewish elders break the divine commandments and lust after this married woman whom they espy nude at her bath. And because they lie and claim to have surprised her with a lover, they are judged and executed.

What remains in this modern picture of a subject so often painted in the past by the likes of Albrecht Altdorfer, Peter Paul Rubens, Artemisia Gentileschi and Rembrandt? The rather murky setting is a cross between a backroom in a café and a theatre box. The flesh-pink divan, the blood-red coat and the hat shimmering like a swarm of fireflies take on the kind of strange importance that we find only in dreams or in memories of certain shameful images. The woman's gaze betrays a professional assurance and a power that verges on sadism. The expressions of the two middle-aged men are hidden behind their ears, pink with pleasure, and their shiny pates, leaning towards the object of their desire.

This *Chaste Suzanne* is, more than a moralistic piece of history, an invitation to immerse ourselves in the unconscious. As in Georges Bataille (*Histoire de l'œil* [*History of the Eye*], 1928), or in Luis Buñuel and Salvador Dalí (*Un chien andalou* [*An Andalusian Dog*], 1929), the representation of the scopic drive (the dialectic between 'seeing' and 'being seen') stands in for the representation of the sex act. The only physical contact suggested by the foreshortening is the way one of the two men's eyelashes brushes against the woman's face, as if laying down a fly, evoking these words from Bataille's story: 'The caress of the eye ... is so extraordinarily gentle.' [CL]

80

Niklaus Stoecklin (Basel, 1896–1982)
Portrait de Tatjana Barbakoff (*Portrait of Tatjana Barbakoff*), 1929
Oil on canvas mounted on cardboard, 55 × 40 cm
Acquisition, 2000. Inv. 2000-031

In 1925, both the Swiss artist Niklaus Stoecklin and his Latvian subject Tatjana Barbakoff began their rise to international fame. Stoecklin was the only non-German artist to take part in the first Neue Sachlichkeit (New Objectivity) exhibition at the Mannheim Kunsthalle, while Barbakoff, a Jewish dancer, presented her first individual programme in Berlin. This was for her the first step to a successful career in the German-speaking world, cut short by exile in Paris in 1933. She was arrested by the Gestapo in Nice in 1944 and deported to Auschwitz, where she died in the gas chambers the same year.

The portrait brings together two seemingly very different temperaments. Barbakoff's performances were expressionist, closer to pantomime than to dance. Her shows featured a series of decorative tableaux and satires on contemporary art (*Dadaismus*, *Wege zu Kraft und Schönheit*), in which self-designed Oriental costumes and masks played a key role. In the 1920s, Stoecklin's art formed part of a broader reaction against expressionism, drawing on a form of magic realism typified by symbolist verismo devoid of social critique.

Tatjana Barbakoff gave a much-admired performance in Zurich in November 1929. The pictoriality of her poses and her very mobile face inspired Stoecklin's portrait, as well as several of Gregor Rabinovitch's prints. They were the last in a long line of artists and photographers who took her as their model. As early as 1924, she sat for the members of Das Junge Rheinland group gathered around Johanna Ey, followed by many expressionist painters and sculptors including her partner Gert Heinrich Wollheim, Waldemar Flaig, Helen Dahm, and Christian Rohlfs, whose house she visited in Ascona in 1931 and who produced a vast cycle of drawings of her. [CL]

81

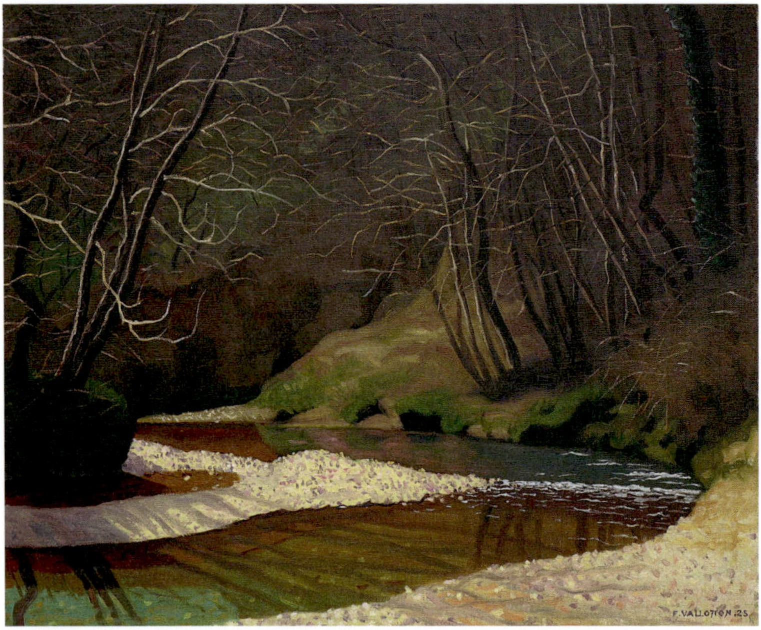

82

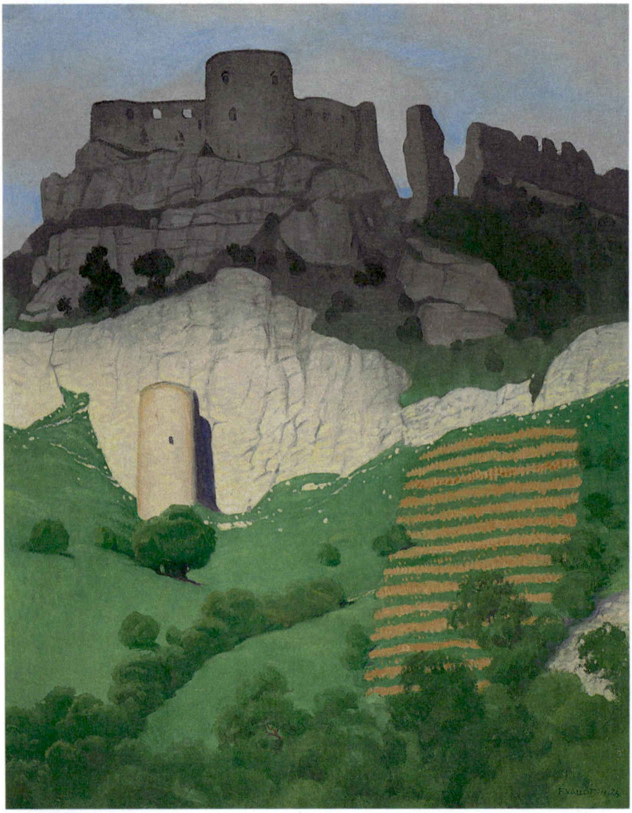

Félix Vallotton, Ruisseau rouille et galets blancs, 1921
Félix Vallotton, Le château Gaillard, 1924

81

Félix Vallotton (Lausanne, 1865–Paris, 1925)
Ruisseau rouille et galets blancs (*Rust Stream and White Pebbles*), 1921
Oil on canvas, 60.5 × 73.5 cm
Acquisition, 2017. Inv. 2017-016

A painful case of sciatica that came on in 1916 prompted Félix Vallotton to decide in late autumn 1920 to spend the winter season in the south of France. He and his wife Gabrielle arrived in Cagnes on 24 November 1920 and stayed in a guest house overlooking the village. They spent the next four winters there until Vallotton bought an old sheepfold in 1924. Vallotton was accustomed to the low, grey skies of Normandy and was initially astonished by the bright winter sun in the south, writing to his brother Paul on 26 December 1920, 'I have started working at long last but I am not at all satisfied with the result; I am a bit disorientated by so much light ... I am not at home with my palette.'

Vallotton did acclimatise to the new light very quickly, choosing hues that he had never used before – intense blues, rust reds, oranges and purples, warm greens and yellows, whose brightness contrasted sharply with the powerfully highlighted colours of the shadows. What guided his choice of hues, even more than the light of southern France, was a new boldness that saw him accentuate their tones and heighten their contrasts.

Here, the stream's almost unreal light extends to the thick forest in the middle ground. The white glints on the rippling water echo the tangle of leafless branches that form a network of long filaments spreading light across the top half of the painting. The curving banks, ripples and pebbles shimmering in the sun filtering through the plants all reflect the heritage of Vallotton's Nabi period, still shaping his landscapes as late as the 1920s. The stream, lying across the pebbles almost like a multicoloured rug, is radically transformed by the artist's chromatic and formal synthesis. [CLC]

82

Félix Vallotton (Lausanne, 1865–Paris, 1925)
Le château Gaillard (*Château Gaillard*), 1924
Oil on canvas, 80.5 × 65 cm
Acquisition, 1940. Inv. 625

In 1924, when travelling to Honfleur, where he rented a villa for the summer in 1909, Félix Vallotton stopped at Les Andelys, a village on the banks of the Seine overlooked by the ruins of Château Gaillard.

To paint this fortress, built in 1196 by Richard the Lionheart, King of England and Duke of Normandy, Vallotton scrupulously studied its composition. His initial pencil drawing is now in the Museum collection.

The exaggeratedly steep upward view, the way the composition separates the château from its modern surroundings, the synthetic approach to the forms with their supple lines and curved extremities (characteristic of the painter's work in the 1920s), as well as the strong contrasts between light and shadow, all help create an image of the site that is at once mysterious and unreal. By leaving the upper part of this white limestone château in darkness, and by putting the sky, ruin and hill all on the same plane, Vallotton unrolls before the viewer a kind of aural tapestry in strident colours.

Vallotton was fascinated by ruins as witness to the disappearance of civilisations both ancient ('Roman ruins are awe-inspiring', he wrote to his brother Paul in May 1907) and contemporary, like the ones created by the First World War. The ones at Les Andelys offered an exemplary setting. Indeed, the small town below was also of interest to him as the birthplace of Nicolas Poussin in 1594. That master of classicism had elevated landscape to the level of history painting by distancing himself from the observed view in favour of a composition recreated by thought and the imagination. Vallotton followed his footsteps. In 1916, the year he travelled to Les Andelys for the first time, he mentioned in his *Journal* the notion of the 'historical landscape', which was now central to his art and is inseparable from the figure of Poussin. [CLC]

83

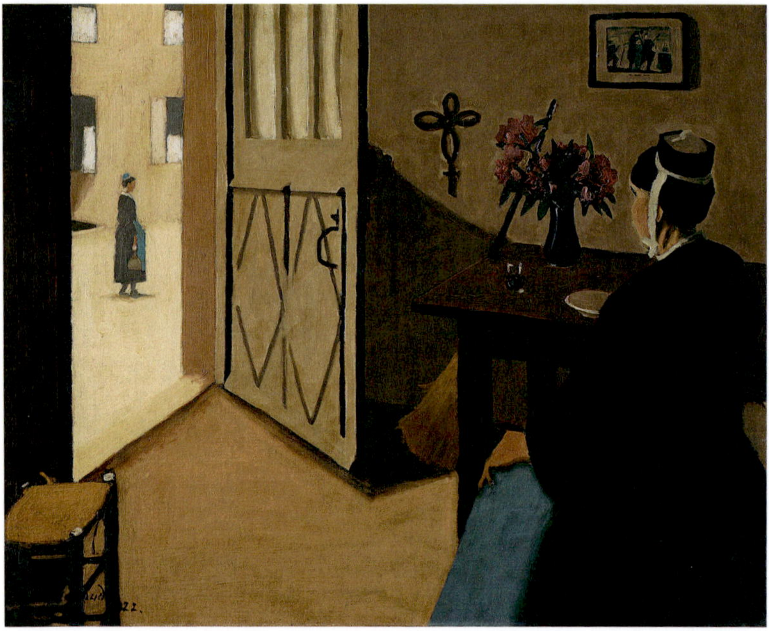

84

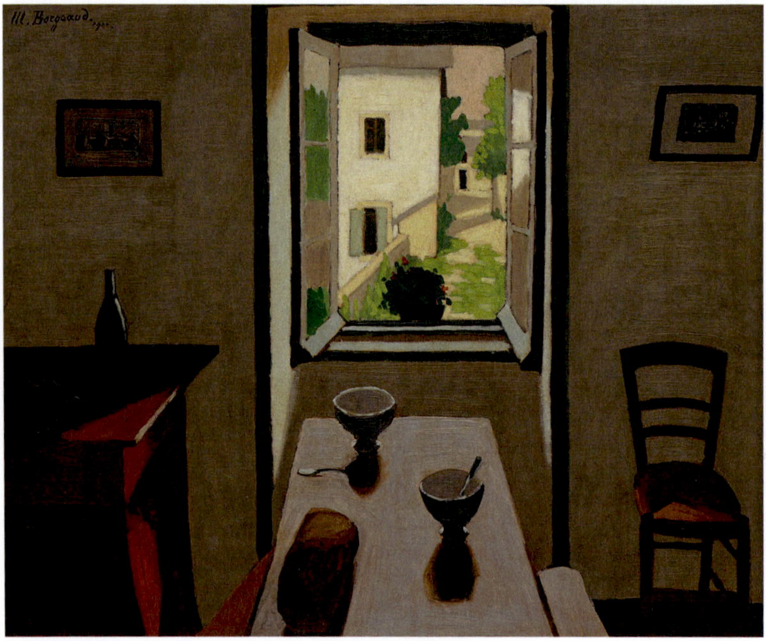

Marius Borgeaud, La Bretonne qui passe, 1922
Marius Borgeaud, La table et les deux bols, 1922

83

Marius Borgeaud (Lausanne, 1861–Paris, 1924)
La Bretonne qui passe (*Breton Woman Passing By*), 1922
Oil on canvas, 65.5×81.5 cm
Acquisition, 1954. Inv. 1954-011

After moving to Paris from his native Lausanne, Marius Borgeaud discovered Brittany in 1908 and from then on to the end of his life spent several months there every year. *La Bretonne qui passe* was painted at Le Faouët, in Morbihan, where the artist stayed between 1920 and 1922.

In a modest interior, a seated woman seems to be taking a break from her everyday tasks to eat. Her traditional costume forms an imposing black mass, not devoid of modelling, from which protrudes a length of blue clothing contrasting with the limited chromatic palette used by the artist. Interiors painted by Borgeaud often include an open door or window that alleviates a possible sense of confinement by creating a link with the outside world, which is also the case here. Despite the impression that the objects are pushed towards the beholder due to the flattening of perspective and the raised viewpoint chosen by the artist, the position of the woman, facing the door, guides the gaze outside the room. A second woman, holding a basket, is framed by the doorway, standing out against the light, bright background of the street, which contrasts with the dark interior. Immobile and silent, each seems locked into her personal solitude.

Contrary to many artists who travelled to Brittany looking for new subjects, Borgeaud does not seem to have been interested in picturesque scenes or local monuments. He set out to represent everyday events and settings, with a strong regional character. The crucifix, seen in many of the artist's canvases, reflects a piety still prevalent in the region. Likewise, hanging on the wall, the print titled *Un des héros de Beauséjour* (*One of the Heroes of Beauséjour*) from the *Grande Guerre* (*Great War*) series (1915) by Eduardo Garcia Benito recalls the popular engravings decorating public establishments in Brittany, but also found in private homes. [CdA]

84

Marius Borgeaud (Lausanne, 1861–Paris, 1924)
La table et les deux bols (*The Table and the Two Bowls*), 1922
Oil on canvas, 65.5×81 cm
Acquisition, 1942. Inv. 513

Marius Borgeaud painted some three hundred canvases, and this is one of a number that represent the quintessence of his aesthetic. Here, his tirelessly explored and always very limited world of subjects – still lifes, scenes of Breton life, interiors – is at its barest, and his art at its most synthetic.

Painted two years before the artist's death, *La table et les deux bols* shows the interior of a house in Le Faouët, Brittany. In the foreground, we see a loaf of bread, two bowls and two spoons, which cast long shadows over the table, underscoring their materiality. The room around them is dim, with the perspective focusing on the window whose open panes reflect the greenery outside. On the wall are two prints – images within the image. Finally, at the centre of the composition is a pot of flowers, which the strong contre-jour reduces to a dark-green mass. Even so, we can make out a few red flowers that catch the sun.

The severity of this painting brings to mind the most austere vanitas paintings, the ones made to encourage Jansenist meditations on death and the fragility of the human condition in seventeenth-century France. However, the panoply of objects assembled by Borgeaud is distinctly poor in symbolism: a barely started loaf and empty bowls signalling, at the very most, an absence. The power of this painting comes from the opening at the rear onto a light-flooded landscape, which stands for the vivifying power of the sun, a rebirth experienced by Borgeaud during his many stays in regions (Algeria, Seville, Brittany) where the strong contrast between shadow and light is like a daily re-enactment of the battle between death and life. [CL]

85

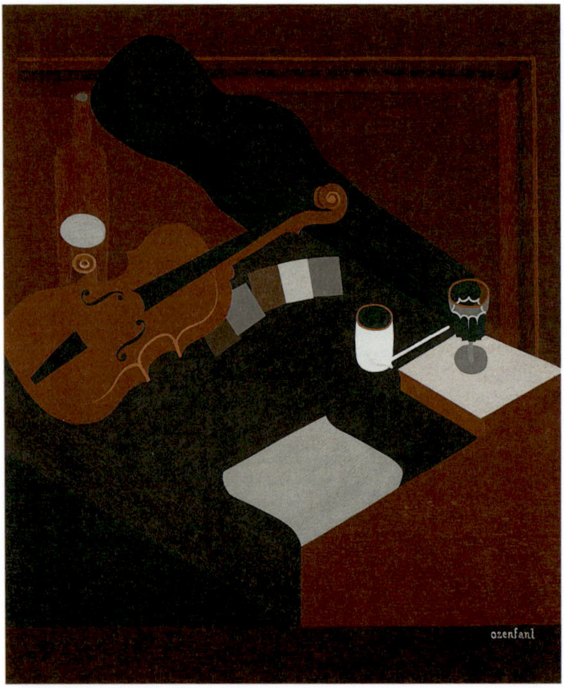

86

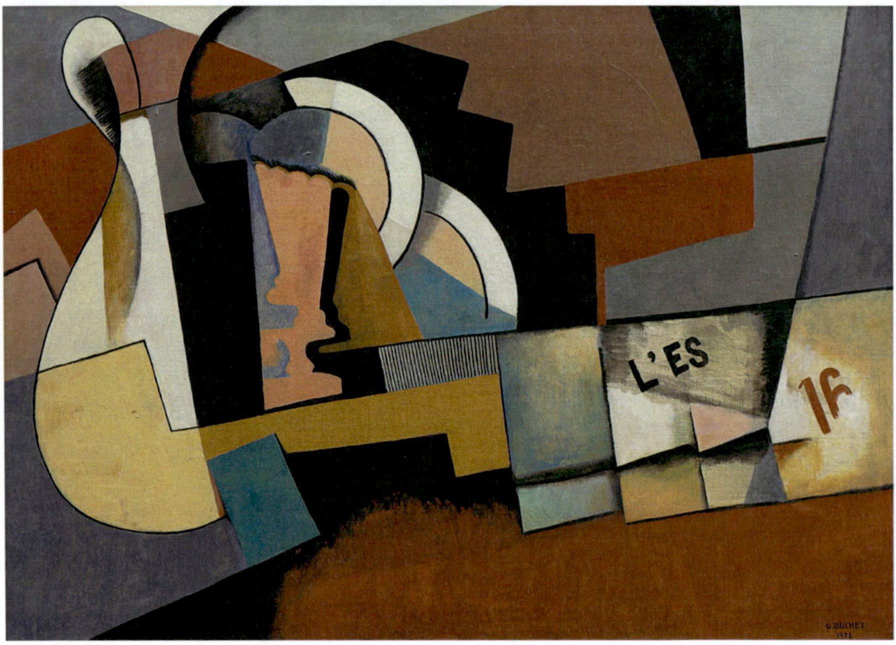

Amédée Ozenfant, Le violon rouge, 1919–29
Gustave Buchet, L'Esprit nouveau, 1925/8

85

Amédée Ozenfant (Saint-Quentin, 1886–Cannes, 1966)
Le violon rouge (*The Red Violin*), 1919–29
Oil on canvas, 53 × 44.3 cm
Acquisition, 1995. Inv. 1995-193

In the aftermath of the First World War, Amédée Ozenfant and Charles-Édouard Jeanneret (Le Corbusier) co-signed *Après le cubisme* (*After Cubism*) [1918], a purist manifesto. In it, they argued for the exclusion of all disorder, be it in the dimension of time, as in impressionism and futurism, or in that of the imaginary, with the wildness of dada, or again in the decorative excesses seen in the epigones of cubism. Their new language would be based on industrial civilisation: paintings would now follow the 'plans of prototype objects that have attained a high degree of invariability'.

In *Le violon rouge*, a half-size copy of a work from 1918–19, Ozenfant alludes to cubism: instead of an industrially produced object, the artist reintroduced an artisanal object, a violin, which was also a popular motif with Georges Braque and Pablo Picasso in the 1910s.

If purism advocated the frontal representation of objects in an almost abstract space, here the artist tempered his intransigence somewhat, choosing a high viewpoint, and basing his composition on oblique lines that generate a slight impression of depth. Arranged around the four sides of a lozenge are the objects in his still life: a table, a violin with its case, a bottle, playing cards, a fluted stem glass, a pipe, a book and a sheet of paper. Here it is not cast shadows that underscore the spatial relations between the objects, but the right-angled intersection of their contours. With no clear grounding, they appear to float free of gravity. The horizontal band along the bottom of the painting, like a modern predella holding the signature, and the panel from a piece of woodwork frame stabilise the ensemble. The visual rhythms between the sheet of paper, the curve of the violin and its F-holes, between the bottom of the bottle and the scrolls of the instrument enliven this painting contained within the 'main scale' or reds, earth, white and black defined by the purists. [CL]

86

Gustave Buchet (Etoy, 1888–Lausanne, 1963)
L'Esprit nouveau (*The New Spirit*), 1925/8
Oil on canvas, 81 × 116 cm
Acquisition, 2011. Inv. 2011-207

The titles of the opening chapters of *Après le cubisme* (*After Cubism*) [1918] reflect the questions of Amédée Ozenfant and Charles-Édouard Jeanneret in the immediate aftermath of the First World War: 'Whither painting?' 'Whither modern life?' Purism, which they sought to promote, opened up new paths inspired by mechanisation, incorporating standardisation, accuracy and economy into the creative process. Order and rigour were their watchwords. They planned their works as 'equations' shaped by rules, rhythm and precision. To bring their ideas to a wider audience, Ozenfant and Jeanneret joined forces with the Belgian literary critic Paul Dermée to found the international journal *L'Esprit nouveau* in 1920.

The title of Buchet's work pays homage to the journal and reflects his adoption of the purist aesthetic. The letters and number refer to the journal's sixteenth issue and are also a reminder of the importance of typography in cubism. The energy of the shapes, arising from straight lines and curves folding into each other, is part of Buchet's theorisation of movement, sparked by his discovery of futurism. The energy attenuates the strict austerity of purism, as does the harmonious palette of reds and greys, with touches of pink, green and white. The brushwork is less rigorous in parts, the line no longer systematically following the shapes, and the colours sometimes gradually meld together. The return of nuance and elegance are part of what makes Buchet's work unique.

The painting was first shown at Buchet's first solo exhibition in Paris in 1926, at Colette Weil's Galerie Mantelet, and was printed on the invitation. It was reworked after the exhibition and dated '1928' by the artist. [CLC]

87

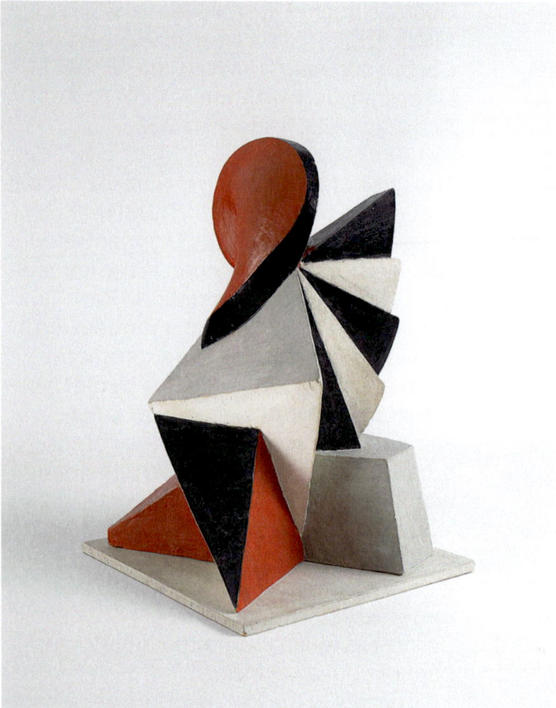

88

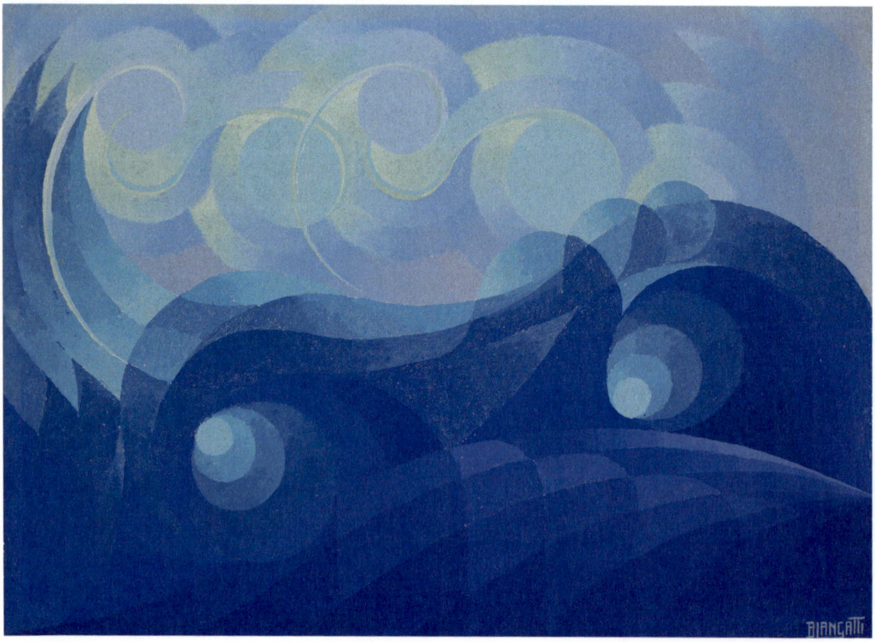

Gustave Buchet, Sculpto-peinture – abstraite –, 1923–4
Charles Blanc-Gatti, Suite bergamasque de Debussy, c. 1930

87

Gustave Buchet (Etoy, 1888–Lausanne, 1963)
Sculpto-peinture – abstraite – (Sculpto-Painting – Abstract –), 1923–4
Plaster and oil paint, 43.8 × 27.5 × 27.5 cm
Gift of Georgette Buchet, 1970. Inv. 1970-020

In the early 1920s Gustave Buchet painted several flat-surfaced canvases, some of them tending towards abstraction. At the same time, he was involved in projects touching on the decorative arts (the opening of a couture house), theatre (costume design) and sculpture, all of which brought him back to three-dimensionality.

In 1923 and 1924 the Swiss artist created several 'sculpto-paintings' made of plaster with oil paint. Three of these have survived; others never got beyond project phase or are known only from references to their existence. These works could be abstract or represent objects (houses, boats, trees) and highly stylised landscapes.

With *Sculpto-peinture – abstraite –* Buchet comes extremely close to geometrical abstraction by translating into three dimensions the principles upheld by the Section d'Or group and the purism of Le Corbusier and Amédée Ozenfant: rigorous, austere and pared-down composition, the geometricising of forms, the flat application of paint and a palette limited to white, black and red. The work consists of a spiral opening out into a fan shape. The projected volume and painted surface participate simultaneously in this effect of unfolding in space, with each 'facet' being associated with a single colour. Although very different, the colours have a subtle harmony while the combination of rounded and hard-edged forms achieves perfect equilibrium. Buchet's work oscillates between rationalism and elegance, order and harmony.

In 1919 Buchet met Alexander Archipenko when the latter was exhibiting at the Kündig bookshop in Geneva. While the Swiss artist may have seen several 'sculpto-paintings' by his Ukrainian colleague on this occasion, his own works were more a development of the cubist sculpture created by Henri Laurens who, in the 1910s, had explored a constructive role for colour by using it as a structural element so that it contributed alongside form to the delimitation of planes and distribution and determination of light. [CLC]

88

Charles Blanc-Gatti (Lausanne, 1890–Riex, 1966)
Suite bergamasque de Debussy (Debussy's Suite Bergamasque), c. 1930
Oil on Pavatex, 32.5 × 46 cm
Acquired with the help of the Association des Amis de Blanc-Gatti, 1955. Inv. 1955-023

In 1911 Charles Blanc-Gatti moved to Paris, then in a state of artistic effervescence, where he worked as a draughtsman. After a period working in fashion in Lausanne between 1919 and 1922, the Swiss artist came back to the French capital and developed an interest in musicalism, the modern theory concerning the equivalences of sensation and value between painting and music. Initiated by the Frenchman Henry Valensi, stimulated by the progress of physics and experimental psychology, musicalism continued from the nineteenth-century interest in synaesthesia, the analogies between differential perceptions explored by Charles Baudelaire in his poem *Correspondances* (1857).

In 1931 the musicalists formed an association. Blanc-Gatti, a founding member, published a manifesto with Valensi, Gustave Bourgogne and Vito Stracquadaini in April 1932: 'We state our awareness, here, that from the aesthetic point of view, the musical spirit dominates in our period and that, in order to continue to translate our life traditionally, "Art must musicalise itself".' Arguing for the dynamic transposition of music and the translation of aural morphology, the signatories stated that they wanted 'to work in obedience to the laws of inspiration and composition in music'.

Blanc-Gatti sought to establish concordances between the vibrations of sound and light, to re-transcribe sound waves, their length, their frequency and their movement. He worked with the music of various composers, from Bach to Saint-Saëns and Rimsky-Korsakov. Here, the painter has executed a pictorial interpretation of Debussy's *Suite bergamasque* for piano (1905) – most probably its third movement, *Clair de lune* (*Moonlight*). In a gradation of blues, he deploys a repertoire of forms derived from the circle. Arabesques and undulating lines, spirals and scrolls follow, interweave and radiate. [CLC]

89

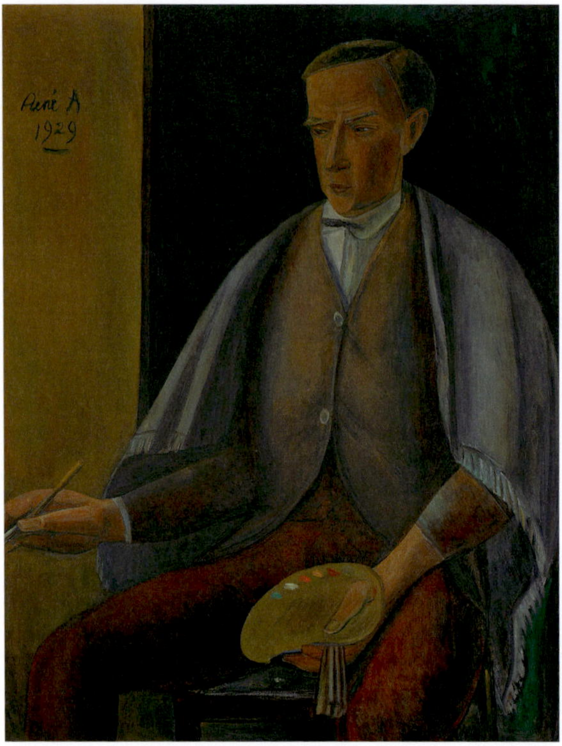

90

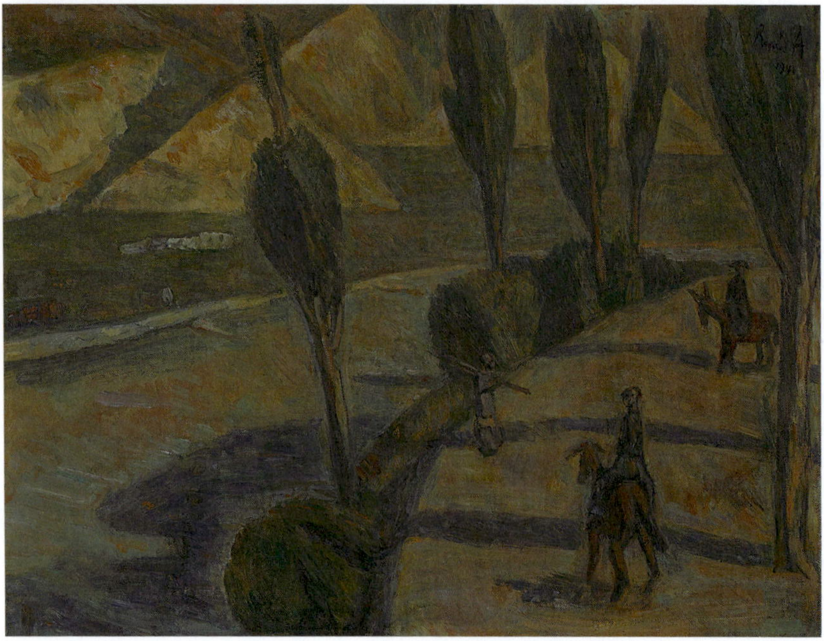

René Auberjonois, Autoportrait, 1929
René Auberjonois, La route valaisanne, 1940–1

89

René Auberjonois (Lausanne, 1872–1957)
Autoportrait (*Self-Portrait*), 1929
Oil on canvas, 105 × 82 cm
Acquisition, 1931. Inv. 609

René Auberjonois frequently tried his hand at self-portraits. He was familiar with the difficulties of the exercise. As he wrote in 1916, 'It is a tough challenge, this silent dialogue that is the painting of oneself.' He also regretted that this confrontation with their mirror image elicited from many artists 'the desire to strike an attitude'. For him, the sole aim of it all was to 'seek my equilibrium within a frame'. This emphasis on form and composition to the detriment of originality of pose or setting was at the heart of his aesthetic. For, him it was always 'poise' that mattered: the solidity of the canvas, the way the body held itself, and even the way the sitter was dressed.

This 1929 self-portrait is a fine example of this austerity, starting with the painter's outfit: rather than his painting clothes, he comes before us in a jacket and fully buttoned waistcoat, complete with white shirt and thin bow tie. The only exception to this sartorial neatness is the fringed blanket, which recalls the loose coat worn by Paul Cézanne over his shoulders in the famous etching by Camille Pissarro (1874). This is Auberjonois's discreet homage to one of his masters.

Sitting up straight on a stool, the painter holds a palette on which he has put pure colours. These recall the fundamental elements of his craft, as do the gigantic hands and the concentration of his gaze. The construction of the painting is simple and severe. Three quarters of the background is occupied by a wide, dark-green panel. Behind the hand holding the brush, a strip of brown offers a transition towards a lighter expanse – a wall, perhaps, or a surface to be painted? The close framing, which excludes the easel from the composition, plays on this ambiguity.

In this self-representation painted for an exhibition held in Geneva in March 1929 and featuring self-portraits of all the major artists on the Swiss francophone art scene, Auberjonois clearly announces his refusal to compromise. [CL]

90

René Auberjonois (Lausanne, 1872–1957)
La route valaisanne (*Road in the Valais*), 1940–1
Oil on canvas, 35 × 45 cm
Acquired with the support of the Association des Amis du Musée, 1994.
Inv. 1994-039

René Auberjonois first stayed in the Valais in 1902 and was stunned by the 'great spectacle of the landscapes'. His life soon acquired a pendulum movement as he alternated between Paris, where he pursued a life in society-followed artistic events, and an exotic elsewhere, which he found in the plain of the Rhône and the hilltop village of Lens. In 1943 his friend, the writer C. F. Ramuz, said that what they both loved about the Valais was the permanence of the unchanging, the simplicity of the way of life and, above all, 'nature, and what it has made of the men who live there'.

In 1940, Auberjonois was preparing for a solo show at the Kunsthalle in Basel. He had long stays in the Valais, was in Lens in January then in September went to Sion, where he painted a dozen canvases, including this *Route valaisanne*. The importance to the artist of the bond between men and their environment is what explains the ambiguous status of this view, which is neither a landscape nor a genre scene, but more a kind of 'chamber landscape' aiming to overcome what for him was the false distinction between outdoor and indoor painting.

Here, the view over a bank of the Rhône flattens onto the same screen realities that we feel to be consubstantial: the peasants riding their mules and the poplar trees bending down towards the water, their shadows merging and crisscrossing on the path and on the water. The hard sunlight cuts out triangles of light on the foothills of the mountains. Typical of the painter's late work, the austerity of the very narrow range of colours and the almost caricatural expressive stylisation demonstrate his lack of interest in colour and naturalism. Auberjonois' formula derives from a formalism concerned mainly with the balance and order of the composition. As a worthy heir of Paul Cézanne, that is where he found his direction, far from the deliquescence of impressionism, and in refusing the path to abstraction opened up by cubism. [CL]

91

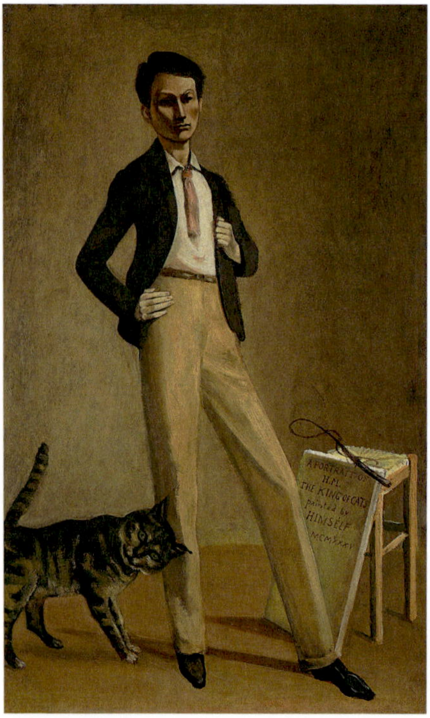

92

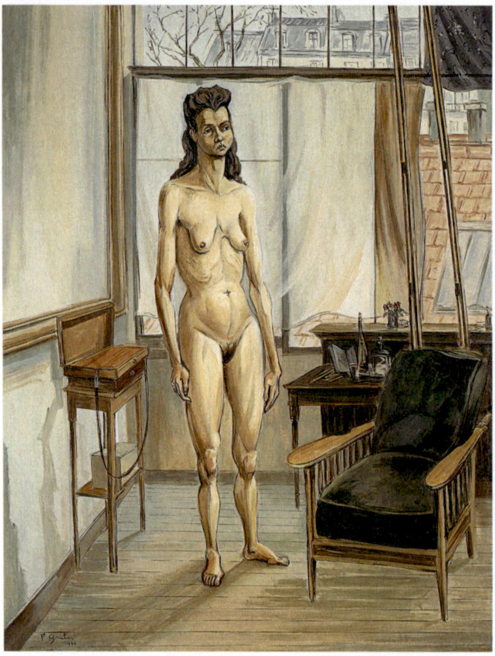

Balthus, Le Roi des chats, 1935
Francis Gruber, Nu dans l’atelier, 1944

91

Balthus (Balthasar Klossowski de Rola)
(Paris, 1908–Rossinière, 2001)
Le Roi des chats (*The King of Cats*), 1935
Oil on canvas, 78 × 49.7 cm
Gift of the Fondation Balthus Klossowski de Rola, 2016. Inv. 2016-048

Balthus's self-portraits depict him with a series of assumed identities in which he never drops his mask. This 1935 portrait shows him standing in an elegant outfit, one hand holding his jacket lapel, the other on his hip. A large tabby cat is rubbing up against his leg. The narrow space and harsh light that seems to fall from a skylight evoke a dungeon. The only objects in the bare-walled room are a stool, a whip and a canvas bearing an inscription in capital letters, which sheds some light on the mysterious work: 'A Portrait of H. M. The King of Cats, painted by Himself'. The self-portrait is that of an artist and monarch who rules over a kingdom of cats.

Balthus's *Mitsou* (1921), begun when he was very young, tells in pictures the story of a cat found and then immediately lost. His obsession with cats would last throughout his lifetime. Cats – part wild animal, part household pet – have represented both freedom and the inner life of artists since the Romantic period. In 1935, the year he painted this portrait, Balthus began signing off his letters to his future wife Antoinette de Watteville as 'King of Cats', having seen off a fellow suitor. The victorious fiancé now reigned over the creatures that resembled him most: as he wrote in his memoirs, 'Very early on, I grasped my secret, mysterious belonging to the world of cats. I shared their urge for independence'. In this painting, one of his subjects is showing due deference, though the whip close at hand transforms the genre painting into an allegory of the savage self that must constantly be tamed.

The ascetic composition and style, drab hues and thickly layered paint owe much to Édouard Manet's *Portrait de Théodore Duret* (*Portrait of Théodore Duret*, 1868, Paris, Petit Palais), with a nod to the English tradition of the swagger portrait. [CLC]

92

Francis Gruber (Nancy, 1912–Paris, 1948)
Nu dans l'atelier (*Nude in the Studio*), 1944
Oil on canvas, 116 × 88.5 cm
Acquisition, 2016. Inv. 2016-028

In 1944, the fate of Paris still hung on the uncertain outcome of the Second World War. That year, Francis Gruber painted his favourite model, Étiennette, standing naked with her arms hanging limply by her sides, thin, perhaps weakened by food shortages. Her skin is stretched taut over the muscles and bones of a body stripped of its sensuality. Her gaze is vacant, her mouth downturned. The space she stands in, powerfully structured by the walls, skirting boards, floorboards and window struts, is oppressive, trapping her in a clutter of cheap furniture that in turn seems frozen by her own immobility. The multidirectional vanishing points and off-kilter proportions heighten the feeling of discomfort, along with the harsh light, dry, fluid paint, dark, drab colours, chilly harmonies, and the dry, hard brushstrokes.

Time stands still in the artist's studio that is part still life, part desolate landscape. The curtains drawn over the windows force us to confront the reality of a female body that is simply there, exposed. The motionless body that could almost be a shop dummy, the unrealistic space, and the significance of the void all nod to Giorgio de Chirico's metaphysical realm, though without its atemporality and anxious, nostalgic ambience. The work's underlying, restrained sense of violence is typical of new objectivist painting, but Gruber has refused its chilly, mechanical approach.

Gruber's painting is both a private and a public undertaking by a man physically unsuited to battle and an artist who believed in art's social utility. In both cases, the work is firmly anchored in the artist's present reality and the harshness of human existence. [CLC]

93

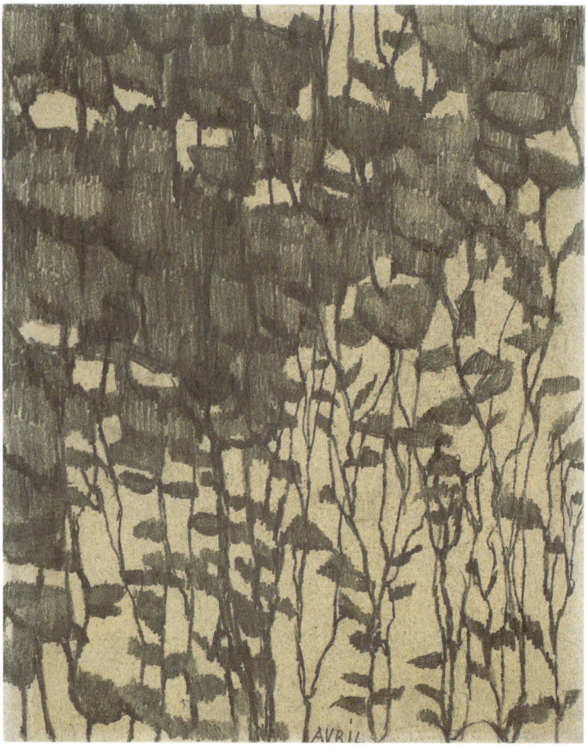

94

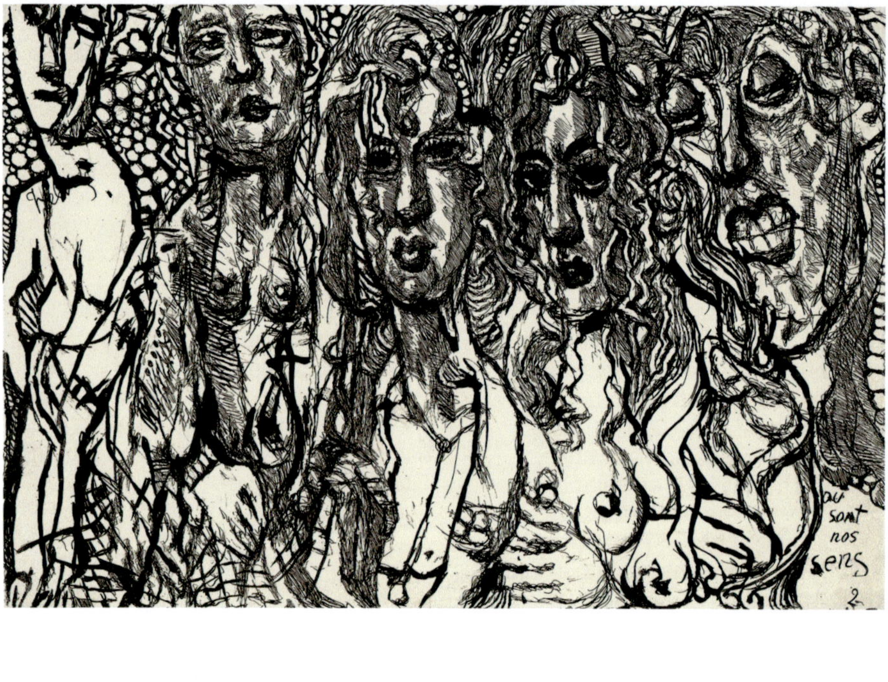

Louis Soutter, Avril, between 1923 and 1930
Louis Soutter, Où sont nos sens ?, between 1930 and 1937

93

Louis Soutter (Morges, 1871–Ballaigues, 1942)
Avril (*April*), between 1923 and 1930
Pencil on paper, 21.9 × 17.6 cm
Acquisition, 1956. Inv. 342

Soutter was fifty-two years old when he was interned against his will in 1923. This mature and extremely cultivated man was about to produce a body of work that is now recognised as a major chapter in the history of modern art. The drawings he made in the twenty years up to his death (some 3,000 have survived) show him to have been possessed of a unique poetic sensibility and creative power.

Before he was sectioned, Soutter studied drawing, painting and architecture in Lausanne, Geneva and Paris. In Brussels, he studied with the famous violinist Eugène Ysaÿe. In the United States, he directed the fine arts department at Colorado College and married Madge Fursman. The couple divorced in 1903, the year he returned to Switzerland. It was around this time that he manifested the first symptoms of a deep melancholy, a physical and mental fragility that would grow steadily worse. After joining the Symphony Orchestra in Lausanne in 1908, Soutter slowly began to fall apart. He took to playing the violin in hotels and cinemas, while his expensive lifestyle and eccentric behaviour impelled his family to have him put in a hospice for old people in Ballaigues, a small village in the Jura Vaudois.

During his first years in the asylum, Soutter drew in grey pencil and Indian ink in school exercise books, which were the only support available to him. Using both sides of each page, he filled them with dense figurative and ornamental compositions, drawn in one go. These notebooks, many of which were later taken apart for their contents to be sold or exhibited, were organised by themes and had titles such as *L'Âme qui s'en va du seuil des fleurs au cycle des pierres noires* (*The Soul Going from the Threshold of Flowers to the Cycle of Black Stones* – as per a cover held at the Museum). *Avril* recalls one of the artist's key sources of inspiration: nature, whose organisation and profusion are mirrored in his extraordinary vision of the world. [CL]

94

Louis Soutter (Morges, 1871–Ballaigues, 1942)
Où sont nos sens ? (*Where Are Our Senses?*), between 1930 and 1937
Pen and Indian ink on paper, 33.9 × 51 cm
Acquisition, 1955. Inv. 409

Soutter was interned in Ballaigues, where he suffered cruelly from the narrow confines of his existence. He adopted an ascetic way of living, forcing himself to fast and go on long walks. He escaped into his imagination, elaborating countless plans to regain his autonomy: 'I want to enter into the life of all beings ... and earn an honest living with my music and my drawings', he wrote to his brother around 1924. In about 1927 he met his cousin Le Corbusier. The encounter would prove decisive: saying he was dazzled by Soutter's drawings, the architect published an article about him in the avant-garde journal *Minotaure* in 1936 and organised an exhibition of his works in the United States. With the attention of a small circle comprising his friend Yvonne Walter-du Martheray, the painters René Auberjonois and Marcel Poncet, the writers Jean Giono and C. F. Ramuz, the publisher Henry-Louis Mermod, and two gallerists in Lausanne, Claude and Maxime Vallotton, Soutter recovered his confidence. This was reflected in a significant change in his art.

The works produced by Soutter in this period are called 'mannerist' because of their new expressiveness and formal distortions. The artist drew in Indian ink, increasing the size of his sheets. *Où sont nos sens?* belongs to a series that is peopled with alluring and suffering creatures inspired by the residents Soutter had observed in the asylum. He called them the 'Without God': '... creatures in pain, a pure caste, raised up by the torturing sickness of isolation.' The women are naked, their only ornament a necklace and a huge head of hair; they display their teeth and made-up lips, their hands alternately hiding and caressing their sex. They strike lascivious poses, teasing the men who vie for their attention. In Ballaigues, these drawings, which speak of the artist's emotional solitude and sexual distress, earned Soutter the nickname of 'the mad pornographer'. [CL]

95

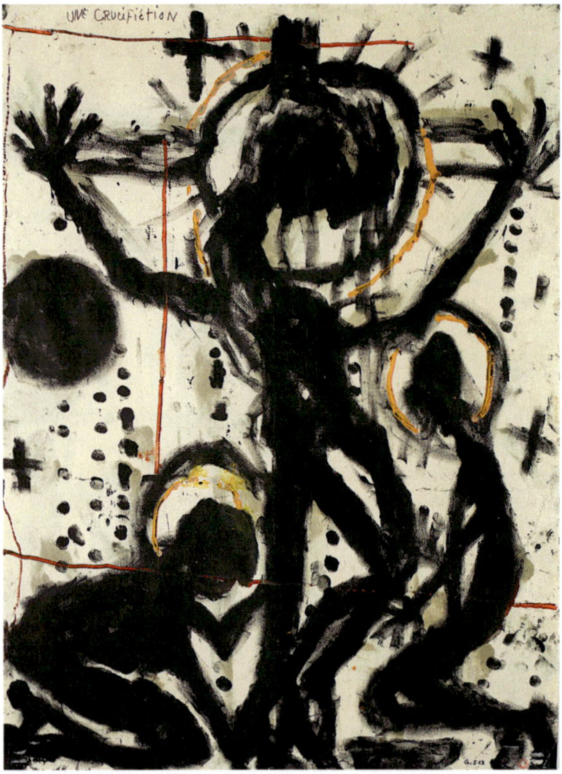

96

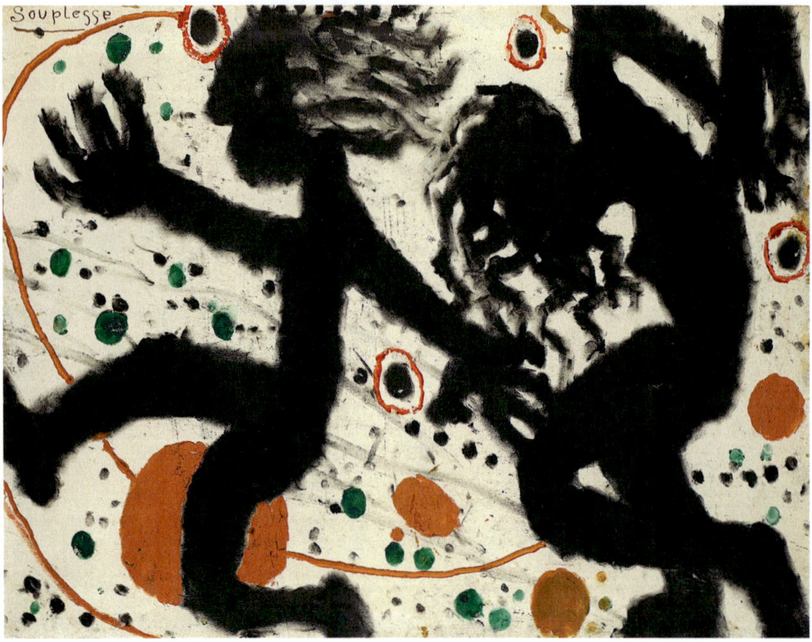

Louis Soutter, Une Crucifiction, between 1937 and 1942
Louis Soutter, Souplesse, 1939

95

Louis Soutter (Morges, 1871–Ballaigues, 1942)
Une Crucifiction (*A Crucifiction*), between 1937 and 1942
Finger painting on paper, 68.4 × 51 cm
Acquisition, 1961. Inv. 512

After 1936 Soutter, now suffering from arthritis of the hands and failing eyesight, began exploring new techniques. Working on the floor, sometimes undressed, he put the whole of his body into making large-scale paintings, applying the colour directly with his fingers. Apart from Indian ink, he used printer's ink, polish, oil, lacquer and sometimes even toothpaste. Whereas his work had previously suggested a certain *horror vacui*, he now worked with the empty space between the forms. Commenting at the time on the white of the paper between the black figures, he told the painter Henri Noverraz, 'Look at the shadows and light on this paper: all I do is interpret them in order to make my drawing.' Although his cousin Le Corbusier responded sceptically to this new development, the so-called 'finger paintings' of Soutter's late period were the ones that would fascinate future generations and artists from Arnulf Rainer to Christian Boltanski.

These finger paintings release sarabands of figures running through space, parallel to the picture plane, constantly moving and busy with multiple activities. *Une Crucifiction* is part of a more static series, infused with a vibrant force, dominated by images from the life of Christ, foremost among them the Passion. Brought up in a Protestant family, at the asylum Soutter was confronted on a daily basis with that rigorist form of Calvinism known as Darbyism. Well established in Ballaigues, this involved the constant iteration of biblical texts, injunctions to humility and mortification. On this sheet, Soutter represents Christ on the cross surrounded by two kneeling figures, also haloed, who may be Mary and John. A black sun reminds us that on this day the sky over Jerusalem went dark, and the crosses punctuating the space recall that in the Christian tradition Jesus is the alpha and omega. There can be no doubt that Soutter identified with this figure who, in his eyes, embodied martyred innocence. [CL]

96

Louis Soutter (Morges, 1871–Ballaigues, 1942)
Souplesse (*Suppleness*), 1939
Finger painting on paper, 44 × 58 cm
Acquisition, 1957. Inv. 418

Two frantic figures cross the space from right to left, parallel to the picture plane, beating a repetitive rhythm with their feet while their waving arms sweep their bodies along in an elemental dance. The melody of the music that leads them on seems repetitive, its tempo unvarying and its theme as insistent as that of Maurice Ravel's *Boléro*. We seem to be watching a ritual celebrating the union of man and the cosmos, a rite of spring or summer solstice celebration. Plunged into a trance, the dancers appear to have reached an apotheosis in which their gyrations have become synchronised with those of the planets that we see orbiting around their suns.

Souplesse is one of Louis Soutter's best-known works. In addition to black, which he uses here to shape his large silhouettes running over the white of the paper, in the final stages of his life, the artist made frequent use of colour, especially yellow, red and blue, and sometimes, as here, also green and orange. These lively hues link the forms already painted in black, consolidate them by surrounding them with a line and, above all, situate them in space.

Tragic subjects (crime, abortion, crucifixion) abound in the work Soutter produced after his internment in Ballaigues. Echoing his own situation, they relate the adventure of a humanity driven out of paradise, moving forward in the dark, weighed down with guilt, driven towards nothingness by some morbid instinct. But there are also drawings and paintings that, like *Souplesse*, almost euphorically express the nostalgia for a lost Eden. Men dance and play here, break free of the contingencies of historical time, in harmony with nature and the cosmos. A society takes shape, passing through the world but not damaging or marking it. A people living away from our gaze, its presence betrayed only by the shadows cast on the great screen of the universe. [CL]

97

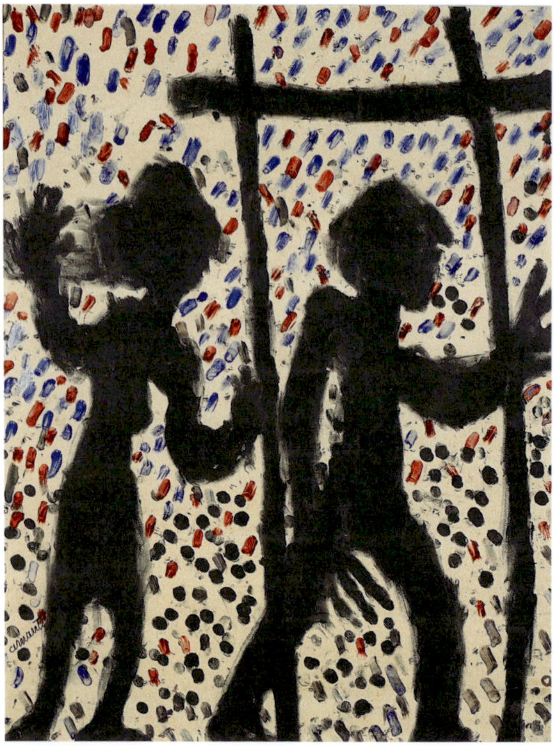

98

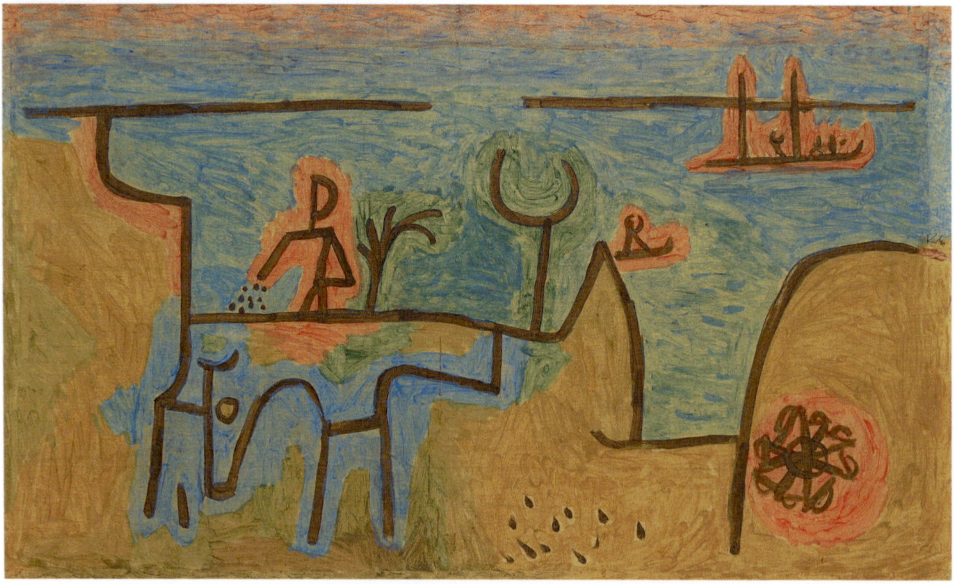

Louis Soutter, Amants. Aurons-nous ? un logis d'hiver, between 1937 and 1942
Paul Klee, Am Nil, 1939

97

Louis Soutter (Morges, 1871–Ballaigues, 1942)
Amants. Aurons-nous ? un logis d'hiver (*Lovers. Will We Have? A Winter Abode*), between 1937 and 1942
Finger painting on paper, 64.5 × 50 cm
Gift in lieu of inheritance tax, estate of Jean-Claude Givel, 2018. Inv. 2018-005

Louis Soutter captures images in movement, freezing them for all eternity. A constant flux of black silhouettes, doomed to eternal rootlessness, are forced to keep going and exist in a world tainted by original sin, in which no desire can be sated and no rest can be found. While Soutter's earlier mannerist paintings depicted women as threatening, emasculating figures and men as their terrified victims, his finger paintings bring the two sexes together in a primitive human society that is prey to the same pitiful fate, subject to the same fears and driven by the same instincts.

Amants. Aurons-nous ? un logis d'hiver depicts a couple wandering aimlessly, in search of shelter, freezing as the snow falls. The man, shown in profile, is walking ahead of the woman, entering a gateway; the woman, seen head-on, is following him but seems to be hesitating on the threshold, her arm raised as if in warning.

The painting reveals the new artistic vocabulary developed by Soutter in his final years. He moved on from filling the surface with a network of lines connecting the figures and ornamentation in a tight-knit web. Now, compact, roughly sketched bodies are positioned in space fleshed out by a few elementary symbols – lines at right angles that sometimes cover the surface like a grid, arabesques that curve and sweep the characters up in their waves, black and coloured dots dabbed on with the finger in chains or a dense scattering filling up any empty spaces. In the late 1930s, Soutter, like other modernist painters, especially his contemporary Paul Klee, sought the utopian possibility of reactivating a universal language of art reaching back to the very origins of mankind. [CL]

98

Paul Klee (Münchenbuchsee, 1879–Muralto, 1940)
Am Nil (*On the Nile*), 1939
Paint with glue on paper mounted on burlap, 75 × 125 cm
Anonymous gift, 2011. Inv. 2011-200

Paul Klee spent four weeks travelling across Egypt, from Alexandria to Cairo and from Luxor to Aswan, from 17 December 1928 to 17 January 1929. Only two drawings are known to have been brought back from the journey itself, but Klee certainly harvested an abundance of rich material, which he turned into art much later, between 1937 and 1940, the year of his death. Like his 1914 tour of Tunisia with August Macke and Louis Moilliet, his brief trip to Egypt was to have a profound impression on him.

Against a background of contrasting warm and chilly hues of dark ochre and muddy blue-green, indicating the mingling of land and water, *Am Nil* makes use of black pseudo-hieroglyphics in a continuous line, extending beneath two lines that serve as a very high horizon. The signs represent an ox, a man sowing seed, a papyrus, two boats and the paddle wheel of a noria, a primitive hydraulic pump with its characteristic yoke for an ox to turn the wheel. This is one of Klee's largest paintings, reflecting the work's 'epic' and personal importance for him.

Paul Klee fled the Nazi regime and settled back in Bern, suffering from a painfully itchy case of scleroderma that erupted in 1936 and would eventually kill him. He launched into a frenzied burst of artistic production, culminating in 1939 with 1,253 works in which his memories of Egypt helped overcome his fear of death. The motifs developed in *Am Nil* draw on the symbolism of the Ancient Egyptian *Book of the Dead*: the boats represent the passage 'to the other side', the dawn of a new day, while the water wheel and the seed promise everlasting return. In this work, Paul Klee, whose initials are hidden all over the painting, wrote his own *Book of the Dead*. [BF]

99

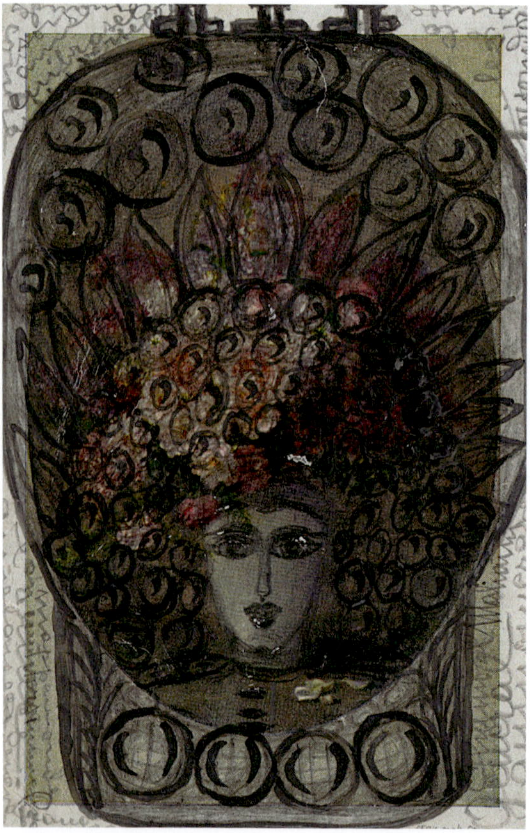

100

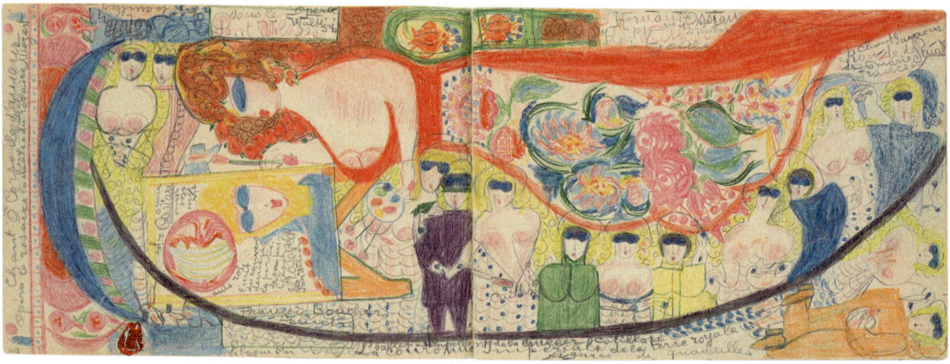

Aloïse, Materdolorosa, 1922
Aloïse, La Couronne Impériale de la terre royale, 1943

99

Aloïse (Aloïse Corbaz) (Lausanne, 1886–Gimel, 1964)
Materdolorosa, 1922
Pencil, ink, coloured pencils on postcard, 14.3 × 9.4 cm
Aloïse Corbaz Succession, 1966. On deposit loan to the Art Brut Collection, Lausanne. Inv. 2011-032

Lausanne-born Aloïse Corbaz was a governess who was employed at the court of Wilhelm II in Germany for a while. On her return to Switzerland in 1913, her religious and anti-militarist mania and turbulent behaviour saw her interned in 1918 in the psychiatric hospital in Cery, near Lausanne. She was transferred to the Rosière asylum in Gimel in 1920 and lived there until her death.

Aloïse started drawing in pencil and ink on whatever small pieces of paper and card she could get her hands on. She produced her first works in secret. In this case, she turned a printed postcard into a portrait with a vast crown of plants on a small woman's head. The diadem's rays refer to one of her favourite sculptures, Frédéric Auguste Bartholdi's *La Liberté éclairant le monde* (*Liberty Enlightening the World*, 1886). The crown resembles a grenadine fruit or a grenade with the pin ready to be pulled.

Aloïse filled the tiniest blank spaces with images and words. Both sides of the card feature a text that is hard to follow, signed '*Lulu*', her nickname, and '*Materdolorosa*', referring to the pain of losing a child. The work also refers to authority figures at the asylum: the '*Pape des protestants*' (Protestants' pope) is Gabriel Chamorel, a charismatic local priest with whom she fell deeply in love. The trauma of the First World War still haunts her in the words '*l'armée anglaise à Genève*' (the English army in Geneva). A number of metaphors describe the floral crown and sunlight: '*la toison d'or*', '*essieux de l'unique roue du soleil*', '*tiare astrale*' (golden fleece, axles of the sun's sole wheel, astral tiara), and refer to roses (perhaps inspired by the asylum's name) that sparked religious associations with '*Rosarie*' (rosaries) and '*materdolo-rosa*'. She also refers to her own inspiration, describing herself as a map of the world as a universe and a body struck by a sunbeam that ricochets off her surface and triggers a stream of images. [CL]

100

Aloïse (Aloïse Corbaz) (Lausanne, 1886–Gimel, 1964)
La Couronne Impériale de la terre royale. Cahier Pâques 1943 (*The Imperial Crown of the Royal Land.* Easter sketchpad 1943), 1943
Pencil and coloured pencils on paper, 24.5 × 66 cm
Gift in lieu of inheritance tax, estate of Jacqueline Porret-Forel, 2016.
Inv. 2016-070

Aloïse was fifty-seven and in her twenty-third year as a patient at the Gimel asylum when she filled the twenty pages of this sketchpad with drawings. Such pads had been her preferred medium since the late 1930s. She was constantly searching for ever larger media and here worked across the double spread, using pencils and coloured pencils, which she licked to obtain a thick layer of colour.

Aloïse did this drawing at Easter, one of her favourite festivals. As is generally the case in her works, the themes combine individual memories and scholarly references, recounting her own joys and sorrows and revealing a life parallel to the daily routine of the asylum: she spent years building her own highly complex imaginary realm with its own powerful internal logic.

The subject has been developed both horizontally and vertically. The upper part is occupied by the blossom-filled body of a red-headed woman wearing a gown with a long red train, kneeling on a cushion. Her eyes, like those of all the other characters, are hidden behind a layer of blue, a colour Aloïse associated with the theatre. The 'empress' holds an artist's palette with multicoloured Easter eggs instead of paints. In front of her is an easel with a painting of the bust of a handsome blond king and a shimmering world map. Across the horizontal axis are the words '*Ô Corse île d'amour*', a hit song by the crooner Tino Rossi. The woman's body lies across the top of a large ship with a mermaid figurehead, in which a number of small couples in eveningwear are preparing to dance a quadrille. The text evokes the children's game 'le jeu de la bague d'or' and refers to great presidents and generals Napoleon, Roosevelt and Wilson, the writer Goethe, the Rococo artist Boucher, and classical music and composers, Mozart and the operas *Ossian*, *The Valkyrie* and *Marie Stuart*, a reminder that as a young woman Aloïse dreamed of becoming an opera singer. [CL]

101

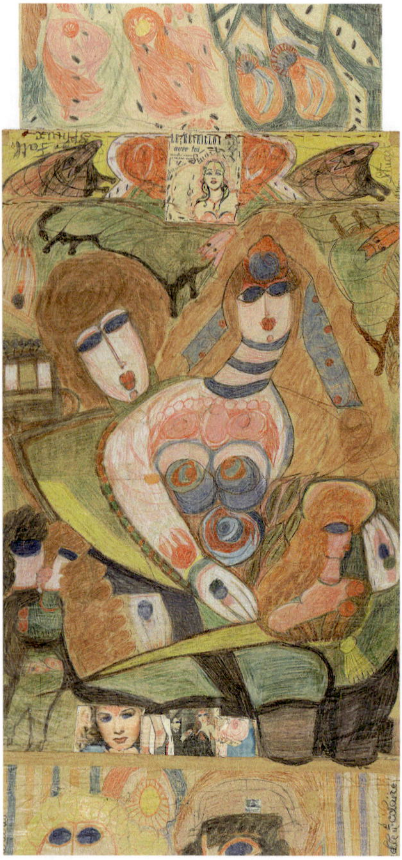

102

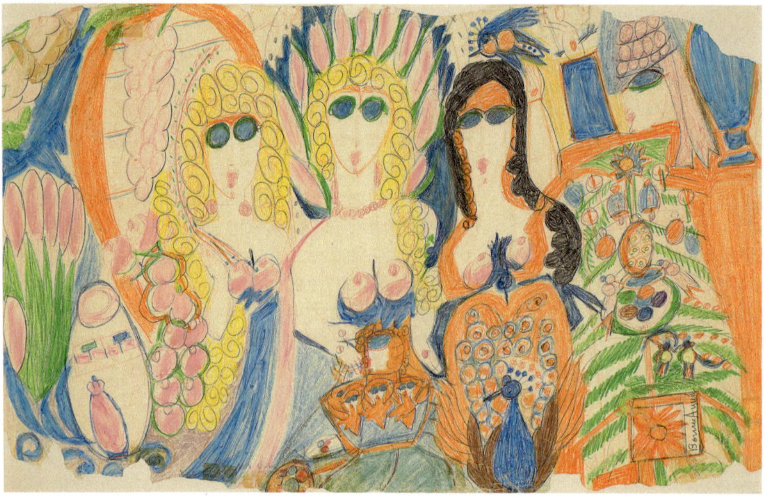

Aloïse, Sphinx Fath – Marie Stuart, 1950
Aloïse, Bonne année, between 1951 and 1960

101

Aloïse (Aloïse Corbaz) (Lausanne, 1886–Gimel, 1964)
Sphinx Fath – Marie Stuart. Feuille du rouleau double face *Le Réveillon avec toi* (*Sphinx-Fath – Mary Stuart.* Sheet of double-sided roll *Christmas Eve with You*), 1950
Graphite, colour crayons and sewn pieces of paper on wrapping paper, 688 × 91 cm
Gift of Professor Hans Steck, 1975.
Inv. 1975-500

Throughout her life, Aloïse was fascinated by needle and thread. Trained at the Professional Couture School in Lausanne, she made her dresses herself and was renowned for her elegance. When interned in an asylum at Gimel, she spontaneously volunteered to mend and iron the linen there. This occupation allowed her to isolate herself in a small room where she made her drawings. That was where she kept her material, including coloured crayons, geranium petals and toothpaste, which, when moistened, served as pigments.

Starting in the early 1940s, Aloïse made several-metre-long rolls from recuperated packaging or wrapping paper, which she ironed flat and patched up, then glued or sewed together. These enlarged formats enabled her to tell her stories in episodes, continuing from one side of the support to the other. In these she also included illustrations cut out from newspapers, postage stamps and labels.

This drawing comes from the roll titled *Le Réveillon avec toi*, consisting of seven metres of sheets sewn together with strands of wool, then strengthened with adhesive paper. At the top and bottom, Aloïse integrated advertising images of elegant women. Their faces are whitened, their eyes blinded with blue. They are being carried away in a carrousel pulled by four little horses positioned in the corners. This is the élan of the eroticism manifested here by the woman's breasts covered with roses and, above all, by the great big gold sabre emerging from her lover's uniform, which she touches with one of her ringed hands. Here the artist demonstrates her remarkable sense of 'suture', managing to keep supports and images together by her talents as a handywoman and by the power of her vision. [CL]

102

Aloïse (Aloïse Corbaz) (Lausanne, 1886–Gimel, 1964)
Bonne année (*Happy New Year*), between 1951 and 1960
Watercolour pencils on paper, 52.8 × 84.1 cm
Gift of Professor Hans Steck, 1971.
Inv. 1971-041

Aloïse did not see herself as an artist but as a scribe: 'I copy what I hear', she wrote. Interned in an asylum for more than forty years, she set out to represent the world that was revealed to her. She claimed to have gained access to it via a 'big viewing glass' that enabled her to 'dash down big paintings'. Some of her figures came to her in her dreams, and she would speak with them as she drew them. 'Miss [?], you are not at all as I saw you that night.'

Aloïse's compositions work with an extensive repertoire of figures, animals and places derived from high and popular culture, from literature, music, philosophy and alchemy. How she acquired all this knowledge is something of a mystery. Formal resemblances, word play and assonance weave a network in which we quickly start to observe certain constants running across the territory of her ideas.

In this drawing we find all the artist's usual figurative procedures: the saturation of space, the dense interlocking of simple forms, emphatic contours, large zones of lively, fresh colour, absence of depth, hieratic figures, and a scale built around the importance of the figures. Here, three bare-bosomed women and a pope coiffed with a tiara with long lappets emerge from a setting of leaves, flowers, bunches of grapes and birds. The associations presented here work as if following a repeated 'it's like': for example, the women's breasts are like camellias, like bunches of grapes, and a painter's palette is like the nest of multi-coloured eggs decorating the Christmas tree, like the eyes of a peacock's tail, or again like birds' crests. The central theme of the painting is made even more explicit by the brush held by the pope, and above all by the palette held by the small kneeling man in the centre, who is kissing the hand of the most marvellous of the three goddesses. [CL]

103

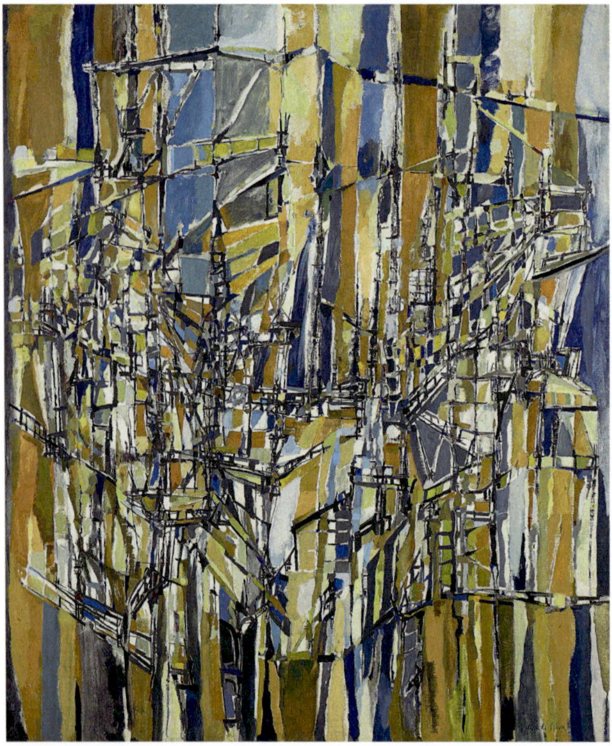

104

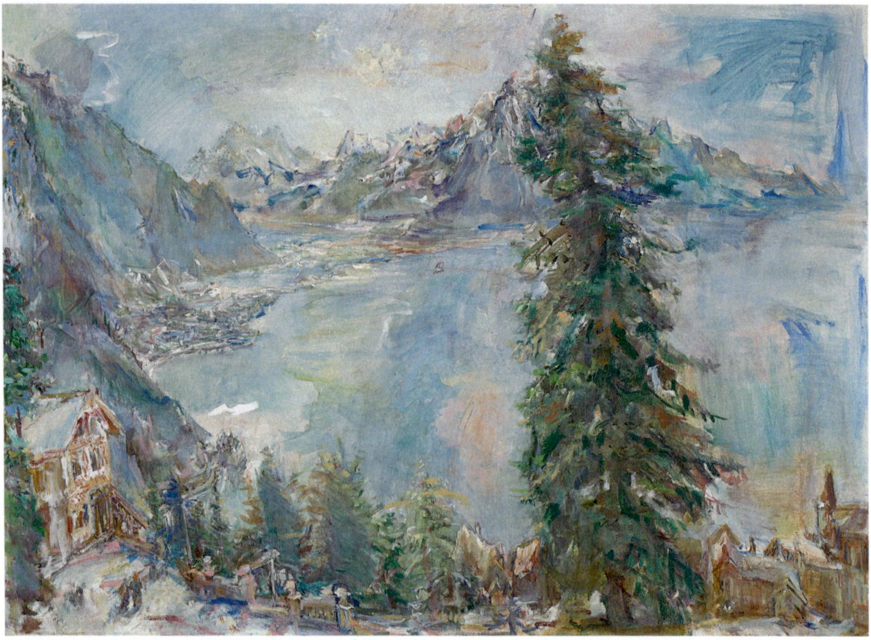

Maria Helena Vieira da Silva, La ville suspendue, 1952
Oskar Kokoschka, Glion, vue sur le lac Léman, 1956

103

Maria Helena Vieira da Silva (Lisbon, 1908–Paris, 1992)
La ville suspendue (*Hanging City*), 1952
Oil on canvas, 137 × 115 cm
Acquisition, 1952. Inv. 1952-015

Maria Helena Vieira da Silva was a member of the Second Paris School, a loose group of post-war artists whose best-known members include Jean Bazaine, Roger Bissière, Maurice Estève and Alfred Manessier. They worked with a form of expressive abstraction based on elements drawn from reality, embracing a degree of 'allusive figuration' while rejecting pure abstraction in favour of 'abstract landscapism'.

In the late 1940s Vieira da Silva began to work on a set of paintings of libraries, train stations, streets and cities, the sorts of urban hubs Michel Foucault described as 'heterotopias'. The labyrinthine, proliferating spaces, interior and exterior, become towers of Babel with outlandish perspectives and a limited palette. *La ville suspendue*, typical of these characteristics, could be Lisbon, the artist's home city, where the houses are indeed built in haphazardly overlapping terraces. The Lisbon cityscape was doubtless a major influence on the art of Vieira da Silva, who left for Paris at the age of twenty. Against a backdrop of vertical yellow-ochre and blue strips, a complex tangle of lines and views presented as fragmentary facets takes centre stage, like a mirror shattered into a thousand shards or a stained-glass window – an art form greatly valued by the Paris School – with a cloisonné effect created by grey-blue brushstrokes.

This seminal work of the early 1950s dates from a period of emerging international interest in the artist and was one of her first works to be acquired by a European museum. The Museum purchased it in 1952 following the exhibition *Rythmes et couleurs*, devoted to major works of French art from the first half of the twentieth century. [BF]

104

Oskar Kokoschka (Pöchlarn, 1886–Montreux, 1980)
Glion, vue sur le lac Léman (*Glion, View over Lake Geneva*), 1956
Oil on canvas, 81 × 114 cm
Work acquired thanks to a major contribution by an anonymous patron, 2010. Inv. 2010-008

Oskar Kokoschka was fascinated by Lake Geneva from the time he first saw it at the age of twenty-four when travelling to Switzerland with the Viennese architect Adolf Loos, to visit the latter's friend, the dancer Bessie Bruce, who was convalescing in the village of Les Avants, above Montreux. During this visit, Kokoschka painted *Les Dents du Midi* as well as several portraits, including one of Auguste Forel in Yvorne. On his second trip to Switzerland, in 1923, he painted his first two views of the lake from Blonay. The view pleased him so much that in 1951 he decided to buy a property up the hill in Villeneuve, which became his home two years later. He died in Montreux at the age of ninety-four, having spent twenty-seven years – nearly a third of his life — in the Canton of Vaud.

Kokoschka painted his last large-scale views of Lake Geneva from Glion and Villeneuve, including this one, between 1955 and 1957. The incredible depth of field here is due to the elliptical compositional plan with two viewpoints. Kokoschka did indeed prefer a bifocal view as he considered an isometric perspective very reductive since 'a man has two eyes'. The tree hiding the mountain peak ensures that the gaze takes in the full extent of the landscape, as if peripheral vision had become clear and been incorporated into it. It feels as though we could look around the tree to see what is behind it. This sumptuous, tormented landscape owes a great deal to Peter Paul Rubens, for whom every landscape is the theatre of a dramatic event. Kokoschka captures the scenery in its last moments of inviolability. What interests him is not the idyll, but nature in its wild, untamed state – the nature that disappeared in the 1960s. *Glion, vue sur le lac Léman* contains a gloomy presentiment of the disfiguring that would be inflicted on the countryside of Lake Geneva. [BF]

105

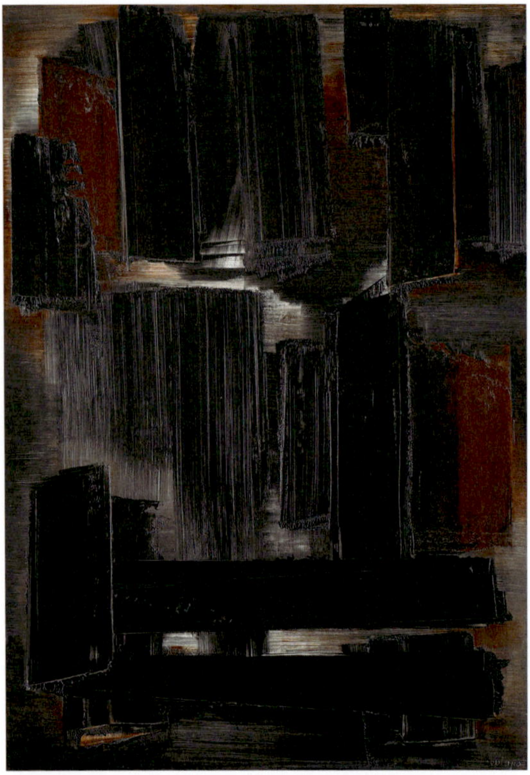

106

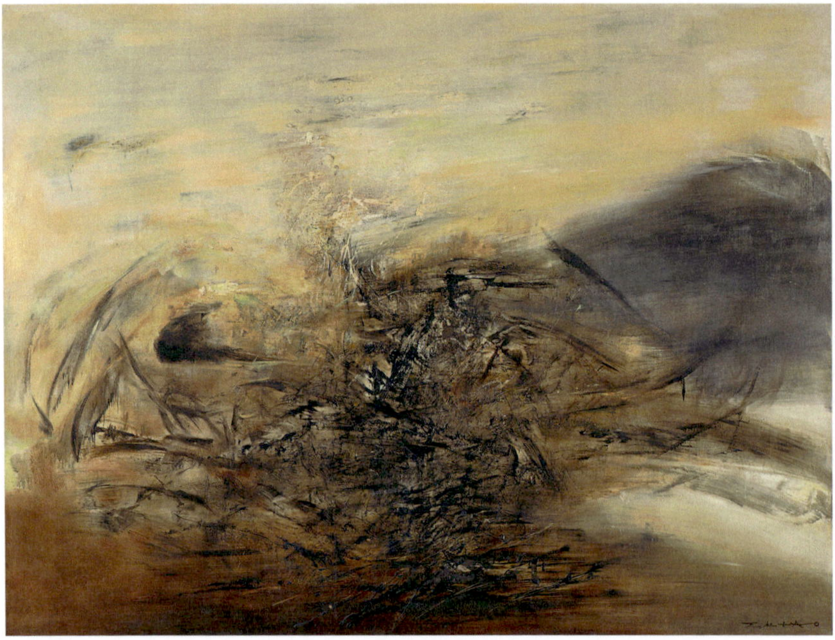

Pierre Soulages, Peinture, 1956
Zao Wou-Ki, Hommage à Edgar Varèse – 15.10.64, 1964

105

Pierre Soulages (Rodez, 1919)
Peinture (*Painting*), 1956
Oil on canvas, 162 × 114 cm
Alice Pauli Donation, 2016. Inv. 2017-005

After having given up an opportunity to study at the École nationale supérieure des Beaux-Arts in Paris in 1937, Soulages returned to the city in 1946 to devote himself wholly to painting. His paintings, already abstract and dark, formed a striking contrast with other postwar schools in the abstraction-creation movement, in which colour and geometry played a key role.

This *Peinture*, a significant work in Soulages's oeuvre, follows from his period using walnut stain on paper, with rich browns and blacks that were 'both transparent and opaque, deeply intense in their darkness', as he later described them, and compositions close to Chinese calligraphy. Around 1955, symbols tended to give way in his work to broad bands of rust and black hues, sometimes horizontal, sometimes vertical, with patches of the white background showing through here and there. The latter half of the 1950s saw Soulages switch from paper to canvas and create an artistic language that opened the way to his 'ultra-black' paintings, confident in their materiality yet simplified to the extreme, with a very narrow palette and criss-crossing or juxtaposed brush strokes.

This generously sized work, painted just after this key transition period, plays with light not only by means of the transparency of the canvas but also in reflections cast by the painting itself. The light seems to well up from the depths of the painting, with its horizontal brushstrokes, while also emerging from the fleshiest black bands. The rust hues form an intermediate zone giving the whole a dramatic effect that is expressionist in inspiration, giving the work an underlying sense of conflict and tension. In the lower part, two horizontal bands block the 'fall' of the blades arranged across two levels. [BF]

106

Zao Wou-Ki (Beijing, 1920–Nyon, 2013)
Hommage à Edgar Varèse – 15.10.64
(*Homage to Edgar Varèse – 15.10.64*), 1964
Oil on canvas, 255 × 345 cm
Gift of Françoise Marquet, 2015.
Inv. 2015-002

The Chinese-born artist Zao Wou-Ki was one of the leading figures of lyrical abstraction from the late 1950s on. He settled in France in 1948 and became friends with Hans Hartung, Alfred Manessier, Henri Michaux, Maria Helena Vieira da Silva and Pierre Soulages, but was never formally part of the Second Paris School.

Zao Wou-Ki was a keen devotee of opera and contemporary music, and Henri Michaux introduced him to Edgar Varèse in October 1954. Shortly thereafter Zao Wou-Ki attended the premiere of *Déserts* at the Théâtre des Champs-Élysées. The score, incorporating electronic sounds, caused one of the greatest scandals in the history of music. Varèse was a pioneering figure in music based mainly on sound or timbre, as opposed to notes, and his work also featured 'noises'. In a 1955 radio interview, he defined his music as a 'movement of planes and masses of sound, varying in intensity and density. When the sounds collide, they generate phenomena of penetration or repulsion.'

Zao Wou-Ki painted *Hommage à Edgar Varèse* a year before the composer's death. It is a key work in his oeuvre, the first in a series of large canvases begun in the 1960s. Like Varèse, Zao Wou-Ki plays with dynamic, rhythmical stresses and shifting masses of colour to create interpenetrating spaces opening onto mystery. Using a range of techniques, from broad brush strokes and impasto to drips, splashes and sgraffito, he stages an epic pictorial drama, a whirlwind, a battle between light and darkness.

Varèse visited New Mexico twice, in 1936 and 1937, discovering its arid landscapes. He saw deserts as a 'scorching whirlwind ... transcending man's attitude'. Zao Wou-Ki's painting offers a lyrical interpretation of Varèse's vision. [BF]

107

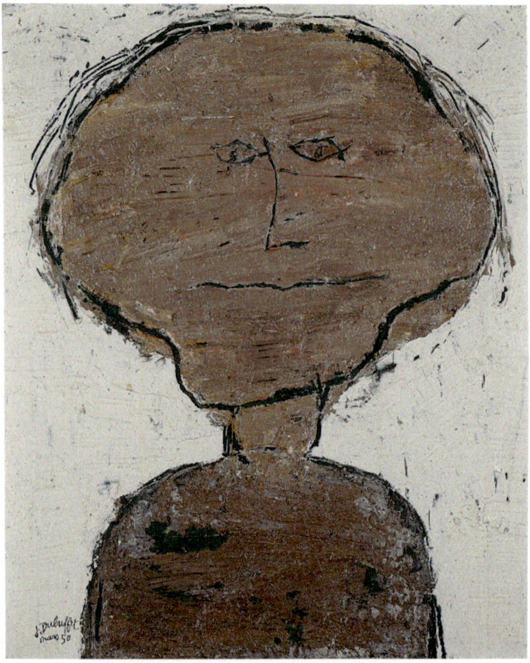

108

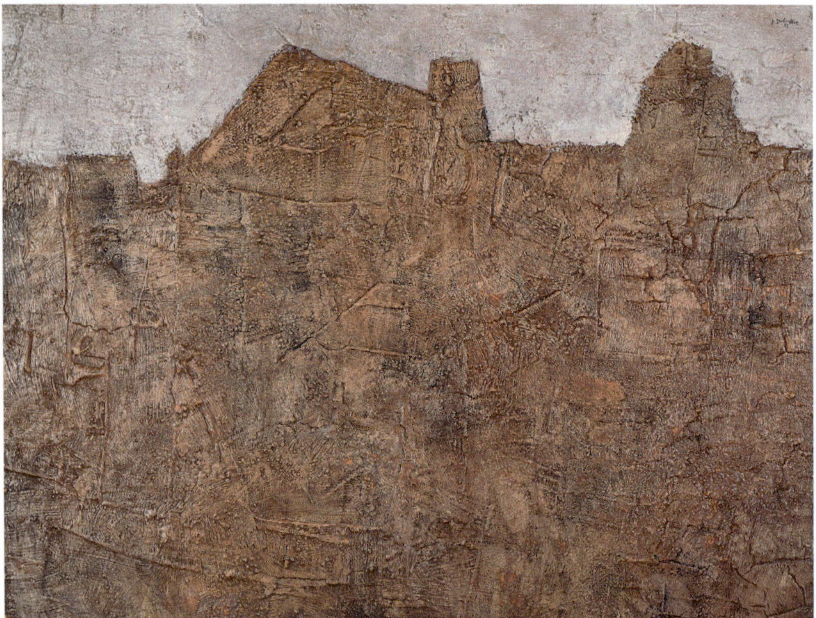

Jean Dubuffet, Petit portrait d'Antonin Artaud, 1950
Jean Dubuffet, Paysage aux murailles, 1952

107

Jean Dubuffet (Le Havre, 1901–Paris, 1985)
Petit portrait d'Antonin Artaud (*Small Portrait of Antonin Artaud*), 1950
Oil on board, 65 × 54 cm
Gift of Mireille and James Lévy from their collection of art by Jean Dubuffet, 2019.
Inv. 2019-023

After studying fine art in his hometown of Le Havre, Dubuffet enrolled at the Académie Julian in Paris in 1918, but left after just six months. He was not enthused by his first paintings inspired by surrealism and cubism and stopped painting for several years, taking up a career in the wine trade. He then went back to painting in 1933, but gave up in 1937 once more. The last time he returned to art, late in 1942, was to prove a turning point, and he never gave it up again. He turned away from 'cultural' art in the Western academic tradition, describing it as 'stifling'. He admired art by the self-taught, 'primitives' and the insane: in his own work, he used rough and ready materials, rudimentary lines and an unsophisticated drawing technique. He experimented with a wide range of materials, plastering his works with a thick layer of paint that he then scratched and scraped.

Turning against the canon of classical art, Dubuffet was on a quest for a new kind of figurative art, as reflected in his numerous portraits of writers and artists he met from 1946 on at the Thursday salons held by the American art patron Florence Gould, a leading light in Paris's cultural life. He tirelessly observed her guests, including Georges Limbour, Francis Ponge, Henri Michaux, and, in this portrait, Antonin Artaud. Drawings, gouaches and paintings show his subjects face on, reduced to their heads with eyes wide open staring at the viewer. A basic black line breathes life into the earthy paint, fixing the face's key features – eyes, nose and mouth. The sitters are deliberately depersonalised as Dubuffet refused to depict their distinctive characteristics. These portraits, which he described as 'anti-psychological' and 'anti-individualist', are intended to capture not the traditional falsity of appearances, but the energy of their presence in the world. [CLC]

108

Jean Dubuffet (Le Havre, 1901–Paris, 1985)
Paysage aux murailles (*Landscape with Walls*), 1952
Oil on hardboard, 92 × 122 cm
Gift of Mireille and James Lévy from their collection of art by Jean Dubuffet, 2019.
Inv. 2019-024

In November 1951, Dubuffet moved to New York for six months. There he produced several paintings, including this *Paysage aux murailles*, displayed in the famous gallery belonging to Pierre Matisse, who masterminded Dubuffet's dazzling rise to fame in America. At this time, Dubuffet covered his canvases with thick layers of putty-like paint, using oil paint mixed with plaster, chalk or glue, and then adding a layer of varnish. The almost living material, with its grooves, blisters and bulges, takes over the entire surface of the painting. It creates a complex, unexpected world that seems to be both the product of physical existence and the fruit of our imagination, prompting the art critic Max Loreau to wonder, 'Wanderings and chimeras of the mind? Or shifting grounds?' The combination generates a realm covering all eventualities arising from the earth and from thought, a disjointed macrocosm that our gaze roams before giving up or getting lost. The painting is divided into two zones, one dark, one pale: it does not follow the reassuringly familiar format of the typical landscape divided into top and bottom, sky and land. Instead, the two-part construction merges, rather than differentiates, the two areas. With the very high horizon line, almost at the top edge, the space of the land seems to be at once in front and behind, above and below, surface soil and geological strata, creating a sense of indeterminacy that makes the viewers question their gaze.

Dubuffet furthered his exploration of the ambiguous frontier between the real and the unreal in a series of landscape drawings, feeling he could no longer count on the random textures generated by his paint mixture. The physical and mental pulse of the earth was then dematerialised and transferred from texture to brushstroke. [CLC]

109

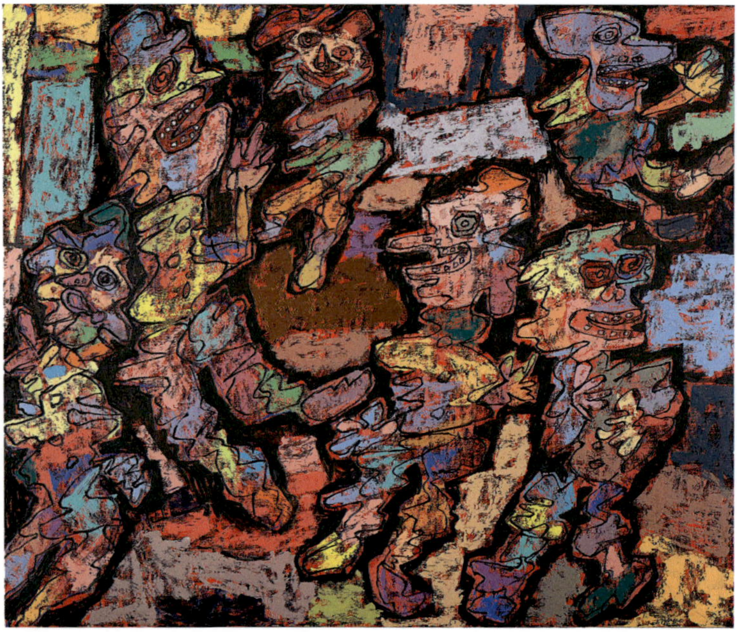

110

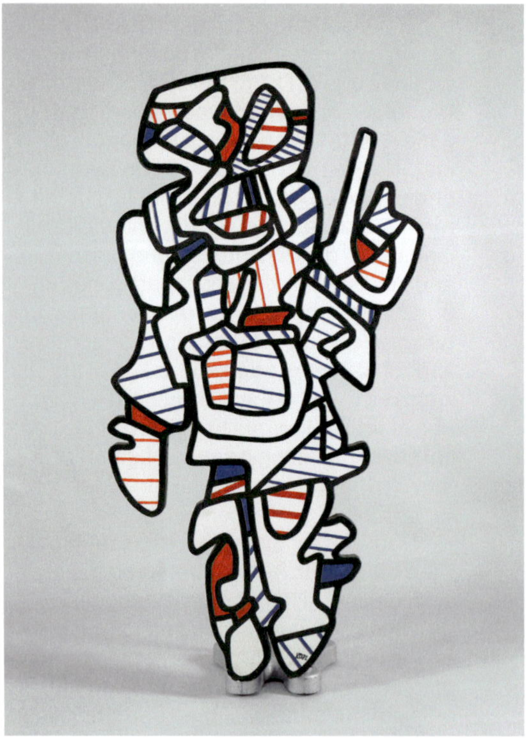

Jean Dubuffet, Affaires et démarches, 1961
Jean Dubuffet, Le précepteur, 1972

109

Jean Dubuffet (Le Havre, 1901–Paris, 1985)
Affaires et démarches (*Business and Steps*), 1961
Oil on canvas, 165 × 199.5 cm
Gift of Mireille and James Lévy from their collection of art by Jean Dubuffet, 2019.
Inv. 2019-026

Dubuffet took his art in a new direction in the early 1960s. His earthy, mineral realm and his drab-hued 'matterist' approach gave way to the colourful chaos of the metropolis and a celebration of urban life in the cycle *Paris Circus* (1961–2). He filled entire canvases with buildings, traffic and crowds, sometimes adding scattered words across the surface referring to signage, popular expressions and character names, often ironically, and adding to the general impression of hubbub. This effervescence was inspired by the French capital, where Dubuffet returned to live in 1961 after six years in Vence. The sgraffito-style oils evoke the textures of his 1950s works, but with a different choice of subjects, drawn from daily life, and with a much brighter palette. The flatness of the image, the thick black lines accentuating how the shapes slot together, and the abundance of detail herald the *L'Hourloupe* series.

Affaires et démarches includes six characters, some grimacing, others smiling, walking up and down the street. Dubuffet created zones of bright colour against a red backdrop before using black to define a thick line around the sinuous bodies and a web of fine lines fleshing out their details. A few splashes of white indicate the teeth of the three characters facing right, drawing the viewer's gaze from one to the next. The gaze barely has time to settle, as the whole picture buzzes with lively energy. The lack of depth also encourages an overall view of the painting. The colours, lent even more vibrancy by the contrast with black, stimulate the gaze. The image of human activity, of anonymous city dwellers thronging the streets as they hurry along, is as frenzied as it is joyful. [LSCH]

110

Jean Dubuffet (Le Havre, 1901–Paris, 1985)
Le précepteur (*The Tutor*), 1972
Acrylic on Klegecell, 178 × 100 × 3 cm
Gift of Mireille and James Lévy from their collection of art by Jean Dubuffet, 2019.
Inv. 2019-031

Dubuffet devoted the years 1962 to 1974 to the major cycle *L'Hourloupe*. He explained that the title was a coinage based on the similarities in sound and meaning of words like '*hurler*' (to howl), '*hululer*' (to hoot like an owl), and '*loup*' (wolf) and on Guy de Maupassant's short story *Le Horla* (1886–7). Dubuffet first used the term to title a brochure featuring doodles in red and blue ballpoint pen produced while talking on the telephone. The drawings encapsulated his new artistic vocabulary of sweeping lines flowing from spontaneous hand movements, multiple cells, saturation and stripes.

From 1966 on, after applying this visual language to drawings and sculptures, Dubuffet developed *L'Hourloupe* in three dimensions in sculpture and architecture, though keeping the works largely flat. The drawings in the original book consisted of figures cut out and mounted on a black background, heralding the sculptures in Klegecell (expanded polystyrene), including *Le précepteur*.

Dubuffet considered all subjects worthy of art, even more when they are outsiders in artistic circles. The tutor is shown raising one commanding index finger; his unsettling appearance is somehow threatening. He is human in scale. His outline and internal structure are singled out with black lines. Various parts of the body, such as the eyes, mouth, hands, legs and so on are identifiable, but the character's identity remains vague as the surface of his body teems busily. The strange creature constantly comes into and out of focus before our eyes, so we never get to the bottom of what we see – or think we see. Dubuffet calls into question the permanence and unambiguity we attribute to reality. The diverse ways the various compartments are handled also add to the sculpture's visual vibrancy. [LSCH]

111

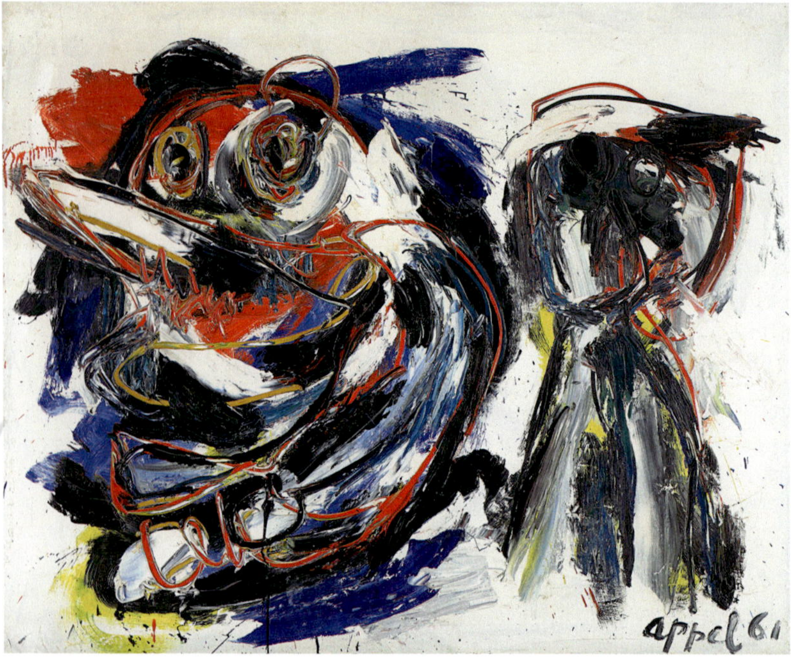

112

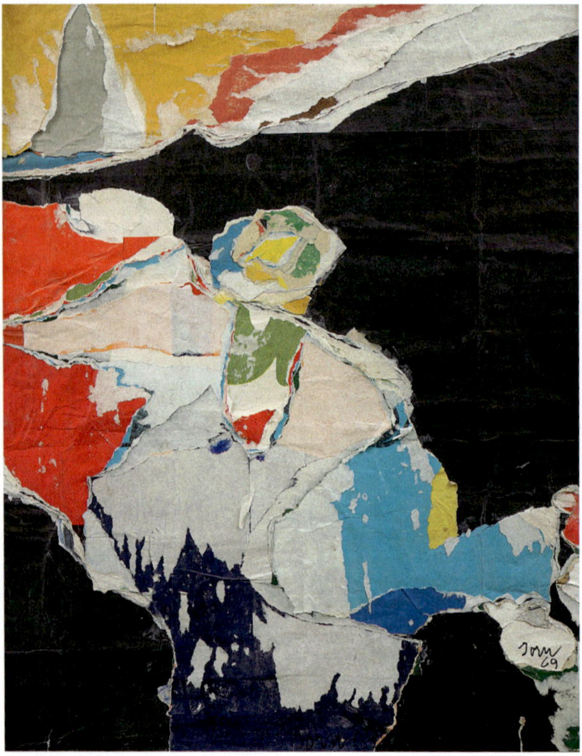

Karel Appel, Varkensmens or L'arcade, 1961
Asger Jorn, Vol de Viol de Fgary de Gambe, 1969

111

Karel Appel (Amsterdam, 1921–Zurich, 2006)
Varkensmens (*Pig Man*) or *L'arcade* (*The Arcade*), 1961
Oil on canvas, 129.5 × 162 cm
Alain and Suzanne Dubois Collection. Promised gift

Karel Appel reacted to the devastation of the Second World War by creating paintings that grappled with the savagery of his experiences while expressing the great joy of painting. 'I paint like a barbarian in a barbarian age', he told André Verdet. Having acquired a solid background in painting, he aspired to unlearn what he knew and rediscover the spontaneity of childhood art.

The urge to break free of the norms of bourgeois art led him to found the Nederlandse Experimentele Groep (Dutch Experimental Group) with Constant Nieuwenhuys and Corneille in Amsterdam in July 1948. In November that same year, the three artists helped found the CoBrA movement (its name referring to Copenhagen – Brussels – Amsterdam) in Paris, with poets and artists including Pierre Alechinsky, Christian Dotremont and Asger Jorn.

Varkensmens features Appel's typically bright colours, such as blue and red, as well as grey. As he explained to Frédéric de Towarnicki, 'Colour is indeed my first stimulant. It strikes me first, then comes the shape, in other words the drawing, and when the drawing begins to take shape, I interpret the story.' This reveals the influence of Henri Matisse's colourism: Appel had seen his work in Amsterdam shortly before the war. As always in his oeuvre, the excess of shapes and colours works towards a crude, roughly outlined face. The features of this *Varkensmens* ('pig man' in Dutch), with a thick neck and raised fist, are so coarse as to be ridiculous. The swift brushwork may look daubed on, but the work is by no means naïve. The shapes in Appel's work stand at the limit of legibility. He sketches in a figure with a few swift strokes that construct, create, denature and destroy the human presence. [LSCH]

112

Asger Jorn (Vejrum, 1914–Aarhus, 1973)
Vol de Viol de Fgary de Gambe (*Theft of a Viola da Fgary da Gamba*), 1969
Décollage, 65 × 50 cm
Alain and Suzanne Dubois Collection. Promised gift

The Danish artist Asger Jorn was a member of several poetic-political groups, including CoBrA (1948–51) and the Situationist International (1957–72). Jorn is best known for his naïve, expressive paintings and the 1959 *Modifications* series of interventions on paintings purchased from junk shops and flea markets. During one brief period, he developed a body of works, using his love of chance and explosive colours saturating the space to shape canvases that were smaller in format, drawing on collage. In 1964, he created his first 'décollages' from layered posters stuck to walls or hoardings across France.

While collage comprises adding material to a support, décollage involves removing material. Asger Jorn enjoyed quickly tearing and slicing off strips of paper to obtain the shapes and colour combinations he wanted. The process was driven partly by chance, since the artist was reliant on his material: he had no idea what he would find underneath and could only partially control how the paper tore. Décollage offers a simulacrum of spontaneity akin to the techniques used by New Realist artists such as François Dufrêne, Raymond Hains and Mimmo Rotella.

Jorn sometimes added paintings or drawings to his décollages, but not in the case of this work dating from 1969, the last year he produced work of this kind. The composition shows striking contrasts between large areas of black and the central zone of white shreds, showcasing a handful of colourful fragments. The artist, who named his works once they were complete, seems in many cases to have tried to interpret the resulting images. Here he invites the viewers to see the theft of a viola da gamba with respect to the work's title, though the work's materiality opens up endless potential interpretations. [LSCH]

113

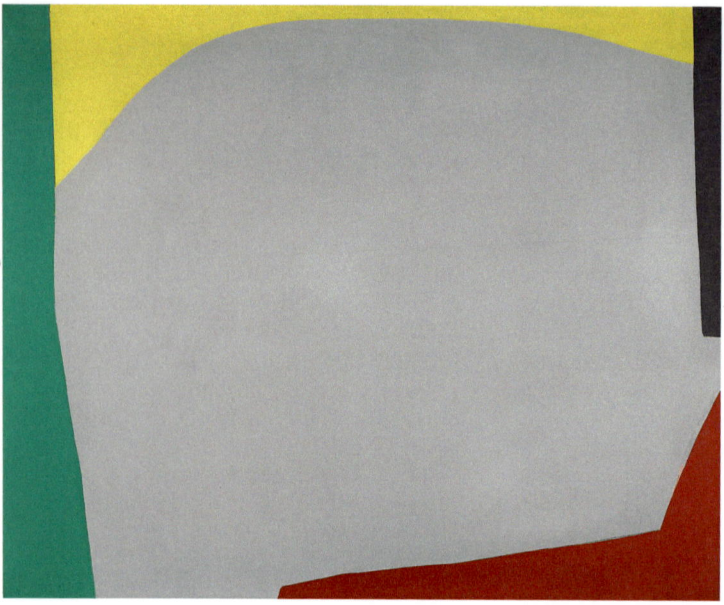

114

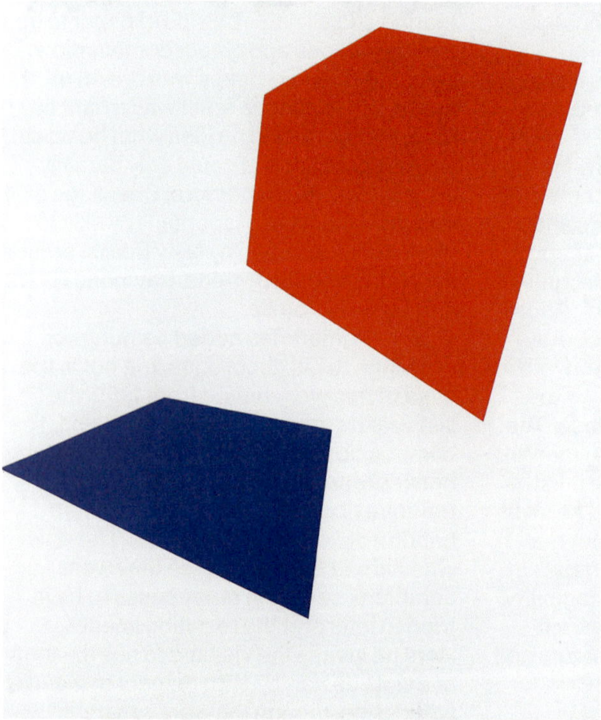

Robert Breer, Sky Chief, 1955
Geneviève Claisse, Soleil des eaux, 1965

113

Robert Breer (Detroit, 1926–Tucson, 2011)
Sky Chief, 1955
Oil on canvas, 80.5 × 100 cm
Acquisition, 2003. Inv. 2003-026

Robert Breer began his career as a painter after studying at Stanford University, near San Francisco, in 1949. That same year he moved to Paris where he applied the principles of neoplasticism, as defined by Piet Mondrian in 1917, but with greater latitude. While he was familiar with the research of the Dutch artist, it was especially concrete art and its offshoots, which were fashionable in Paris at the time, that encouraged him to pursue geometrical abstraction.

Sky Chief is emblematic of this period. Each element exists in relation to the others, and all, in spite of their irregularities and their differences, contribute to the temporary stability of the composition. Indeed, the potential movement that one perceives is actually played out in the films that Breer starts making from 1952, and notably in *Form Phases IV* (1954).

The work has neo-plasticism's areas of flat colour, its bi-dimensionality and its absence of symmetry. Unlike Mondrian, however, Breer does not limit himself to primary colours or to black, grey and white, and he does not limit himself to strict horizontals and verticals. The supple linearity of his forms was probably inspired by Henri Matisse's cut-outs. Within the rectangle of the canvas, the coloured segments with their uneven edges neither interlock nor clash. As if frozen in their own movement, they seem to form a random composition, Breer was influenced by Jean Arp and John Cage's interest in chance. The work's title may refer to the advertisement for 'Sky Chief' petrol, named after Frank Hawks's aeroplane, whose colours were, apart from yellow, similar to those of Breer's canvas.

Breer stopped painting in 1959 and returned to the United States, where he concentrated on making the films and kinesthetic sculptures for which he became known. Although regularly exhibited by the Galerie Denise René in Paris in the 1950s, his paintings were not shown to the American public until 2000, when an exhibition was held at Staff USA, New York. [LSCH]

114

Geneviève Claisse (Quiévy, 1935–Dreux, 2018)
Soleil des eaux (*Sun of Waters*), 1965
Oil on canvas, 150 × 130 cm
Acquisition, 1967. Inv. 1967-015

Geneviève Claisse's first steps in art in the latter half of the 1950s took her into geometric abstraction, exploring its most elementary possibilities over the course of her career. Her rigorous approach involved considering the surface of the canvas as a given space where tension was generated by the arrangement of simple geometric shapes in bold colours. The paint was laid thinly and evenly on the canvas, with the expanses of colour and the relationship between them as the sole vector of an artistic utterance striving for balance. Claisse's pictorial experiments drew on the periodical *Art d'aujourd'hui* (1949–54), and her friendship with the artist and art theorist Auguste Herbin. Herbin likewise influenced many other artists such as Victor Vasarely who lent abstract and kinetic art such vibrancy in postwar France.

This painting is one of a series dating from 1965–6, forming a sharp contrast with the busier paintings of Claisse's earlier period. The earlier profusion has been stripped back entirely, with large, irregular geometric shapes floating on the canvas, covering much of its surface. In some cases, though not here, black lines connect the shapes to a network. The colours are not necessarily bright, but add to the playfulness of Claisse's abstraction. While abstract painting might seek to distance itself from direct depictions of nature, that does not preclude any reference to it. Here, the work can be read as a landscape, taking the 'sun' of the title as the red polygon towards the top of the canvas and the 'waters' as the blue trapezium whose slanting sides create the illusion of depth of field. In a similarly titled smaller watercolour from 1965, the star is green, suggesting an element of symbolism. In both cases, the eye is immediately drawn by the elements that seem to quiver imperceptibly, foreshadowing the dynamic energy of Claisse's later works. [LSCH]

115

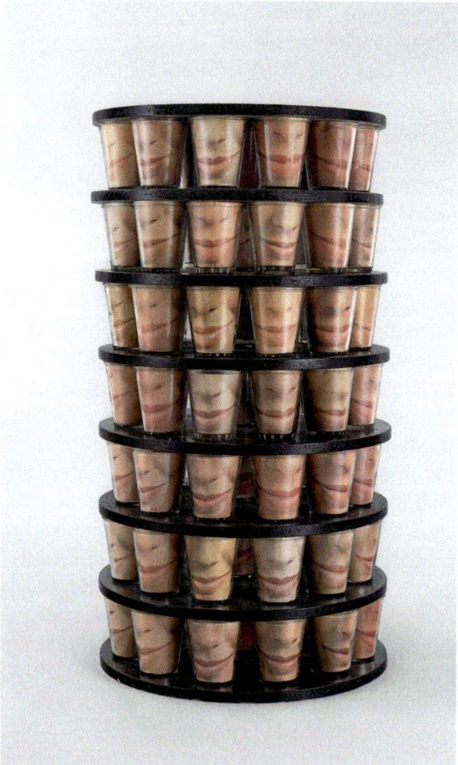

116

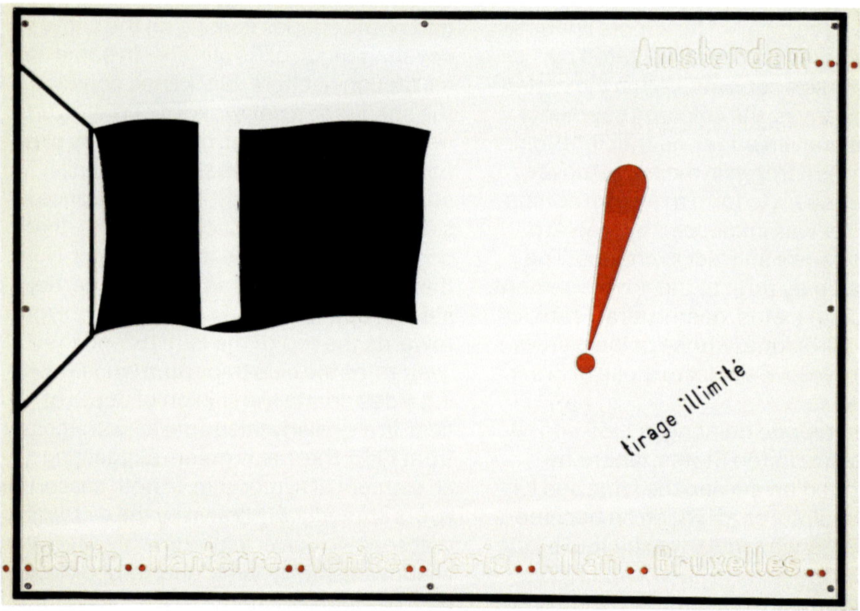

Marcel Broodthaers, Tour de Babel, 1966
Marcel Broodthaers, Le drapeau noir, 1968

115

Marcel Broodthaers (Brussels, 1924–Cologne, 1976)
Tour de Babel (*Tower of Babel*), 1966
Glass jars, prints, cotton, wood, 95×50×50 cm
Gift of the New Smith Gallery, Brussels, 1966. Inv. 1966-031

Marcel Broodthaers's career was as prolific as it was brief, giving rise to books, films, photographs, sculptures, objects, drawings and installations, among others. His career as an artist began with his first exhibition at the Galerie Saint-Laurent in Brussels in April 1964, which he titled *Moi aussi, je me suis demandé si je ne pouvais pas vendre quelque chose et réussir dans la vie. Cela fait un moment déjà que je ne suis bon à rien. Je suis âgé de quarante ans…* The exhibition featured his very first sculpture, *Pense-Bête* (*Memory Aid*) [Ghent, S.M.A.K., on long-term loan from the Collectie Vlaanderen], a bundle of fifty copies of his final slim poetry collection set in plaster. This wry display set the tone for the rest of his career, characterised by sharply witty interplay between image, object and writing.

In 1966, the Museum showed two of Broodthaers' works at the second Salon international de galeries-pilotes, one of which was this *Tour de Babel*. It comprises seven rows of glass jars, each holding the same image of a woman's nose and smiling mouth, taken from a magazine. The jars are arranged in a ring on seven, round, wooden planks, piled to form a tower that could possibly grow higher forever. That same year, Broodthaers built his *Tour visuelle* (*Visual Tower*, Edinburgh, Scottish National Gallery of Modern Art) on the same principle, featuring a wide-open eye rather than a smile. Building on the work of the new realists and pop art, Broodthaers' first pieces stage everyday items – in this instance, glass jars and advertising imagery, in other works mussels and eggshells – and underline their serial nature by means of repetition and accumulation. While *Tour de Babel* does not include any text, unlike other works from the same period, its title does point to a further reading, the repetition of identical mouths countering the multiplicity of languages in the biblical Tower of Babel, the crowning metaphor for the ambiguity inherent in human language. [NS]

116

Marcel Broodthaers (Brussels, 1924–Cologne, 1976)
Le drapeau noir (*Black Flag*), 1968
Painted vacuum-formed plastic plate, 83×120 cm, unlimited edition
Acquisition, 1969. Inv. 1969-027

In 1968 Marcel Broodthaers started making plastic panels onto which he thermoformed texts sometimes accompanied by an image or punctuation marks, in the manner of rebuses or political or commercial slogans. He grouped this series of works together under the title *Poèmes industriels* (*Industrial Poems*).

Acquired by the Museum a year after its creation, *Le drapeau noir* is a major example of this series. Comprising a black flag divided by a white line and confronted by a big red exclamation mark combined with the words '*tirage illimité*' (unlimited edition), the panel also bears the names of seven cities – Amsterdam, Berlin, Nanterre, Venice, Paris, Milan, Brussels – all of which were the scene of major uprisings during the protest movements of 1968. Seen in relation to the names of these cities, the flag can therefore be read as an explicit reference to the anarchist movements that it has symbolised ever since the late nineteenth century, and to its recuperation by the student movement in 1968.

Like the slogans that sprouted on walls, '*tirage illimité*' is an injunction to make a clean sweep of what makes a work of art, that is, its uniqueness. So it was that the artist stated in an interview in 1968: 'I don't believe … in the unique artist or the unique work of art. I believe in phenomena and in people who put ideas together.' Unlike certain of Broodthaers's plaques, limited to seven copies, no limits were placed on this one's numbers, giving it the status of a manifesto. Yet the 'pop' character of this work, like his other panels, with their palette of primary colours, use of industrial plastic, and playful rebus form, undermines the activist potential of the contents, underlining Broodthaers' scepticism about the utopia of a radical reformulation of social and artistic norms. [NS]

117

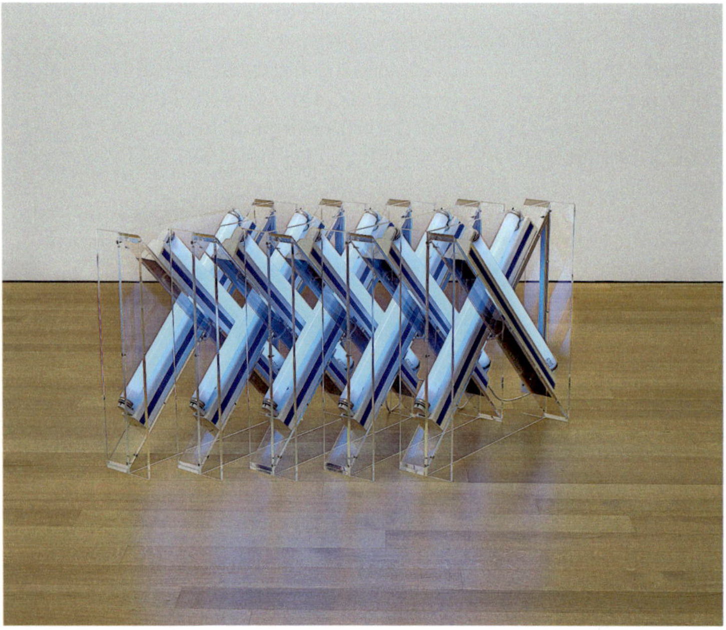

118

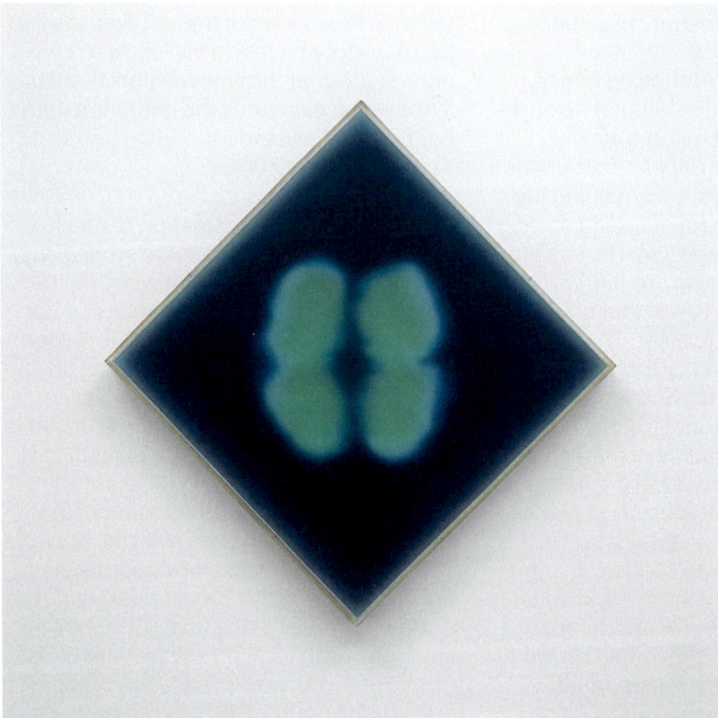

René Bauermeister, Animation lumineuse, 1966–8
Janos Urban, Construction n° 6, 1969

117

René Bauermeister (Neuchâtel, 1930–Gland, 1985)
Animation lumineuse (*Luminous Animation*), 1966–8
Plexiglas and neon, 49 × 49 × 75 cm
Gift of the artist, 1976. Inv. 1976-440

Animation lumineuse is one in a set of six sculptures made by Bauermeister between 1966 and 1968 which he donated to the Museum in 1976, several years after he had begun making experimental films and videos, a practice that he pioneered in Switzerland alongside his friends Jean Otth, Janos Urban, Gérald Minkoff and Muriel Olesen.

Trained at the schools of applied arts in Biel and in La Chaux-de-Fonds, Bauermeister later frequented the Parisian studios of André Lhote and Fernand Léger in 1953 and 1954. After initially working in two dimensions (painting), he started to explore volume, constructing the models for his sculptures and then drawing up the plans for their factory production. Iron, aluminium, chrome-plated metal, polyester, acrylic glass, neon – he used industrial materials to make forms that were simple and surfaces that were uncluttered.

Animation lumineuse was shown at Galerie Templon, Paris, in 1969 along with three more of the six sculptures held by the Museum. It is the only one of the set that is made up of neons and one of the only luminous sculptures by this artist to be found in a public collection. Comprising a succession of neons forming crosses and set in transparent Plexiglas cases, the sculpture appears to be a module that could be repeated ad infinitum. This principle is characteristic of the minimalist sculpture of the day and seems to anticipate later developments in Bauermeister's work, notably his exclusive focus on moving images after 1970. Indeed, the question of how we perceive a volume in a given space is already linked to that of temporality here, by the 'animation' from the glow of the neon. As the artist noted in an interview given in 1970, 'Ultimately, an object in three dimensions refers only to its own obviousness, whereas an image has its repetitions, infinite echoes .... The core of my approach consists in exposing the mechanisms of perception by following the different paths that it takes.' [NS]

118

Janos Urban (Szeged, 1934–Lausanne, 2016)
Construction n° 6, 1969
Insulac with polyester moulding, fluorescent pigment, Plexiglas, phosphorus, 126 × 126 × 12.5 cm
Acquisition, 1969. Inv. 1969-020

In 1956 Janos Urban reached Switzerland as a political refugee from his native Hungary. Having begun his artistic training in Budapest, he now continued at the École cantonale des beaux-arts in Lausanne, where he also started teaching in 1964. A pioneer of conceptual art in Switzerland, he began working with new materials such as phosphorus and Plexiglas in his research into optical phenomena and questions of perception and duration.

Construction n° 6 belongs to a series of works that harness the luminescence of phosphorus. It comprises a concave polyester moulding set into a block of chipboard in order to prevent thermal expansion. On top, two sheets of translucent Plexiglas are fixed at a certain distance from each other. The hollow form is covered with pigments mixed with phosphorus, which glows in the dark as it continues to emit the light to which it was exposed. 'I am interested', wrote Urban, 'in the physical properties of phosphorus, both as a "survival" of autonomous luminous energy and, in connection with the radio waves of the electromagnetic spectrum, as an extension of the audible as random visual intensity.' His fascination with the physical possibilities of matter – Urban worked in dialogue with a physicist friend when making this series – was because they made it possible to show light's relation to time in visual form, here captured by the material and then restored to the spectators at a later point in time.

When a work from the same series, *Construction n° 15* (1970, private collection), was shown at the 35th Venice Biennale, the artist put in place an installation protocol that made it possible to observe both phases (the capturing and the emission of the light) by presenting the work in a dark space with lighting coming at regular intervals from a spotlight. [NS]

119

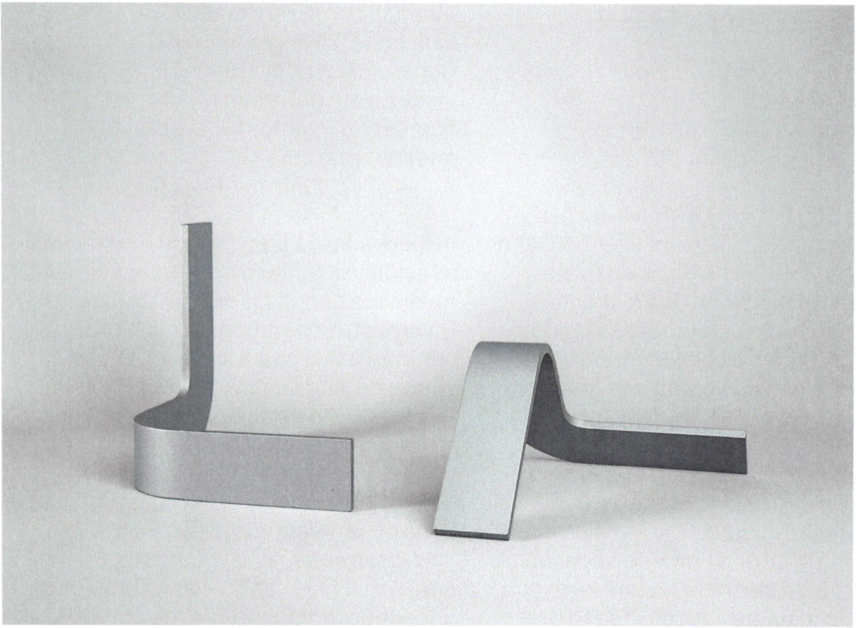

120

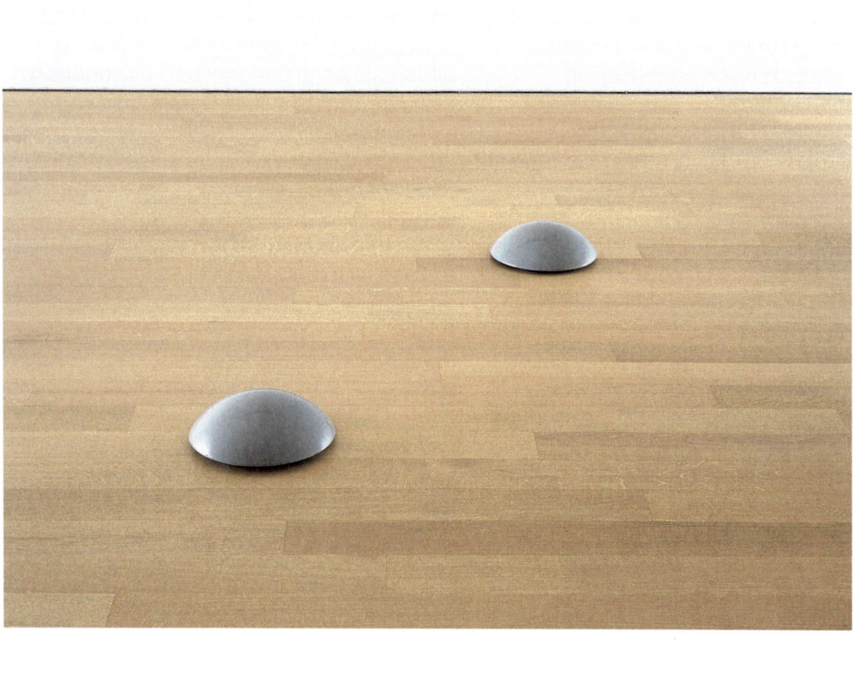

Tony DeLap, Tango Tangles II, 1966
Robert Breer, Jumelles, 1970

119

Tony DeLap (Oakland, 1927–Corona del Mar, 2019)
Tango Tangles II, 1966
Silver lacquer on moulded acrylic, 20 × 46 × 33.5 cm (each element)
Acquisition, 2002. Inv. 2002-063

In the 1960s, the American art scene was divided between the east and west coasts and underwent a profound shift in artistic practice, due in large part to the development of sculpture. Tony DeLap was part of this change in San Francisco, as were Donald Judd, Robert Morris, Richard Serra and others in New York, whose works, manufactured by subcontractors in industrial materials, are regular in volume.

The lack of artifice is one of the major features of minimalism. DeLap's work is characterised by the broadness of his approach as he plays with the limits of moderation. The sculpture *Tango Tangles II* meets the requirement of pared-down modularity. Yet the curves of its two parts give it a somewhat whimsical air, as do the variety of positions and connections between the two, which can be changed whenever it is put on display, changing how it is perceived, and the title, which refers to a Charlie Chaplin film.

Tango Tangles II is one of a set of sculptures, some flat, some three-dimensional, representing sections of the same 'ribbon', all with titles taken from Chaplin films – *Modern Times*, *Triple Trouble*, and so on. The series is rooted in the infinite potential of the variations of three shapes and four colours, all standardised and capable of being combined. None of the works has a fixed composition; instead, all can be assembled and rearranged in space. The 'tango tangle' of the title perfectly describes the sculpture, 'dancing' with itself, and the two words, differentiated by just a couple of letters, suggests change in constancy and constancy in change.

The work was shown at the Dilexi Gallery of San Francisco stand at the second Salon international de galeries-pilotes curated at the Museum in 1966 under the leadership of its then director René Berger. [LSCH]

120

Robert Breer (Detroit, 1926–Tucson, 2011)
Jumelles (*Twins*), 1970
Resin cast, acrylic, motors, 9 × 25 × 25 cm (each element)
Acquisition, 2002. Inv. 2002-062

In 1952 Robert Breer started making films parallel to his practice of painting. The first of these, *Form Phases I*, shows his interest in movement and transversality between mediums. In the mid-1960s he conceived the first of what he calls his *Floats* (in the sense of both buoyant vessels and carnival vehicles) – small, dome-like sculptures moved by a motor (their size and form would evolve over the years). Their movement is slow and hard to perceive and follows no predetermined itinerary. The *Floats* are not immediately visible, and only an attentive viewer will be aware of their motion.

The *Floats* create fixed points in the exhibition room. With each position, they invite viewers to look at the spatial field from a new perspective, like these *Jumelles,* which move autonomously and randomly in relation to each other: viewers see the relation between them as soon as they become aware of their presence. The dynamic of the site is thus renewed not only by their co-presence but also by their successive positions.

Unlike some *Floats* that stand out by their bright colour and that Breer liked to show at eye level, the neutral character of the *Jumelles*, of their form and colour, and the fact that they are placed on the ground, without a base, evokes the minimalist sculpture that developed in New York, where the artist lived from 1959, when he returned to the United States after ten years in Paris. These works should also be viewed as a caustic commentary on this artistic tendency, even if the *Floats* themselves engage in the same reflection on the space of the beholder as its proponents. [LSCH]

121

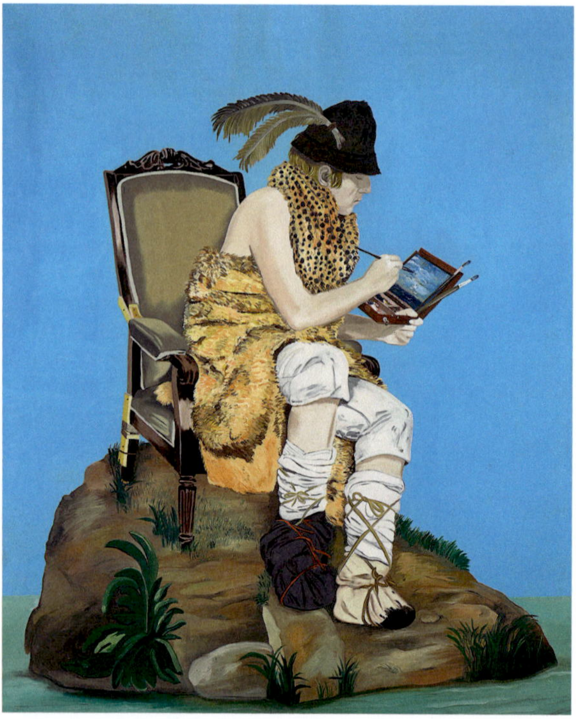

122

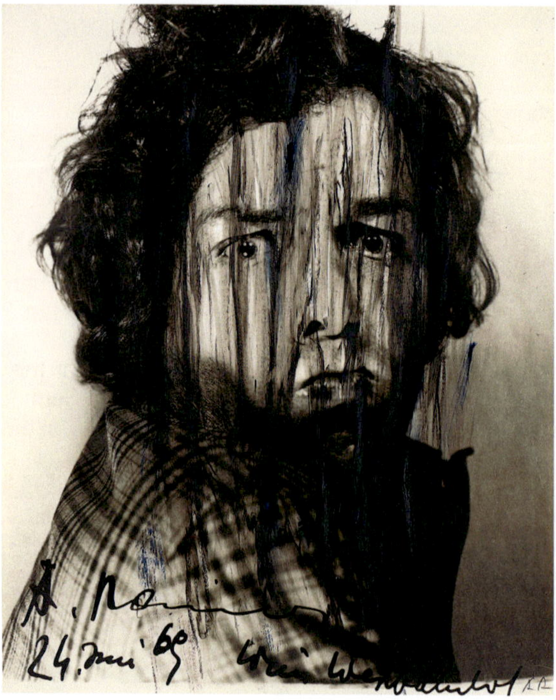

Eduardo Arroyo, Robinson Crusoé, 1965
Arnulf Rainer, Ohne Titel (Face Farces), 1969

121

Eduardo Arroyo (Madrid, 1937–2018)
Robinson Crusoé, 1965
Oil on canvas, 220 × 180 cm
Gift of Éric Meyer, 1968. Inv. 1968-012

The figure: a man dressed in animal skins, with rags wrapped around his feet and a Tyrolean style hat with feathers on his head. His skin is a waxy white. The setting: a tiny island supporting a patched-up chair, the rickety throne of an exotic painter-king. The man hardly seems surprised by his incongruous situation but is concentrating on the small seascape he is painting on a traveller's palette. Because the man is shown in half profile, viewers – no more of interest to him than his surroundings – can also see what he is working on, an aquatic landscape as blue as his own setting. *Robinson Crusoé* is in fact a self-portrait of the artist, based on a photograph in which he is shown wearing this garb.

In 1958, Arroyo fled Franco's Spain, and his home town of Madrid, for Paris. In 1964–5 he took part in exhibitions by the figuration narrative movement, whose content was often highly political and, together with Erró, Bernard Rancillac, Hervé Télémaque among others, became one of its leading figures. *Robinson Crusoé* dates from this period. It ironically presents a painter who has chosen exile, an artist cut off from the world, concentrating on his work and on the miniature universe shown by his palette.

In his use of collage (bringing together fragments from different realities on the same canvas), his rejection of illusionism (absence of depth and the modulation of shadow and light, except for certain elements), and the use of flat blocks of colour (the sky is simply a big blue monochrome), Arroyo was influenced by British pop art (he was closer to David Hockney, for example, than to Roy Lichtenstein). *Robinson Crusoé* turns out to be very much a product of its time. However, the theme of the artist's solitude places this painting within a philosophical tendency that extends much further than the 1960s; it originated with *Thus Spoke Zarathustra* (1883–5) by the philosopher Friedrich Nietzsche. [BF]

122

Arnulf Rainer (Baden, 1929)
Ohne Titel (Face Farces) (*Untitled [Face Farces]*), 1969
Acrylic on b/w photograph, 59.6 × 50 cm
Acquisition, 1984. Inv. 1984-050

Arnulf Rainer created the first of his *Übermalungen* (overpaintings) in 1952, covering reproductions of art works with paint; to the point of making them in part unrecognisable. He painted over his own canvases and attacked his own face with the same energy in *Face Farces* (1969–75), a series of self-portraits based on photo booth head shots enlarged and touched up with paint.

The photographs, in which he stares at the camera while pulling a face or pouting, are energetically slashed over with paint. Rainer is interested in depictions of madness. The series is also heir to the Northern school tradition of the series of modified, expressive self-portraits, from Rembrandt's successive changes to his own engraved portraits to Franz Xaver Messerschmidt's 'character heads'.

Rainer disfigures himself doubly. First, he sits for the camera without seeking a flattering pose. He explores the resources of bodily communication by adopting the most absurd facial expressions, simultaneously contorting various parts of his face: the resulting expressions are disconcerting in terms of meaning and are not particularly pleasant to look at. Rainer then adds to the work by hand, as in this case, daubing black and blue acrylic over his own face. Rather than destroying the work's legibility, he brings in a note of tension between himself and the viewer who is confronted with his odd attitude.

Facing a man whose individuality is denied triggers a certain discomfort in the viewer. The artist's intervention on the photograph echoes a taboo and an iconoclastic act: the handwritten inscriptions on the lower part of the photograph – signature, date and place on the negative – temper the action somewhat by foregrounding its place within the artistic process and affirming Rainer's identity through his name. The work is located in the context of the Viennese actionists who recorded their own performances in photography and made their own bodies a surface for painting. [LSCH]

123

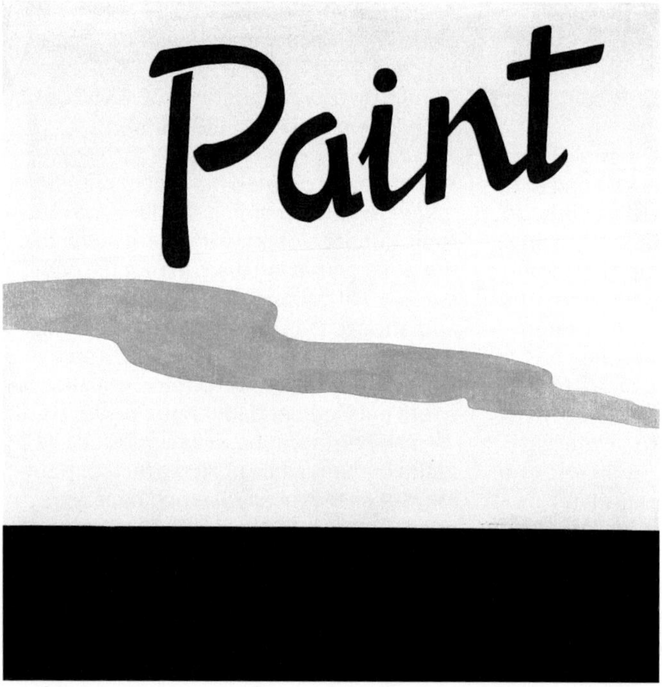

124

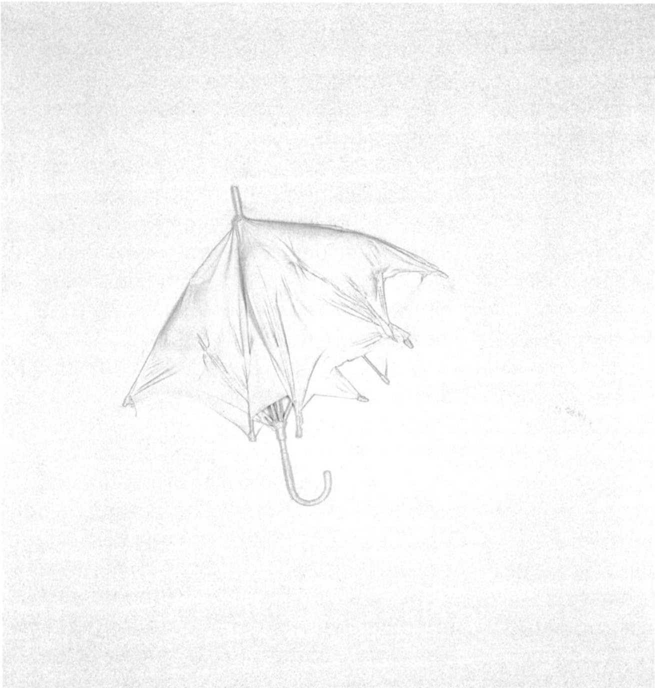

Jannis Kounellis, Untitled Paint, 1965
Tadeusz Kantor, Multipart, 1970

123

Jannis Kounellis (Piraeus, 1936–Rome, 2017)
Untitled Paint, 1965
Acrylic on canvas, 207×207.7 cm
Alain and Suzanne Dubois Collection. Promised gift

Jannis Kounellis left his native Greece for Rome in 1956. During his studies, he was influenced by artists such as Lucio Fontana and Alberto Burri and by the rich cultural and historical heritage of his adopted city, which rivalled that of his native country.

Prior to 1965, Kounellis focused on painting. He rose to acclaim with canvases stencilled with large black letters, numbers and symbols, but soon decided to turn his back on what was quickly becoming recognised as his signature style. *Untitled Paint* is one of a group of works from the period just before he distanced himself from painting and joined the arte povera movement, taking up natural materials such as jute, coal, cotton and stones, which then became his preferred media.

Its composition reflects the artist's hesitations over his future artistic path. Echoing contemporary developments in art, it incorporates three directions. It nods to pop art with a touch of surrealism in the appropriation of words taken from everyday life and referring to the object itself as an artefact (in this case, the stylised word 'paint', as if written with a reed pen, evoking an advertising billboard). It refers to figurative art with the motif of the cloud or smoke, and the horizon line that gestures towards landscape painting, and it also hints at geometric abstraction in its large square format and the black strip against a white background.

Untitled Paint offers a synthesis of various artistic languages and self-referentially describes itself as a painting. The stripped down, highly efficient composition, structured by one straight line and two diagonals, each consisting of a single element, generates a range of unresolved tensions: linguistic utterance or representation? Figurative or abstract? Black, grey or white? [LSCH]

124

Tadeusz Kantor (Wielopole Skrzyńskie, 1915–Krakow, 1990)
Multipart, 1970
Mixed media on canvas, 121×111 cm
Gift of Galeria Foksal, Warsaw, 1970. Inv. 1971-023

A visual artist and creator of happenings, Tadeusz Kantor was a major figure on the Polish experimental theatre scene as production designer, director and author. In 1955 he was one of the founders of the avant-garde theatre group Cricot 2, and in 1957 he united artists who rejected the doctrine of socialist realism around the second Krakow Group. He became a noted presence on the international art scene as of the late 1950s (documenta 2 and 6 in Kassel, 15th Venice Biennale, 9th São Paulo Biennial, etc.)

Practical objects presented in a non-functional context are a constant in Kantor's work. As of the early 1960s he wrapped objects from everyday life, or associated with personal memories – suitcases, letters, umbrellas – to make what he called *Emballages*. The title of the work kept at the Museum, *Multipart* (a contraction of 'multiplication' and 'participation') later also became the name of the series to which it belongs. This piece is the result of the eponymous happening organised by Kantor at Galeria Foksal, Warsaw, in February 1970. Forty identical works, made to the artist's instructions, were exhibited. Each consisted of an open umbrella flattened and glued on a canvas, the whole thing painted white and titled *Parapluie-emballage*. The buyer's contract stipulated that owners of the works were allowed to write on the canvas, to burn it, to sell it or to speculate with it: in short, to do what they wanted with it, on the condition that it should then be made available to the artist so that he could re-exhibit it after it had been used. Twenty-five of these owned works were exhibited in Warsaw in 1971. These did not include the Lausanne piece, which was given to the Museum by Galeria Foksal during the third Salon international de galeries-pilotes, and as a result was already in the collections, having been withdrawn halfway through its performative process. [NS]

125

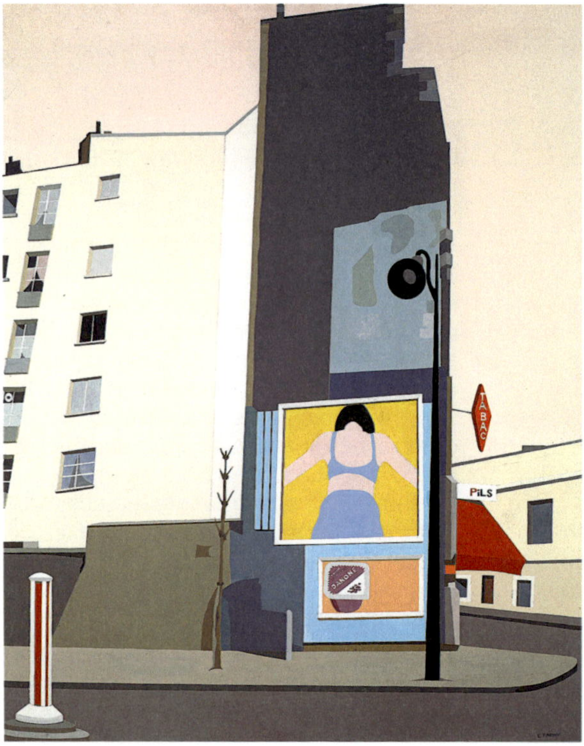

126

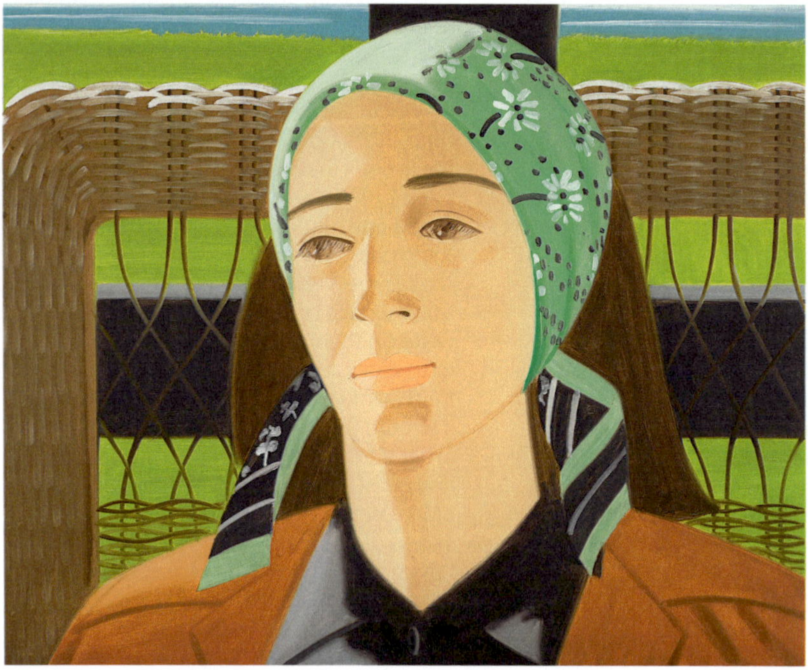

Émilienne Farny, Rue de l’Armorique (Façade), c. 1970
Alex Katz, Green Scarf, 1975

125

Émilienne Farny (Neuchâtel, 1938–Lausanne, 2014)
Rue de l'Armorique (Façade), c. 1970
Acrylic on canvas, 100 × 81.5 cm
Acquisition, 1971. Inv. 1971-003

From 1962 to 1972 Émilienne Farny lived in Paris, in the 14th arrondissement. As a painter, her focus was always on reality. In the French capital she found a big city in the throes of change, with the alternation of old neighbourhoods and construction sites, bared façades and the irruption of giant advertisements – in a word, the contemporary urban scene in all its violence and beauty. Another decisive discovery was American pop art, then being brought to Paris by exhibitions of Robert Rauschenberg, Andy Warhol, Roy Lichtenstein and Tom Wesselmann at the Ileana Sonnabend gallery. Finally, Adam Montparnasse, where Farny purchased her supplies, started selling acrylic paint. The artist had found both a new theme and the idea of a new figurative style.

Rue de l'Armorique (Façade) is one in a series of works showing the fronts of houses, car parks and factories. The painting clearly shows her debt to pop art, but also the individuality of her style. Rather than sticking to the hallowed themes of the new American painting – advertising, comics and gadgetry – as did many other Swiss and French painters of her generation, she represented her immediate surroundings with great documentary precision.

As in all the paintings from this series, the street here is deserted, devoid of both pedestrians and cars. Perhaps the artist felt that such anecdotal presences would distract viewers from the pictorial idea. In any case, this absence brings out a sociological, economic and ideological reality that is signalled by its heterogeneity: the syncopated times of old Paris and property speculation, the irruption of advertising and road signage, a dead tree heralding ecological concerns, etc. Likewise, the coherence of the coloured surfaces, fitting together like the pieces in a puzzle, paradoxically highlights the disparities of the urban landscape. [MTh]

126

Alex Katz (New York, 1927)
Green Scarf, 1975
Oil on canvas, 122 × 152.5 cm
Alain and Suzanne Dubois Collection. Promised gift

Influenced by pop art, Alex Katz produced a body of figurative painting dominated by portraits and landscapes. His subjects are broken down into large sections of colour enriched with careful detailing in a smooth, neutral style.

In this work, a cross of dark wood is placed slightly off-centre behind a woven wicker frame, perhaps the back of a chair or bench, whose left-hand side lies along the edge of the canvas, its weave forming a regular, delicate pattern. In the foreground, in front of the cross and wicker frame, are the head and shoulders of a woman looking off slightly to one side. She is wearing a black blouse and brown jacket and on her head is the item that gives the work its character and its title, a green headscarf. The scene takes place in nature: a green meadow can be seen in the background with a high horizon line opening onto a turquoise strip that suggests water rather than sky. The natural world is also present in the fabric printed with white-petalled flowers.

While the shadows on the face and neck are simplified to the extreme, the artist has created a subtle interplay of visual echoes between the woman's eyebrows, the flower stems, the wickerwork, and the folds and details of the jacket. The anonymous portrait, in harmonious chilly hues of blue and green and warmer yellows, ochres and browns, is timeless. The woman's gaze, lost in the distance as if seeking something outside the artist's restrictive frame, adds a touch of melancholy. The decision to place the figure in a precise construction and the woman's minimal yet majestic expressiveness may gesture to Piero della Francesca, an artist Alex Katz admired greatly. [BF]

127

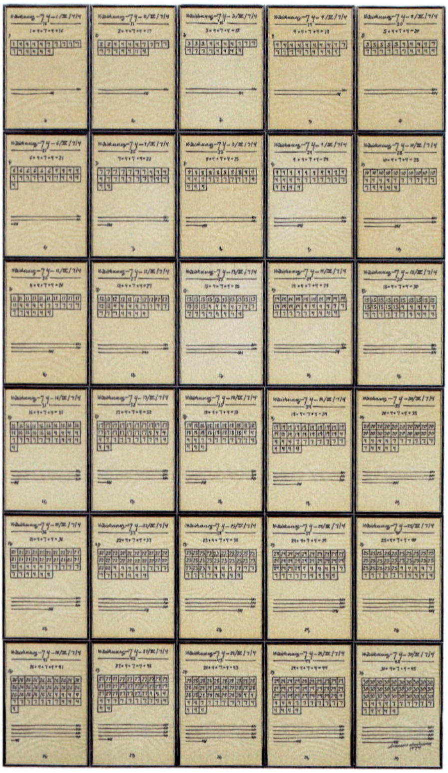

128

Hanne Darboven, K – Zeichnung – 74 – 1/IV/7/4 – 16 à – 30/IV/7/4 – 45, 1974
Giuseppe Penone, Svolgere la propria pelle (Pressione su carta), 1974

127

Hanne Darboven (Munich, 1941–Hamburg, 2009)
K – Zeichnung – 74 – 1/IV/7/4 – 16 à – 30/IV/7/4 – 45, 1974
Indian ink on paper parchment, 29.5 × 21 cm (each sheet)
Alain and Suzanne Dubois Collection. Promised gift

Hanne Darboven, the daughter of a wealthy shopkeeper, grew up surrounded by art. She started playing the piano as a child – many of her drawings visually echo musical scores – but she gave up music in 1962 when she began her studies at the Hamburg Hochschule für bildende Künste. She spent the years 1966 to 1968 in New York, where she met Sol LeWitt and Carl Andre, who were keen supporters of her art. This was when she created her first works on squared paper, much in vogue among artists at that time. On her return to Hamburg, she determined what she called 'K-Wert' (K value) for 'Konstruktion', the sum of the numbers in a given date, which became the key to her own system of notation. She developed numerical sequences that were part-writing, part-drawing, based on K-Wert numbers for dates in the Gregorian calendar. She considered herself more a writer than an artist.

Darboven's works offer a meditation on the passage of time and thus the ebb and flow of life itself, like those of On Kawara. They take the form of an index progressing across a wall, as in this work, *K – Zeichnung – 74 – 1/IV/7/4 – 16 à – 30/IV/7/4 – 45*, or across an entire room. The drawing, based on complex logic, consists of thirty sheets produced over the course of thirty days in April 1974. Darboven records the passage of time and life flowing past. Encoding dates and their written expression was her way of acting and being in the world. She based her work on a system invented to organise time, the calendar, highlighting its relative artificiality. Her art, which over time developed towards installations including photography and sculpture, can be read as part of the emergence of conceptual art, exploring issues of seriality and the mechanical progression of shapes, at the limits of figuration. [LSCH]

128

Giuseppe Penone (Garessio, 1947)
Svolgere la propria pelle (*Pressione su carta*) (*Developing Your Own Skin* [*Pressure on Paper*]), 1974
Graphite and adhesive tape on paper mounted on canvas, 130 × 160 cm
Alice Pauli Donation, 2018. Inv. 2018-026

In the early 1970s, Giuseppe Penone, the youngest member of arte povera, then just twenty-five, developed a series of works that literally involved him lying flat. He applied his own body to glass plates, took a photograph, then pieced the fragments together in one large composition. He soon moved on to copying enlargements of his own skin in drawings on paper or even over entire walls. One of his favourite themes is still the (often invisible) imprint left by human bodies on nature.

At the centre of the composition *Svolgere la propria pelle* (*Developing Your Own Skin*) is a small black rectangle. This is a piece of transparent adhesive tape bearing a print of a patch of the artist's own skin dusted with graphite. Penone transferred the print to the paper as the starting point for his composition, enlarging the 'skin print' in soft-lead pencil. The resulting *Pressione su carta* (*Pressure on Paper*) is a drawing of skin that could almost be tree bark or a landscape. This work is a personalised landscape. The artist's careful choice of materials – graphite gesturing to the mineral world, paper to the plant kingdom – and choice of direct and indirect techniques in printing with the adhesive tape and drawing bring humanity into its own various environments, linking microcosm and macrocosm, and creating a poetic world filled with complex relationships.

Penone foregrounds skin as the screen that records even the slightest sensations while leaving its own prints, giving our sense of touch pride of place rather than sight, which has long been central to the Western art tradition. In a world ever more subject to dematerialisation, Penone's works help us maintain physical contact with nature. [BF]

129

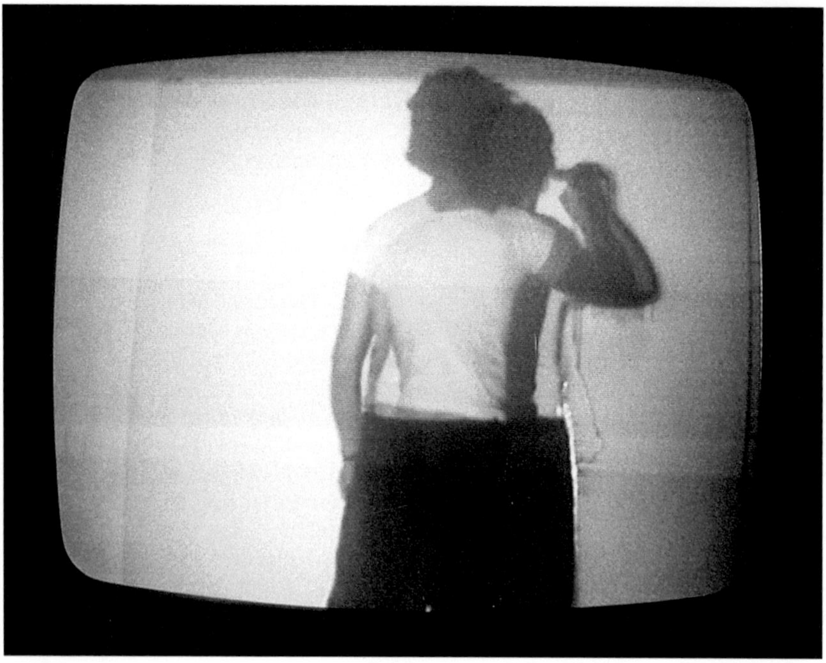

130

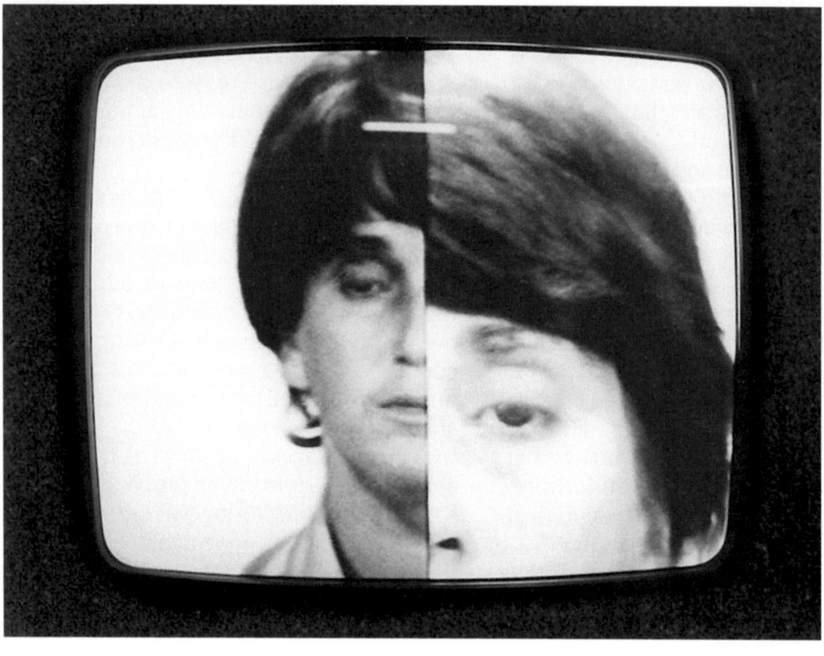

Jean Otth, Limite E, 1973
VALIE EXPORT, Space Seeing – Space Hearing, 1973–4

129

Jean Otth (Lausanne, 1940–Chavannes-près-Renens, 2013)
Limite E (*Limit E*), 1973
Video, b/w, sound, 21 min 40 sec
Acquisition, 1973. Inv. 1973-036

Jean Otth made his first video works in 1971 and showed them the following year at Galerie Impact in Lausanne (*Action Film Vidéo*) and at the Museum (*Musée expérimental 3 : Implosion*). These two exhibitions are considered as marking the beginnings of Swiss video art.

Limite E was the first video to enter the Museum collection, alongside other tapes by Otth, such as *Limite A* and the *TV-Perturbations* series. It makes use of the aesthetic potential of electronic technology (closed-circuit, mise en abyme of the image). We see the artist from behind, standing in front of a white wall that also serves as a screen. Otth draws the outline of his own shadow, his static image (a projected transparency) and, finally, his dynamic image (a projected Super-8 Film), suggesting a reflection on the different natures of the image – in this instance, drawing, projected or filmed, and static or in motion. The pictorial result of this action was a canvas measuring 170 × 170 cm, also in the Museum collection, which cannot be exhibited without the video which recorded its making.

Limite E belongs to a series whose subtitle, *Interrogation sur les 'réalités' de l'image* (*Interrogations on the 'Realities' of the Image*), not only sums up what interested the artist at the time, but also offers a diagnosis of the video scene of the day. As Otth puts it in the catalogue *Vidéo 1970–1980* (1980), 'the *Limit* is a theme that chokes on its own obviousness. Drawing, scrawling the outline of a form is a primitive act to be preserved and developed. As the common denominator of all images and all codes (with time as a new plastic dimension), video brings forth a pictorial space whose specificity still needs to be determined.... But one thing is certain: matter. Rather than passively receiving images (a movie projection), this electronic material produces them with the fine doggedness of light, in a perpetual "techno-imaginary" happening.' [NS]

130

VALIE EXPORT (Linz, 1940)
Space Seeing – Space Hearing, 1973–4
Video, b/w, sound, 6 min 19 sec
Acquisition, 2013. Courtesy of the artist and Electronic Arts Intermix (EAI), New York. Inv. 2013-072

In 1967, VALIE EXPORT abandoned her birth surname for that of a brand of cheap cigarettes, 'Smart Export', which became her artist and legal name. This powerful feminist act, refusing to perpetuate the tradition of inheriting the father's surname, is typical of her artistic undertaking, which, while drawing on the work of the earlier Viennese actionists, explores issues of power inherent in gender relations. All her earliest works, including performances, experimental films, photographs and videos, question the social order and its norms, bringing the female body into confrontation with urban space. Like other performance artists, VALIE EXPORT takes over public space, stepping outside the boundaries that traditionally legitimise artistic actions or objects (the studio, the exhibition space), and outside the spatial and symbolic space available to women (the private sphere, the household).

The video *Space Seeing – Space Hearing* arose from a performance by VALIE EXPORT at the Kölnischer Kunstverein. It reflects her work on the perception of space. For the performance, the artist stood upright and motionless in the centre of an empty museum room. Four video cameras filmed her, broadcasting still frames of her body on four screens. The screens broadcast six different images of the artist, on the right or left of the screen, in the foreground or background, full-length or in close-up. Each position in space was characterised by a change in volume, the duration of the repetition, or the pitch of the sound. The result was broadcast on a fifth monitor with a split screen that synchronised sound and image. It shows VALIE EXPORT becoming her own twin, splitting in two, distancing herself from and coming close to the camera, representing the complex relationship between body and space. [NS]

131

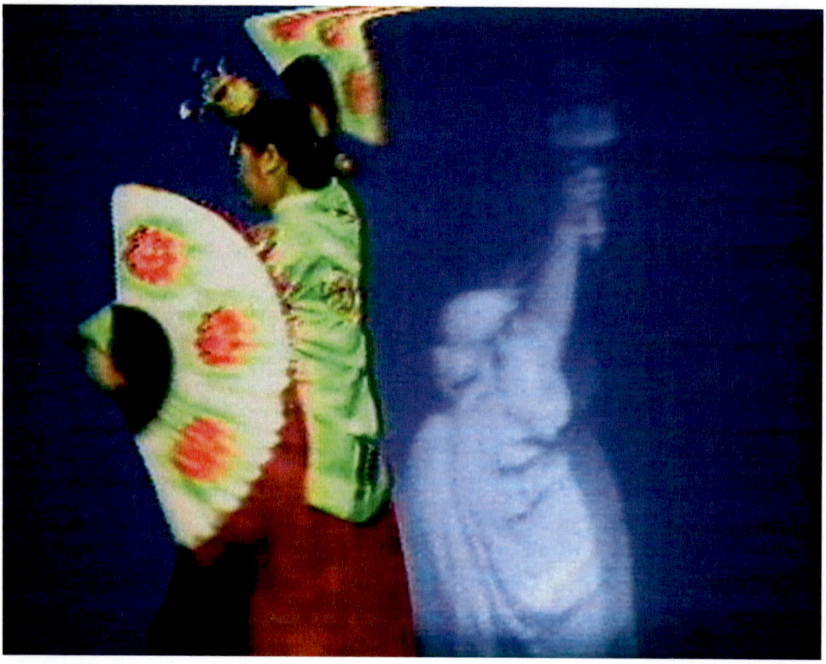

132

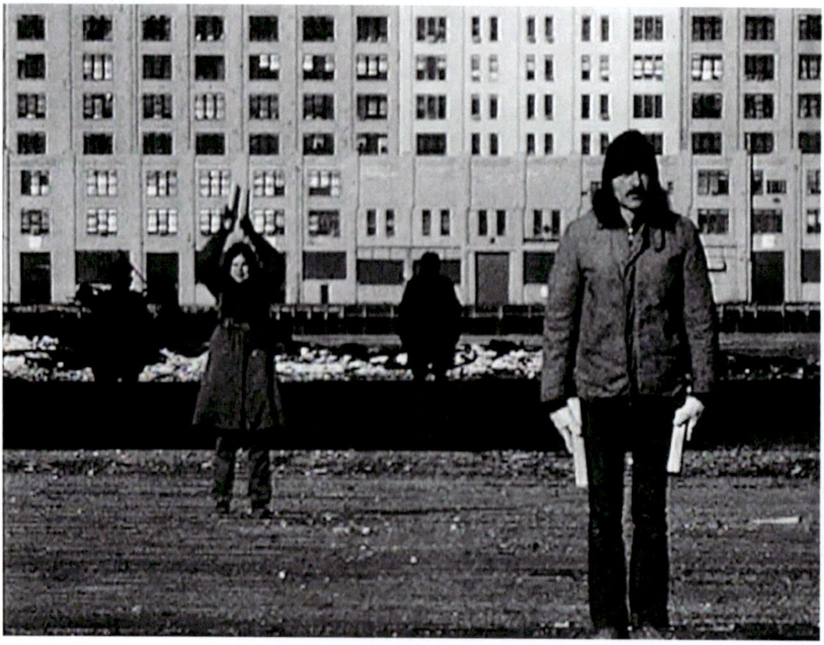

Nam June Paik, Global Groove, 1973
Joan Jonas, Songdelay, 1973

131

Nam June Paik (Seoul, 1932–Miami, 2006)
Global Groove, 1973
Video, colour, sound, 28 min 30 sec
Acquisition, 2013. Courtesy of Studio Nam June Paik and Electronic Arts Intermix (EAI), New York. Inv. 2013-073

One of the founders of video art, Nam June Paik produced a vast corpus of works comprising video tapes, televisual productions, performances and installations. In 1963 he presented his first Fluxus-inspired video and musical works in an exhibition titled *Exposition of Music – Electronic Television* at Galerie Parnass, Wuppertal. Looking back, this can be seen as marking the beginnings of video art. In 1965 Paik bought a Portapak, one of the first hand-held video cameras, the technical possibilities of which (live recording, autonomy of the production tool) would enable him to carry out new experiments on the medium.

'This is a glimpse of a new world when you will be able to switch on every TV channel in the world and TV guides will be as thick as the Manhattan telephone book.' These are the opening words of *Global Groove*, now a cult work in the history of video art. This radical manifesto concerning globalised communication in a media-saturated world explores the potential offered by the manipulation of video signals and magnetic tape. It takes the form of an electronic collage, a pastiche of sounds and images that subverts the language of television – excerpts of films and music clips are interspersed with scenes of traditional Korean dance, the face of Richard Nixon disfigured by the action of a magnet on the television follows a musical excerpt from Karlheinz Stockhausen, etc. The images and sequences themselves are treated as plastic objects: processing by the synthesiser transfigures the faces into a kaleidoscope of bright colours, while inlays and superimposition transform and complexify the images that follow at a frantic rhythm. Paik humorously has fragments of different works and disciplines cohabit in a flux of sequences in which planetary space is reduced to the television screen and time to the present moment. [NS]

132

Joan Jonas (New York, 1936)
Songdelay, 1973
16 mm film transferred to video, b/w, sound, 18 min 35 sec
Acquisition, 2013. Courtesy of the artist and Electronic Arts Intermix (EAI), New York. Inv. 2013-074

Initially trained as a sculptor, Joan Jonas was involved in the development of performance art in the late 1960s alongside other artists of the New York avant-garde, such as Robert Smithson, Richard Serra, Yvonne Rainer, Gordon Matta-Clark and the members of Fluxus. She acquired a Portapak camera in 1969 and made her first video, *Organic Honey's Visual Telepathy*, two years later. In her first works, performance and filmed images are always closely linked; performance is often preceded and extended by videos and films, and sometimes by installations.

Between 1970 and 1974 Jonas produced five outdoor performances, working with the rural and urban landscape. The fourth of these, *Delay Delay*, was made along the Hudson River in Lower Manhattan, on the banks of the Tiber in Rome, and at documenta 5 in Kassel. Reprising certain aspects of this performance, *Songdelay* was filmed in 16 mm and uses a highly cinematic vocabulary (wide angles, varying camera distances and a disjunct between sound and image). The action takes place on the riverfront in Manhattan. The performers, among them Jonas, make sounds, notably by striking pieces of wood, and draw circles and lines on the ground. The audience was kept at a distance from the place of representation, which it watched from a raised position. The discrepancy between the actions watched by the viewers and the different sounds that reach them help define the spatiotemporal relations and provide a sensation of the topography. The rhythm, the distance and the different forms of desynchronisation enable Jonas to deconstruct space and duration in a performance that is at once precisely choreographed and open to improvisation. [NS]

133

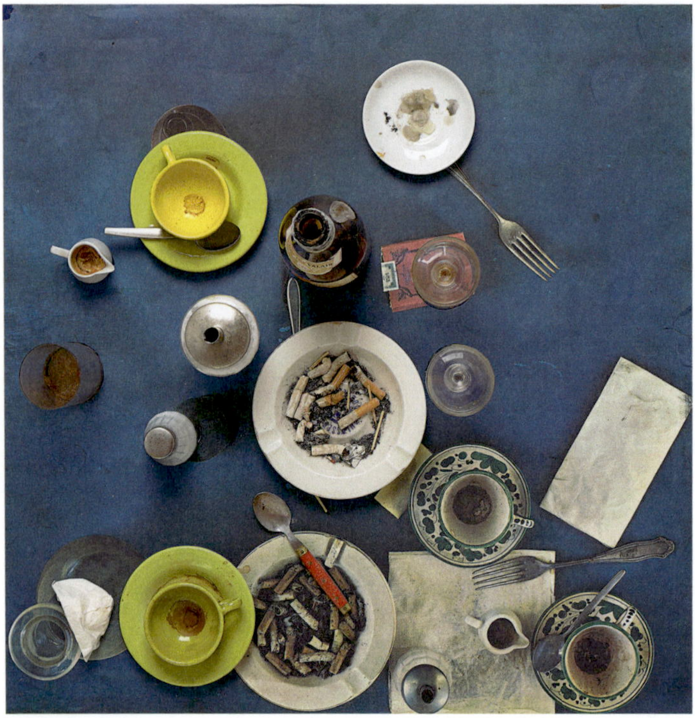

134

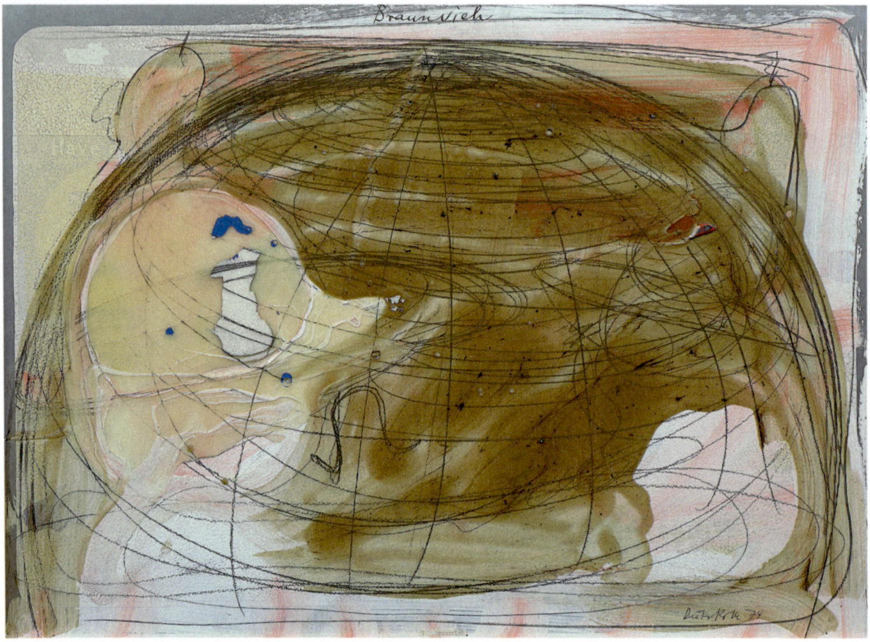

Daniel Spoerri, Aktion Restaurant Spoerri. Tableau-piège, 1972
Dieter Roth, Braunvieh, 1974

133

Daniel Spoerri (Galati, 1930)
Aktion Restaurant Spoerri. Tableau-piège (Aktion Restaurant Spoerri. Trap-Painting), 1972
Assemblage of various objects on printed image glued on wood, 71 × 71 × 40.5 cm
Acquisition, 1988. Inv. 1988-037

In 1960, Pierre Restany and Yves Klein created the new realist group. Many artists, including Daniel Spoerri, Arman, Martial Raysse and Jean Tinguely, signed the group's manifesto, with the intention of drawing on reality for the concrete content of their art. As early as 1912, Georges Braque and Pablo Picasso had started incorporating scraps of newspaper into their cubist paintings; now, torn posters, crushed cars and accumulated objects became works of art in their own right.

Spoerri first showed his *Trap-Paintings* in Paris in 1960. Created in the tiny twelve-metre-square room in the Hôtel Carcassonne he called home from 1959 to 1965, they show the remains of meals and crockery frozen in time. At this point, he did not rearrange the items at all, simply preserving the banal, chance image as a snapshot. He was particularly interested in freeze-framing objects that were usually handled and moved around during an evening meal. Once they had become static, he set the whole table up vertically on the wall. The shift from horizontal to vertical – Spoerri's only input – strips the everyday scene of its ephemeral nature. The visitors are invited to engage in head-on study of elements that they would never have glanced at if sitting at the table.

Food and eating are recurrent themes for Spoerri, who sees them as an expression of the cycle of life. This work dates from when he ran a restaurant in Düsseldorf. He opened it in 1968 to study what leads to mess on dinner tables. This work features the 'trapped' traces of a meal eaten on 6 December 1972, with cigarette butts, coffee dregs, an empty bottle and used cutlery transformed into a lasting still life. The objects are stuck to a photocopied picture of crockery, forming a trompe-l'œil tablecloth that in turn explores the nature of representation. [LSCH]

134

Dieter Roth (Hanover, 1930–Basel, 1998)
Braunvieh (Brown Cow), 1974
Mixed techniques on board, 52 × 70 cm
Alain and Suzanne Dubois Collection. Promised gift

Dieter Roth made art using whatever came to hand. He enjoyed using materials such as foodstuffs, including chocolate, banana, salami and cheese, that not only produced interesting aesthetic effects, like rings of grease, but also evolved over time, developing from one physical state to another or decomposing, for instance. He observed such changes with a certain melancholy, seeing them as symbolising life itself.

Roth was a free spirit with a compulsion to create art, mainly drawings, which could be produced anywhere with the most basic of materials. He used an exceptionally broad range of materials and techniques, from pencil, felt tip and collage to stamps with one or two hands, working on the telephone in collaboration with other artists, and drawing in notebooks, on desk blotters, tracing paper, among many others. He took what he found and turned it into art.

Braunvieh is emblematic of his range of techniques and the random nature of his creative process. He poured vinyl adhesive onto cardboard, let it spread out, then roughly fleshed out the earthly sphere in brown, leaving out the space for his own right-hand profile, recognisable by the bald pate and pointed nose. A scrap of torn paper represents the eye, topped by a simplified eyebrow in blue felt tip. The time zones are also sketched in.

Typically, Roth has saturated the entire surface of the medium with successive layers. The drawing, with the artist hugging the world in his arms, can be read as a manifestation of his appetite for everything that comes his way and his sense of oneness with the world itself: his work *is* the world. He *is* the world. [LSCH]

135

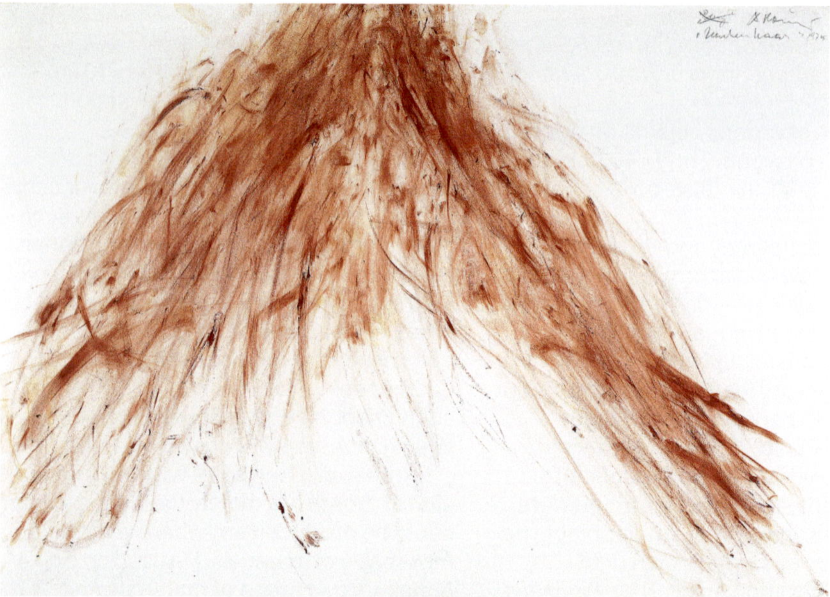

136

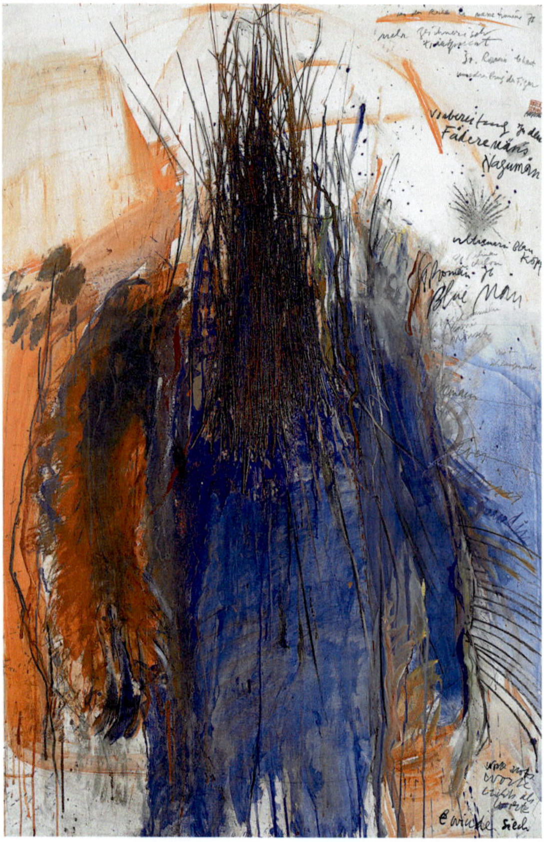

Arnulf Rainer, Nackenhaar, 1975
Rolf Iseli, Blauer Homme du jonc, 1976

135

Arnulf Rainer (Baden, 1929)
Nackenhaar (*Neck Hair*), 1975
Oil on cardboard, 51×73 cm
Acquisition, 1986. Inv. 1986-015

From as early as 1952, Arnulf Rainer developed a painting style typified by the nervous energy of the artistic process. His work on reproductions of famous paintings and photographic self-portraits is characterised by his physical commitment to the work and its intense, often violent energy. *Nackenhaar* accentuates the artist's physical labour: he painted it with his fingers, as if they were a direct connection between artistic impulse and action, stripping out any intermediaries between him and his medium. He started finger painting in 1973 after breaking a paintbrush while working and carrying on with his hands so as not to interrupt the flow of his inspiration. It is also doubtless a deliberate reference to Louis Soutter, who produced numerous finger paintings: Rainer admires him and collects his work.

In *Nackenhaar*, the artist has used both hands to paint an almost symmetrical composition, working from instinct. Two aspects of the work are unusual for Rainer. He has painted on a previously unused medium, pointing to a certain sense of unfussy simplicity. The use of non-black monochrome is likewise atypical: his art usually combines bright red and yellow, hemmed or split with black or blue lines. The use of cardboard rather than paper reflects the need for a less flimsy base.

Only the title indicates the subject of the finger-painted lines that come together at the top of the card. With a considerable economy of means, Rainer has thus sketched out the hair on the nape of a neck, as suggested by the work's title. The work has been painted swiftly. Without this information, the link between the triangular form, the marks, and their colour might suggest a volcanic eruption, a blazing fire, or bloody finger marks. A symbolically brutal imaginary is distilled in the vision we project onto this milky skin and strands of red hair. [LSCH]

136

Rolf Iseli (Bern, 1934)
Blauer Homme du jonc (*Blue Bulrush Man*), 1976
Gouache, earth and bulrushes on paper, 150×100 cm
Acquisition, 1977. Inv. 1977-079

Rolf Iseli first came to public attention in the mid-1950s for canvases in which pictorial technique and physical energy were themselves the object of the painting. He produced his first tachist work in 1954 and was instrumental in bringing informal art to Switzerland as the movement spread across Europe in the wake of American abstract expressionism.

Iseli gave up oil painting in 1966, moving from canvas to the more fragile medium of paper, which can be folded, torn and otherwise mistreated. This led to an research period that achieved a balance between figurative art and pure expression in the early 1970s. His preferred subject became man and his environment, with no sense of nostalgia for an imagined lost connection with nature. The shift drew on his experience with planting and growing vines in Saint-Romain, Burgundy in 1971, on land he had purchased ten years earlier and where he spent half the year working. This work, typical in its use of natural materials – earth, straw, feathers, leaves and so on, all feature in Iseli's art – is part of a series on the theme of the *Bulrush Man*. A male silhouette, the artist's own shadow, hidden by a spray of dried bulrushes, maps fully onto the painted surface. Projected on the paper as it would be on the ground, it is an image of humanhood.

This image translates the experience of an almost mystical moment. The man, stripped of any notion of identity, is in symbiosis with his natural surroundings. His body, radiating blue, blends into the orange gouache and ochre earth. The sheer power of the strokes applying gouache to paper causes drips to run off uncontrollably in vigorous lines to each side. The comments in various languages written during the course of the creative process, mainly in the right-hand margin, transcribe the artist's train of thought. [LSCH]

137

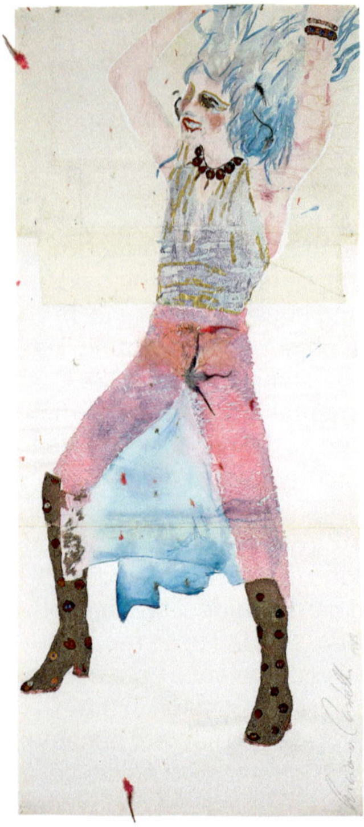

138

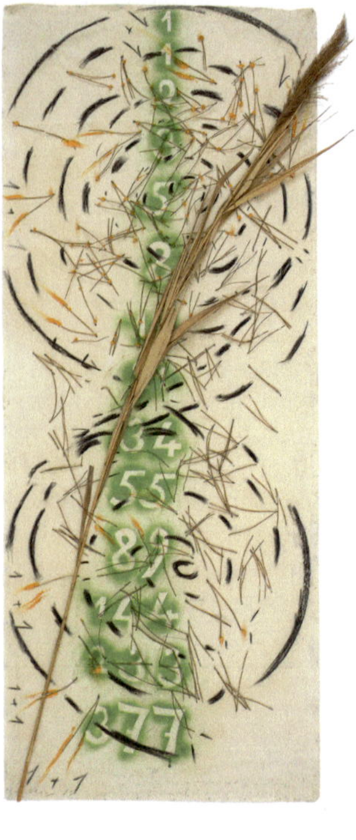

Luciano Castelli, Haarzupfer, 1973
Mario Merz, 8 che riporta 8 – La natura interloquisce sempre e solo con se stessa? Paesaggio con vento – Fibonacci, 1978

137

Luciano Castelli (Lucerne, 1951)
Haarzupfer (*Hair Fleecing*), 1973
Watercolour and various materials on several sheets of paper, 205 × 90 cm
Acquisition, 1986. Inv. 1986-005

Like Urs Lüthi, who also came from Lucerne, Castelli began his career in the early 1970s with representations of his own body, whether in performances or made-up self-portraits. Numerous photographs show him in various roles, outfits and poses, usually outrageously made up and decked out with accessories assigned to the feminine. He was inspired by glam rock culture and the androgynous style and extravagance embodied by David Bowie and Lou Reed. For Castelli, the notion of beauty, the right to live freely and identity stereotypes are all essential questions.

The artist also paints from his own photographs. The watercolour *Haarzupfer*, from the *Glitter Pictures* series, reveals his fascination with transsexuality. Heeled boots, make-up, long hair – Castelli appears here as his alter ego Lucille. The verticality of the support corresponds to the life-size figure's slender form, facing viewers. Lucille's presence is emphatic, with parted legs and arms raised, drawing on her blue locks. Shown in half profile, her body overflows the image. The support is constituted by seven sheets of paper. Some have been folded and crumpled and one of them has been cut to simulate the lower edge of Lucille's shiny tank top.

Lucille's joyous face and her unfolded body express her pleasure in living. The extravagance of the materials used also conveys this: the fishnet trousers are done in glue with pink sequins and the crotch is covered with feathers; the golden boots are covered with dried flowers, the eyelids with gold leaf, etc. Still lightly applied, the vivacity of Castelli's painting here heralds the more expressionist style he would develop in Berlin in the 1970s as a result of his contact with the Neue Wilde (New Fauves). [LSCH]

138

Mario Merz (Milan, 1925–Turin, 2003)
8 che riporta 8 – La natura interloquisce sempre e solo con se stessa? Paesaggio con vento – Fibonacci (*8 Which Reports 8 – Does Nature Always Interact Only with Itself? Landscape with Wind – Fibonacci*), 1978
Charcoal, acrylic, reed and pine needles on canvas, 226 × 98 cm
Alain and Suzanne Dubois Collection. Promised gift

In the 1960s and 1970s, the Fibonacci sequence ([0], 1, 1, 2, 3, 5, 8, 13, 21, and so on) was a constant reference for artists such as Mel Bochner, Donald Judd and Sol LeWitt, who used it as a principle of progression, for instance, for their sculptures. The rule is that each term except for the first two is the sum of the two before. The Fibonacci sequence is thought to be found widely in nature most notably in spirals.

Mario Merz first used the sequence in 1968 when he was thinking about ways to combine art and social activism. Over his oven in Turin, he hung five neon tubes with the numbers '1, 1, 2, 3, 5', creating the work *Fibonacci Santa Giulia*. He only truly integrated the sequence into his art from 1970 on, however. Being associated with arte povera, he had already shown an interest in organic harmony, considering igloos the ideal shape and habitat, for instance.

This work illustrates the numerical sequence by stencilling it in acrylic alongside two spirals in charcoal. The two elements are often juxtaposed in his oeuvre, as if to display both the principle and illustration: one example is *The Philosopher's Egg*, on display at Zurich station since 1991. What he liked about the Fibonacci sequence was less the minimisation of randomness than the growth of the animal and plant realms it symbolised. The question in the work's title – 'Does nature always interact only with itself?' can be explained as a consideration on how living matter is arranged. Alongside the references to the mathematical sequence, he makes use of natural materials. A single reed lies across the sheet diagonally and pine needles are scattered across its surface, suggesting the 'landscape with wind' of the title, introducing a simulacrum of chaos into the carefully arranged work. [LSCH]

139

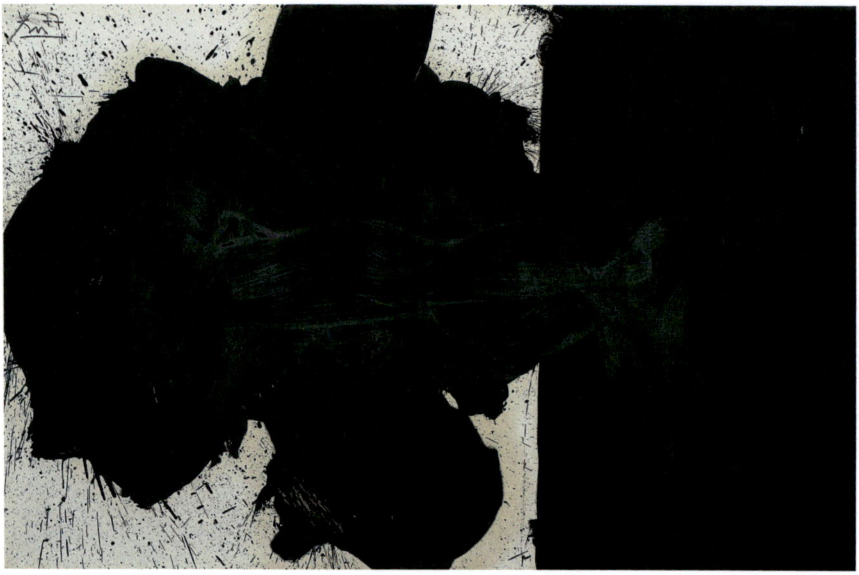

140

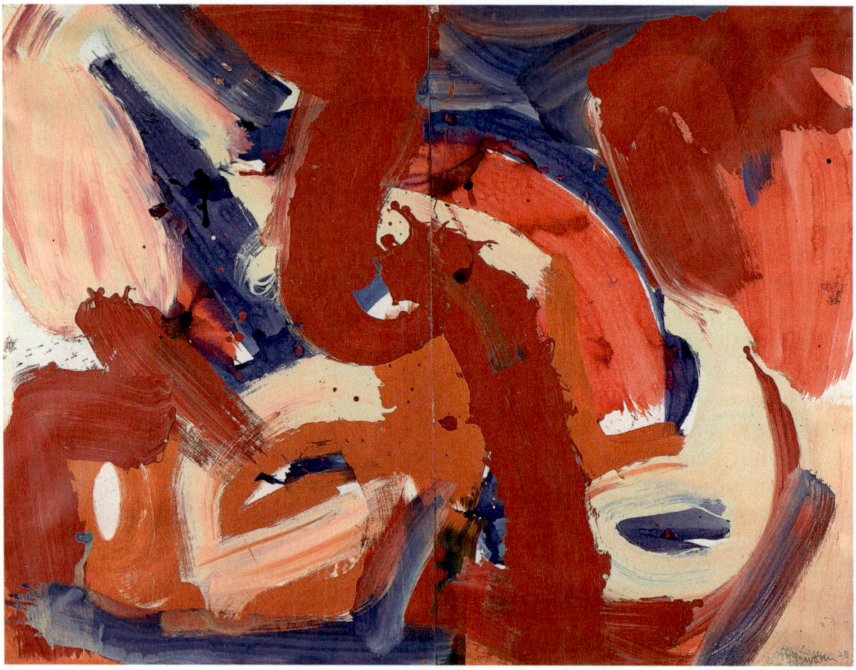

Robert Motherwell, Elegy Study A, 1977
Francine Simonin, Composition, 1978

139

Robert Motherwell (Aberdeen, 1915–Provincetown, 1991)
Elegy Study A, 1977
Oil on paper mounted on cardboard on canvas, 36 × 53.5 cm
Alain and Suzanne Dubois Collection. Promised gift

Robert Motherwell studied at Stanford and Yale universities. His intellectual interests spanned philosophy, literature, art history and psychology. In 1940, on returning to America after extensive travels in Europe, where he also had his first solo exhibition (Paris, 1939), he settled in New York and confirmed his decision to be a painter. At the time he frequented European surrealists then in wartime exile, and, particularly in their advocacy of the creative powers of the unconscious (automatism), they would have a decisive influence on him as well as other future proponents of American abstract expressionism, including Jackson Pollock.

This study is part of a sizeable ensemble of works responding to the Spanish Civil War (1936–9), which Motherwell continued to work on throughout his career. Paintings, prints and drawings in a variety of formats constitute a memorial to this conflict that the artist, following from Pablo Picasso, took as a symbol of oppression and injustice. From one *Elegy* to the next, the size, medium and other details of the works may vary, but the motifs remain the same: ovoid forms and broad vertical bands alternate and extend over horizontal supports. These forms have been interpreted as anything from uteruses or phalluses to architectural structures, but Motherwell himself described them as the testicles of a dead bull in the ring, exhibited to the view of all. The cycle of life and death is indeed what underlies this particular composition.

The palette is limited to black, so that there is a strong contrast between the painted and the unpainted zones. The massive forms, attracted to the right by a zone saturated with black, contrast with the lightness and swiftness of the artist's gesture whose spontaneity, paradoxically rehearsed and somewhat attenuated by repetition (the first *Elegies* date to 1948), is betrayed by the splashes. Motherwell was constantly striving for a balance between accident and control, between emotion and self-mastery, between fluidity and structure. [LSCH]

140

Francine Simonin (Lausanne, 1936)
Composition, 1978
Acrylic and Indian ink on paper, 120 × 157 cm
Acquisition, 1978. Inv. 1978-106

Francine Simonin works in painting, drawing and engraving. Her physical approach to her art differs according to the medium, but always displays the same sheer power. She enrolled at the Lausanne School of Fine Arts in 1953, at which point her drawings were inspired by her reading, already with a particular interest in unusual female forms. The power of her interaction with the medium made her work increasingly hard to read as figurative art. Some silhouettes appear clearly in outline and some places are hinted at: Lake Geneva, for instance, is recognisable by its blue ripples. In most cases, however, Simonin's numerous references are clear only from her titles. Landscapes, cityscapes, bodies, works of art, literature and music are her favourite subjects, all assimilated in one great sweep of creativity. She has stated that she depicts them without striving for photographic accuracy.

A great admirer of abstract expressionists, particularly Jackson Pollock and Willem de Kooning, Simonin paints on a flat surface and prefers to use paper, which is less costly than canvas and allows her to experiment and paint without worrying about the result. She works with brushes, her hands and fingers, and rags, always with the same determination. The energy of each new work covers the surface of the paper (in this case two sheets mounted together) with a deep, inner current that flows from her own moving body. This composition's sense of teeming abundance stems from the accumulation of marks on the paper. The first lines providing the work's broad structure have been buried under successive layers. *Composition* is an interplay of colour applications with no sense of cohesion that are nonetheless in dialogue with each other. What counts for Simonin is that once the painting is placed upright, it should express her urge to transmit the energy she felt at the moment of creation. [LSCH]

141

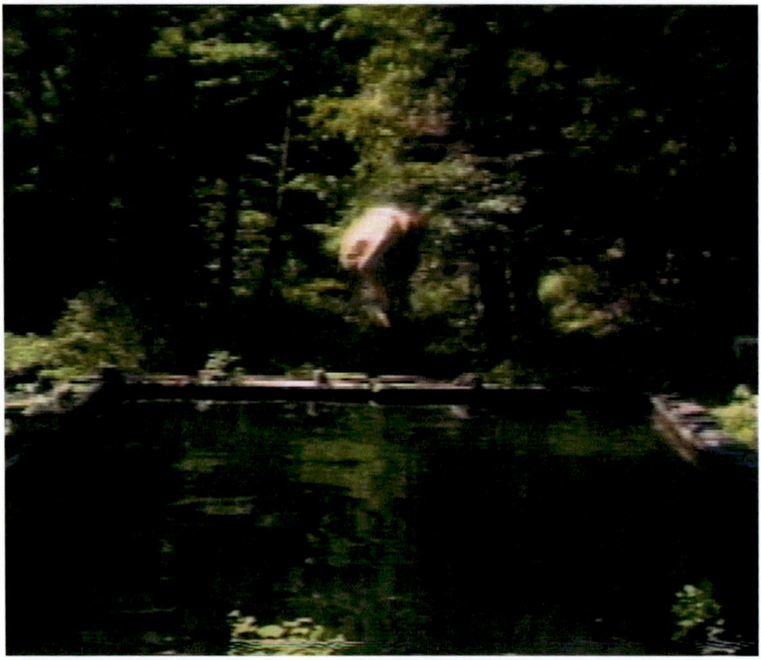

142

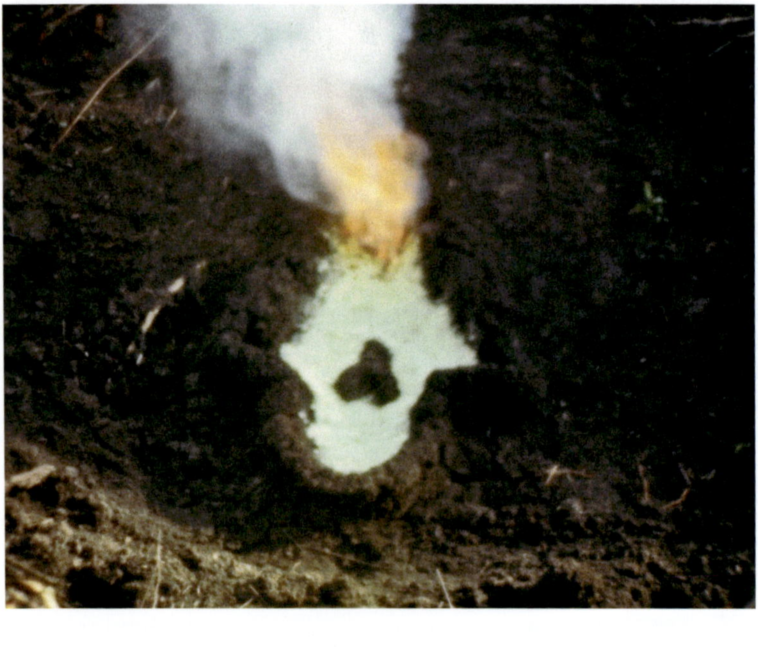

Bill Viola, The Reflecting Pool, 1977–9
Ana Mendieta, Fundamento Palo Monte: Silueta Series (Gunpowder Works), 1980

141

Bill Viola (New York, 1951)
The Reflecting Pool (from *The Reflecting Pool – Collected Work 1977–80*), 1977–9
Video, colour, sound, 7 min
Acquisition, 1993. Inv. 1993-018

Viola is among those artists who have most powerfully influenced the development of video art since the late 1970s. Trained at Syracuse University in New York State, he first exhibited his video work in 1972, in the United States. Two years later he had an installation in the show *Action Film Vidéo* organised by the Impact group in Lausanne. Here he forged links with actors in the local scene, including Jean Otth.

The Reflecting Pool belongs in a series of five independent fragments which, taken together, describe the stages in a personal journey using images of transition – day to night, movement to fixity, time to timelessness. In these works Viola also explores the possibilities for special effects afforded by magnetic tape. We see a man come out of the woods and take up position beside the pool at the centre of the image. His body is reflected in the water. Suddenly, he leaps up and his body stops in mid-air, like a freeze-frame. Meanwhile, the other elements in the image continue to move normally (the branches, the water, forest noises). Interviewed by Raymond Bellour in 1986, the artist said of this work that, 'The image is fragmented into three distinct levels of time (real time, suspended time, time lapse) and reconstructed in such a way that it looks like an image in a single space. ... It really is like sculpting time.'

In addition to the way video makes it possible to bring together several temporalities, the symbolic dimension of the relation between man and water is also at the centre of this piece. Indeed, water is omnipresent in Viola's work, where it signifies different states of consciousness (dream, waking) but also different stages leading from birth to death, from amniotic fluid to baptismal water or even the apocalyptic waters of the flood. [NS]

142

Ana Mendieta (Havana, 1948–New York, 1985)
Fundamento Palo Monte: Silueta Series (Gunpowder Works), 1980
Super-8 film transferred to high-definition digital support, colour, silent, 5 min 56 sec, ed. 4/6
Acquisition, 2013. Inv. 2013-078

Created mainly outdoors (on the US East Coast, in Iowa, Indiana, Canada, Mexico and Cuba), the works of Ana Mendieta are all about the relation to the earth, the body and time. The artist was exiled from her native Cuba at a young age and brought up far from her parents in Iowa. In the course of her short career this double heritage helped her produce work that stands at the intersection of conceptual art, land art and performance art, while showing a marked interest in pre-Columbian cultures and prehistoric art.

Fundamento Palo Monte belongs to the *Siluetas*, a series of ephemeral works that the artist made between 1973 and 1981 and then recorded on film or in photographs. In the first *Siluetas*, the artist's body is still visible, while in later works only traces remain. Mendieta imprinted her body into the earth to create forms that recall stylised Neolithic statuary but also, by the material used, arte povera. Whether temporarily occupied by the artist's body, filled with organic materials like blood or ashes, or in a state of combustion, these *Siluetas* set up a dialectic between presence and absence, plenitude and lack, past and present.

Made in Iowa, *Fundamento Palo Monte* shows a form hollowed from the ground and filled with white gunpowder, with three stones in the position of the heart. The fire consumes the silhouette from the base to the head. At times, the flames and thick white smoke obscure the form in the ground, which then reappears through the thinning wisps of smoke as the powder burns out. What remains is the charred figure, the work of earth, fire and air. The time of combustion and the time of the film are one. [NS]

143

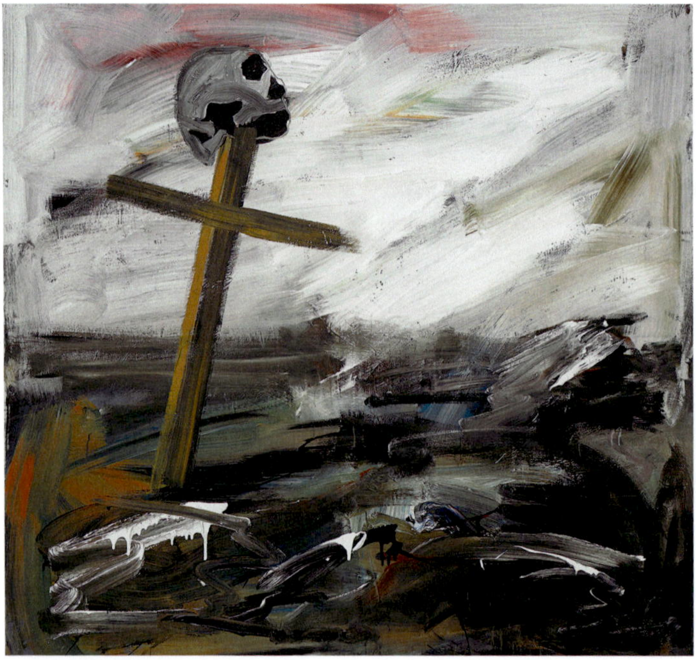

144

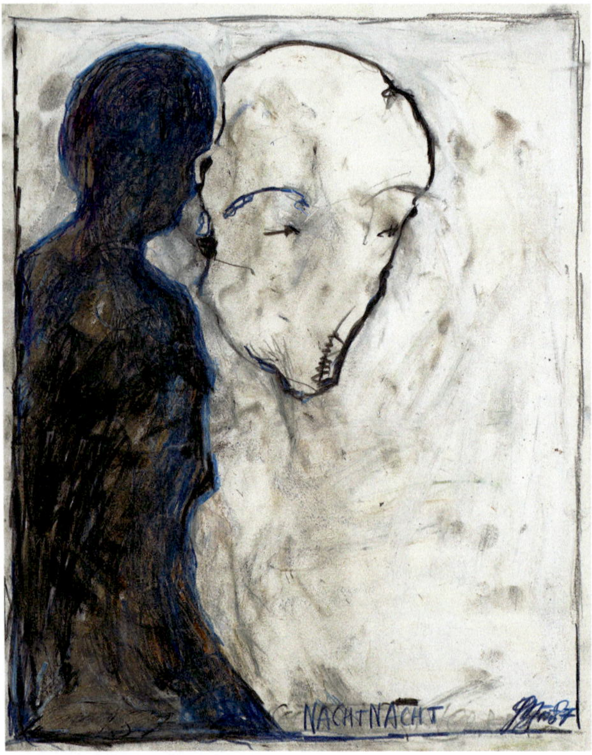

Albert Oehlen, Ohne Titel, 1981
Günter Brus, Nachtnacht, 1987

143

Albert Oehlen (Krefeld, 1954)
Ohne Titel (*Untitled*), 1981
Acrylic on canvas, 150 × 160 cm
Acquisition 2004. Inv. 2004-066

Having trained at the Hamburg Hochschule für bildende Künste in the late 1970s, Albert Oehlen is part of the generation of artists who have focused on painting and its potential for criticism as a reaction against minimalist and conceptual art. In 1981, when he produced this painting, he had his first solo exhibition and initiated his collaboration with Martin Kippenberger and Werner Büttner.

Ohne Titel thus dates from the very beginning of the artist's career, and as such is deeply influenced by the brushwork of the Neue Wilde (New Fauves), typified by a powerful sense of expression and a return to figurative art. For Oehlen, however, the key question was how to keep contemporary painting beyond the boundaries of conformism, as indicated by the title of his first canvas, *Gegen den Liberalismus* (*Against Liberalism*, 1980, private collection). He rejects the notion of pictorial virtuosity, both in brushwork and composition. Yet the work's expressive aura and its perfectly balanced composition, falling neatly into two halves – dark at the bottom and pale at the top – simply punctuated by two iconographic elements with powerful connotations, the cross and the skull, make it tempting to suggest that Oehlen is a virtuoso master of anti-virtuoso paintings. The ample application of thick paint, to the point that in places it has dripped, in shades from white to black via a whole palette of dark, 'dirty' colours, mean *Ohne Titel* can be read as the young Oehlen's manifesto: as he stated in 1991, 'The aim of our stage at that point was to torture painting with motifs that were as striking as possible, and above all burdened with associations, to leave technical constraints behind'. While the cross and the skull refer both to the history of painting and of Germany itself, the key issue at stake is the relationship to the very materiality of painting, probing the conditions for its potential survival. [NS]

144

Günter Brus (Ardning, 1938)
Nachtnacht (*Nightnight*), 1987
Coloured pencil and wax crayon on paper, 39.6 × 32 cm
Acquisition, 1988. Inv. 1988-008

Günter Brus is a representative of Viennese actionism, alongside artists such as Otto Muehl and Hermann Nitsch. This movement, which developed in the 1960s, was characterised by the violence of the actions performed by its protagonists in reaction to the conservatism of Austrian society. Like the Austrian expressionists Oskar Kokoschka and Egon Schiele before them, the actionists sought to liberate human beings of their taboos, such as sexuality, and to reveal the drives whose repression, they argued, had led to fascism.

Brus put on performances in which his own body was tormented. The images of Jackson Pollock's intense involvement in the creative process, standing over his canvas with his brush in one hand and a pot of paint in the other, inspired him to want to recreate the same tension in his own pictorial practice, but by limiting his expressive resources to his own body: if art is energy, then it can be reduced to an action. Initially a support for painting, Brus's body was later exhibited naked, mutilated, or spattered with its secretions, in performances denouncing societal norms by the disgust that they provoke.

Brus went back to drawing in the early 1980s. This work refers to the censorship suffered by the Viennese actionists, who were regularly arrested by the police. The artist, identified by his profile and bare skull, shows himself with his mouth sealed, as if no longer allowed to express himself. His figure is preceded by a silhouette in the half-light, referring to the double 'Nacht' (night) of the title. The energetically drawn image shows emphatic and lively pencil strokes, while the wax crayon marks give it a somewhat gestural look, in a literal expression of the unhampered forces of the unconscious. [LSCH]

145

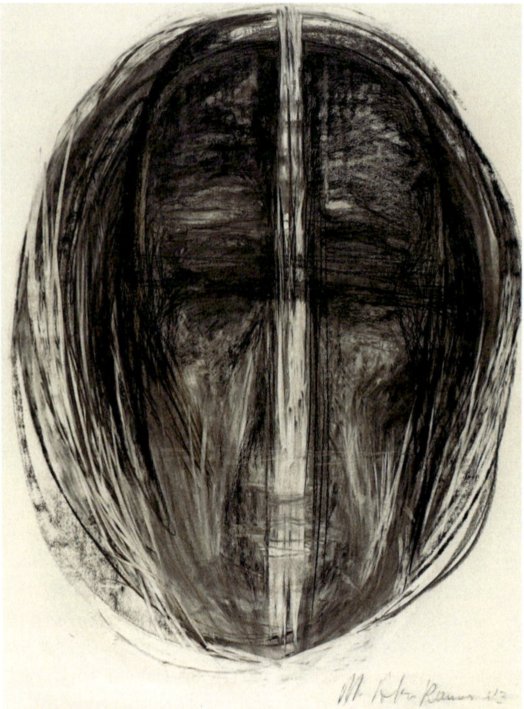

146

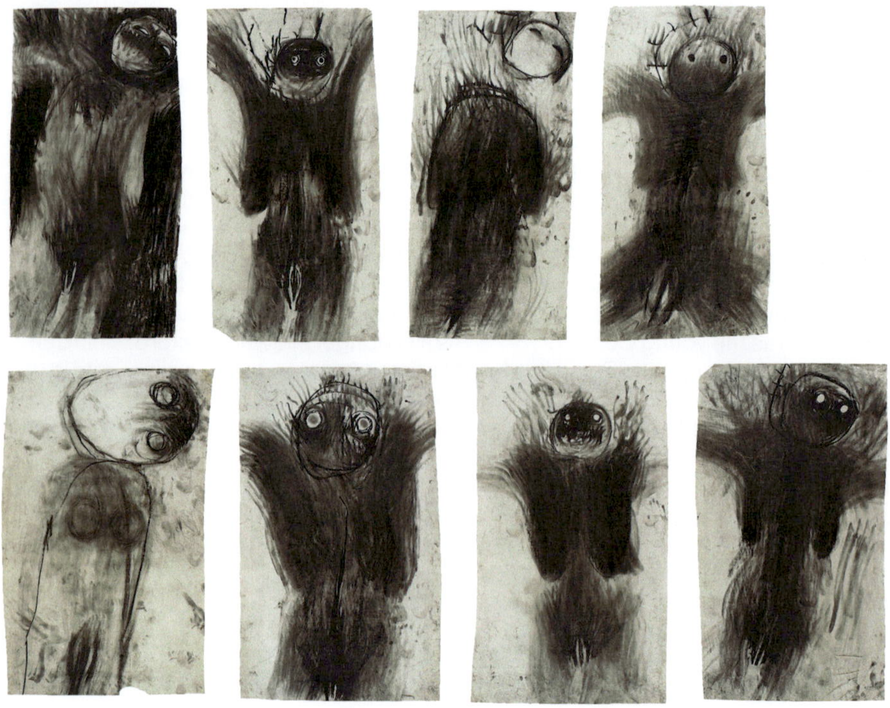

Magdalena Abakanowicz, Tête, 1983
Miriam Cahn, das klassische lieben – femmes, 1981

145

Magdalena Abakanowicz (Falenty, 1930–Warsaw, 2017)
Tête (*Head*), 1983
Charcoal and stumping on paper, 100 × 75 cm
Acquisition, 1986. Inv. 1986-042

Exhibited at several editions of the Lausanne Tapestry Biennal organised at the Museum between 1962 and 1995, Abakanowicz's woven works, the *Abakan*s (1966–75), shown hanging in space, made a powerful impact on the public. The *Têtes* series, which she made using charcoal and lithography in the early 1980s, in some ways recalls the form of the simplest *Abakans.* These faces split down the centre display both flatness and volume. This dual effect is produced, in part, by the curve of the expansively drawn head and partly by the face itself, rendered in short, multidirectional strokes. Abakanowicz allows two states of drawing to coexist: the working drawing and the illusion of three-dimensional form that gradually emerges.

Each of these big faces is structured around a cross whose horizontal axis locates the level of the eyes and whose vertical axis marks the place of the nose, and the zone between the arches of the eyebrows. Abakanowicz drew with the support laid flat on the floor. Her work explores the range of effects of charcoal. In certain areas, she works with the tip of the rod, leaving dense black marks; at others, she stumps them. She also makes the most of the width of the charcoal that she rubs on; the pulverulent material then attaches to the grain of the paper and reveals its structure. Finally, the artist takes advantage of the fact that the charcoal is easily removed because of its weak adhesion to the support, using an eraser to open up luminous interstices or accentuate the relief of the face.

Eyes closed and mouth silent, this *Tête* seems immersed in silence. The attitude of withdrawal, like the suggested thinness of the face, reach out to the viewer and create a feeling of empathy. Of Polish origin, Abakanowicz was marked by the horrors of the Second World War. Body fragments that are like concentrates of introspection, her *Têtes* remind us of the interiorised suffering of human beings inhabited by tragedy while evoking the image of a deceased person wrapped in a shroud. [LSCH]

146

Miriam Cahn (Basel, 1949)
das klassische lieben – femmes (*classic love – women*), 1981
Series of eight drawings in charcoal and coal on tracing paper, from 136×170 cm to 157×110 cm
Acquisition, 1983. Inv. 1983-030

For Miriam Cahn, the body is more than just a tool; it is also her subject. It makes perfect sense to her to depict the body that enables her to create. She produces art from her own inner being, as though her body were an echo chamber for various memories and experiences that are purged through creativity. The physical effort involved in producing her works goes hand in hand with the subjective perspective she postulates.

das klassische lieben is a major creative cycle in which Cahn pitilessly scrutinises her parents' relationship and how they handled gender roles. Her various sets of drawings depict nudes in simplified form, with no individual characteristics other than clear sexual dimorphism. She conveys heterosexual relationships, describing them with a hint of irony as 'classic love', denouncing their social and normative construction. The large drawings on tracing paper were produced on the floor. Displayed vertically and heightwise on a wall, they turn the gaze of the female figures outward to the viewer, calling on us as witness to a dazzlingly aggressive private moment, as if readying to launch themselves at us.

In the set of eight drawings entitled *das klassische lieben – femmes*, the principle remains the same but the effect is different. Cahn places us beneath the bodies, making us the partner they have collapsed onto. Her women have no waistline or hair. Their arms and legs are barely sketched in. They lose their outline because they are experienced inwardly. Only their breasts and genitals are marked, sometimes outrageously so as in this case, proclaiming their gender identity. The marks left by the artist's fingers generate a spectral tremor. Her hands become those of the women she depicts, who are both individuals in their own right and representatives of womanhood in general. [LSCH]

147

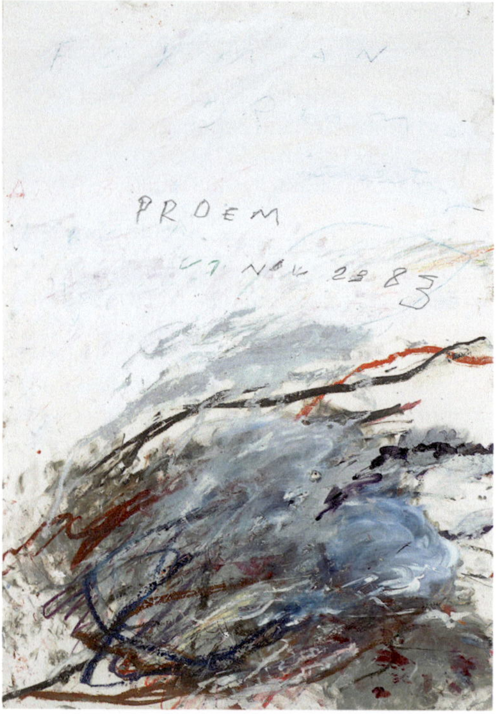

148

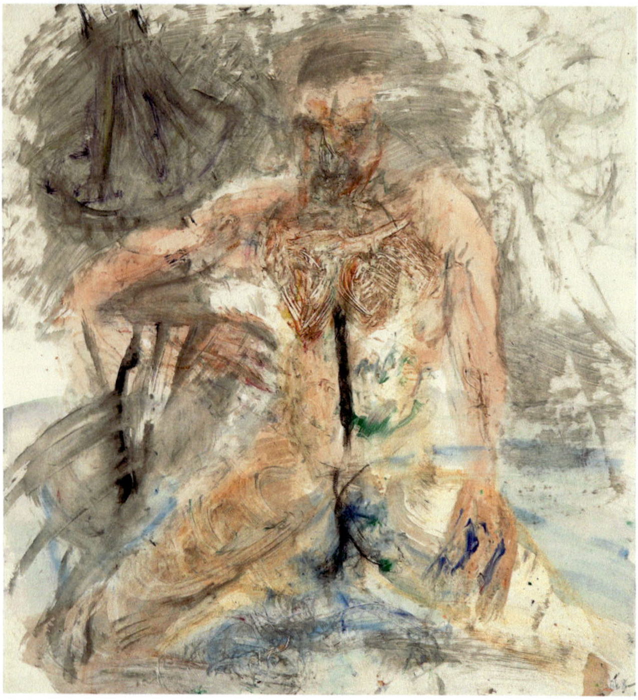

Cy Twombly, Proem, 1983
Martin Disler, Ohne Titel, 1986

147

Cy Twombly (Lexington, 1928–Rome, 2011)
Proem, 1983
Oil, crayon and pencil on paper, 100 × 70 cm
Alain and Suzanne Dubois Collection. Promised gift

Cy Twombly's work draws on a deep well of scholarship. The artist displayed boundless intellectual curiosity from a very young age. In 1952 he travelled across Europe and North Africa with Robert Rauschenberg. He visited Rome and came back to live there five years later, but regularly returned to the United States. His paintings and drawings are influenced by contemporary abstract expressionism, although he was a marginal figure in the movement: while he eschewed figurative art like other artists in the same school, he did introduce depth of field into his works.

Proem results from the same creative force and makes use of the same visual language as much of Twombly's work: eruptive intensity, marks that seem to mimic writing, and interference between drawn elements and verbal fragments. Each work offers a synthesis of the artist's own memory, knowledge, and experiences, transformed into emotional energy.

This drawing was produced in Rome. The date, 23 November 1983, and the title, taken from an 1847 poem by John Greenleaf Whittier that is a vibrant ode to nature, float over the centre of the sheet. The information, presumably added at the end of the creative process, are rare instances of explicit detail in Twombly's oeuvre, while also forming part of the work itself. The way they are written suggests they emanate as much from the cloud above which they hover as from the background spattered with words, for instance 'F O R M I A N D R E A M S', that are largely illegible, having been covered with white oil paint. The composition thus feels balanced between the pared-down upper part and the dense, frenetic lower part. Twombly organises controlled chaos that can also be seen in the black and brown lines that run off to the right, smudged by the brush. [LSCH]

148

Martin Disler (Seewen, 1949–Geneva, 1996)
Ohne Titel (*Untitled*), 1986
Acrylic and watercolour on paper, 167 × 156.5 cm
Acquisition, 1987. Inv. 1987-027

Although Martin Disler was never part of the Neue Wilde (New Fauves), his work has often been linked with this movement because of the closeness of his concerns and similarity of his engagement. This group of artists, which emerged in a number of German and Austrian cities in the early 1980s, contributed to the renewal of figuration that had begun in the previous decade. Affirming the expression of subjectivity in art, they invented a raw, free and fiery form of painting, capable of expressing the themes of the body and sexuality with a very personal truthfulness. In Switzerland, Disler adopted the same approach.

His paintings are the fruit of an introspective process which leads him to exhume images that are buried deep within. Emotions, often violent ones, clash in these swiftly executed works. The intensity they exude is due to their imposing formats and saturated surfaces and, even more, the power of the artist's gesture. The subject of the composition is not immediately legible. As here, abundant traces of paint teem on the surface of the paper. This chaotic profusion gradually gives way to the images of an immense, hostile-looking naked figure, reminiscent of Willem de Kooning's *Woman* paintings. But Disler does not represent a subject; he conveys an inner agitation, an emotional state.

Legs apart, the folded right arm resting on the hips, and the left hand resting on a thigh, this figure, which is sometimes read as the artist's self-portrait, is on his knees, in an offensive position. The body, which occupies most of the centre of the work, is at once evanescent and solid, a diffuse island of flesh. The artist paints energetically, using different tools (brushes, knives, fingers) and scrapes the acrylic in certain areas. The pictorial surface thus bears the marks of Disler's passionate élan in the heat of creation. [LSCH]

149

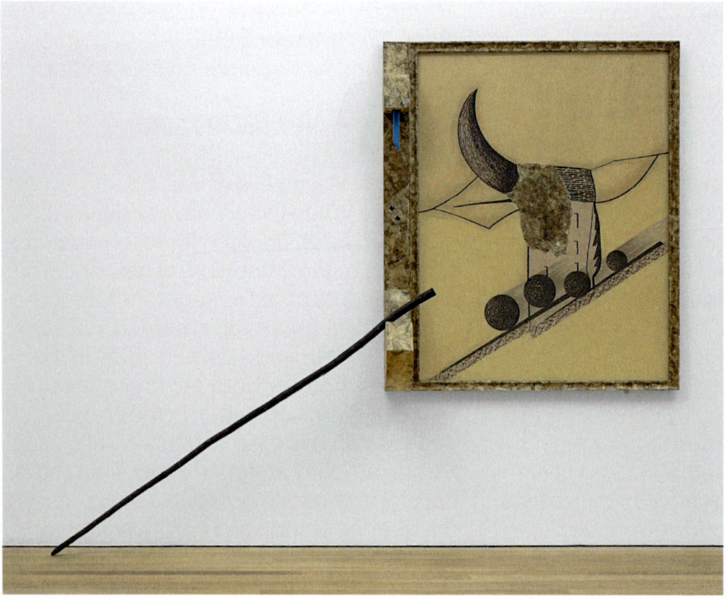

150

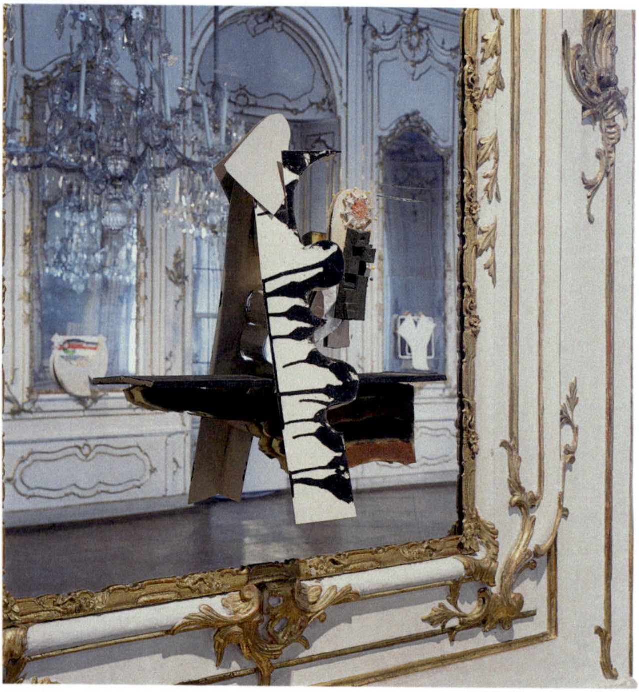

Flavio Paolucci, Peinture objet, 1983
Richard Tuttle, The Baroque and Color VII, 1986–7

149

Flavio Paolucci (Torre, 1934)
Peinture objet (*Painting Object*), 1983
Wood, paper, paint, collage and charcoal, 235 × 360 × 50 cm
Acquisition, 1987. Inv. 1987-012

Having studied at various schools and studios in Lugano, Locarno and Milan from 1949 to 1957, Flavio Paolucci was influenced early in his career by Parisian tachism and neo-dadaism, then briefly by pop art. His first encounter with the Moroccan desert in 1964 also had a profound impact on him. In this first period, he already showed an interest in the relationship between man and nature. This meditation is a constant thread throughout his work: he has developed a more abstract language in which leaves, branches and stones evoke the fragile equilibrium of the living world.

In around 1973–4, Paolucci began to use plant matter such as branches in his art. *Innesto* (*Graft*, 1974), created in a forest near Biasca, was a turning point in his career. He placed scions in an ash tree cut down to one metre off the ground, attributing the concept of grafting central significance in his art. At this point, he was on the fringes of the arte povera movement, alongside figures such as Giuseppe Penone, who was also keenly interested in the relationship between man and the living world.

Peinture objet is typical of Paolucci's work in the 1980s. It combines drawn or manufactured elements with natural objects that are sometimes found or altered in some rudimentary fashion, particularly by the addition of colour. The stick resting on a wooden shape protruding from the frame is placed parallel to the wall, echoing the diagonal in the main drawing. A house – another of Paolucci's recurrent motifs – is decorated with shapes reminiscent of horns and leaves. It is partly hidden behind a scrap of paper mimicking rock, while four spheres rush down the slope, their speed suggested by charcoal traces. *Peinture objet* presents a broad range of potential relationships between nature and culture, reality and artificiality. [LSCH]

150

Richard Tuttle (Rahway, 1941)
The Baroque and Color VII, 1986–7
Cardboard, wood, foam, aluminium and adhesive on graph paper, 74 × 74 × 16 cm
Acquisition, 1989. Inv. 1989-014

Although often associated with the post-minimalist tendency, Richard Tuttle is in fact one of the most disconcerting and hard to pin-down American artists of the last fifty years. He 'tinkers' with poor materials such as wood, paper, wire, synthetic foam and fragments of sheet metal, fabric or plastic. His drawings and collages are like experimental sketches rather than finished objects. They are works in process that avoid any kind of insistence or conventional aesthetics.

The *Baroque and Color* series reflects the reviving interest in the Baroque on the part of artists like Frank Stella and thinkers like Gilles Deleuze that took place after the mid-1980s. The references behind this sculpture-assemblage are Kazimir Malevich's *Suprematist Composition: White on White* (1918, New York, Museum of Modern Art) and the reliefs of Ivan Puni. The work was originally part of an installation made for the baroque Spiegelsaal at the Neue Galerie in Graz, where it was positioned opposite a mirror. It became an autonomous piece when Tuttle decided to duct tape it onto a sheet of paper.

The square piece of graph paper to which the relief is now attached recalls the works of Agnes Martin, a close friend of Tuttle's. It also constitutes the base or plane of the compositions against which the pieces that look like the negative form of the body and head and pegs of a violin now stand out. That instrument is a complex assemblage of pieces made from noble materials; in Tuttle's hands it becomes an extremely precarious piece of bricolage, held together only by adhesive tape, a few nails and pins. This is his take on the great cubist adventure of deconstructing the motif. [BF]

151

○

152

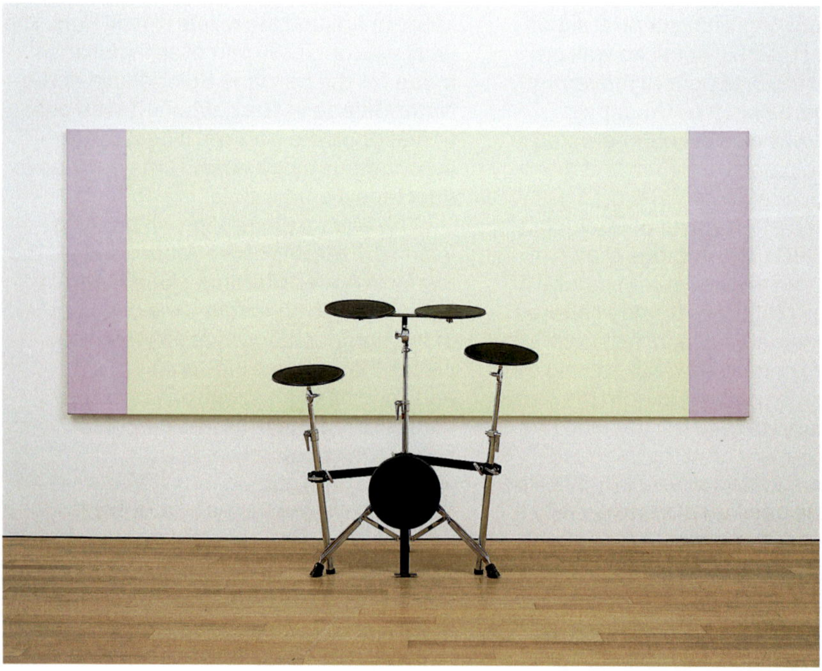

Olivier Mosset, Sans titre, 1975
John M Armleder, Furniture Sculpture 189, 1988

151

Olivier Mosset (Bern, 1944)
Sans titre (*Untitled*), 1975
Acrylic on canvas, 300×300 cm
Acquisition, 2006. Inv. 2003-017

Between 1966 and 1972, Olivier Mosset painted some two hundred white canvases measuring a metre square, with a black circle of unvarying diameter at their center – targets or 'O's. These followed his earlier canvases featuring the letter 'A'. He had moved to Paris in 1965 and worked for Jean Tinguely and Daniel Spoerri. Above all, he later met there the painters Daniel Buren, Michel Parmentier and Niele Toroni, with whom he would form the short-lived group BMPT, its name the acronym of their surnames. Their painting positioned itself in a dialogue with the history of abstract art while at the same time critiquing pure painting. As Mosset put it in an interview with Christophe Cherix and Lionel Bovier in 2003, 'I considered my painting a critique of the market and of the uniqueness of the art object, and a critique, as well, of sensitive and expressionist aspects of the painting of that period. I found similar preoccupations in the works of my fellow comrades BPT. ... We were trying to develop an artistic practice with a more political approach.'

The painting kept at the Museum cannot really be included in the series of two hundred targets because, while the dimensions of the circle are the same, the canvas itself measures 300×300 cm, and by 1975 Mosset was already in his third year of making the vertical stripe paintings that he had 'borrowed' from Buren. However, when gallerist Gerald Piltzer asked him to produce a canvas for his Parisian apartment, the artist decided to make one last black circle and chose a monumental format with his mind on the position planned for it by the collector. Here, he considered not only that the size of the circle was independent of the surface on which it was painted, but judged, retrospectively, that it was this painting in particular, combined with his interest in American painting of the 1950s, that made him decide to work with the larger formats that would henceforth characterise his practice. [NS]

152

John M Armleder (Geneva, 1948)
Furniture Sculpture 189, 1988
Acrylic on canvas and silent drum kit, 110×270 cm (canvas), 91×86×66 cm (drum kit)
Acquisition, 2018. Inv. 2018-019

In 1969, John M Armleder organised his first public event, the Ecart Happening Festival, in Geneva. This marked the creation of the Ecart group, part of the broader Fluxus movement. Armleder continued to hold happenings and musical performances, similar in mood to those of George Brecht and John Cage, until the early 1980s. In 1979, he painted his first gouache on a chair, later titling the piece *Furniture Sculpture 1*, heralding a corpus of works typical of his artistic output in the 1980s, combining abstract painting and items of furniture or objects.

Furniture Sculpture 189 is a quasi-symmetrical composition consisting of a silent drum kit standing in front of a horizontal yellow canvas with two strips of mauve at each end, hung very low, so that the drums share the same visual space. The drum kit's upper pads form black circles that stand out against the yellow background, forming a composition that echoes the dot paintings that Armleder was producing parallel to the *Furniture Sculptures*, the circle motif harking back to both historical avant-garde artists and pop culture.

If other *Furniture Sculptures* similarly stage instruments, such as cymbals, horns and a cello, the title of the series itself is a nod to its musical genealogy. Indeed, the *Furniture Sculptures* echo Erik Satie's experiments in *Furniture Music* from 1917 on. This was music designed to create a mood rather than be listened to: as Satie himself wrote, it 'claims to contribute to life in the same way as a private conversation, a painting in the gallery or the seat one is, or is not, sitting on'. While the *Furniture Sculptures* may be read by analogy as installations contributing to an 'art of ambiance', the use of a silent drum kit in *Furniture Sculpture 189* also gestures to Cage, a major influence on Armleder's performances. The work is thus an assemblage of abstract painting and drum kit, holding the potential for infinite scores of musical silence. [NS]

153

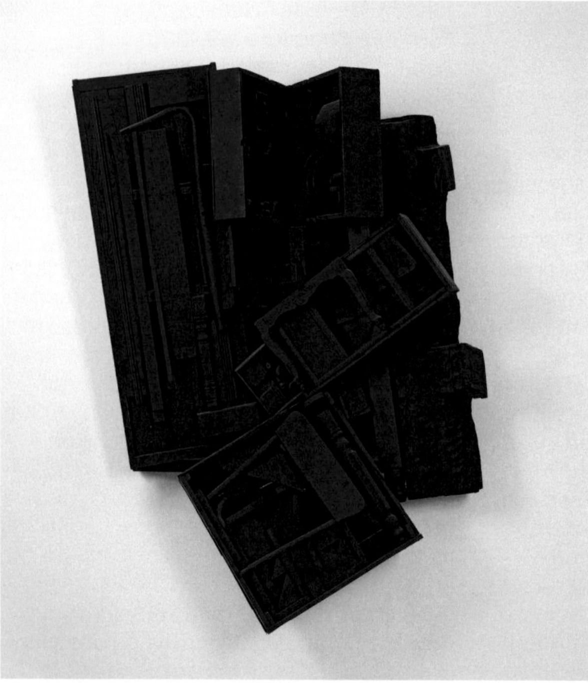

154

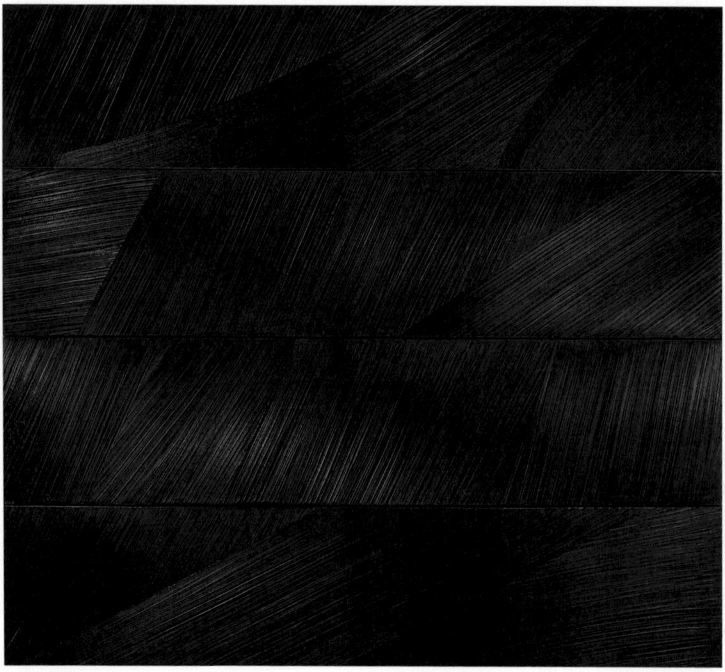

Louise Nevelson, Mirror Shadow XV, 1985
Pierre Soulages, Peinture 324 × 362 cm (Polyptyque J), 1987

153

Louise Nevelson (Pereiaslav-Khmelnytskyi, 1899–New York, 1988)
Mirror Shadow XV, 1985
Wood and black paint, 223 × 134 × 71 cm
Alice Pauli Donation, 2019. Inv. 2019-254

Louise Nevelson was born Leah Berliawsky to a Jewish family in what was then the Russian Empire, now Ukraine. She emigrated to Maine, in the United States, with her mother, sister and brother in 1905 to join her father, who worked in the timber industry, first as a lumberjack; his own father had been in the timber trade. Wood became Louise Nevelson's main creative material, though she also worked in other media including steel, aluminium and Plexiglas. She left for New York in 1920, where she studied art and theatre.

Influenced by Pablo Picasso, Marcel Duchamp and pre-Columbian architecture, Nevelson spent several years producing and exhibiting her early works, developing a form of mural sculpture whose structure consisted of assembled found objects, painted black, gold or white. The 1950s saw her create carefully-arranged large-scale compositions consisting of montages of wooden crates that in turn contained carefully-arranged objects. She often let herself be guided by the objects available to her, organising them and nailing them together. On the same principle, she also designed 'walls' that were perfectly rectangular in shape. *Mirror Shadow XV* is part of a series of the same name, dating from a few years before her death. It differs from her earlier work in that it is more compact, dynamic and voluminous. The objects are juxtaposed, bringing together multidirectional lines in their key elements and entering three-dimensional space.

The use of a single colour subordinates the details to the overall shape. The neutral colour gives no further information, and the elements, stripped of their individuality and function, lean towards abstraction. As the artist told Diana MacKown, 'When I fell in love with black, it contained all colour. It wasn't a negation of colour. It was an acceptance. Because black encompasses all colours. Black is the most aristocratic colour of all.' [LSCH]

154

Pierre Soulages (Rodez, 1919)
Peinture 324 × 362 cm (Polyptyque J)
(*Painting 324 × 362 cm [Polyptych J]*), 1987
Oil on canvas, 324 × 362 cm
Gift of Pierre Soulages in memory of Olivier Pauli, 2017. Inv. 1999-063

Following a period of dark shapes standing out against pale backgrounds, Pierre Soulages's work became increasingly dominated by black, creating powerful contrasts. In a 1990 interview with Olivier Pauli, he recalled, 'One day in 1979, I was painting when the colour black took over the canvas. It struck me that there was no way out, no hope.' Soulages then began a series of black canvases in which the surface is painted with various textures, reflecting the light. He invented black as a carrier for light, naming it 'Outrenoir' (Beyond Black). In 1996 he defined the concept to Pierre Encrevé as 'Outrenoir means beyond black, light reflected and transmuted by black. Outrenoir is black that, stopping being black, starts emitting clarity and secret light. Outrenoir is a mental field other than plain black.'

The surface textures are formed by the brush striating the paint in uneven strokes or by a blade spreading and smoothing it. Each texture draws and reflects the light in its own way, causing it to bounce off the surface at a multitude of different angles. By creating an interplay of blackness and light, laying the paint on the canvas so that it is thin or thick, smooth or rough, matte or shiny, Soulages keeps monochrome at a distance.

In the early 1980s, Soulages extended the same approach to monumental formats, increasingly producing his work in the form of polyptychs with several panels joined together. This allowed him to introduce a new discontinuity in the paint from panel to panel, triggering further vibrations by complicating the interplay of vertical and slanting lines. In *Peinture 324 × 362 cm (Polyptyque J)*, the combination of an almost square format consisting of four panels joined lengthwise draws the viewer's gaze both horizontally, from panel to panel, and vertically, to take in the work in one sweep. [BF]

155

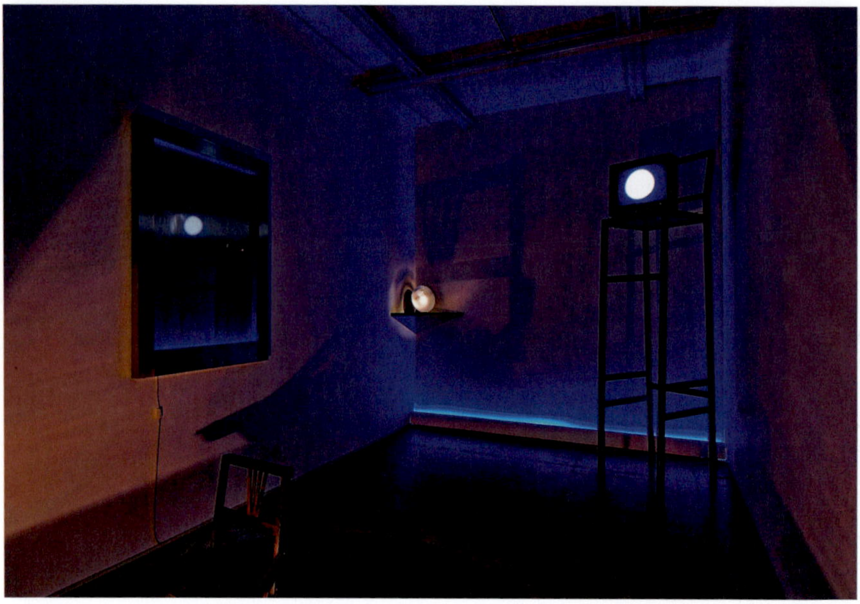

156

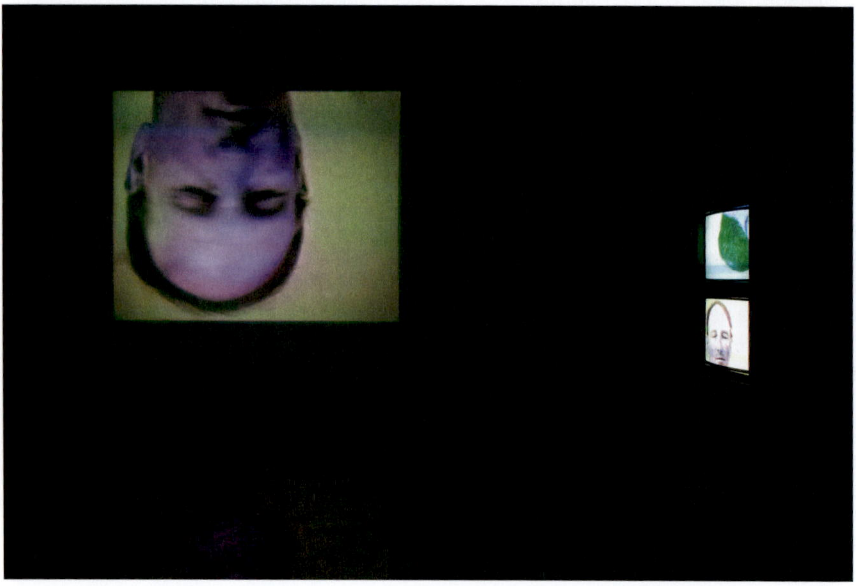

Silvie and Chérif Defraoui, La nuit, les chambres sont plus grandes, 1987
Bruce Nauman, Raw Material 'MMMM', 1990

155

Silvie and Chérif Defraoui (Sankt Gallen, 1935 and Geneva, 1932–Vufflens-le-Château, 1994)
La nuit, les chambres sont plus grandes (*At Night, Bedrooms Are Bigger*), 1987
1 video on monitor, 1 window, various objects, dimensions variable
Acquisition, 2017. Inv. 2017-028

In 1975, after respective careers in the visual arts (for her) and in writing and cultural criticism (for him, after training as a historian), Silvie and Chérif Defraoui decided that they would henceforth work together. Under the general title *Archives du futur*, they reflected on the image, on its role, value, degree of reality and power, and on its relation to time and memory, asking how we still manage to *see* when we are assailed by so many images that not only accumulate but also proliferate thanks to the various media channels. Video and installation, two mediums that in those days were still relatively new, enabled them to better capture the life of images and their continual metamorphoses.

La nuit, les chambres sont plus grandes explores the memory of a bedroom enveloped in a nocturnal atmosphere. This silent, recreated room is bathed in a blue penumbra and only lit by a ray of light that suggests a door left ajar. Combined with this disorienting evocation are objects that simultaneously construct and deconstruct the fiction of the image. In the corner of the room, a china plate echoes the perfectly round and white moon that appears on a screen, placed atop a chair with abnormally long legs – as if to situate it, just as artificially, in the sky – and is reflected in the window. The dimensions of the chair more or less correspond to the cast shadow of the folding child's chair that is placed on a round, black rubber carpet, in front of a crystal ball, one of its feet resting on a small metal panther. Everything in this installation is illusory. Each object is reflected several times, in different materials and with different proportions. If, at first glance, this vision appears familiar, nothing in it seems normal. The bedroom is the place of the imaginary, where everything is dreamed, where reality grows distorted and images suffuse the unconscious. [LSCH]

156

Bruce Nauman (Fort Wayne, 1941)
Raw Material 'MMMM', 1990
2 videos for monitors and 1 projection, colour, sound, 24 min 50 sec
Acquisition, 1992. Inv. 1992-115

Raw Material 'MMMM' is part of a series of six video installations in which Bruce Nauman combines the movement of the body and vocal exercises. A projection and two monitors, one atop the other, show the artist's head slowly spinning, now upside down, now the right way up, in changing colours of blue, green and yellow, while emitting a piercing murmur (Nauman was filmed by a fixed camera turning in a spinning chair). This series sees the artist returning as the main protagonist of his video works after the filmed performances of the late 1960s. He is at once artist and material, perceiver and perceived, manipulating his own body in order to transform personal subjectivity into an objective demonstration. The motif of the suspended head spinning like a mad top also recalls the wax head sculptures made by the artist in the 1980s and his *Carrousels* of animal sculptures turning mechanically in an endless round.

Following on from Nauman's researches into the questions of the body as sculpture, of sculpture as defining space, and of the video device as modifying our spatial perception, *Raw Material 'MMMM'* plays insistently on the sound element that, since then, has become preponderant in his work. Pulled into the space of the installation, viewers are made almost dizzy by the endlessly repeated action and sound, in a blind face-to-face made even more complex by the multiplication of the image. The decisive material here is indeed the one signalled by the title of the installation – 'MMMM', a sound that is not music nor yet speech, a sound that refuses to communicate anything more than its own space of utterance.

In 2004, when he was invited to make a work for the Turbine Hall at Tate Modern, London, Nauman reprised the sound from this video, along with that of twenty-one other works, to make a vast installation, *Raw Materials*, in which sound, but also the bodies of the viewers moving around the space from one aural source to another, constituted a sculpture. [NS]

157

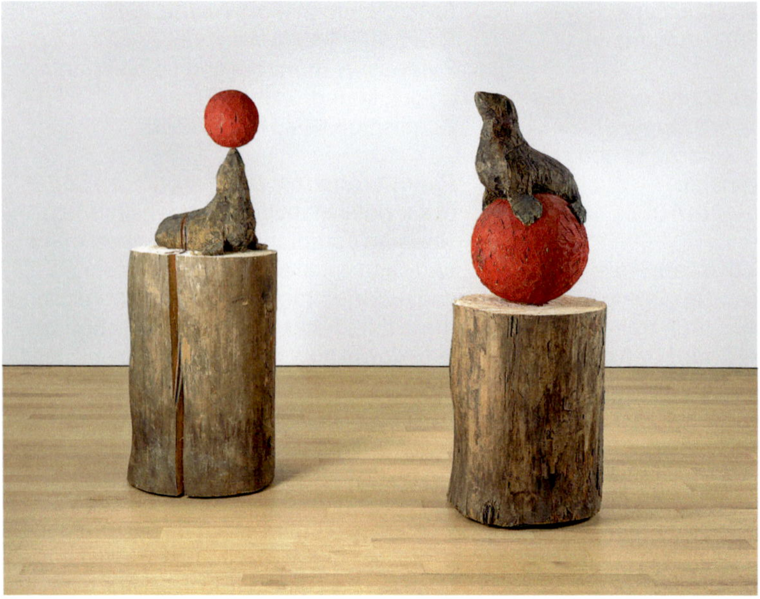

158

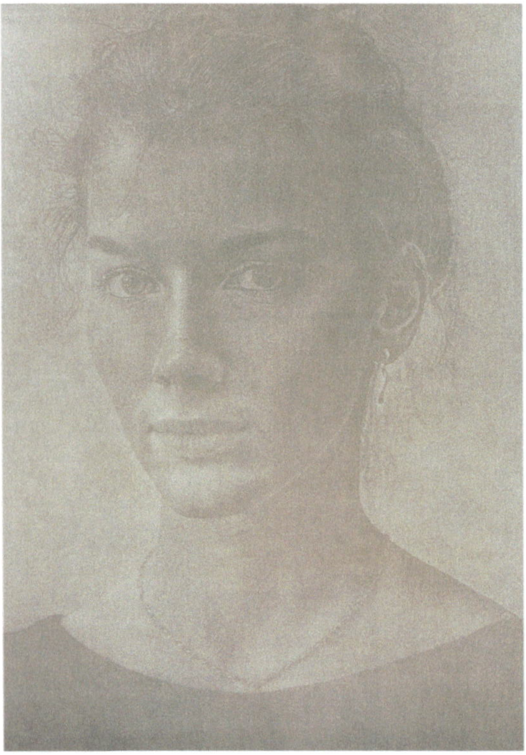

Stephan Balkenhol, Phoque I and Phoque II, 1989
Franz Gertsch, Doris, 1989–90

157

Stephan Balkenhol (Fritzlar, 1957)
Phoque I and *Phoque II* (*Seal I* and *Seal II*), 1989
Carved and painted wood 143 × 57 × 57 cm (each sculpture)
Acquisition, 1990. Inv. 1990-019 and 1990-020

After visiting documenta 5 in 1972 while in his teens, Stephan Balkenhol decided to become a sculptor. He then studied at Hamburg Hochschule für bildende Künste from 1976 to 1982. In the early 1980s he successfully turned his focus to a form of sculpture that might have seemed anachronistic at a time when German art was dominated by the minimalism of Ulrich Rückriem, who was in fact one of his teachers, and the raw expressionism of Georg Baselitz. The German tradition of figurative wood carving had previously been reinvented by German expressionism. He produced numerous self-portraits in two and three dimensions, full-length and busts, alongside contemporary men and women shown larger or smaller than nature, clothed or nude, sometimes in series, and animals, such as this pair of seals.

The bases and figures are carved from the same block of wood. The tool marks remain visible where the wood was roughly chopped and chiselled, with chips left hanging. Balkenhol prefers to use green wood, which generates cracks that widen over time. The theme of nature tamed by the artist is thus countered by ongoing changes in the living material of the tree trunk: it remains solid and the sculpture thus risks splitting over the years.

Like most of Balkenhol's works, the seals are painted (except for the bases), gesturing to polychrome religious statues of the medieval period and to children's toys, combining both high art and popular culture. The two red balls, one large, one small, at different heights, stand out in space in an ironic reference to abstract sculpture. The juggling seals are an ironic illustration of Balkenhol's overarching artistic project, which treads a narrow path between tradition and modernity, banality and refinement. [BF]

158

Franz Gertsch (Mörigen, 1930)
Doris, 1989–90
Colour woodcut on Japan paper, 218 × 158 cm, ed. 8/18
Alain and Suzanne Dubois Collection. Promised gift

Franz Gertsch's earliest paintings can be read in the light of pop art, with compositions based on photographs, figures reduced to silhouettes, a lack of detail, simplified shapes and stretches of colour. In the early 1970s, however, he began to mimic the precision of photography by producing such detailed paintings that from a distance they appeared more lifelike than life itself. These large-format works, based on photographs often taken by Gertsch himself, recount an era through portraits of artists and genre scenes.

When Gertsch was looking for new approaches to art in 1986, he experimented with his first woodblock prints using a technique he had recently perfected. He pressed a gouge knife onto a block of wood to obtain a copy of the source image that was as detailed as possible thanks to thousands of tiny points of varying depth. The original image was screened onto the printing surface, coated in a thin layer of blue dye, letting the artist follow the progression of his work by visualising every mark left in the holes made by the points. The surface left standing out in relief was inked and printed, while the hollows left the paper white.

Gertsch makes his own ink from pure pigments purchased in Kyoto and orders his paper from one of Japan's finest paper makers, Heizaburo Iwano. Each sheet is carefully hand-printed, a process inspected through large magnifying glasses, requiring input from several people including the artist himself. The eighteen prints in the *Doris* edition are printed in different colours in three chromatic groups. This work is one of the grey group, with an added touch of sepia pigment inspired from the colour of ash. Each variant has its own aura, but all provide an extraordinary tactile sensation, opening up a new perception of the image. [LSCH]

159

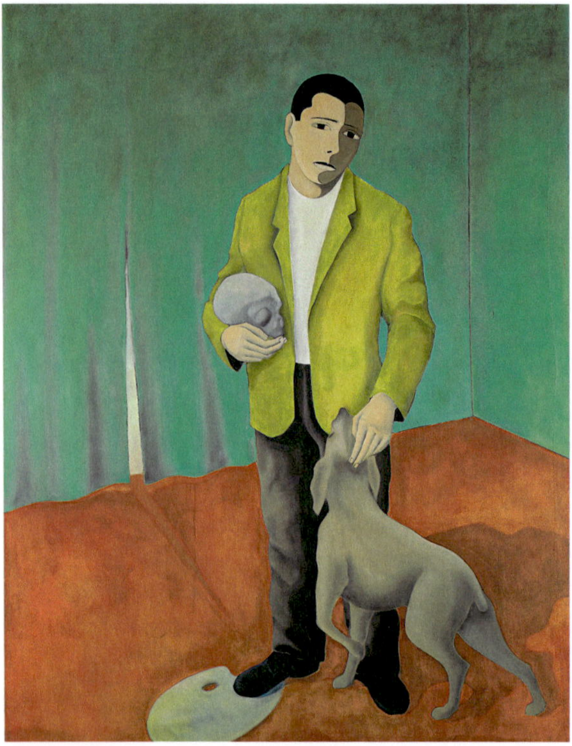

160

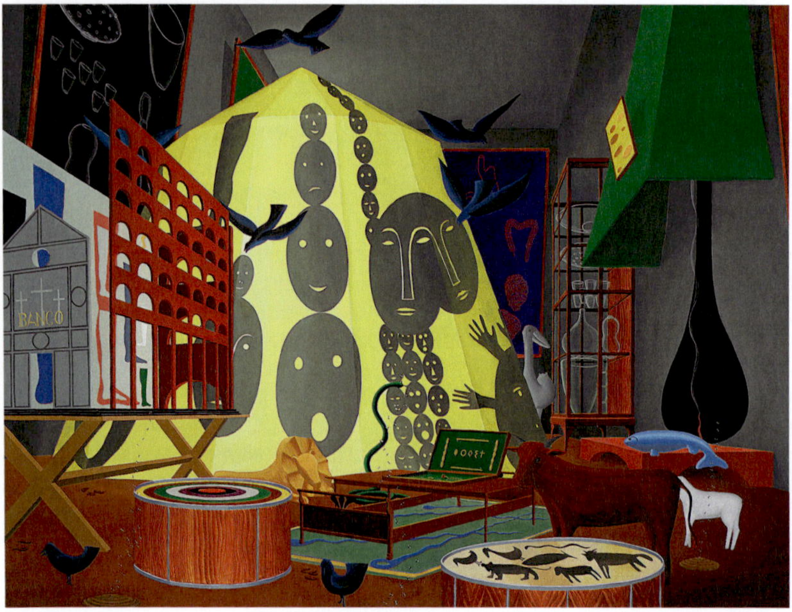

Albrecht Schnider, Ohne Titel, 1989
Thomas Huber, Studio II, 1991

159

Albrecht Schnider (Lucerne, 1958)
Ohne Titel (*Untitled*), 1989
Oil on canvas, 230 × 180 cm
Acquisition, 2000. Inv. 2000-036

Albrecht Schnider enjoyed critical acclaim in the mid-1980s for his icon-like portraits, whose austerity has often been compared to that of Félix Vallotton. This canvas, which also echoes Vallotton's handling of colour and space, is a vanitas painting in the tradition of the self-portrait with skull indicating man's mortality, a genre that has remained current since the golden age of Dutch painting until the present day, from Frans Hals to Sarah Lucas. Taking inspiration from a self-portrait by François Barraud (*Le mélancolique [The Melancholy Man]*, 1931, private collection), Schnider has nestled a skull in the crook of his arm.

While the large-format, full-length self-portrait appears deceptively plain, it is in fact full of symbolism. The artist is patting a dog, symbolising fidelity, while gazing out at the visitor. He does not show himself painting, as is often the case for self-portraits of artists at work. His work is hinted at only by the palette without paint under his foot, an odd shape that could almost be an anamorphosis of a skull. The background is a corner wall covered with a curtain with folds and a split, hinting at the theatricality of the scene and of life in general.

Schnider looks sad, with a downturned mouth and downcast eyes. The stylised face, with simplified lines, smooth skin and close-cropped hair, also features in other works from the same period, in which Schnider wears the same outfit. Sometimes he is alone with his painting kit, at other times he has a brush and palette in hand and a child by his side. The dog also appears regularly, while the range of colours is invariably the same. The set of works heralds the schematic faces of his paintings from the period after the turn of the millennium, which have become featureless contours. [LSCH]

160

Thomas Huber (Zurich, 1955)
Studio II, 1991
Oil on canvas, 150 × 200 cm
Acquired with the support of the Union Bank of Switzerland Jubilee Foundation, 1992. Inv. 1992-004

Thomas Huber studied at the Basel Kunstgewerbeschule, the Royal College of Art in London and the Düsseldorf Staatliche Kunstakademie. He now lives and works in Germany, having moved from near Düsseldorf to Berlin in 2008. Towards the end of his studies he painted a trilogy that can be read as programmatic of the oeuvre to come: *Rede über die Sintflut* (*Talk on the Great Flood*) (1982, Gabriele Henkel collection), *Rede zur Schöpfung* (*Talk on Creation*) (1982, Gabriele Henkel collection), and *Rede in der Schule* (*Talk in the School*) (1983, Darmstadt, Hessisches Landesmuseum). All three paintings contain Huber's key motif of a painting within a painting as a way of coming into contact with both the real and imaginary worlds and foregrounding the gateway between the two.

Studio II was the first of Huber's works to be acquired by the Museum, followed by a series of watercolours and drawings that explore in detail the themes he handles both in the planning stages and while working on the canvas itself. *Studio II* is part of the 'banks' series in which Huber draws a parallel between the process of converting and growing ideas, values and energies, and the work of bankers. The title refers to Huber's view of banks as a metaphor for a place of creation and alchemy, where gold turns into beauty and animal tallow turns into soap bubbles. As Huber wrote in a 1992 text entitled *Die Bank – Eine Wertvorstsellung* (*The Bank. Representing Value*): 'Are we not strangely similar, us artists and bankers? Changers, multipliers of money, manufacturers of gold, shimmering speculators in appearances. Charlatans? Charmers promising miraculous increase? We both paint pictures of a happier time.' [NS]

161

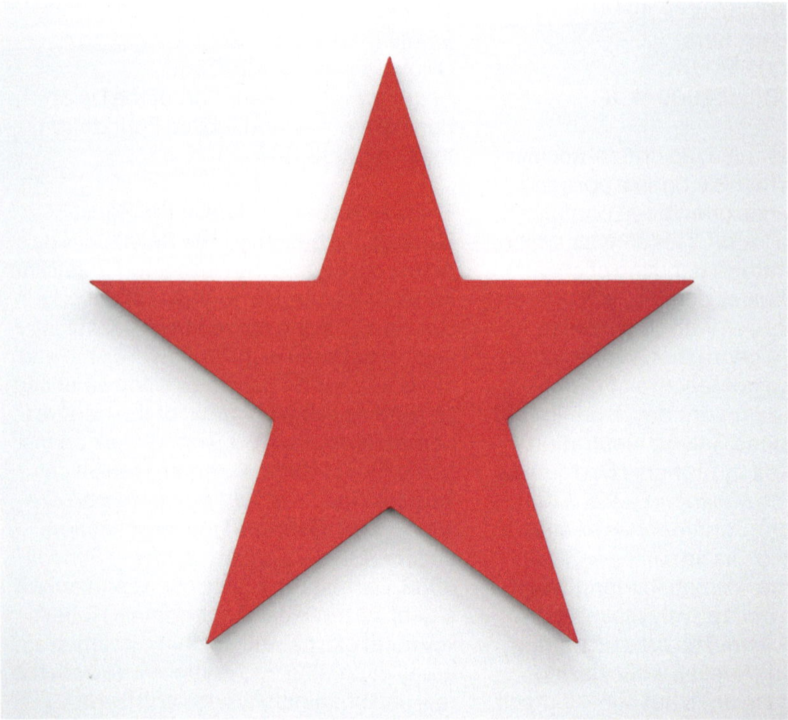

162

Olivier Mosset, Pink Star, 1990
Jean-Luc Manz, Les pleurs de cendres IV, 1996

161

Olivier Mosset (Bern, 1944)
Pink Star, 1990
Acrylic on canvas, 200 × 200 cm
Acquisition, 2003
Inv. 2003-018

Olivier Mosset moved to New York in 1977 after more than ten years in Paris. In an artistic context influenced by its minimalist heritage, he began working in monochrome rather than his earlier series of targets and canvases with vertical bands. He took part in the American exhibitions *New Abstraction* (1983) and *Radical Painting* (1984) while still keeping one foot in the Swiss and European art scene, representing Switzerland at the Venice Biennale in 1990.

His first shaped canvases, including this work, appeared in 1977. This allows the artist to explore the relationship between painting and sculpture, in other words, the painting as object. Shaped canvases, i. e. those that are non-rectangular or with surfaces that are not flat, are mainly associated with the 1960s art scene in New York, including artists such as Frank Stella, Kenneth Noland, Barnett Newman, Ellsworth Kelly and Richard Tuttle. Mosset developed his practice alongside works in three dimensions. His thinking on the relationship between object/sculpture and painting was also marked by his time in Paris, where he was friends with artists in the new realism movement, including Daniel Spoerri [n. 133] and Jean Tinguely, who turned objects into paintings. Mosset produced canvases in the shape of circles, crosses, parallelepipeds, ovals and stars (red and pink), which gave way over the following decade to triangles, arrows and L shapes. As the artist explained in a 2003 interview, 'The "shaped canvas" must, of course, be seen as a critique of the traditionally rectangular format of painting. When I produced these works they already belonged to a potential repertoire of solutions. The idea was also to suggest a re-reading in my practice, of motifs previously used (for example, the star once painted and once cut out).' [NS]

162

Jean-Luc Manz (Neuchâtel, 1952)
Les pleurs de cendres IV (*Tears of Ashes IV*), 1996
Acrylic on canvas, 140.6 × 140.6 cm
Acquisition, 1996. Inv. 1996-017

Jean-Luc Manz's work follows a particular, indeed unique path through the geometrical abstraction movement that developed in and around Geneva and Lausanne from the 1980s on. His artistic endeavour incorporates an affective dimension proper to the references that comprise it. This anchoring point in reality is a strategy used by Manz to avoid yielding to pure formalism. The artist developed his appropriationist vocabulary after an initial period of non-figurative creation from 1974 to 1977. He moved towards geometry after coming into contact with new influences such as Chérif Defraoui's studio and John M Armleder. He then discovered Cairo in 1992, where the popularity of decorative forms led his work to allude to elements drawn from reality, such as fabrics and mosaics. The colourful chessboard patterns of the series *Bari's Paintings* (1998–9) and *Bari's Fields* (1999) refer to the way fields are laid out in the Bari region, viewed from a plane heading to Egypt.

Heralded in a series of twenty-one drawings (1995, Zurich, Kunsthaus), *Les pleurs de cendres* is a series of seven paintings, the fourth of which is in the Museum's collection. All seven share the same composition, with alternating horizontal lines in two colours against a white background. Only the two colours – in this case yellow and red – change. The series pays hommage to the artist's friend Chai who died of cancer at the age of thirty-one. Grief is not approached directly or with any great sense of tragedy. Instead, it takes the form of a melancholic allusion through the dialogue of the lines, in an ode to the encounter between two souls. The lines, rare in Manz's oeuvre as a whole, refer to the Canadian-American artist Agnes Martin, his aim being for *Les pleurs de cendres* to recreate the emotion felt on seeing her canvases, and to Richard Paul Lohse. This series of paintings is a homage to a loved one, an all-too-brief encounter, recording a sense of life and loss and the tangible presence of memory and its infinite expanse. [LSCH]

163

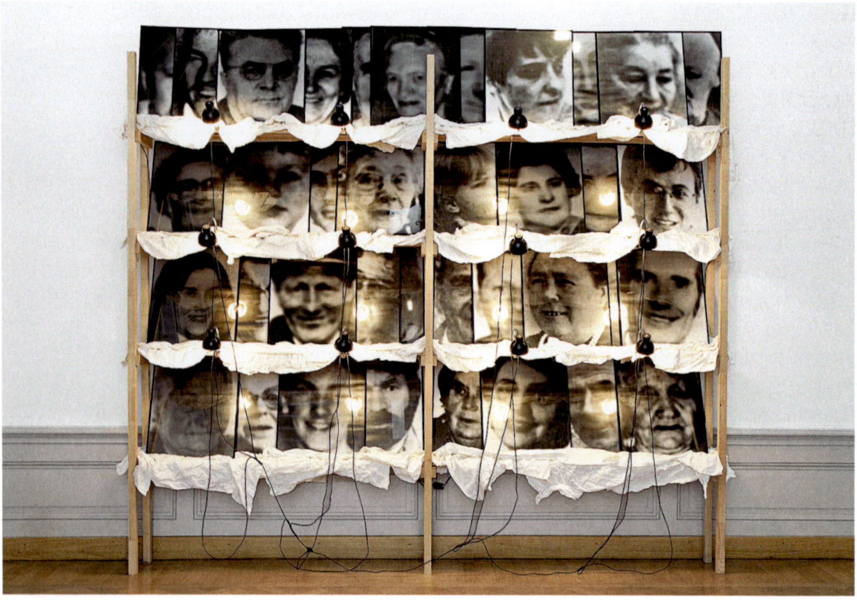

164

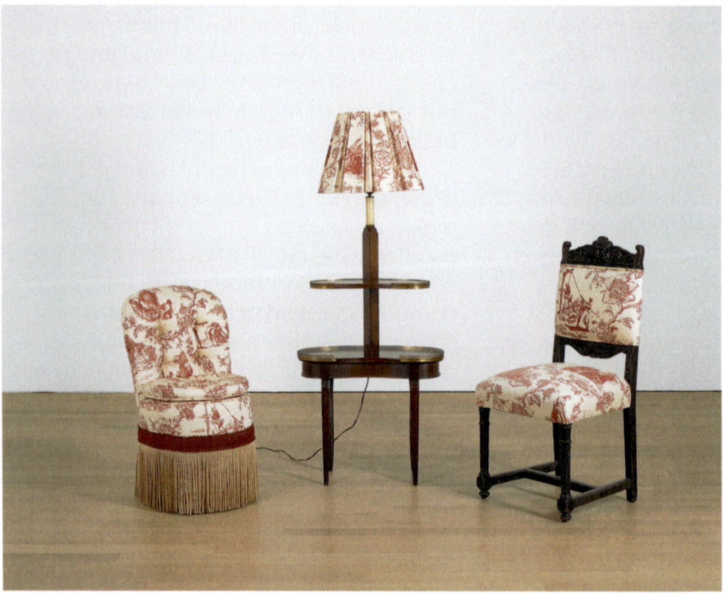

Christian Boltanski, Réserve des Suisses morts, 1990
Renée Green, Commemorative Toile, 1992

163

Christian Boltanski (Paris, 1944)
Réserve des Suisses morts (*Reserve of Dead Swiss*), 1990
39 b/w photographs, sheets, wood shelves, lamps, 280 × 330 × 40 cm
Acquisition, 1993. Inv. 1993-013

Christian Boltanski was a painter before turning to photography and film. He is renowned for his installations that are part inventory, part archive, exploring our relationship with history and memory, particularly what he refers to as the 'small memory' meaning 'the opposite of the great memory found in books'. Born during the Second World War to a Catholic-born mother and a converted Jewish doctor who spent two years hiding from the Gestapo under the floorboards of the family apartment, Boltanski has constantly returned to the history that left its inexorable mark on his own life, that of his family and millions of other people.

He first openly broached the Holocaust in the installation *Les Archives* at documenta 8 in Kassel in 1987, raising the question of the individual and the mass, the one and the multiple. The installation *Réserve des Suisses morts* builds on this work. It consists of a series of photographs of faces taken from death notices in the Valais newspaper *Le Nouvelliste*, re-photographed and enlarged before being arranged on shelves as nameless portraits that are deliberately stripped of any historical frame of reference. The images include portraits of living people cut out of the same newspaper, undercutting the narrative of death. The lighting and the sheets on which the photographs are arranged give the character of a memorial or an altar to these individuals. While Boltanski has defined *Les Suisses morts* as a work on the Holocaust, the use of portraits of Swiss men and women, who, as the artist points out, had no history-driven reason to die, allows him to explore the issue without taking up any particular stance in terms of historical representation or memorialisation. 'Working on dead Swiss men and women raises the question, "why the Swiss?". That's what I'm interested in. The Swiss also die, because they are human.' [NS]

164

Renée Green (Cleveland, 1959)
Commemorative Toile, 1992
1 table with a built-in lamp, 2 upholstered chairs, dimensions variable
Acquisition, 2004. Inv. 2004-069

Renée Green collects words, images, narratives and sounds. She journeys back and forth between past and present, between real and imaginary spaces, between disciplines, layering the personal and the political in her installations, videos, sound pieces and writings. Educated in New York and at Harvard University, Green, who has worked both in Europe and the United States, most frequently conceives her works in association with a specific place, questioning its visible or suppressed history, whether dealing with Lisbon, Berlin, Amsterdam or Los Angeles.

Invited to work in collaboration with the city of Nantes, Green developed *Commemorative Toile* to explore relics of the city's colonial past, especially its key role in the triangular trade, which saw goods manufactured in Europe being exchanged for African women and men who were then sold as slaves in the West Indies in exchange for raw materials. The fabrics designed by the artist refer to the floral prints produced in great quantity in eighteenth-century Nantes, used to pay for slaves in Africa and also to decorate wealthy, genteel French interiors. The pattern of violent scenes of enslavement and revolt was inspired by traditional Toile de Jouy fabric, with its rustic and illustrative prints. Green borrowed illustrations from engravings and narratives popular at the time, such as the Senegalese nun who was the heroine of the 1824 novel *Ourika* and the disturbing image of a European licking an African's face to determine his state of health and thus his market value. Yet by inserting the image of a Frenchman hanged during the Haitian revolution amidst the wreaths of flowers, Green also commemorates the first successful slave revolt of modern times, ushering in Haiti's independence in 1804. The work thus subverts the seemingly innocent comfort of bourgeois furnishings, as well as that of the period rooms popular in museums across the English-speaking world, to foreground narratives that are all too often absent from them. [NS]

165

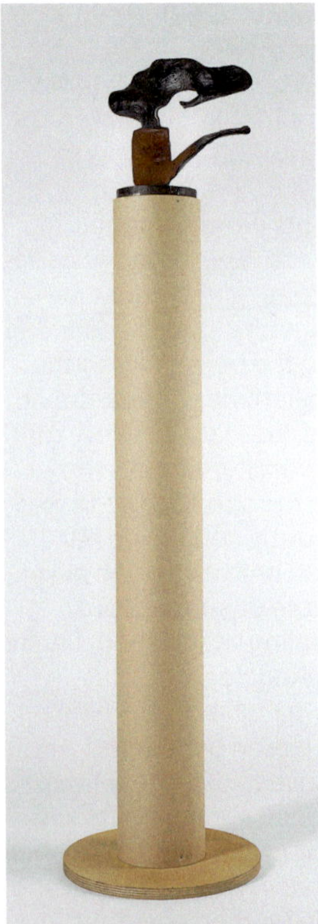

166

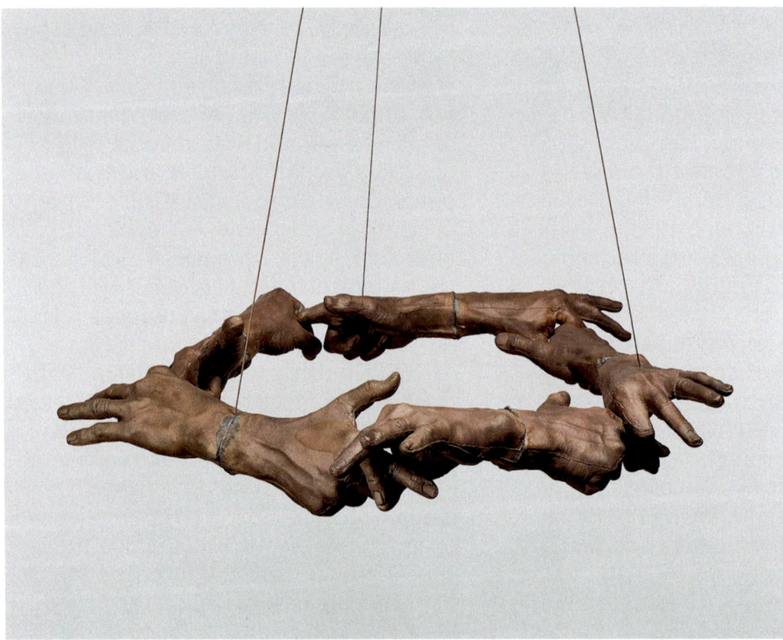

Markus Raetz, Nichtrauch/Non-fumée, 1990–2
Bruce Nauman, Untitled (Hand Circle), 1996

165

Markus Raetz (Büren an der Aare, 1941–Bern, 2020)
Nichtrauch/Non-fumée (*Notsmoke*), 1990–2
Partially rusted cast iron painted with scorched linseed oil on a cylindrical cardboard base, 196.2 × 50 cm
Acquisition, 1995. Inv. 1995-087

Markus Raetz's drawings, engravings and sculptures play with the viewer's visual perception: shapes are unveiled or they shift before our very eyes as we move around the artwork, revealing the illusory nature of reality. The artist plays with the transition between polar opposites, whether in the form of a word that simultaneously encompasses its own opposite, one motif hiding another, or a shape turned on its head, as in this work, *Nichtrauch/Non-fumée*.

This sculpture is an anamorphosis that can be seen for what it is from only two standpoints. Visitors must walk around it to find one of the right vantage points. With each step, the matter shifts from a vague outline to an object, from a cloud of smoke to a smoking pipe, as though it were fluid. Another step, and the image breaks up again to form anew as an upside-down pipe with smoke pouring onto the base.

The motif echoes an emblematic avant-garde masterpiece of the early twentieth century, René Magritte's painting *La trahison des images* (*The Treachery of Images*, 1929, Los Angeles County Museum of Art), with its iconic subtitle and text '*Ceci n'est pas une pipe*' ('*This is not a pipe*'). Magritte undermines painting's power to create illusion by foregrounding the pipe's figurative nature. Indeed, he goes even further, using the performative power of language to suggest that the image is not of a pipe at all. Raetz plays with the two layers of meaning in turn. The smoke is an illusion: the material used and the stability of its substance run counter to the very nature of smoke, and all it takes is one step to see it vanish and another to see it turn into a pipe. The playful ambiguity invites viewers to contemplate the reality and outward appearance of things. [LSCH]

166

Bruce Nauman (Fort Wayne, 1941)
Untitled (Hand Circle), 1996
Phosphor bronze, copper, silver solder, 12.7 × 67.3 × 63.5 cm, ed. 9/9
Acquisition with the support of a friend of the arts, 1996. Inv. 1997-003

Bruce Nauman is undeniably one of the most important artists of the latter half of the twentieth century, with a lasting influence on conceptual and performative art practices. From his earliest works in the mid-1960s, he used his own body both as subject and as material in his performances, films, videos, drawings, and sculptures. For instance, in the films *Thighing (Blue)* (1967) and *Pulling Mouth* (1969), he massages his thigh and pulls at his mouth with his hands as if moulding clay. Later he even cast parts of his body (*From Hand to Mouth*, 1967, Washington, D.C., Hirshhorn Museum and Sculpture Garden). His face and head frequently recur in his oeuvre, while his hands also came to play an increasingly central role from the mid-1990s on.

Nauman's 1994 series of etchings in the Museum holding showcases his own hands in pairs or by fours. One of their gestures, the index of the left hand poking the hole formed by the right hand's thumb and forefinger, is repeated five times in the print *Untitled (Fingers and Holes Series)* to form a circle. The image was the model for the sculpture *Untitled (Hand Circle)*, produced from a cast of Nauman's hands.

The deliberate obscenity is confirmed by a neon work of 1985 representing the same gesture, *Human Sexual Experience* (private collection), whose title is as explicit as the pose of the hands. The interlinking of the hands creates a sense of movement referring to sexual intercourse, though the decision to cast the work in bronze, one of the noblest materials, attenuates its obscenity, even violence. As a technique, casting, like printing, allows for the limitless repetition of a single element, highlighting the circular, inextricable character of the cycle. [NS]

167

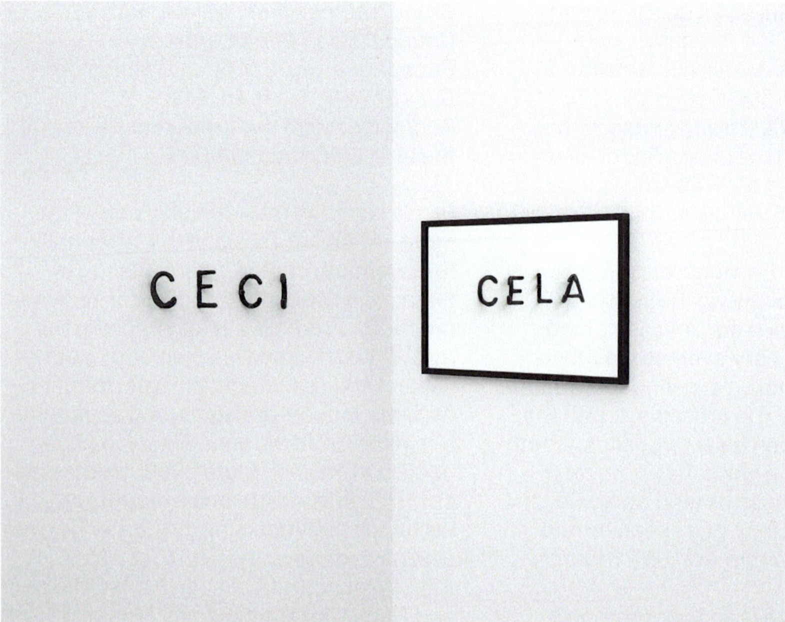

168

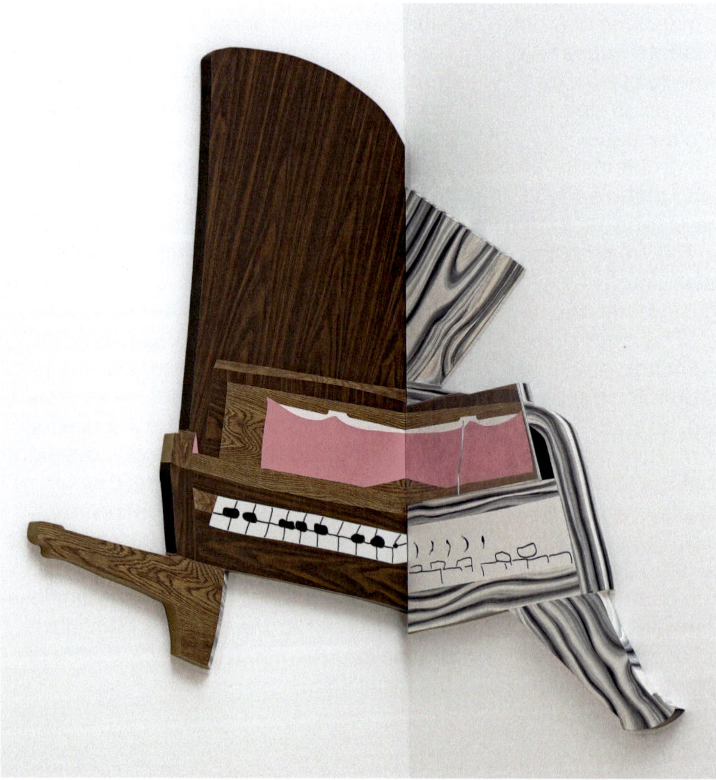

Markus Raetz, CECI – CELA, 1992–3
Richard Artschwager, Splatter Piano II, 1995

167

Markus Raetz (Büren an der Aare, 1941–Bern, 2020)
CECI – CELA (THIS – THAT), 1992–3
Brass, wood, mirror, 8 cm (height of each letter) and 33 × 43.3 × 8 cm (mirror)
Acquisition, 1998. Inv. 1998-007

Markus Raetz has been interested in perception since the 1960s. He uses simple, ingenious tricks to design sculptures that are transformed by movement: either some external force makes them move and change as the visitor watches, or the visitor's own movement makes the sculpture seem to shift progressively from one state to another. As if watching a conjuring trick, we marvel as we watch the matter transform, a motif reverse or turn into something else, a word represent itself and its own opposite, a silhouette burst into three dimensions.

CECI – CELA works on the same principle using a new stratagem in the form of a mirror. Four brass capital letters, 'CECI' ('THIS'), are attached to the wall near the corner. They are reflected in a mirror on the other wall, spelling 'CELA' ('THAT'). How can 'CECI' also be 'CELA'? Why does the mirror not reflect the exact same image as the model? This shows that reality always has two faces, two opposite sides that co-exist, and therefore one is *also* the other. Raetz invites us to mistrust appearances, which can often be deceptive.

Mirrors produce images that are reversed from reality, which is not the case here. Raetz has added elements to each letter to turn it into another that can still be read from left to right in the mirror. 'CECI' is therefore also 'CELA' because the artist has himself undercut the principle of his own stratagem to create an image that is a legible word in its own right. [LSCH]

168

Richard Artschwager (Washington, D.C., 1923–Albany, 2013)
Splatter Piano II, 1995
Formica and varnish on wood, aluminium, approx. 170 × 127 cm
Alain and Suzanne Dubois Collection. Promised gift

Richard Artschwager's oeuvre was influenced by his mother, an artist, and his father, a botanist. Though he studied science and then earned a living for his family as a furniture maker, he never entirely turned his back on art: for instance, he was Amédée Ozenfant's assistant in Paris in 1949. When his flourishing furniture workshop burned down in 1958, he took up drawing classes, reawakening his passion for art.

Aiming to make the most of his skills, Artschwager soon took his art in a new direction. He explored the use and aesthetic value of objects by drawing on his own craft skills to produce fine art. He first produced small wall sculptures, then experimented with pieces on a human scale. His works featured interplaying geometric shapes, colours including acid brights, and industrial materials generating both volume and pictoriality. A typical work such as *Description of Table* (1964, New York, Whitney Museum of American Art) is a rectangular parallelepiped bearing a Formica image of a wooden table covered with a white tablecloth, with a negative (black) space between the four legs.

Splatter Piano II is one of a series of later works in which the artist engages in more sophisticated play with the same basic idea. A grand piano is reduced to two dimensions and then 'splattered' across a corner of the room. The work is a response to the use of space, which is often wasted. The instrument is divided in two along the vertical axis, with one side made of Formica, the other side in imitation 'wood' with paint mimicking its grain. The right-hand side is also inset with an aluminium plaque that reflects the pink book of scores and the brown fake wood, further undermining the viewer's understanding of the 'cubist' object. The piano's formal and functional qualities are taken so far that the effigy develops a certain degree of kitsch. [LSCH]

169

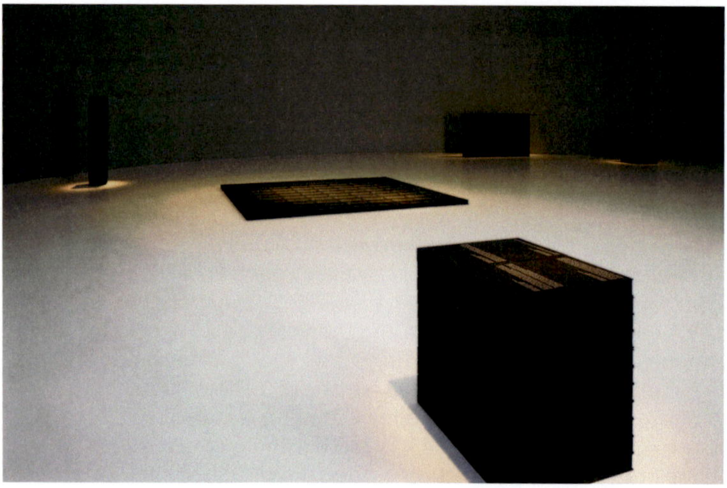

170

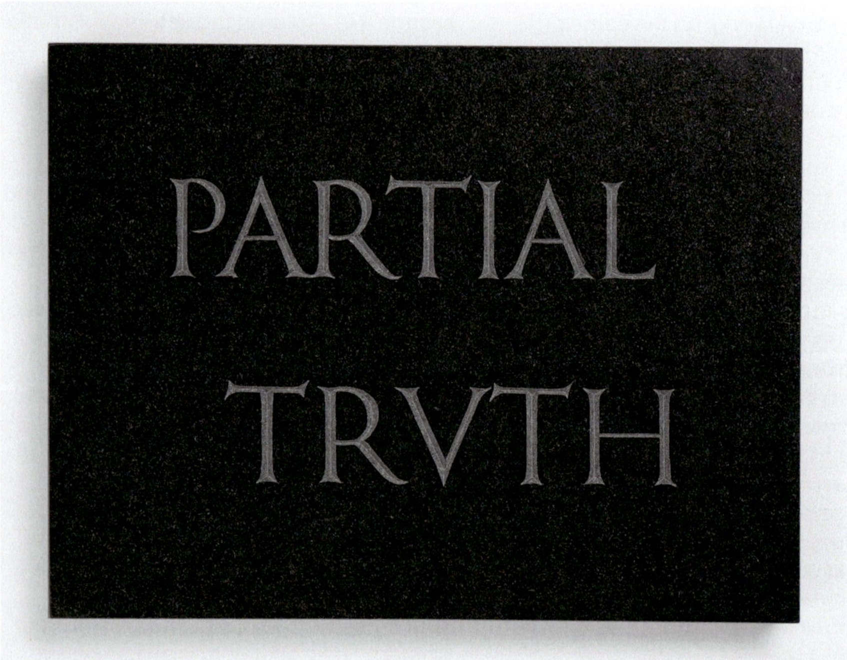

Alfredo Jaar, Real Pictures, 1995–2007
Bruce Nauman, Partial Truth, 1997

169

Alfredo Jaar (Santiago, 1956)
Real Pictures, 1995–2007
6 monuments consisting of 291 silkscreen printed filing boxes, each containing a single photograph, dimensions variable
Acquired with the support of the Association des Amis du Musée, the artist and an anonymous donor, 2007.
Inv. 2007-015

Alfredo Jaar's public interventions, installations, photographs and videos all explore the nature of images and our relationship to them. His work closely follows current events while seeking to counter sensationalist reportage, preferring instead to freeze-frame single images, thereby opening up the potential to flesh out the political background of what might appear to be one-off events.

Three weeks after the end of the Rwandan genocide, which saw nearly a million people killed in less than a hundred days, Alfredo Jaar travelled to Kigali and then the border with Zaire. He met survivors and visited massacre sites and refugee camps, collecting almost a month's worth of words, images, and eyewitness accounts and thousands of photographs. The material had a profound impact on him and he spent the next six years trying to give it the shape that would do justice to it, as it so deeply challenged his relationship with representation, images as witness and his own role as an artist.

One of the major works to come out of this project is *Real Pictures*. The set of rectangular elements are gestures to the pared-down aesthetic of minimalist sculpture. However, each box holds a photograph by the artist of various aspects of the Rwandan genocide. The pictures are not on display. On each box Jaar has described the content, creating an installation that is part graveyard, part archive. The unimaginable mass of nameless victims gives way to individuals with names, identities, families and connections, in an attempt to give them back a scrap of humanity, or, as the artist himself has put it, to 'offer an absence that could perhaps provoke a presence'. [NS]

170

Bruce Nauman (Fort Wayne, 1941)
Partial Truth, 1997
Black granite, 45.7 × 61 × 5.1 cm, ed. 10/25
Acquisition, 1997. Inv. 1997-018

One of Bruce Nauman's best-known early works is a neon spiral incorporating the words *The True Artist Helps the World by Revealing Mystic Truths* (1967), an ambiguous, complex statement on the artist's status and the question of truth. A number of Nauman's works foreground sentences or wordplay in neon, sound, drawing, print and more rarely sculpture, as is the case for his first series of black granite works engraved with lettering, entitled *Seven Virtues / Seven Vices* (1983–4), or this work, *Partial Truth*.

This sculpture, a rectangular slab of black granite like the earlier series, is hand-lettered with the words 'PARTIAL TRUTH'. It is designed to be placed directly on the floor, propped up against a wall or placed on a shelf. Nauman originally planned to use the words 'partial truth' in a neon work, inspired by a conversation with the gallery owner Konrad Fischer, who represented him. However, Fischer died while the work was still in the planning stage and Nauman decided to use granite in his honour. The choice of material and *scriptura monumentalis* lettering evoke a gravestone, giving the work the air of a funeral monument or memorial.

Alongside this granite work, Nauman produced fifty prints with the same epitaph using the same lettering for the exhibition *Bruce Nauman 1985–1996: Drawings, Prints, and Related Works* (Aldrich Contemporary Art Museum, Ridgefield, 1997). The Museum has two of these in its collection, as well as an embossed print of the sculpture. On one print the lettering is printed in reverse, multiplying the possible readings of this 'partial truth' in a nod to Ludwig Wittgenstein, a philosopher who had a profound influence on Nauman, and his understanding of language as a mirror held up to the world. [NS]

171

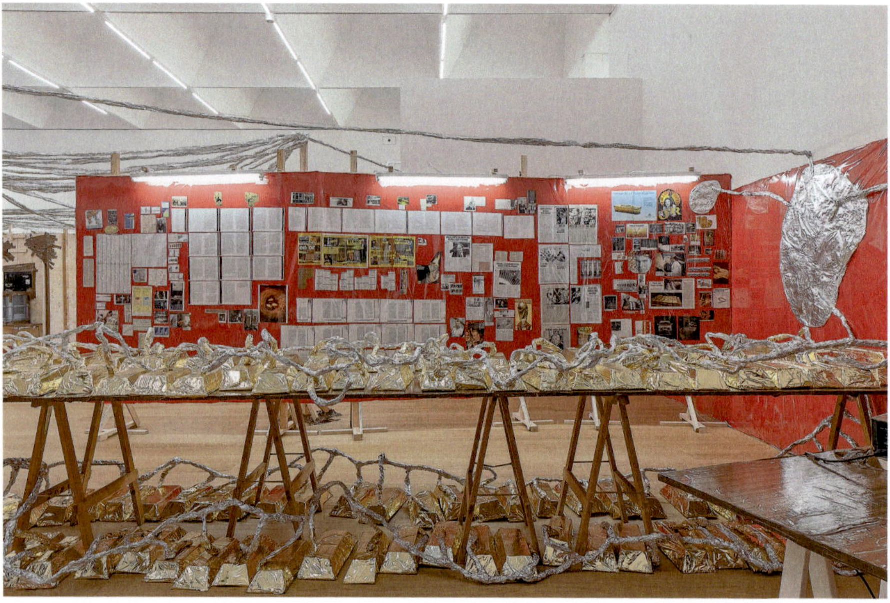

172

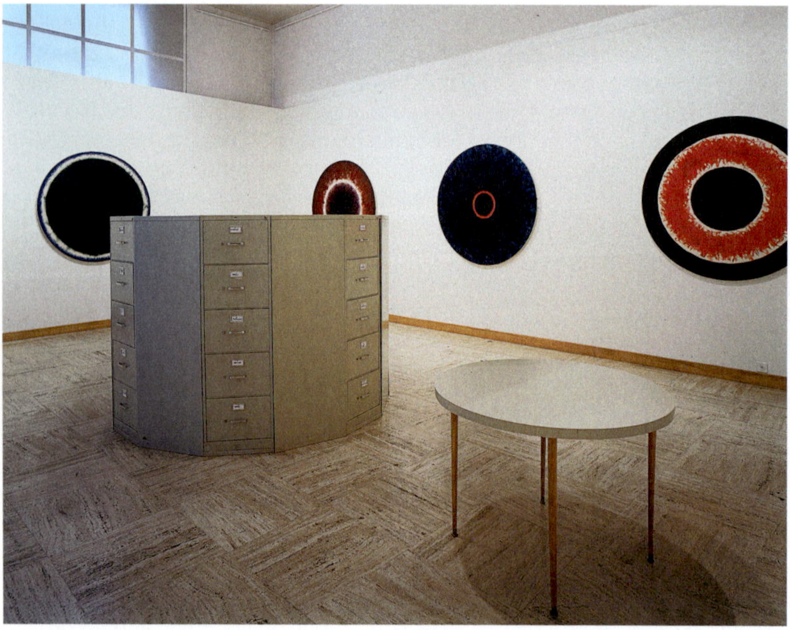

Thomas Hirschhorn, Swiss Army Knife, 1998
Jim Shaw, The Goodman Image File and Study, 2002

171

Thomas Hirschhorn (Bern, 1957)
Swiss Army Knife, 1998
Mixed media, approx. 400–500 m^2
On deposit loan from the Walter A. Bechtler Stiftung. Inv. 2012-012

In 1984, Thomas Hirschhorn moved from Switzerland to Paris, where he still lives today, in order to join Grapus, a graphics collective with roots in the events of May 1968. The collective seeks to combine artistic research with social engagement and therefore to work for a new world. This attitude has been manifest in Hirschhorn's work since 1986. Precarious, sometimes even ephemeral, his installations convey an image of tumult, of a great jumble. They immerse viewers in a dense magma of thought mashing together philosophy, literature, art and politics, to assemble them in a network via snatches of ideas and with simple techniques (collage, recycled material, fragments of texts, etc.).

The artist made the installation *Swiss Army Knife* for his 1998 exhibition at the Bern Kunsthalle, where it occupied the entire ground floor. Made up of fifteen themes or 'condensation points', as Hirschhorn calls them, this seemingly chaotic installation works like the traditional Swiss army knife after which it is named: it is a multifunctional tool that can cut, perforate and file, but also repair and mend. Hirschhorn applies this Swiss army knife approach to fifteen chapters from Swiss history and culture (including the army, Nazi gold, luxury watches, globalisation, concrete art and Ferdinand Hodler), sometimes mocking and deconstructing myths, sometimes celebrating misfits like Robert Walser who were never understood by the Swiss system. Using poor materials such as wooden panels, folding tables, red cloth, photocopies, cardboard, plastic and sheets of aluminium, Hirschhorn makes art with a do-it-yourself aesthetic on a grand scale, producing work that is concise, energetic and immediately effective, a connected ensemble with no hierarchies whose formal appearance is the direct result of the urgent message to be communicated. Here, the Swiss army knife, a global symbol of Swiss success, ends up turning against those who produced it. [BF]

172

Jim Shaw (Midland, 1952)
The Goodman Image File and Study, 2002
7 oil paints on canvas, 1 table, 7 metal filing cabinets full of archival images, dimensions variable
Acquisition, 2003. Inv. 2003-189

After studying at the California Institute of the Arts alongside artists such as Mike Kelley, John Miller and Tony Oursler, Jim Shaw developed his own body of work in cycles, exploring fictional realms that resonated from one work to the next. His *Dream Drawings*, *Dream Objects* and *My Mirage* cycles were followed in the late 1990s by 'Oism', an imaginary religion whose rituals, principles and characters he defined as a parody of American spiritual movements such as the Mormons. Taking his inspiration from sources as varied as American popular culture of the 1950s and 1960s and history books, the large-scale project drew on a process of accumulation and free association. It can be read as a critique of totalitarian thought systems, whether political, ideological, religious or artistic in nature.

The installation *The Goodman Image File and Study* is part of the 'Oist' series. It is a fictional archive of documents supposedly collected by an artist by the name of Adam O. Goodman, surrounded by seven of his abstract paintings, juxtaposing popular, worldly images and the mythical purity of abstract art. The filing cabinets contain a vast range of figurative imagery from American magazines of the 1950s and 1960s, including *Life Magazine*, *National Geographic*, *Ebony*, *Esquire* and *Playboy*, organised alphabetically by theme – men, women, children, stars, artists, religion, sport, architecture, mammals, reptiles, birds, design, landscape, fashion, food, alcohol, tobacco, weapons, science and so on. Visitors are invited to consult the archive, which is part obsessive repertoire, part visual record of a particular moment in history. [NS]

173

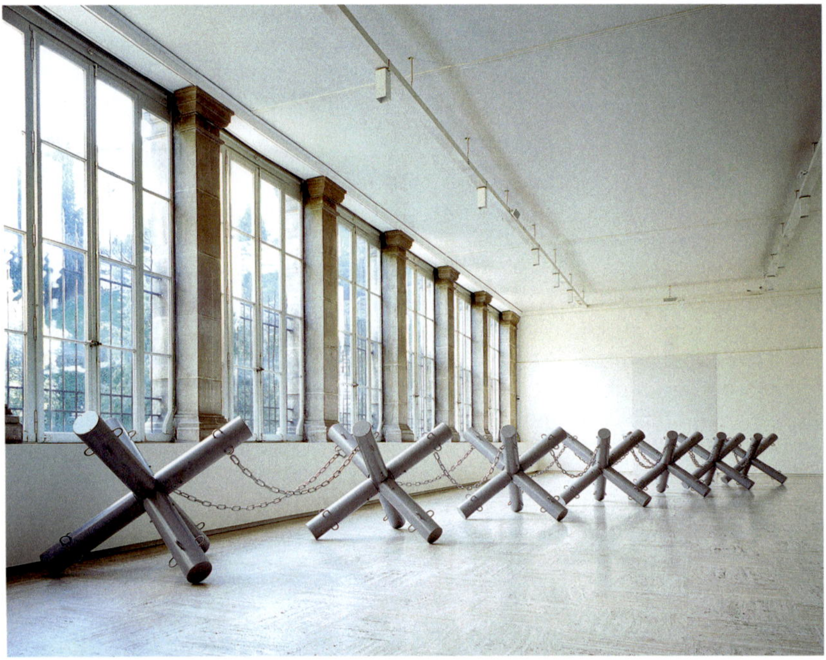

174

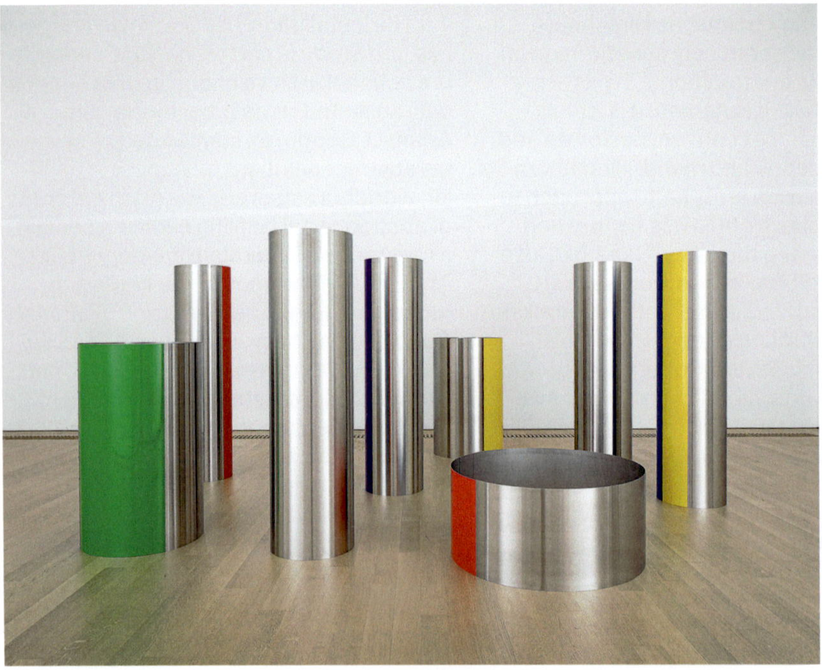

Fabrice Gygi, Crossblocks, 2001
Stéphane Dafflon, SAI010, 2011

173

Fabrice Gygi (Geneva, 1965)
Crossblocks, 2001
7 steel elements, paint, iron chains, 120 × 150 × 165 cm (each element)
Acquired in co-ownership with the Swiss Confederation, Federal Office of Culture, Bern, 2005. Inv. 2005-032

Fabrice Gygi's sculptures are inspired by barriers, sandbag walls, airbags, road-blocks, control towers, pylons and water cannons, all forms of street furniture that play a role in maintaining social order and protecting and controlling individuals. Trained at the École des arts décoratifs from 1983 to 1984 and the École supérieure des arts visuels from 1984 to 1990 in Geneva, he soon turned to a primarily sculpture-based practice, first with temporary structures such as *Cabane* (1986) and then with object-based performances such as *Always Upright* (1995). He developed a formal vocabulary inherited from minimalism, both in his use of materials and in the focus on space and the role of the audience, exploring themes related to displays of power and authority. Street barriers designed to protect, separate, channel and enclose are a recurrent theme in his work.

Crossblocks is an alignment of steel elements linked by chains to form a barrier that looks impassable and threatening, but also contains the seeds of its own transgression, as hinted at by the title. The smooth painted steel contrasts with the aggressive shape, making the installation part minimalist sculpture, part street furniture, while the chains connecting the elements gesture to torture and sadomasochism. The sculpture, built on a human scale, forces visitors to contemplate their own bodies and their relationship with the space surrounding them – the urban setting and the museum itself – and question its constraints and potential for reconquest. [NS]

174

Stéphane Dafflon (Neyruz, 1972)
SAI010, 2011
8 stainless steel cylinders, coloured adhesive sheeting, rivets, dimensions variable
Acquisition by the Commission cantonale des activités culturelles, 2011. Inv. 2011-197

Stéphane Dafflon's development as an artist was shaped by his studies and an art scene that encouraged geometric abstraction. The influence of Swiss graphic design, the precedent of concrete art in Zurich in the 1930s and 1940s and the neo-geo movement that was already harking back to the work of the concrete artists in the 1980s all shaped his use of abstraction, drawing on the aesthetic potential of elementary shapes. Artists such as Luigi Lurati, Piet Mondrian, Ellsworth Kelly, Robert Mangold, Olivier Mosset, Alan Charlton, Alan Uglow, Peter Halley, Marcia Hafif and Steven Parrino have also influenced his work.

Dafflon initially designs his works on a computer. After his first paintings, in which he reshaped logos, he has now reduced his vocabulary to lines and shapes without direct references. He arranges them in a 'fictional' two-dimensional space that allows him, for example, to work with brand new perspectives, creating anomalies that can then be transferred to real space.

Dafflon gives his works neutral codes for titles, starting with acronyms referring to the material (in this case 'SAI' for 'Sculpture en Acier Inoxydable', or sculpture in stainless steel) followed by the work's number in the order of creation. When designing them, he records how his works are placed in an architectural or other setting to play with optical effects. *SAI010*'s eight hollow cylinders of riveted steel were drawn with design software. Their surface does not produce a perfect reflection of the surrounding elements, but rather, a slightly distorted one. The shapes are stretched height-wise and intercalated with broad strips of coloured adhesive on each cylinder. Visitors cannot see their own reflection; they can only contemplate the solid yet airy presence of the cylinders. [LSCH]

175

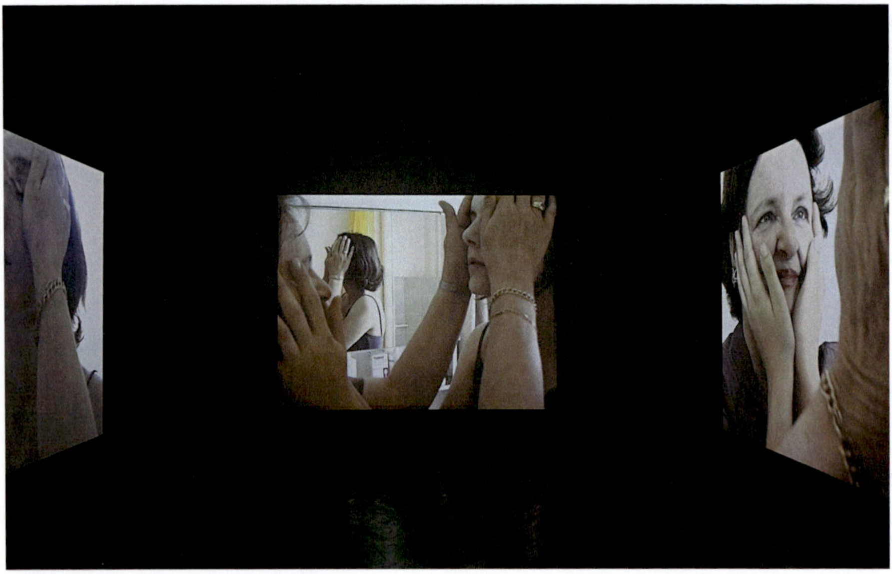

176

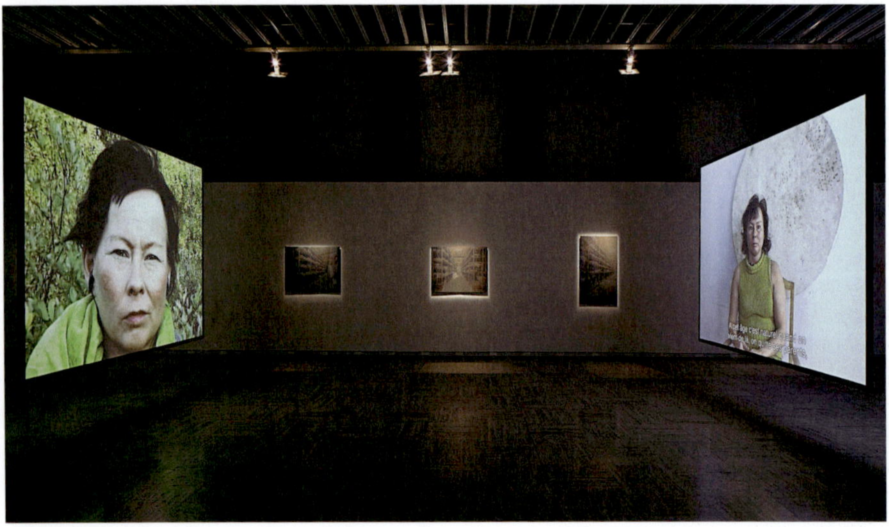

Emmanuelle Antille, As Deep as Our Sleep, As Fast as Your Heart II, 2001
Esther Shalev-Gerz, White Out – Between Telling and Listening, 2002

175

Emmanuelle Antille (Lausanne, 1972)
As Deep as Our Sleep, As Fast as Your Heart II, 2001
3 synchronised video projections, colour, sound, 10 min 2 sec, ed. 2/3
Acquisition by the Commission cantonale des activités culturelles, 2001. Inv. 2001-049

Emmanuelle Antille studied at the École supérieure des arts visuels in Geneva and the Rijksakademie van Beeldende Kunsten in Amsterdam and has been working in video and installations since the early 1990s. Her work lies at the juncture between fiction and documentary, with recurrent themes exploring human relations, rituals, social expectations, individual relationships, and power struggles within various communities such as families, step-families and groups of teenagers.

As Deep as Our Sleep, As Fast as Your Heart II is shown on three screens hanging in a room, taking viewers into a fascinating dreamscape simply by the way it occupies space. As the artist said in a 2001 interview, 'I started working on the installation because I wanted to tell stories and I didn't know how to go about it, which bit of the video and editing to start with'. The scenes shown on the three screens do not follow the logical narrative structure that still typifies most film productions. The same scene is repeated on the three screens from different angles, not only offering different points of view of the same event, but also opening up an infinite spectrum of points of view for the same scene.

Antille's work, filmed indoors, subtly draws the ambivalent, tense relationship between a mother and her daughter through interactions that alternate between rituals and children's games, halfway between waking and sleeping, dreaming and reality. As in many of her works, the artist and her own mother embody the protagonists. The repetition of their actions across three screens foregrounds the routines and social expectations driving them, while the symbolism of the staging, with the red dress, mother tucking in her daughter and washing her back, and so on, highlights how slender the gap between reality and fiction really is. [NS]

176

Esther Shalev-Gerz (Vilnius, 1948)
White Out – Between Telling and Listening, 2002
2 synchronised video projections, colour, sound, 40 min, 7 Diasec-mounted colour photographs, 6 texts laminated on aluminium, ed. 1/3
Acquisition, 2012. Inv. 2012-049

Esther Shalev-Gerz was born in Lithuania, brought up in Israel, and now lives in Paris. Her art explores the construction of individual and collective memories. Her fresh reading of history is anchored in the present of her protagonists. Most of her works are created in dialogue with the inhabitants of a particular place or witnesses of a particular event. The past is always read through the present of those who remember it or work with its relics.

White Out – Between Telling and Listening draws a portrait in two phases of a woman between two cultures, two places, and two times. Two still frames focused on Asa Simma, a Sami woman living in Stockholm, are projected facing each other, one filmed in Stockholm, the other in her home landscape in Lapland. In the first, she reacts to quotes about Swedish and Sami culture, while in the other she listens to her own words. The contrast between the two Asas is striking. On the one hand, the energetic urbanite moves her arms and hands expressively as she shares her story, while on the other, her face is calm and reserved as she listens. The work divides the I into the subject of the utterance and the subject that receives it, but also into two lifestyles. Unlike the video *On Two* (2009), which plays with the contrast between two inhabitants of Paris who share the same time and space (the French philosopher Jacques Rancière and the young Lebanese philosopher Rola Younes), the contrast in *White Out* focuses on one single individual. The 'betweenness' of the title is the space constantly crossed from one contemporary identity to another, the permanent to-and-from between two positions. Echoing the country's official history, the photographs that complete the installation depict objects from Stockholm's Historiska Museet. [NS]

177

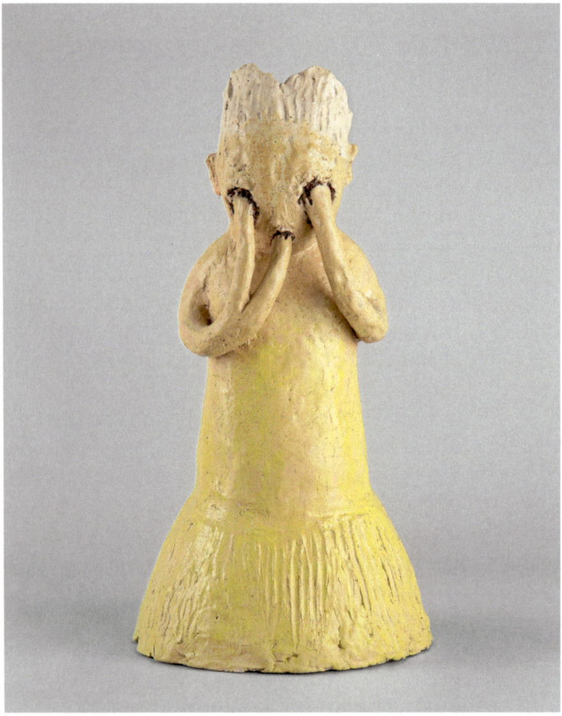

178

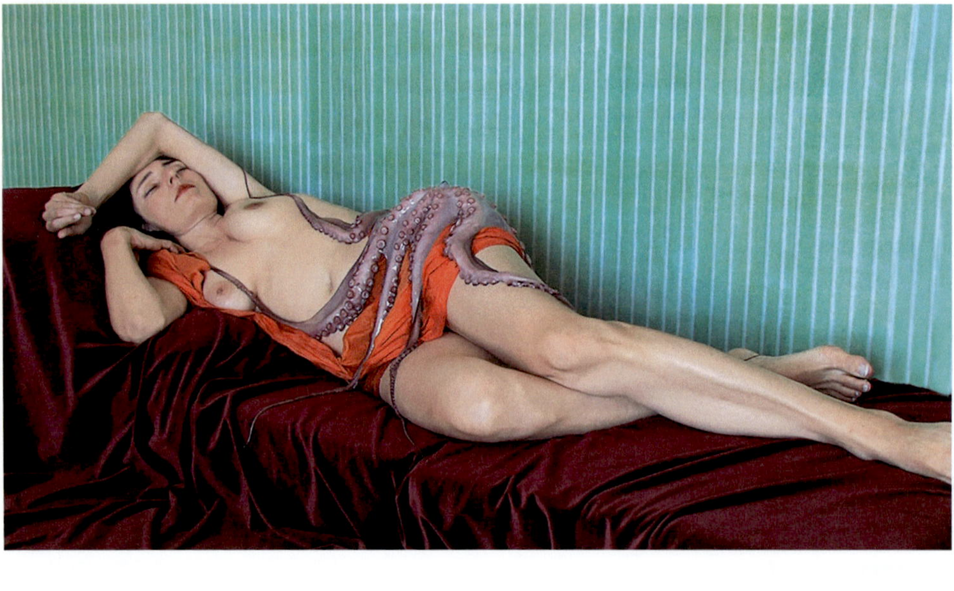

Leiko Ikemura, Gelbe Figur mit drei Armen, 1996
Judith Albert, Nu à l'écharpe orange, 2009

177

Leiko Ikemura (Tsu, 1951)
Gelbe Figur mit drei Armen (*Yellow Figure with Three Arms*), 1996
Terracotta and glaze, 65×31×31 cm
Acquisition, 2001. Inv. 2001-018

Leiko Ikemura left her native Japan for Europe in 1972 and began developing her oeuvre after studying drawing at the Seville School of Fine Arts, later exploring the potential of drawing in her Zurich studio from 1979 to 1983. Her rapid, powerful strokes of pencil and charcoal filled the paper with strange human and animal creatures, hybrids and plant-like beings. She then turned to painting in the mid-1980s.

By this time, she had moved to Germany where she took up terracotta sculpture alongside painting, shaping female bodies reminiscent of her early drawings – headless beings or large ones with multiple organs, singly or in groups, reclining or standing. She sculpts her figures directly from the clay, with no preliminary models or sketches: the clay's own potential for textures, volumes and hollow spaces shapes the final work.

Gelbe Figur mit drei Armen is a terracotta sculpture with a glaze that varies in hue from flesh to luminous yellow. The figure is a little girl, judging by her size and her yellow dress. Her head is lowered and her right forearm is split into two, one part reaching into her mouth, the other into her right eye. The left arm reaches into her left eye. Her hair forms two peaks over her face, leaving an opening that shows the work is hollow. In an interview given the year before she made this sculpture, Ikemura said: 'the eyes are questionable organs that surreptitiously close on the world'. This small figure, turned in on itself in a closed circuit, is part realist, figurative depiction, part metaphorical evocation of the pain of being in the world, in which sight, taste and breath are momentarily annihilated. [NS]

178

Judith Albert (Sarnen, 1969)
Nu à l'écharpe orange (*Nude with Orange Scarf*), 2009
Video, colour, sound, 8 min, ed. 1/7
Acquisition, 2009. Inv. 2009-019

From the mid-1990s on, Judith Albert worked with moving images, exploring their potential for capturing subtle variations such as almost imperceptible changes in light, pose and movement, in simple, poetically staged scenes that draw both on art history and her own imagination.

Nu à l'écharpe orange features a woman reclining on a divan draped with purple fabric, one arm thrown back. She seems to be asleep. Her body lies diagonally across the screen, standing out against the turquoise wallpaper. She is naked other than some orange fabric draped across her left hip, on which lies a huge mauve octopus whose tentacles extend across her thighs and torso. The animal follows the calm, regular rhythm of her breathing, the two movements intermittently falling out of synch. Someone can be heard repeating a brief snatch of Erik Satie's *Gnossienne n° 1*, stopping and starting again.

The soundtrack not only strengthens the scene's domestic nature, but also underlines its timelessness and potential to extend to infinity. The static shot, unmoving pose, repeated music and looped display also turn the work into a *tableau vivant*. And indeed, the work is directly inspired by Félix Vallotton's *Nu à l'écharpe verte* (*Nude with a Green Scarf*, 1914, La Chaux-de-Fonds, Musée des Beaux-Arts). Where Vallotton simply has a green scarf that both hides and reveals the nude woman's genitals, Judith Albert has changed the colours and brought in an incongruous element in the octopus: the relationship between painter and model has been turned on its head, as the artist in this instance takes both roles. The octopus' sensual, threatening overtones, inspired by Hokusai's erotic engraving *Kinoe no komatsu* (1814), interrupts the viewer's gaze with a quasi-surrealist juxtaposition of iconographic elements. [NS]

179

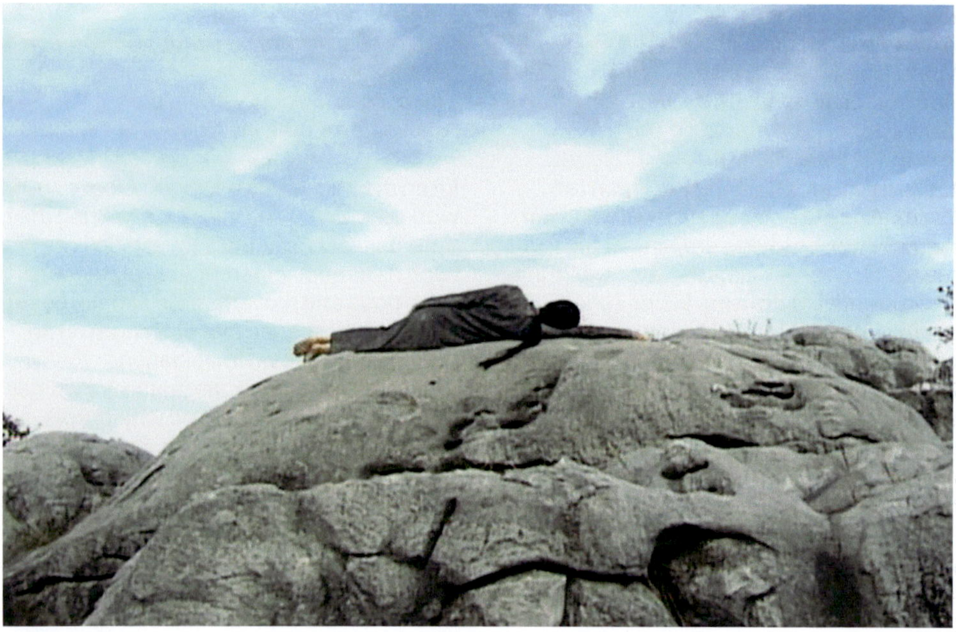

180

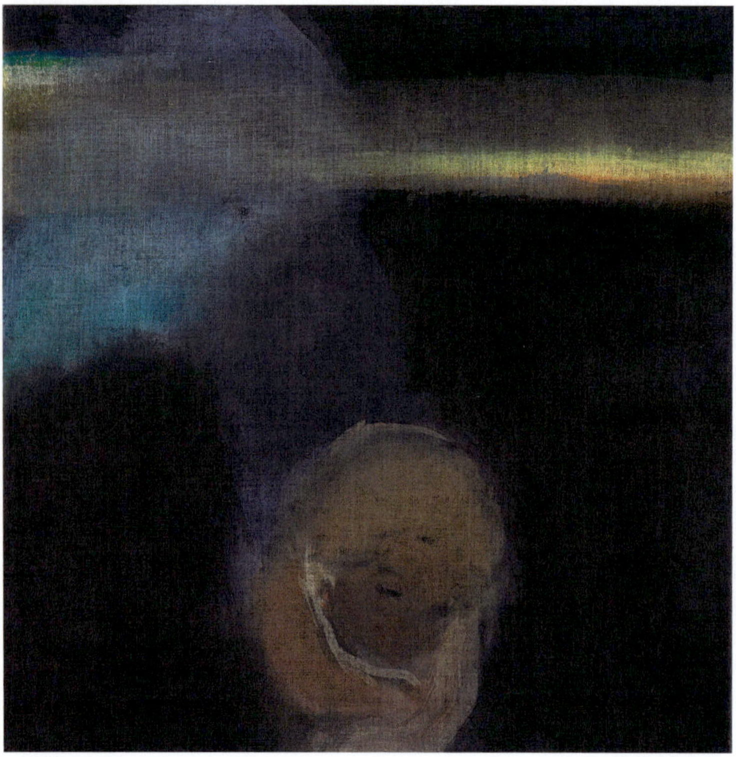

Kimsooja, A Needle Woman – Kitakyushu, 1999
Leiko Ikemura, Eintauchen, 1999

179

Kimsooja (Daegu, 1957)
A Needle Woman – Kitakyushu, 1999
Video, colour, silent, 6 min 33 sec, ed. 2/4
Acquisition 2018. Inv. 2018-078

Trained at Hongik University in Seoul and then at the École nationale supérieure des Beaux-Arts in Paris, Kimsooja has divided her time between New York and Seoul for the past thirty years. Since 1999, she has put on a series of performances for the camera in a number of locations, mainly urban ones. Their title, *A Needle Woman*, refers to the centrality of fabric in her performances and installations, and can also be read metaphorically as referring to the way the moving body weaves connections with new contexts and new situations.

A Needle Woman – Kitakyushu is a performance that was put on in Kitakyushu, Japan. It consists of a single fixed shot, without sound. The artist, dressed in dark grey, her feet bare, her hair gathered by an elastic band, lies on a crevassed rock with her back to the camera. Above her, a blue sky with fine white clouds moved by the wind. Whereas other performances show the artist moving or remaining still amidst moving crowds (*A Needle Woman*, 1999–2001), here the body is perfectly immobile. Placed exactly at the centre of the image, overlooking the horizon, it is positioned between heaven and earth, between the pull of gravity and the fluidity of the azure, between mineral weight and the lightness of air, as if it were one with the stone and at the same time was providing a link with the celestial element. As the artist said in 2013: 'My body functions as a central point of four different elements: earth, sky, nature, and human being.'

While the immobile, reclining body may evoke death, the fact that it is in a dynamic position, with one leg on top of the other and the head resting on an arm, and not in a position of abandon, suggests the performative choice of a meditative, concentrated position rather than the body collapsing into nothingness. [NS]

180

Leiko Ikemura (Tsu, 1951)
Eintauchen (*Submerging*), 1999
Oil on burlap, 100 × 100.5 cm
Acquisition, 2001. Inv. 2001-019

Leiko Ikemura's pictorial practice took a new turn in the early 1990s. Her expressive early paintings gave way to a more restrained form, with strokes of colour of almost transparent brightness, landscapes between sea and mountain with young girls floating, walking, reclining or diving, on the border between the world of the living and the spirit realm.

In *Eintauchen*, a young girl gently falls or dives, as the title suggests, from a horizon line placed very near the top to the lower third of the canvas, her two arms folded round her face, her eyes half-closed, in a pose close to sleep. She is strangely disembodied: her legs cannot be seen though her garments are transparent, and nor can the feet that would anchor her to the ground. Her torso and head stand out against a very dark ground, while her blue skirt floats above her, showing the yellow horizon line through it, creating two separate spaces on the canvas: one for the figure, part black night, part opaque subaquatic world, and the other hinted at by the bright, vibrant line of light. The horizon line can also be read as a dividing line or a threshold between sea and sky, falling and rising, the here and the beyond, two states of being, also underscored by the floating figure. The girl's torso and head are below the line, but her skirt overlaps it and takes flight beyond it. The figure is thus connected to the two realms, crossing between the two with ease. When asked in 2001 about the omnipresent horizon in her canvases, Ikemura replied, 'The horizon does reveal itself to us like a line, but the line does not exist. Yet it is the most beautiful line of all. It represents both our bond with the earth and nostalgia for infinity'. [NS]

181

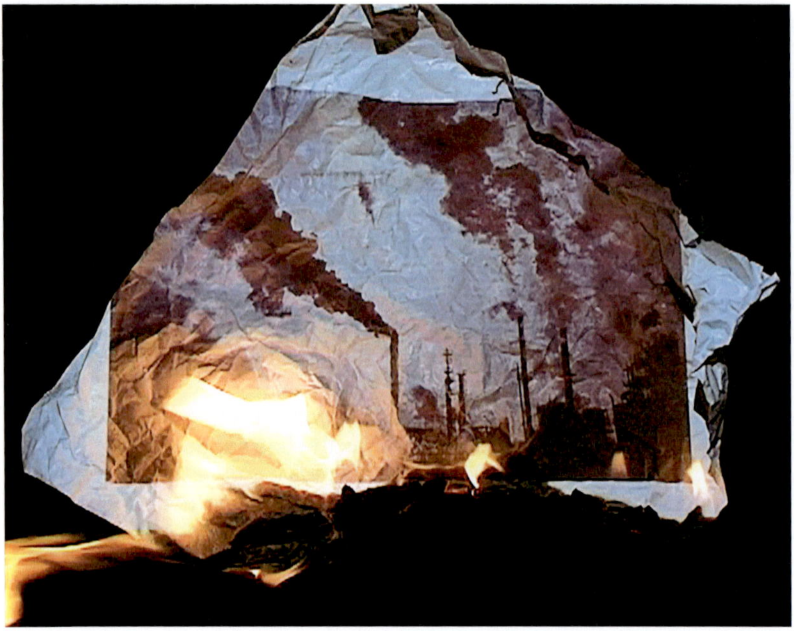

182

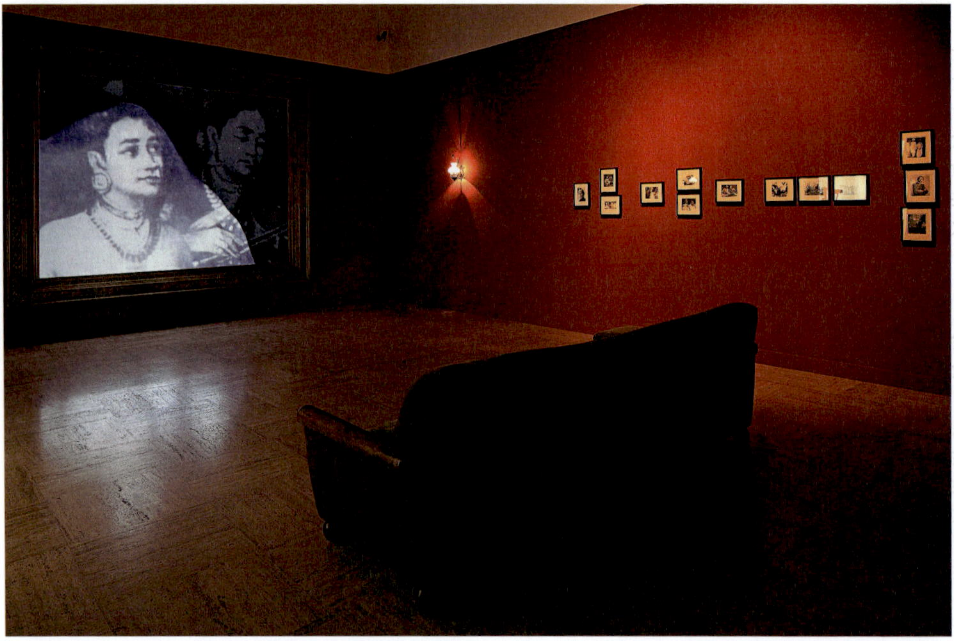

Silvie Defraoui, Plis et replis, 2002
Nalini Malani, Unity in Diversity, 2003

181

Silvie Defraoui (Sankt Gallen, 1935)
Plis et replis (*Folds and Re-Folds*), 2002
Video, colour, sound, 17 min 45 sec, ed. 3/5
Acquisition by the Commission cantonale des activités culturelles, 2007.
Inv. 2007-020

Silvie Defraoui studied painting at the School of fine arts in Algiers and then ceramics at the École des arts décoratifs in Geneva. After a period working alone, she teamed up with Chérif Defraoui. Between 1975 and 1994 the couple pursued a reflection on the image, on its status and meaning in a society where visual reproductions had been circulating for centuries and where their production was growing ever more intensive. After Chérif's death, Silvie Defraoui continued to work within the framework of the research project they had established together, *Archives du futur*.

This video applies one of their principles, that of reusing pre-existing images and showing them in a new light. Against a black ground, a ball of glossy paper is thrown onto a table and opened by two gloved hands, gradually revealing the contents of the photograph. The crumpled paper is taken away and another piece thrown in, another image revealed. The action is repeated with a single variation: some of the images are set on fire. The procedure, reminiscent of earlier videos, is certainly simple, but it seems to involve some kind of illusion. Hence the viewer's growing fascination and interest in the rustling and crumping of the paper, which is the only sound.

Like a slide show, the successive photographs are taken from the press, forming a kind of collective memory of current events (war, seal hunting, famine, etc.). Each one seems familiar but it is impossible to identify a precise place, date or situation: everything happens too fast for us to really recognise them. Defraoui digs into the folds of our memory ('*plis*') and brings back to consciousness some of the countless images we consume and forget every day, then makes them disappear again ('*replis*'). [LSCH]

182

Nalini Malani (Karachi, 1946)
Unity in Diversity, 2003
1 video, colour, sound, 8 min 7 sec, 3 lamps, 13 b/w photographs
Anonymous gift, 2010. Inv. 2010-016

Nalini Malani is a politically committed artist who sees her work as an active, eyewitness account of modern society. The work mimics a middle-class Indian sitting room, with red walls, photographs of characters and scenes from history on the walls bathed in dim light, and a large painting that comes to life before our very eyes. It is a video shown in a large gilded frame holding Ravi Varmâ's undated canvas *Galaxy of Musicians*, shown at the Chicago World Congress of Religions in 1893, where the philosopher Swami Vivekananda warned of the dangers of religious orthodoxy. At the time, India was witnessing the rise of a nationalist school of thought alongside powerful reformist movements. The painting depicts eleven female musicians in regional costume playing traditional instruments, symbolising 'unity in diversity', the paradoxical motto chosen by India at the country's independence following the partition of Pakistan in 1947.

In the video, Malani confronts Varmâ's painting with recent Indian history, particularly the 2002 genocide of the Muslim population of Gujarat, on the border with Pakistan. The outbreak of violence between communities was the bloodiest in India since independence, shaking the democratic nation to its foundations. What starts out as a harmonious composition, with all parts of the nation playing sweet music together, ends in a bloodbath. Gunfire rattles as the music gives way to screams and lamentations. The orchestra morphs into an army where women carry rifles to protect themselves from abuse. Images of a surgical abortion symbolise the failure of a promising future. A voice that sounds like Nehru evoking the unfinished task of liberal nationalism delivers a pessimistic manifesto borrowed from Heiner Müller's play *Der Auftrag* (*The Task*), inspired by a 1933 text by Bertolt Brecht. [BF]

183

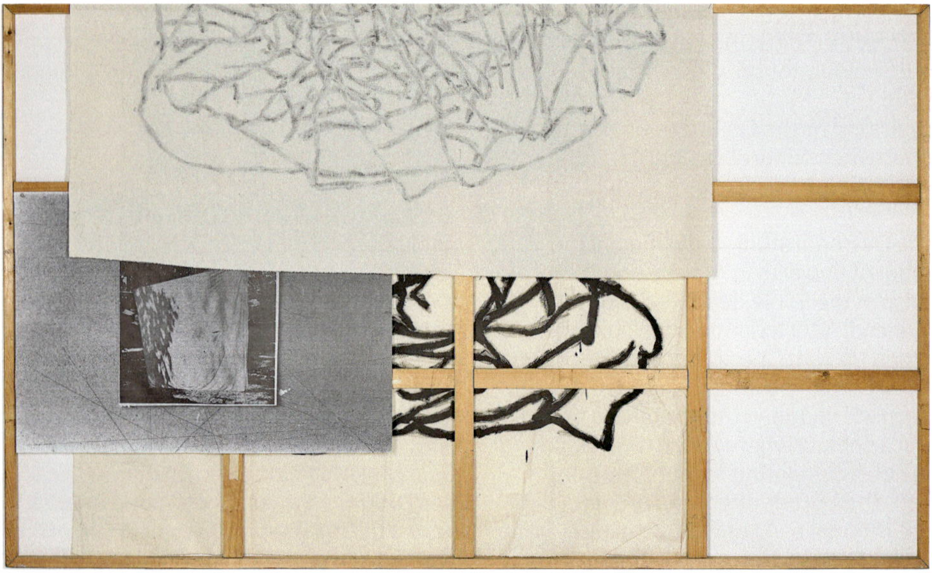

184

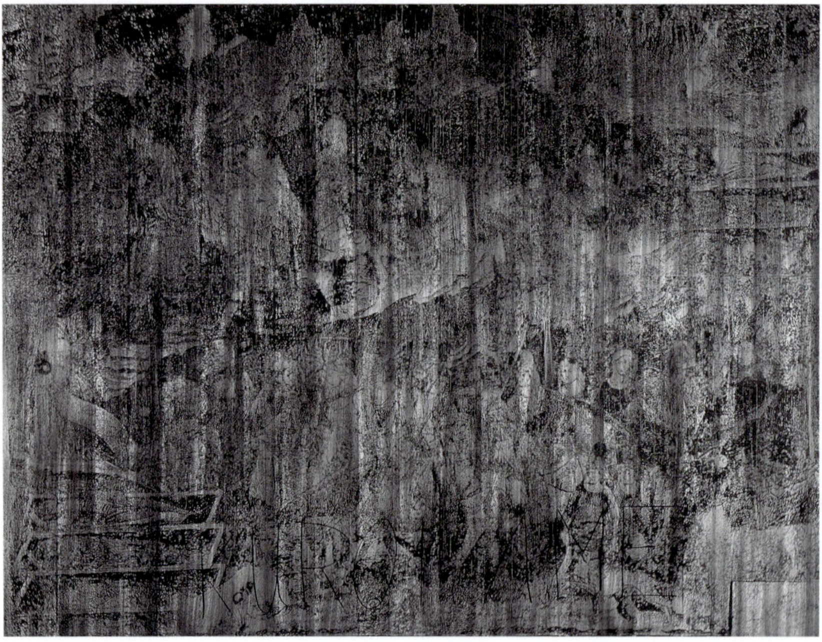

Robert Ireland, Dépendances, 2000
Alain Huck, Kuroi Ame II, 2008

183

Robert Ireland (Dallas, 1964)
Dépendances (*Dependencies*), 2000
Paint on canvas, ink jet print on paper, wood stretcher, 160×270 cm
Gift of the artist, 2019. Inv. 2019-008

Robert Ireland is an artist and also author of theoretical texts on the questions he explores in his oeuvre. His considerations on the history of painting, its unspoken rules and conventions, as well as the affects it embodies, always start from the material conditions in which an image is produced: canvas, stretcher, paper, paint and so on.

Dépendances is part of a series of works shown at Robert Ireland's 2004 solo exhibition at the Museum, *Speaking of Pictures*, which spatialised his thoughts on museums as a locus of memory. The work consists of a rectangular stretcher with crossbars holding a painted canvas, the reverse of which partly covers a photograph pinned to the stretcher. Everything is contained within the space of the stretcher, but the various elements only fill it partially, such that empty space – or, to be precise, the wall – becomes a vital part of the composition. Reversing Alberti's idea of the painting as a window opening onto the world, Robert Ireland is interested above all in the 'window' – the material layers of the painting itself. He forges relations between fragments of images, which in turn become an image in their own right by a process of montage, or creates a mise en abyme effect using visual echoes.

Indeed, the photograph of a sheet drying in the wind points not only to the canvas literally hanging over the stretcher but also to the question of the pictorial surface as a screen, while the slight tear that can just barely be seen in it summons up associations with the history of painting, in this case Lucio Fontana and his slashed canvases. A further association arises from the canvas, on which a painting of drapery can be made out, while it is itself draped over the stretcher like a garment, as it refers to the history of painting since the Renaissance. Moreover, the use of stencilling evokes the history of techniques, marking the distance between an idea, its implementation and what the viewer sees. [NS]

184

Alain Huck (Vevey, 1957)
Kuroi Ame II, 2008
Charcoal on paper, 250×368 cm
Gift of the Arts Visuels Vaud, 2008.
Inv. 2008-371

Kuroi Ame II is part of the *Salons noirs* (*Black Salons*) series of huge charcoal works begun in 2006. Alain Huck explores great human tragedies in these works, freely associating personal, literary, iconographic and historical references, and superimposing different images.

'Kuroi ame', written in capitals in the bottom quarter of the drawing, means 'black rain' in Japanese. It is the title of a 1966 book by Masuji Ibuse recounting the lives of survivors of the 1945 Hiroshima bombing. The author describes the radioactive, ash-laden rain that fell after the atomic bomb was dropped on the city. In the foreground, Huck depicts the lashing rain with vertical sweeps of charcoal pigment using rags and brushes. The carbon black of the charcoal echoes the ashy, death-dealing rain. The spectator must peer through the 'curtain' to make out the underlying composition.

Beneath the layer evoking Hiroshima are open coffins contemplated by a cohort of horsemen. This is a reference to the left-hand side of the *Triumph of Death* (c.1338–9), the right-hand side of the same work inspiring this work's 2008 companion piece *Kuroi Ame*, held in a private collection. The fresco, now attributed to Buonamico Buffalmacco, was painted in Pisa shortly before the outbreak of the Black Death that ravaged Tuscany in 1348.

In juxtaposing eras, circumstances and memories of these tragedies, Huck offers a subjective reading of our human fate. The history of civilisation is seen as a succession of events striving to eradicate human existence, while at the same time preserving it despite the misfortunes that afflict us. [LSCH]

185

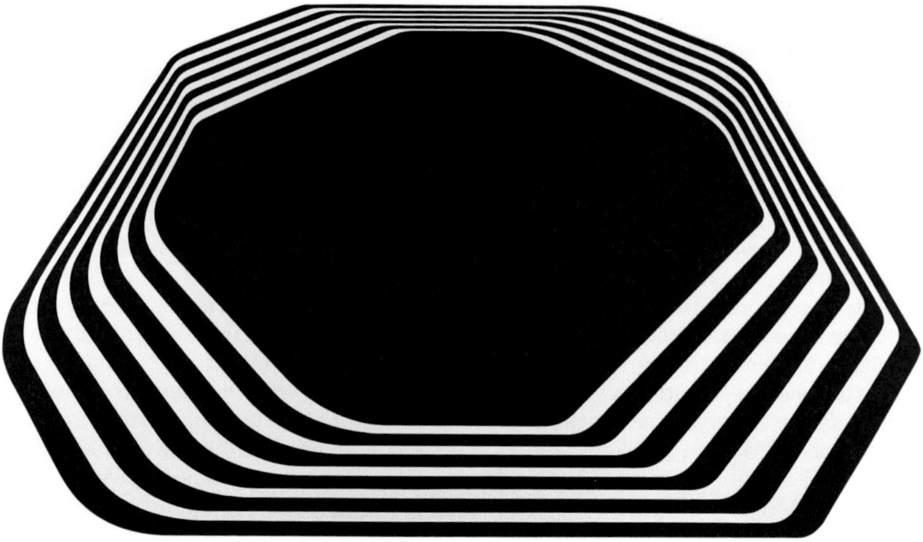

186

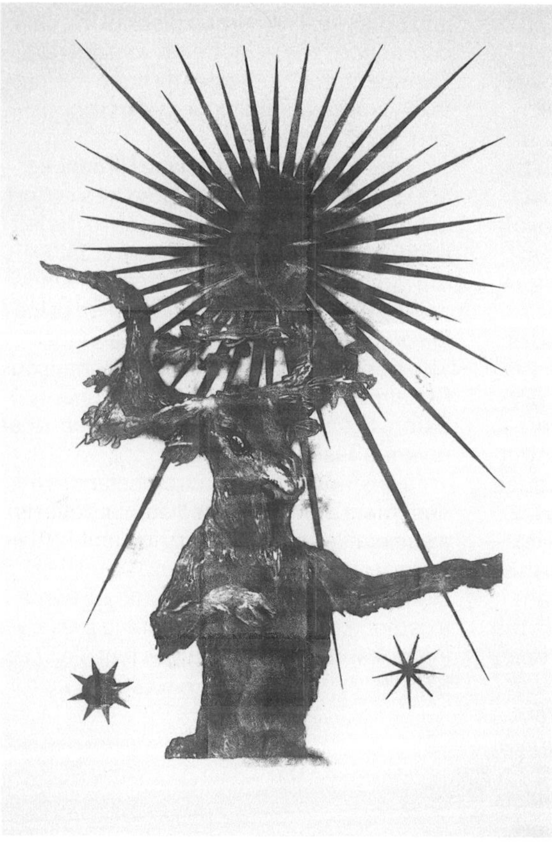

Philippe Decrauzat, Sans titre, 2001
Didier Rittener, Bouc, 2004

185

Philippe Decrauzat (Lausanne, 1974)
Sans titre (*Untitled*), 2001
Acrylic on canvas, 140 × 245 cm
Acquisition by the Commission cantonale des activités culturelles, 2002.
Inv. 2002-004

After graduating from the École cantonale d'art in Lausanne, Philippe Decrauzat co-founded Circuit, an artist-run space in the same city, in 1998. His paintings, murals, installations and films are influenced by the rich heritage of abstraction and op art, drawing on references borrowed from the fine arts, experimental film, popular culture, and music. While the artist returns to the issues of vision, perception and movement dear to the twentieth-century avant-garde movements, his work is by no means a mere patchwork of quotations; rather, it reformulates the same questions in the space of paintings and installations.

Decrauzat produced the polygonal canvas *Sans titre* for the exhibition *Get Angry. Perspectives Romandes 3*, curated at the Museum in 2001. It features five alternating pale and dark bands of varying thickness that follow the curve of the canvas, with a black centre identical in shape to the shaped canvas itself. As the bands narrow and widen, they generate an optical illusion whereby the lines seem to vibrate, challenging our understanding of the painting as a flat surface. It seems to shift from two to three dimensions, from painting to sculpture, while the black centre acts as a bottomless space, an opening, a void. In a 2007 interview, the artist recalled that as he was working on the painting he was watching the film *Alien*, whose space ship reminded him of Frank Stella's *Black Paintings* (1958–60): 'From Stella to *Alien*, you go from a frontal image to a space ship. For Stella, the edge determines the centre; in my paintings there is an impression of depth of field that deforms the centre of the drawing that emerges from the contour.' The painting's shape and optical properties make it 'float' on the wall, challenging our perception of space and our visual grasp of the work when standing in front of it. [NS]

186

Didier Rittener (Lausanne, 1969)
Bouc (*Billy Goat*), 2004
Chemical transfer on paper, 210 × 150 cm, ed. 1/5
Acquisition, 2004. Inv. 2004-016

Didier Rittener designs his transfers, prints, sculptures and murals based on an archive of pencil drawings on A4 tracing paper. The drawings depict faces, animals, ornamental motifs, various patterns and words, that the artist picks out of the flow of images that constantly assails him. Once de-contextualised on paper, they are isolated, modified, resized and/or combined with other subjects, with each step distancing them further from their original source by altering their material nature, with pencil playing the largest role.

The first such drawing dates from 2001, while the archive itself was published in 2004 and 2010 with the title *Libre de droits* (*Out of Copyright*), defining the parameters of Rittener's artistic undertaking. His iconographic repertoire, which he is still developing, is heir to medieval books of motifs used by apprentice copyists for practice and to establish norms for figurative representation by means of examples. Rittener foregrounds the fact that such collections belonged to all and were designed for constant reuse.

Art history is one of Rittener's sources. This large-format *Bouc* juxtaposes the central figure of the devil wearing a vine-leaf wreath, as he was often depicted from the fifteenth century on, in Francisco de Goya's *El aquelarre* (*Witches' Sabbath*, 1797–8, Madrid, Museo Lázaro Galdiano), and stylised and radiant stars, one of which may resemble a virus. Didier Rittener does not necessarily expect visitors to identify the elements he has taken from other works of art. Instead, he aims to conjure up a feeling of déjà-vu and demonstrate the extent to which our visual culture is a pool of intertwined images that we appropriate for our own use. [LSCH]

187

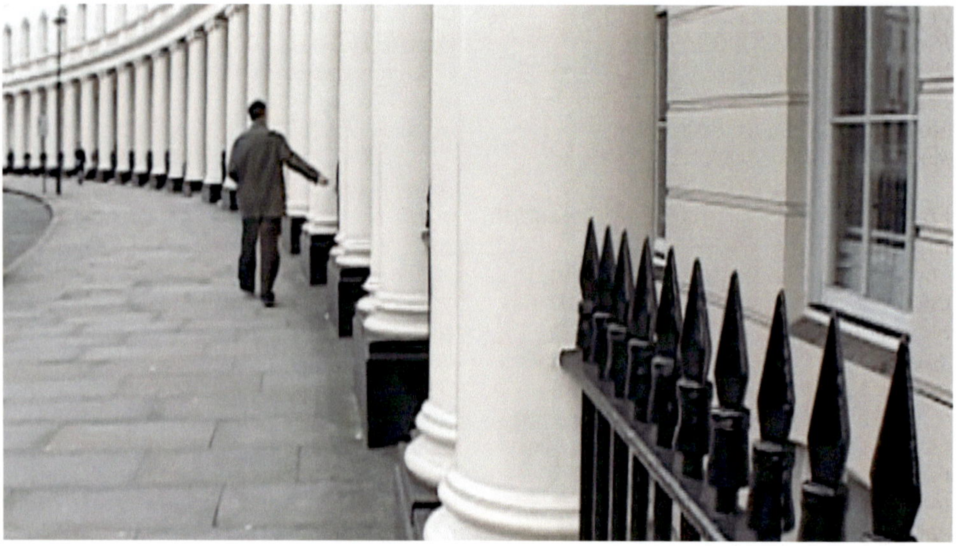

188

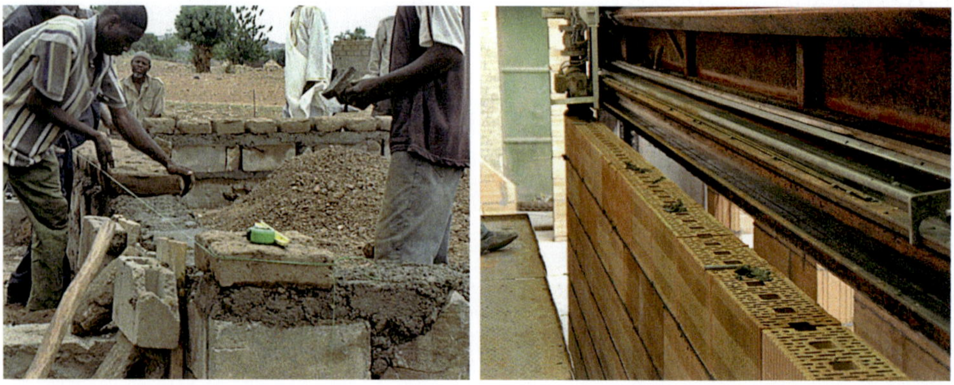

Francis Alÿs, Railings, 2004
Harun Farocki, Vergleich über ein Drittes, 2007

187

Francis Alÿs (Antwerp, 1959)
Railings, 2004
Video, colour, sound, *Park Crescent*, 3 min 25 sec; *Sample 1*, 1 min 35 sec; *Onslow*, 1 min 21 sec, ed. 3/4
Acquisition, 2014. Inv. 2014-001

Francis Alÿs has been walking since 1990. He started his walks in Mexico City, his chosen home since 1986, and has continued in São Paulo, London, Istanbul and Jerusalem, among others. Alÿs is the 'artist as walker' par excellence, one who explores and re-imagines the city by the routes he follows through it.

In *Railings*, Alÿs walks around London, running a drumstick along railings in order to create an urban sound specific to its setting. This gesture, which at first recalls a children's game, may also bring to mind some of the music of John Cage or Steve Reich; it produces a vast repertoire of rhythms produced by the different kinds of railings that the artist walks past. Added to these sounds produced by the gesture of his hand are various accidental noises – a barking dog, a siren, the roar of traffic. But it is the specific score that the artist superimposes over the ambient noise that produces the music here. If his gesture makes the space itself resonate – its structure and linearity, its architectural ruptures and rhythms –, then the impact of the stick on the railings and walls in turn underscores the rhythm of his steps, the movement of his body in space, the passing of time as a movement.

Railings recalls an earlier work by Alÿs, *Time Is a Trick of the Mind* (1998), which consists of a video animation based on drawings, shown as a double projection. We see a man walking alongside a fence with a wooden stick in his hand and we hear the sound of the stick touching the metal, sometimes in synch with the gesture and sometimes out of synch, the two rhythms combining to form a third. *Railings* can thus be read as the culmination of work begun several years earlier, with drawing giving way to performance and musical simulation to capturing reality. [NS]

188

Harun Farocki (Nový Jičín, 1944–Berlin, 2014)
Vergleich über ein Drittes (*Comparison via a Third*), 2007
Double projection video, colour, sound, 24 min, ed. 3/3
Acquisition, 2010. Inv. 2010-018

The work of filmmaker, video artist, and photographer Harun Farocki explores with rare incisiveness the question of the image, especially the documentary image and its various devices. Born in Nový Jičín in Czechoslovakia, which at the time had been annexed by Germany, he later studied at the Deutsche Film- und Fernsehakademie in Berlin, then worked mainly as a filmmaker. He also edited the journal *Filmkritik* from 1974 to 1984, in which he developed an important body of theoretical work on the image.

In the video installation *Vergleich über ein Drittes*, the central idea is the question of work and its representation. The consequences of the processes of rationalisation and automation are interrogated through the example of the production and transformation of bricks. Farocki shows the different work processes in traditional, recently industrialised, and highly industrialised societies. Images filmed in factories in India are projected individually or side-by-side, alternating or juxtaposed with scenes shot in European factories. A linear presentation of increasingly automated production processes is followed by montages of images that blur this kind of one-sided reading. By looking for similarities and contrasts between different temporalities and geographies through the simultaneous montage of two different images, Farocki sets up a dialogue between realities that seemed distinct, while retaining the specificity of each of the contexts.

As the artist explains in a 2004 text, 'In a double projection, there is succession and simultaneity, links from one image to the following image and to the image alongside. Links to what has been seen and to what is being seen at the same time. Imagine the three double bonds between the six carbon atoms in a benzene ring jumping back and forth – that is how ambiguous I imagine the links to be between one element in an image sequence and the one after or beside it.' [NS]

189

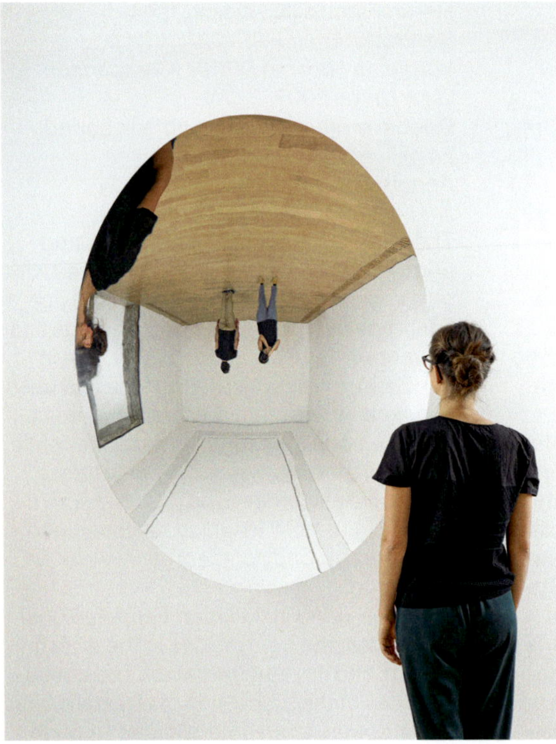

190

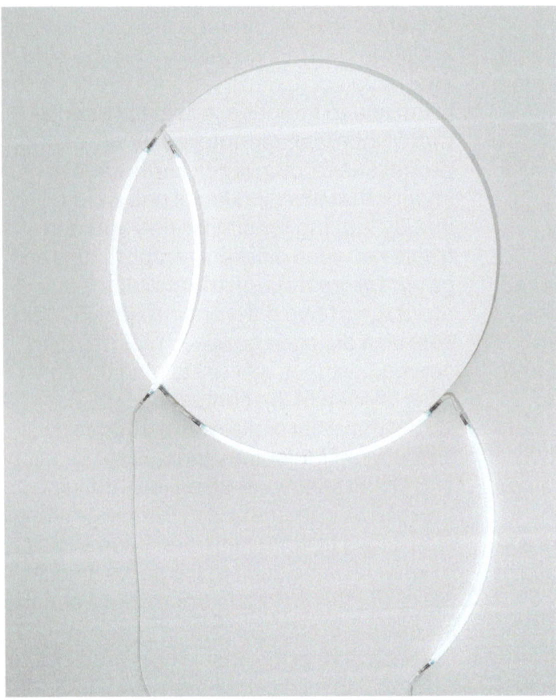

Anish Kapoor, Untitled, 2002
François Morellet, Décrochage n° 4, 2005

189

Anish Kapoor (Bombay, 1954)
Untitled, 2002
Polished stainless steel, 150 × 120 × 33 cm
Alice Pauli Donation, 2018. Inv. 2018-025

Born in India to a cosmopolitan family, with an atheist father from a Hindu background and an Iraqi Jewish mother, Anish Kapoor initially planned to become an engineer before moving to London in 1973 to study art. He has lived there ever since. The Romanian artist Paul Neagu was one of his earliest influences. On a visit to India in 1979, Kapoor found himself drawn to the bright colours of the clothes and spices in the markets and outside the temples. He began using pure pigments in reference to both the modern Western tradition of monochrome painting and Hindu symbolism. He used the pigments to coat strange shapes installed according to a detailed plan, generating visual echoes in a system of internal relations that he saw as freeing up energy. Powerful colour defined the soft, delicate, tactile bodies of his sculptures.

Kapoor's work later took an introspective turn. He made much use of concave shapes and darker colours, and his sculptures grew larger. These combined characteristics created the illusion of an 'empty' space for the viewer to dive into and explore. Matte pigments gave way to reflective materials, such as bronze and polished stainless steel. These 'mirrors' let Kapoor develop the relationship between his works and space even further: they reflect and deform their surroundings and the visitor, who is absorbed into their surface.

This is one such work. We are fascinated to contemplate the large ellipsoid that reverses our bodies, stretching them to exaggerated proportions when we step forward and propelling them into the distance when we step back. Locating the work in the Duchampian and minimalist tradition where art does not exist without an audience, Kapoor compares the close bond between the work and its audience with the married Hindu deities Shiva and Parvati. Once hung on the wall, the concave shape draws in and distorts its surroundings, as if questioning the stability of the real world and our own certainties. [LSCH]

190

François Morellet (Cholet, 1926–2016)
Décrochage n° 4 (*Coming Undone n. 4*), 2005
Acrylic on canvas and neons, 235 × 153 cm
Alice Pauli Donation, 2018. Inv. 2018-103

Despite the severe, bare appearance of his artistic language, François Morellet shows great invention and humour in his approach to geometrical abstraction. After a short figurative period in the late 1940s, the artist rejected expressiveness of style or brushstroke and, in evacuating these signs of subjectivity, followed instead the rigour of mathematics and geometry. In this he was influenced by his friend, the artist Pierre Dmitrienko, and by his discovery of Max Bill and Piet Mondrian. Another source of inspiration was the geometrical motifs that he observed in the productions of various cultures. While Morellet later subjected the making of his works to pre-established constraints, or rigid systems, he also included an element of chance in his approach, for example by using random distributions. In this way he developed a kind of absurd rationality.

Morellet first used neons in 1963, at a time when these tubes were coming to the fore in art (Martial Raysse, Dan Flavin, Mario Merz, etc.), and they remained a central part of his work thereafter. *Décrochage n° 4* belongs to a series that continues his experiments with light and the destabilisation of forms by means of superposition, juxtaposition or fragmentation. As the title of this work indicates – as early as 1956, Morellet began using the names of his pieces to indicate the protocol they involved – it involves a *décrochage*, or unhanging, which means in this instance that two of the neon tubes fixed around the edge of a canvas painted in white acrylic have come loose. This organised catastrophe introduces disorder into order, and injects humour into seriousness. There is a kind of pleasure to be had in considering the way this circle gets out of kilter by breaking up and repositioning itself with an almost ornamental grace. The work shows no more than its constituent elements, yet it reorients them by means of a minimal intervention that is immediately comprehensible to the ordinary viewer. [LSCH]

191

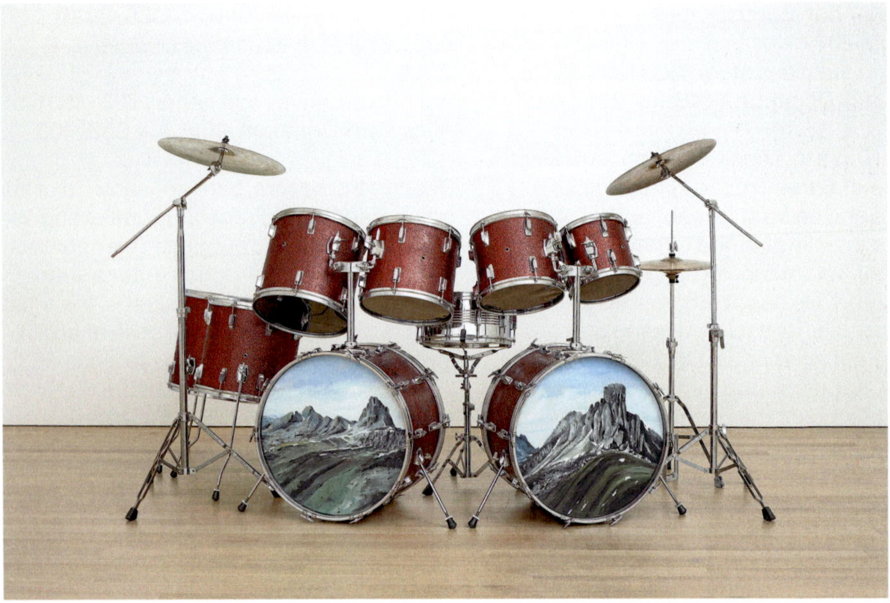

192

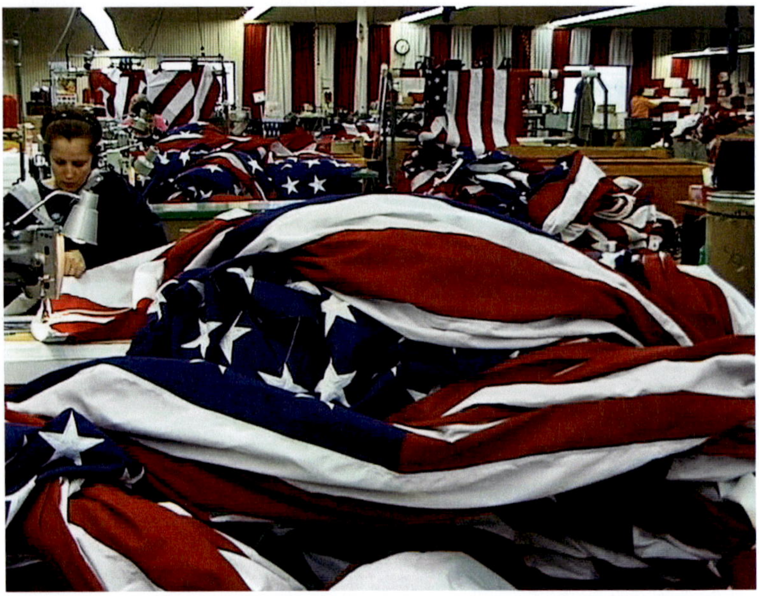

Vincent Kohler, Vintage Drums Ensemble, 2004
Anne-Julie Raccoursier, Grace-Notes, 2005

191

Vincent Kohler (Nyon, 1977)
Vintage Drums Ensemble, 2004
Drums, glitter paint and oil paint on skin, approx. 200×200×300 cm
Acquisition by the Commission cantonale des activités culturelles, 2013. Inv. 2013-039

Vincent Kohler appropriates familiar objects and takes them as far as his imagination will carry him, towards popular culture and, sometimes, childhood. He oversizes and transforms them, giving them a humorous, grotesque or fantastical quality. *Charlotte* (2001, Geneva, Mamco), for example, is a female monster made of giant potatoes whose parts are articulated with toothpicks. *Cervelas* (2008) is a grilled sausage whose ends have been split crosswise, and *Cancan* (2013) is a limited edition of concrete legs inspired by the ones used to display tights.

Music is a favourite theme with this artist, who also plays drums for the group Kunst, and this youthful work, *Vintage Drums Ensemble*, refers to this passion. There is no play on scale here, simply the kind of extensive drum kit used to boost the visual impact of a hard rock band. The artist has decorated the skins with crudely done alpine paintings based on photographs. The instrument no longer seems to serve its usual function, unless one imagines a very iconoclastic drummer. Instead, it has become a device for displaying painting: these tondo windows open to nature, as if we were looking at a landscape through a telescope. For example, a panorama extends across several drums, echoing the 'toms going down', a rhythmic figure typical of rock and jazz.

Vintage Drums Ensemble marks the meeting of two cultures, that of folklore and its picturesqueness, and that of rock. Behind its surprising appearance, verging on bad taste (red glitter and mediocre paintings), the absurdity of this work interrogates the kitsch aesthetic while evoking 'customisation', the practice of appropriating mass-produced objects by adding unique details. [LSCH]

192

Anne-Julie Raccoursier (Lausanne, 1974)
Grace-Notes, 2005
Video, colour, sound, 7 min 30 sec, ed. 1/3
Acquisition by the Commission cantonale des activités culturelles, 2006.
Inv. 2006-017

Anne-Julie Raccoursier's video work stands at the intersection of recorded live scenes and spectacularly staged images. She starts from real life, working on the images to reframe them and give them a fresh rhythm, isolating particular elements and playing with the sound.

Grace-Notes, shot in Pennsylvania in one of the three American factories that makes flags for official use, is the result of a long process of research, interviews and editing, foregrounding the paradoxes involved in 'producing' a national identity. While the work literally explores how the national emblem is made, it is delivered to the viewer by means of ellipsis, since recorded reality too, by definition, precludes a global overview.

Filmed with a camera on a tripod, in classic documentary fashion, *Grace-Notes* opens with a shot of a seamstress at work, wearing noise-cancelling headphones and frowning in concentration, her hands constantly feeding through metres of Stars and Stripes fabric. The shots follow one after the other at a fast pace, framing first each seamstress bent over her monotonous task, then the group as a whole – an army of women at work, almost motionless except for their hands. Only the fabric that quickly piles up in the foreground seems to have a life of its own. We hear the chatter of the machines and a hypnotic soundtrack of looped guitar chords, but there is no off-screen voice commenting on or interpreting the images. The only words framing the video are those on the label the artist has displayed alongside the video wherever it is shown: 'When you buy an American flag ... You wouldn't like to see a tag on it ... with the words "Made in China".' [NS]

193

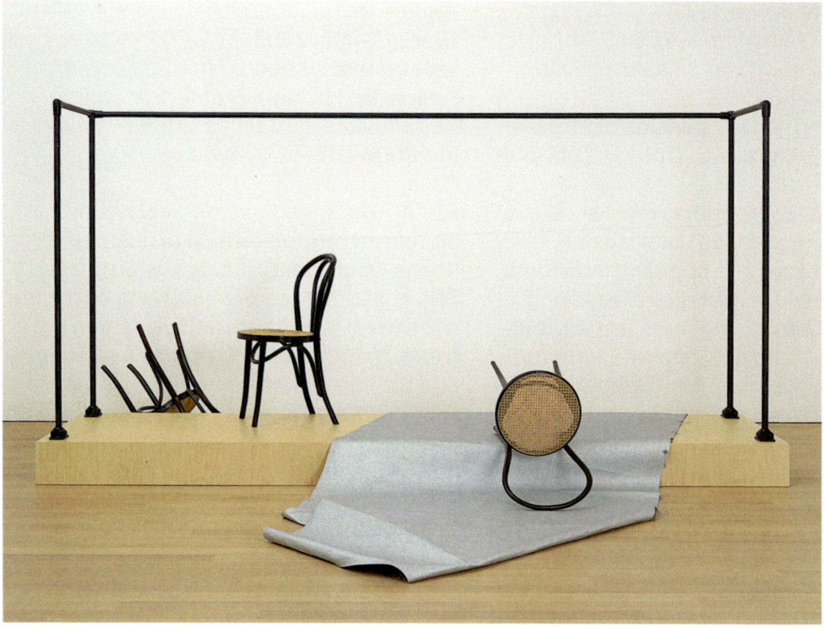

194

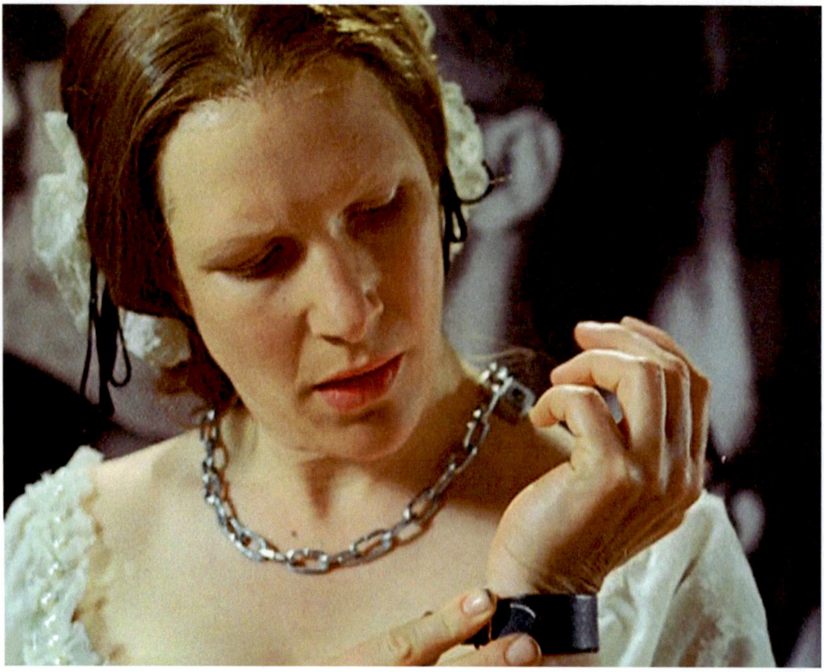

Tom Burr, Abstract Lausanne II / Lausanne Abstrait II, 2006
Pauline Boudry / Renate Lorenz, Normal Work, 2007

193

Tom Burr (New Haven, 1963)
Abstract Lausanne II / Lausanne Abstrait II, 2006
Plywood, steel, canvas, paint, eyelets, hooks, 3 chairs, 184×365×92 cm
Acquisition, 2006. Inv. 2006-007

Tom Burr produces works – photographs, sculptures and installations – that revisit the formal vocabulary of the avant-gardes, especially minimalism and post-minimalism, and combines pop iconography, gay culture, architecture and contemporary design with musical, cinematic and literary influences. The artist reprises the appropriation found in the art of the 1980s as a strategy that can be used to revisit works from the past and to reveal new meanings.

For his show at the Museum in 2006, Burr made two installations, *Abstract Lausanne I* and *II / Lausanne Abstrait I* and *II*, their titles based on that of a small abstract canvas painted by Francis Picabia in Lausanne in 1918, when he was being treated for addiction after several years spent in New York (*Abstrait Lausanne*, private collection). It is this biographical echo which enables Burr to situate these works within a definite geographical and temporal framework, that of his own presence in Lausanne. As the artist says, 'During this time I developed the desire to merge the concerns of space and design and physicality... with thoughts of subjectivity, sexual identity, and audience, as well as a nascent concern with *autobiography*'.

Abstract Lausanne II consists of three chairs set within a space created by a base delimited by metal bars, with a curtain laid on the ground, like a kind of small platform or stage devoid of characters. Here, Burr is revisiting minimalist sculpture and its connection to space and the viewer's body, by exacerbating its theatricality, its literality and its apparent emptiness. However, in contrast to minimalist forms, *Abstract Lausanne II* seems to be on the verge of collapse, on the fragile border between a presence structured in space and its lurch towards chaos (overturned chairs, the curtain on the ground). The narrative, associative, and even allegorical potential of this three-dimensional 'collage' thus vies with its capacity to form an image in space. [NS]

194

Pauline Boudry (Lausanne, 1972) /
Renate Lorenz (Bonn, 1963)
Normal Work, 2007
16 mm film transferred to high-definition video, colour, sound, 13 min, and 13 photographs (each 102×102×12 cm)
Acquisition, 2007. Inv. 2007-016

Born in Lausanne and based in Berlin since the late 1990s, Pauline Boudry has developed a practice that embraces film and video on the one hand and music on the other. Since 2007 she has produced all her projects in collaboration with Renate Lorenz. One recurring theme in their art concerns the links between work and sexuality, be it the work of constructing sexual identities or work as the place where these identities are tirelessly produced and reproduced.

The film *Normal Work* was inspired by archive photographs taken in 1860s England, which are themselves an integral part of the installation. These are portraits and self-portraits by Hannah Cullwick, a woman who all her life worked as a servant. In them, she poses in her working clothes, but also in 'class drag' or in 'ethnic drag' – that is, playing the roles of a bourgeois woman or black slave. These pictures were part of her secret sado-masochistic relationship with Arthur Munby, a London-based barrister, writer and photographer.

Normal Work raises the question of transgressing the limits between social hierarchies, classes, genders and races that Cullwick represented, hierarchies of which she was both the object and the protagonist, in that the images in these photographs enabled her to produce changes of social position that she also experienced in her daily life, notably when she travelled with Munby disguised in 'bourgeois drag'. By having the performance artist Werner Hirsch replay four of Cullwick's poses, the film interrogates the topicality of the questions raised by these archive photographs, that is to say, the fragile intersection between roles and identities in a world of work that continues to be traversed, albeit in different forms, by class and gender relations. [NS]

195

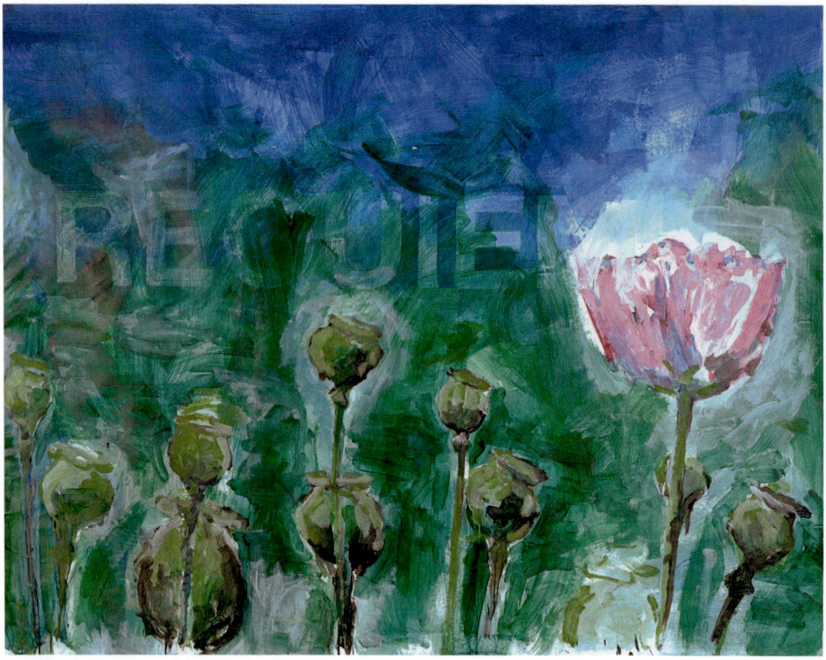

196

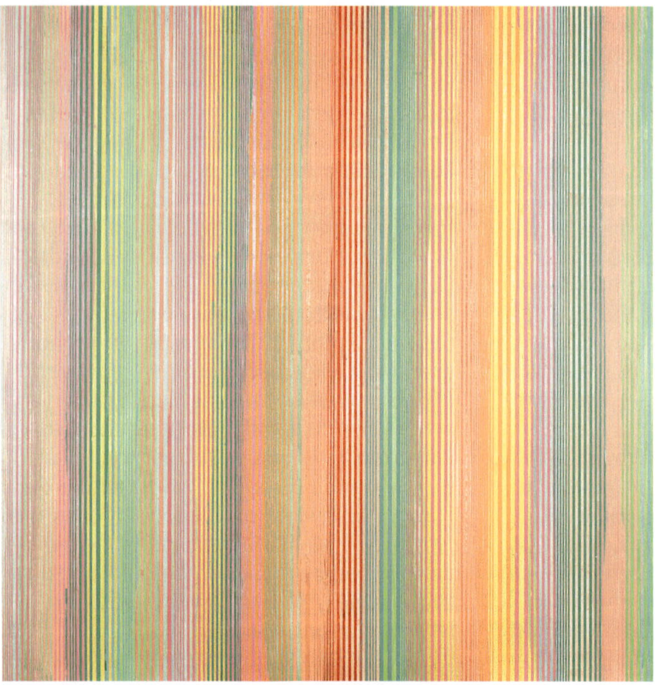

David Hominal, Flowers, 2006
Michael Scott, ATHTTSTW # 7, 2009

195

David Hominal (Évian, 1976)
Flowers, 2006
Acrylic on paper, 148 × 190 cm
Gift of the artist, 2009. Inv. 2009-002

David Hominal mixes images from different sources and references with different arts and pictorial traditions in order to take on the great narratives of painting, and even to partake in them, with the gravity of a person forging their own path, despite the doubts. For him, painting is an imperative duty: a space of respite as well as of tyranny, which in spite of it all, remains a realm of endless possibility.

Hominal's love of classical music and jazz is regularly echoed in his work, notably in the words – musical terms, names of musicians, titles, etc. – that he inscribes there in block print. Here, a diaphanous 'REQUIEM' (from the Latin word for 'rest') is bannered across the cusp of a flowery meadow and an electric-blue sky. The iconography of *Flowers* is thus rich in symbols. In the foreground, filling more than half the image, the capsules of opium poppies – the opiate latex oozes from the incisions made in them – surround the last blooming flower. A bright, luminous pink, this dominates the picture like a lighthouse in the night, piercing the sky with its gleams. A dreamlike vision of luxuriant nature in the chiaroscuro of consciousness, this work exudes a serene melancholy.

Hominal usually works in series and it is tempting to see another, larger work of his, *Requiem* (2006, held at this Museum), also made on the same fragile paper support as the pendant of *Flowers*. It certainly helps orient our reading: blazoned across its surface, the words 'PAINTING', 'REQUIEM', 'PAINTING' are obscured by a layer of white paint, and over the second 'PAINTING' is another 'REQUIEM', this time its white letters formed by a black outline. The artist seems to be defying the often-proclaimed death of painting with his own persistence. At the same time, he evokes the vain desire to represent things that do not last. [LSCH]

196

Michael Scott (Paoli, 1958)
ATHTTSTW # 7, 2009
Enamel paint on aluminium, 152 × 152 cm
Acquisition, 2014. Inv. 2014-024

In 2014, Circuit, an artist-run space in Lausanne, held an exhibition of works by Michael Scott, including *ATHTTSTW # 7*, which paid homage to his influence on artists in the french-speaking part of Switzerland, most notably Philippe Decrauzat. As Decrauzat stated in a 2007 interview, he obtained the shimmering effect in his first paintings by reproducing scans taken from Scott's kinetic black and white *Stripes Paintings* (1988–94) as colour gradations.

ATHTTSTW # 7 is part of a series of paintings begun in 2009. It takes its title from the initial letters of the sentence 'And Then He Tried To Swallow The World', chosen by the artist when he first showed the series at the Gering & López Gallery in New York in 2009 to reflect the fact that it was his most ambitious exhibition since the 1990s.

The hand-painted lines – part brushstrokes, part drips – make *ATHTTSTW # 7* almost musical in scope, with subtle variations that generate a sense of slow movement rather than the intense optical pulsation of his black and white paintings of the late 1980s. The intuitive process of creation and its inherent imperfections are visible: the rhythm of the lines swings between a regular pattern and variations, with three thin lines alternating with broader ones that expand and shrink, returning to the original rhythm. The artist could almost have carried on forever, the edge of the panel bringing the process to an arbitrary end. The lines of colour, from pale to bright pink and from dark green to blue-grey and orange, stand out against a background of large bands of colour in an interplay of alternations, echoes, and repeats of colour that imbue the painting and its composition with a sense of energy. [NS]

197

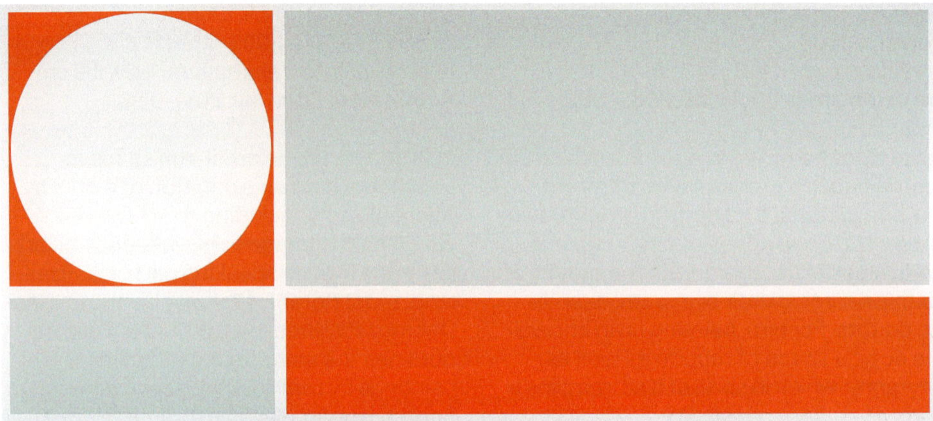

198

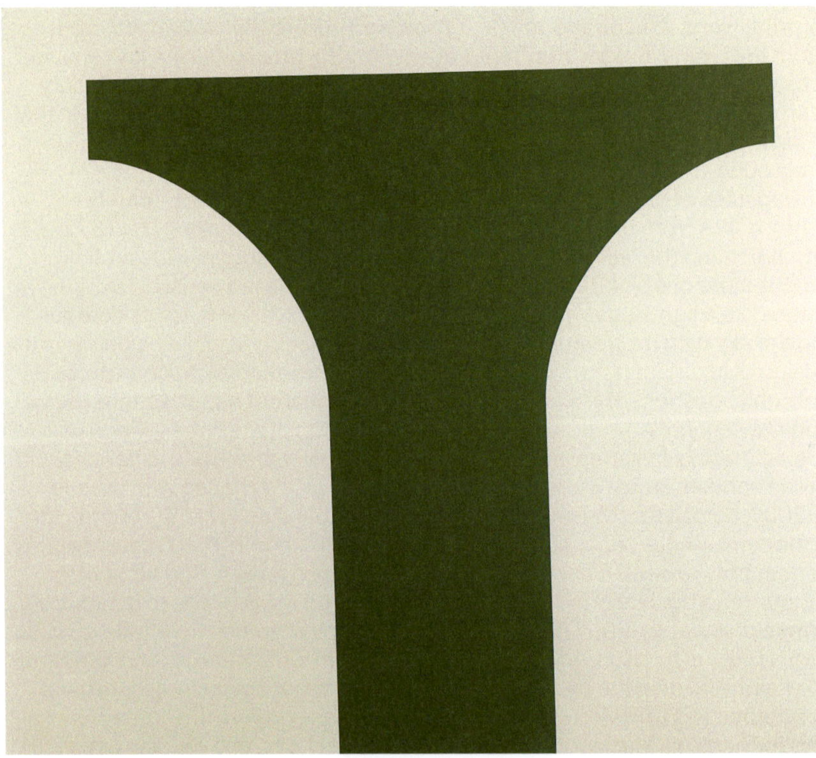

Francis Baudevin, Sans titre (Talens), 2008/10
Christoph Gossweiler, Peinture, vert olive, 2008

197

Francis Baudevin (Bulle, 1964)
Sans titre (Talens) (*Untitled [Talens]*), 2008/10
Acrylic on canvas, 110 × 250 cm
Acquisition by the Commission cantonale des activités culturelles, 2009. Inv. 2009-061

Since 1987, Francis Baudevin has been producing a referential form of geometrical abstraction. He postulates that it is impossible to create even abstract art without referring to preexisting images, if only involuntarily. Each of his works faithfully repeats the forms and colours, as well as the proportions of a composition derived from a logo, packaging or record cover, removing the words and considerably enlarging what remains. Sometimes, the title of the resulting work alludes to its origins but usually the reference is manifest only in the formal elements repeated by the artist.

This approach reflects the omnipresence of blocks of colour and the language of geometry in our visual environment, but also the endless possibilities of the abstract repertoire, despite its limited vocabulary. It also bears witness to the way different forms of abstract art, particularly concrete art, have influenced graphics (Baudevin has worked as a designer in that field, as did Max Bill, the chief proponent of concrete art). In this sense, he is taking forms back to their origins. Finally, the artist shows how deeply advertising images penetrate our memory; it is not unusual for his images to cause a feeling of déjà-vu.

Sans titre (Talens) is typical of Baudevin's work. Four quadrilaterals are fitted into a white rectangle, two are a light grey colour and two an orangish red. One of the red squares has a large grey-white circle cut out of it. This small grid contains a maximum number of oppositions (of colour, shapes and sizes). The painting is applied in as neutral a fashion as possible, with no trace of brushstrokes, no detectable gesture. Voided of the original typography, the composition now appears as an image, asserting its uniqueness against the multiplicity of Royal Talens products– supplier of fine arts materials–, for which it was first created. [LSCH]

198

Christoph Gossweiler (Hüttlingen, 1950)
Peinture, vert olive (*Painting, Olive Green*), 2008
Acrylic on canvas, 135 × 154 cm
Acquired with the support of Circuit, espace d'art contemporain, Lausanne, 2011. Inv. 2011-199

A self-taught painter, Christoph Gossweiler began his career in the mid-1970s, adopting the practice of seriality that played an important role, especially in minimalist art and in conceptual art. Also evident in his work is the influence of Zurich concrete art. Gossweiler developed a style of painting based on the subdivision of the pictorial surface or logic-based variations of geometrical forms. He also produced monochrome works.

This work, which is presented without a stretcher, was created for a joint exhibition in 2008, *La chute d'eau*, celebrating ten years of activity of Circuit, an artist-run space in Lausanne. The artists were invited to explore the theme of the waterfall, the subject of a poster left by the previous occupants of the exhibition space, and the background to Marcel Duchamp's installation *Given: 1. The Waterfall, 2. The Illuminating Gas...* (1946–66, Philadelphia Museum of Art), a photograph of the Forestay waterfall at Chexbres in Switzerland. Gossweiler chose to contribute *Peinture, vert olive*, selecting it from the model of a solo exhibition planned for 2002 but never held.

The work's title doesn't offer any clues to its subject. It provides only objective information concerning the medium ('peinture') and colour ('vert olive'). Visitors are thus encouraged to read the green form for itself. The shape is formed by offcuts of sticker sheets for miniature cars on a normalised scale of 1:43, which the artist found in a model-making shop and transposed back into a scale of 1:1, including the paper background. This explains the unusual format and slightly off-kilter shape, which results from its original position on the sheet of stickers. [LSCH]

199

200

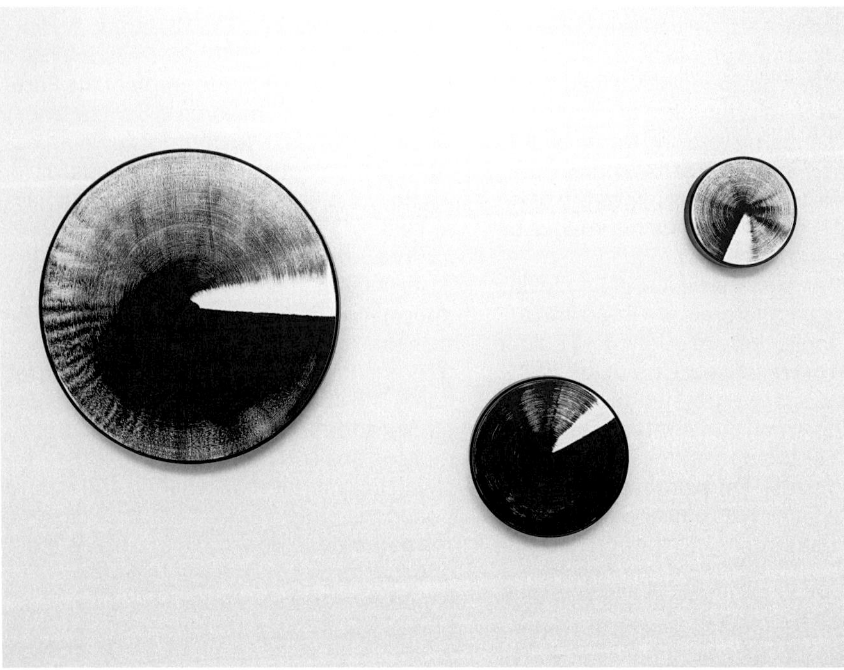

Pierre Schwerzmann, Sans titre, 2010
Claudia Comte, Turn and Slip 120, 4/4, Turn and Slip 40, 1/4, Turn and Slip 60, 4/4, 2015

199

Pierre Schwerzmann (Aubonne, 1947)
Sans titre (*Untitled*), 2010
Acrylic on canvas, 130 × 180 cm
Alain and Suzanne Dubois Collection. Promised gift

Since the 1970s, Pierre Schwerzmann has been exploring the condition of painting as a space of perception rather than as a cultural object. At times his work has focused on the painting's stretcher, at others on the canvas, which he has folded, torn, incised and partially left visible. He has incorporated objects into the surface of the painting, layered canvases of the same colour but different formats, and worked with mirror-paintings. These strategies, often destined to undermine the illusion of the pictorial space, all share in the same theoretical approach to the act of painting and what focusing on painting allows us to understand.

Schwerzmann has often set gradations of colour in the background of his works, enjoying the sense of distortion generated by the process. Gradations of colour open up a space in the painting thanks to the depth created by the shading of black to white, opening up a patch of light in the centre of the canvas, to the left or right, top or bottom. In some instances, the disruptive presence of a painted monochrome shape, full and flat, lies across the gradation of colour, disturbing the gaze, which finds it difficult to settle on any one point: the form is legible, while the space it rests on contradicts it. In a 2000 interview with the artist Robert Ireland, Schwerzmann explained that he saw the background of his paintings as 'a participant in its own right that works to dilate and contract the scale of grey'. He added that 'if it is not in colour, it is because colour would distract us from the function that I here attribute to value: producing this spatial effect, this groundswell'.

This 2010 work does not include a shape interfering with the relationship with the background; rather, it speaks with one single pictorial language. The gradual contact between black and white generates a zone of vibration and the optical illusion of an area that might equally be concave or convex, drawing the viewer in for a closer look to realise that it really is just part of the painted surface. [LSCH]

200

Claudia Comte (Grancy, 1983)
Turn and Slip 120, 4/4, *Turn and Slip 40, 1/4*, *Turn and Slip 60, 4/4*, 2015
Acrylic on canvas, resp. 120 cm (diam.), 40 cm (diam.) and 60 cm (diam.)
Acquisition by the Commission cantonale des activités culturelles, 2016.
Inv. 2016-030, 2016-031 and 2016-032

Claudia Comte revisits the history of forms, with references ranging from sculpture of the first half of the twentieth century (Hans Arp, Constantin Brancusi, Barbara Hepworth, etc.) to artistic movements of the mid-century and beyond (concrete art, op art, pop art, etc.), but also to vernacular and popular culture (cinema, cartoons, etc.). She relates these to one another while creating a new visual system. Her preference for wood as her main material, which she works on with a chainsaw, is rooted in her childhood years living in a village near a forest. Comte emphasises closeness to nature and an artisanal finish in her works. Whether organic or geometrical, these are often inserted in a powerful graphic environment, as in the case of mural paintings with op art motifs, or a set of paintings on stretchers. Comte physically juxtaposes the quotations that she summons up in relations that are always precise, and in a dialogue between the second and third dimensions, driven by visual playfulness and pleasure.

Turn and Slip 120, 4/4, *Turn and Slip 40, 1/4* and *Turn and Slip 60, 4/4* belong to a series of circular paintings whose diameters range from 40 to 140 cm. They were made using a brush whose width matched the radius of the support, which was applied in a single movement of the hand. The progressive unloading of the paint produced striations and then white when there was no more acrylic left. The indication '1/4' means that Comte dipped her brush in the paint once in order to obtain a given chromatic density, whereas '4/4' means that she dipped it four times. As is her habit, this artist followed simple rules. Here, too, she explores the random dimension of a compositional method that, by its principle, demands scrupulous application. The pictorial condition of abstraction is reduced to a protocol, the execution of which is calibrated by an instrument, a gesture and a geometrical support, and therefore by the 'turns' and 'slips' of the brush mentioned in the title. [LSCH]

201

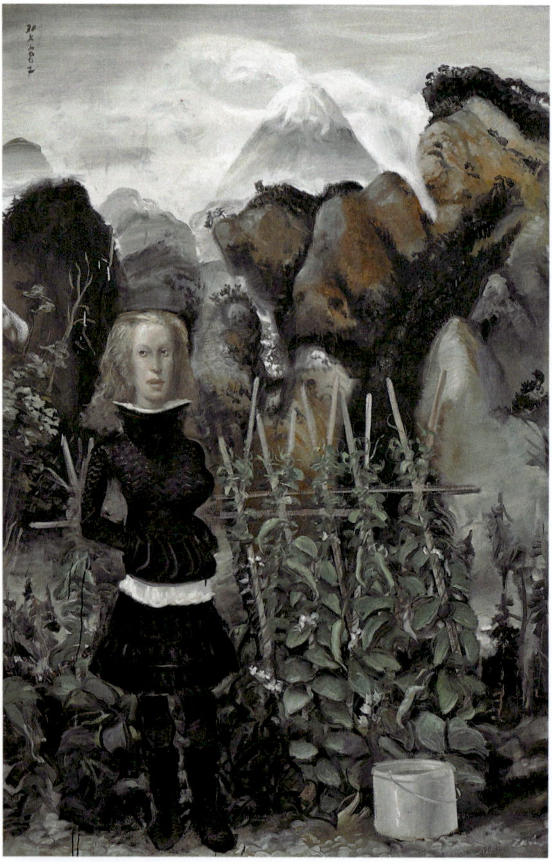

202

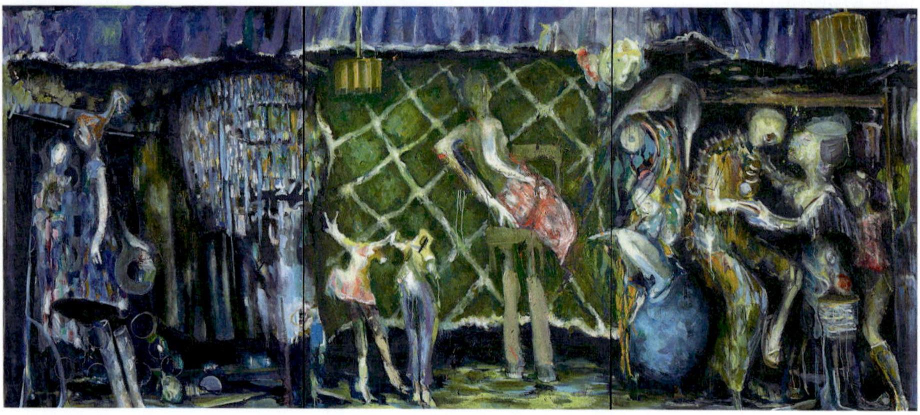

Stéphane Zaech, Pearl Harbor (Madonna dell'Orto), 2007
Valérie Favre, Crystal Palace, 2014–16

201

Stéphane Zaech (Vevey, 1966)
Pearl Harbor (Madonna dell'Orto), 2007
Oil on canvas, 195 × 130 cm
Acquisition by the Commission cantonale des activités culturelles, 2009.
Inv. 2009-016

Entering Stéphane Zaech's imaginary realm and his studio are equally reassuring experiences. The visitor feels a sense of familiarity on seeing genres canonised by art history such as portraits, landscapes and history paintings and joy at witnessing a solid mastery of the artist's trade, judging the ambition of his formats, and seeing the classical techniques of drawing and oil painting still in use. Yet the sense of celebration soon dissolves: there is no trace of Greek beauty, harmonious proportions, or transparent subjects. Zaech's art seems to hang together solely by its virtuoso execution, playing with references to the geniuses whose work he has studied in depth, from the Baroque masters to Pablo Picasso, Francis Bacon and Alex Katz.

The painting's title is another take on his approach, combining literary ideas and caustic reveries. It conjures up the Second World War (Pearl Harbor) and the Venice church decorated by Tintoretto and where he lies buried (Madonna dell'Orto) – two times and spaces that collide on the canvas. In concrete terms, the work features the almost forced inclusion of a figure inspired by the seventeenth-century Spanish painter Diego Velásquez, with contemporary faces, attitudes and clothing. The preciosity of the cross-dressing figure ('Pearl') contrasts with the bucolic countryside panorama ('orto', the orchard).

'The beans come straight from the neighbourhood kitchen gardens, and the mountain landscape is also based on my surroundings, corrupted by my memory that arranges things to suit itself as it goes along', the artist explains. All sorts of 'arrangement' and 'corruption' are apparent in this sardonic pastiche of an eighteenth-century masquerade, influenced by classical Chinese landscape painting, down to its very composition and even the artist's signature. [CL]

202

Valérie Favre (Évilard, 1959)
Crystal Palace, 2014–16
Oil on canvas, 170 × 390 cm (triptych)
Acquisition, 2017. Inv. 2017-017

Before devoting herself to the visual arts in the 1980s, Valérie Favre worked as a theatre actress in Geneva and Paris. After a brief stab at performance art, she turned to painting as a medium that was sufficiently physical to please her. She engages fully with its materiality and paints for hours on end, sometimes without stopping to eat, spending months on each work. Her total involvement is accompanied, paradoxically enough, by a kind of pragmatism in her attitude to the 'impossible' undertaking of making things visible.

Crystal Palace belongs to her *Les Théâtres* series, begun in 2007. Over three panels forming a kind of panorama, the artist lays out a frieze of figures (dancers, acrobats, animals, skeletons – some of these dressed in harlequin suits) that recalls the dance of death motif. The curtains and lamps tell us that they are on a stage. Because of the tight framing, viewers cannot say whether they are standing on the rostrum or among the audience. Favre heightens this sense of uncertainty by having her *Théâtres* hung relatively low, the better to embrace the world around them. She thus opens up a frontal narrative about the darkness and beauty of humanity, about the tragedy and comedy of all life, about what she calls 'the madness of the world'.

Favre paints without preliminary sketches. She lays out her setting and then puts in the individual figures, which she is constantly correcting – a first state of *Crystal Palace* was exhibited in Strasbourg in 2015, after which she reworked the positions and postures of certain figures, as well as their clothing. On the left, for example, she has substituted a chandelier for a figure in an aquarium. And she has removed tables that served as stages. The great narrative power and aura of this triptych result from its teeming composition, its imaginative richness and its expressive treatment of the paint (colours, drips, impasto, accidents). [LSCH]

203

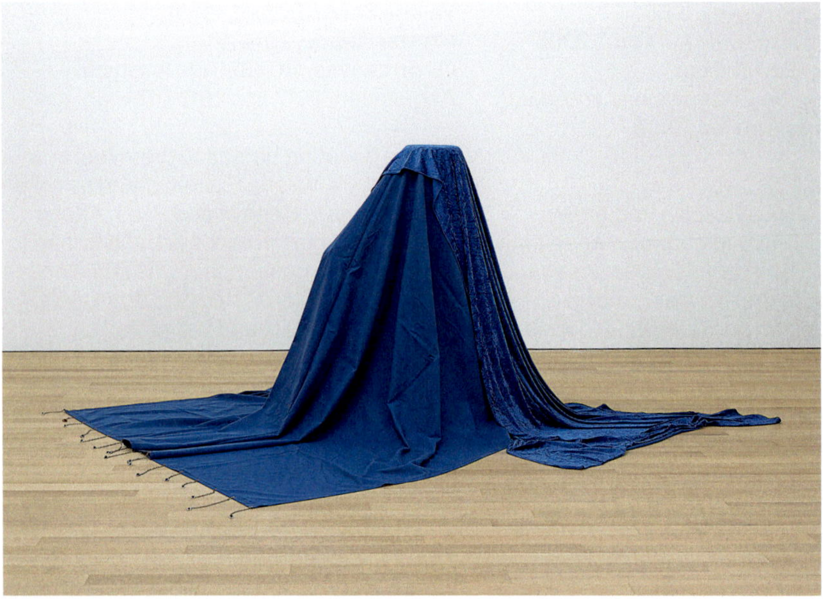

204

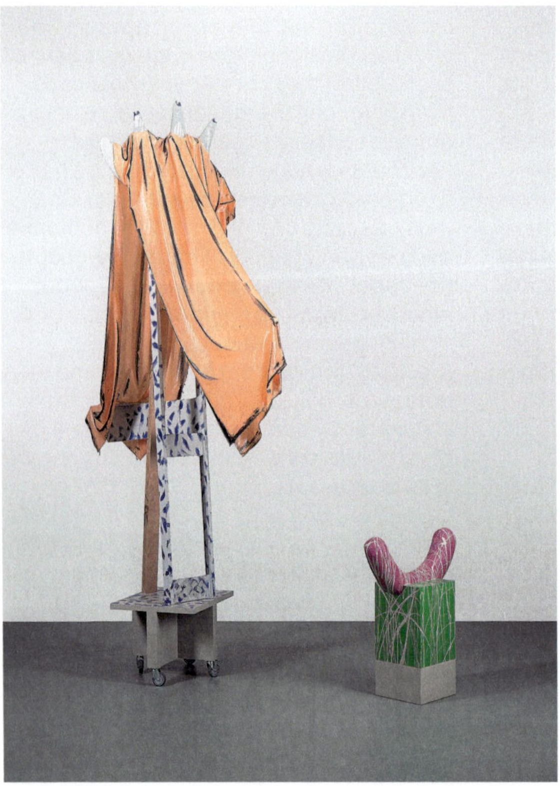

Delphine Coindet, Le cyclope, 2011
Christopher Füllemann, The Peeks and the Kiss, 2013

203

Delphine Coindet (Albertville, 1969)
Le cyclope (*Cyclops*), 2011
Machine tool, fabric, metal, glass, dimensions variable
Gift of the artist, 2014. Inv. 2014-006

After studying at the École des Beaux-Arts, Nantes, and at the Institut des Hautes Études en Arts Plastiques, Paris, Delphine Coindet spent several years in Lausanne, where she was an active member of the artist-run space Circuit and a teacher at École cantonale d'art in Lausanne.

Le cyclope was created in her studio in Lausanne. Part found object, part surrealist assemblage, the sculpture is 'as beautiful as the fortuitous encounter on a dissecting table of a sewing machine and an umbrella', to quote Lautréamont's well-known observation taken up by André Breton. It is a machine tool, a relic of the studio's industrial past, with two rectangles of blue cloth draped over it, hiding it completely. One of the rectangles is blue synthetic velvet, the other cotton canvas edged with glass buttons held on by small gilded metal chains.

The machine draped with fabric suggests a series of contrasts – solid/soft, rough/smooth, utilitarian/decorative – deconstructed by the fabric hiding the machine: the sculpture is simultaneously on view and hiding from view. While the title evokes its anthropomorphic shape and the question of perception, the cyclops of Greek mythology with one eye in the middle of his forehead also points to the monstrous creature's link with metalworking, and hence to the 'soul' of Coindet's sculpture. The artist is heir to the legacies of both assemblage and minimalist sculpture, imbuing what seem to be abstract sculptures with all the poetry, theatricality and tactility that had been stripped from them. As she wrote in a note of intent when she was artist in residence at the Villa Medicis in Rome in 2011–12, 'Sculpture is an art of transition and I am interested first and foremost in it as an incomplete form'. [NS]

204

Christopher Füllemann (Lausanne, 1983)
The Peeks and the Kiss, 2013
Wood, fabric treated with epoxy, expanding foam, acrylic, enamel, rollers, 317 × 175 × 100 cm
Acquisition by the Commission cantonale des activités culturelles, 2013. Inv. 2013-036

A graduate of the École cantonale d'art de Lausanne and the San Francisco Art Institute, Christopher Füllemann works at the intersection of sculpture and performance. Ephemeral or fragile materials (wax, latex, mirror glass, fabric and ceramics) combine with bright colours to exist in space, not as isolated objects, but as so many elements of a movement of which the viewer is an integral part.

Thus, for his exhibition *Forms and Lovers*, held at the Museum in 2013, Füllemann created a series of seven monumental sculptures, among them *The Peeks and the Kiss*. The artist froze in mid-movement an orange fabric with folds underscored in blue, draped over a wooden structure crowned with spines and suggesting a ladder – and treated it with epoxy resin. On an arm of the structure, a metal handle is placed at hand-height, whereas the sculpture rests on a base fitted with casters. As the artist formulates it in a statement of intent from 2012, the idea is not only to evoke the possible feel or movement of the sculpture, but also to allow the viewer to genuinely activate it: 'The anthropomorphic aspect of my works, evoked both by their form and by their dimensions, results from a desire to see these three-dimensional collages as performers.' And in fact, *The Peeks and the Kiss* occupies space like a monumentally proportioned dancer. The dynamic relationship between immobility and movement, between viewers' bodies and the body of the sculpture, between the space occupied by the work and the potential space of its displacement, is perceptible. The only thing grounding it in a precise place is the chair that comes with it: *You and Me Both (Green and Purple)*, a coloured cube with a half-moon set into it in the style of Franz West. But if Füllemann's work lays claim to a heritage, it is that of the 'eccentric abstraction' of an Eva Hesse or a Bruce Nauman, somewhere between the visual and the tactile, the conceptual and the sensual, abstraction and figuration. [NS]

205

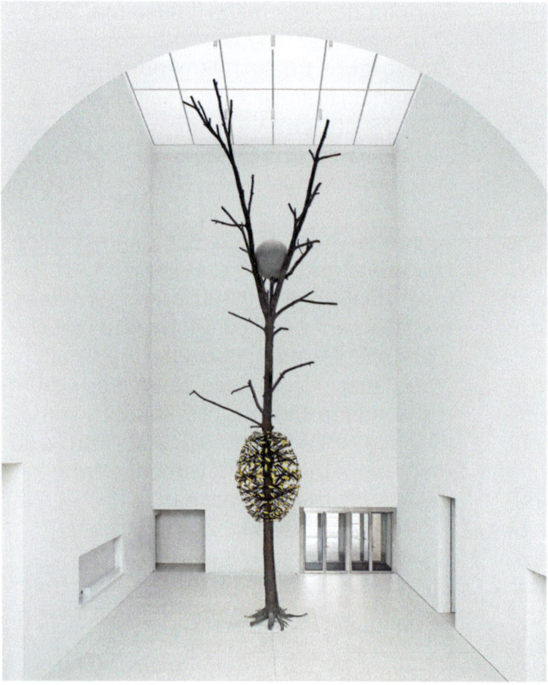

206

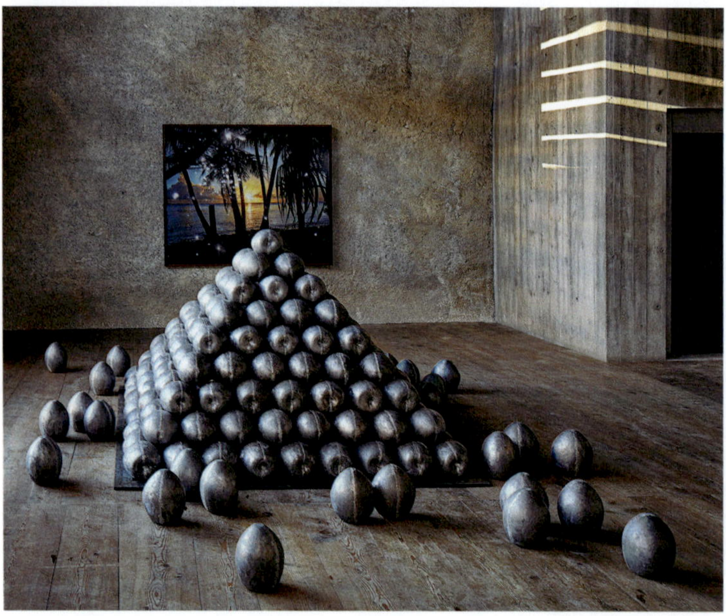

Giuseppe Penone, Luce e ombra, 2011
Julian Charrière, Pacific Fiction – Study for Monument, 2016

Giuseppe Penone (Garessio, 1947)
Luce e ombra, 2011
Bronze, gold and granite,
1450 × 470 × 490 cm
Gift of Alice Pauli in memory of her son Olivier, 2016. Inv. 2017-006

Trees as a motif and wood as a material are constant presences in Giuseppe Penone's work. He has exhibited blocks of wood, carved trunks into a tree trunk and sculpted them in marble, assembled branches into a base, exposed roots, made prints from bark, and turned growth rings into fingerprints, exploring the connection between man and nature.

A leafless bronze tree standing fourteen metres tall, an ellipsoid outgrowth of gilded leaves, and a granite sphere are the three elements and materials of this sculpture, a surprising blend of organic and geometric, with surrealist echoes of Max Ernst and René Magritte. Giuseppe Penone commented on the work: 'The tree reaches for the sky and the foliage broadens into an ample sphere to gather as much light as it can. This is why the leaves are gilded. Bronze, on the other hand, is an element subject to the force of gravity that pulls us down towards the depths of the earth, to darkness.' The granite ball perches atop the tree as if it had fallen from the skies. The perfect geometric form creates a striking contrast with the tree, an organic element that for Penone is the prototype of the ideal sculpture.

According to the Book of Genesis, the first act in the creation of the world was separating light and darkness. The theme of light and shade is materialised in Penone's work in a superb, eminently sensual, and somehow enigmatic work of art. Standing in the Museum entrance lobby, a neutral space where people come and go, the sculpture marks its territory, defining it as part of the realm of art. It explores a question that is fundamental to the act of perception, as light and shade are the absolute prerequisites for visibility. [BF]

Julian Charrière (Morges, 1987)
Pacific Fiction – Study for Monument, 2016
259 coconuts encased in lead, steel frame,
128 × 330 × 440 cm
Acquired with the support of Evangelos Stassinopoulos in memory of Jacques Treyvaud, and the Commission cantonale des activités culturelles, 2017. Inv. 2017-020

Faithful to the heritage of conceptual art, fascinated by land art and especially by Robert Smithson, influenced by Olafur Eliasson's teaching at the Institut für Raumexperimente in Berlin, Julian Charrière sets in motion research processes that give rise to performances, photographic records, films and installations. His materials, including decaying organic matter, cryogenically frozen plants, sediment and salt bricks reflect particular times and spaces, both as tangible traces of what he calls a 'geology of history' and as explorations of humanity's interdependent relationship with our environment.

Pacific Fiction – Study for Monument is one of a set of works created by Charrière following his exploration of the Marshall Islands and the Bikini atoll, part of his research into former nuclear testing sites as dystopian places *par excellence*. The United States test-fired nearly seventy nuclear bombs in the Marshall Islands from 1946 to 1958, including Castle Bravo, the single most powerful H-bomb, which wiped two islands from the map.

Pacific Fiction, a pyramid of coconuts encased in lead, can be read as the model for a future memorial. The coconuts refer to the etymology of the Bikini atoll, which takes its name from the local Melanesian name 'Pikinni', 'pik' meaning 'surface' and 'ni' meaning 'coconut palm'. The lead is used for its physical property of withstanding radiation. While the pile of coconuts echoes a stock of cannon balls, the work's pyramid shape and its subtitle, *Study for Monument*, also conjure up images of a tomb, Egyptian pyramids, the architecture of the bunkers on the Bikini atoll shoreline, and the angular iron monoliths that slumber in the depths of the Pacific. [NS]

207

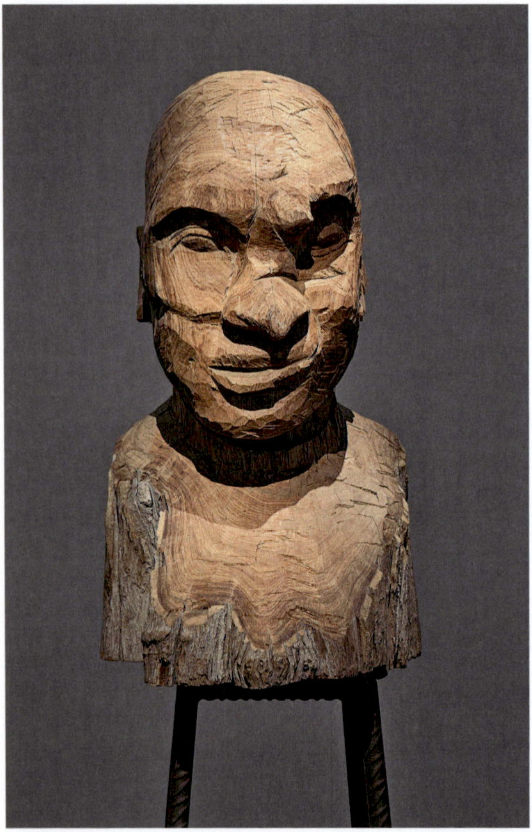

208

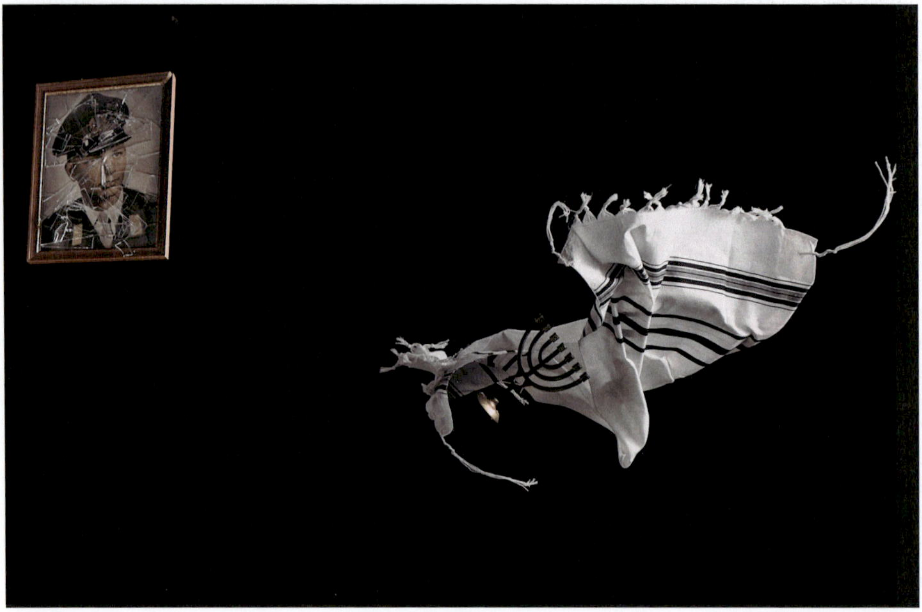

Kader Attia, Culture, Another Nature Repaired, 2014
Yael Bartana, Tashlikh (Cast Off), 2017

207

Kader Attia (Dugny, 1970)
Culture, Another Nature Repaired, 2014
Wood and metal support, 221 × 50 × 50 cm
Acquisition, 2015. Inv. 2015-140

For nearly twenty years, Kader Attia has been interested in the question of repair, understood in both senses, as the action of repairing – an object, a wound – and reparation. Hence the importance of the object and the archive in his work as the tangible traces of history and of the wounds that require reparation. The space of the installation then becomes a space of memory, but also a space for rethinking the intrinsic links between political, personal and aesthetic histories that are distinct in appearance.

The series of busts, *Culture, Another Nature Repaired* (2014), from which the Museum has three works, was created in collaboration with artisans in Bamako (Mali) and Brazzaville (Republic of the Congo). Conceived using photographs of soldiers mutilated in the First World War (known as *gueules cassées* in France), it offers another reading of the cultural transfers and exchanges between the African and European continents, continuing along the lines of *The Repair from Occident to Extra-Occidental Cultures*, the monumental work conceived by Attia in 2012 for dOCUMENTA (13). Indeed, if these busts remind us that the great figures of modern Western art history – from the German expressionists to artists like Georges Braque and Pablo Picasso – were inspired by the Other, such was their fascination with African sculpture, then this sculpture here presents its own vision of Western man in all his destructive savagery.

If we remember that the Great War was 'global', that many of the belligerent nations were also nations that colonised sub-Saharan and North Africa, and that they recruited large numbers of soldiers from that part of the world, that after the war the more or less long-term consequences for the colonised countries were disastrous, then the significance of Attia's proposition becomes clear. In his work, the artist poses the question of what can be done now to repair, to make reparation for history. [NS]

208

Yael Bartana (Kfar Yehezkel, 1970)
Tashlikh (Cast Off), 2017
Video, colour, sound, 11 min 5 sec, ed. 4/6
Acquisition, 2017. Inv. 2017-022

Yael Bartana shot her first videos at the turn of the millennium, and has since built a body of work that shifts between a documentary approach and the fictional construction of historical events and even political utopias. Her work reflects her fascination with ceremonies and social ritual and their role in building communities and individuals.

The video installation *Tashlikh (Cast Off)* takes its title from the tashlikh ritual, held to mark the Jewish New Year. It involves throwing small bits of bread or other objects into a stream, symbolically casting off the sins of the past year and preparing for the year to come. The video is a sort of invitation to a collective tashlikh ceremony, or at least a record of such an event.

Objects are filmed in slow motion against a black background, falling at different rates, singly or in groups, with a hypnotic soundtrack of wind or waves, a roaring aeroplane, a blasting siren, a voice counting down, interspersed with moments of silence. A life jacket, photographs, letters, newspapers, a prayer shawl, uniforms, a rifle, yellow stars, flags, crockery – the objects are both part of the private sphere and touching upon a broader context. Each represents an episode of collective trauma, from the Armenian genocide to the Eritrean civil war, the Holocaust and the Nakba. Yet the victims are not alone in telling their stories: their persecutors also share in the tashlikh. The objects are the tangible trace of a history, of all these histories, as well as the protagonists of a fictional moment staged by the artist. In this sense, *Tashlikh (Cast Off)* is part of Bartana's overarching exploration of the construction of individual identities and collective memory. [NS]

209

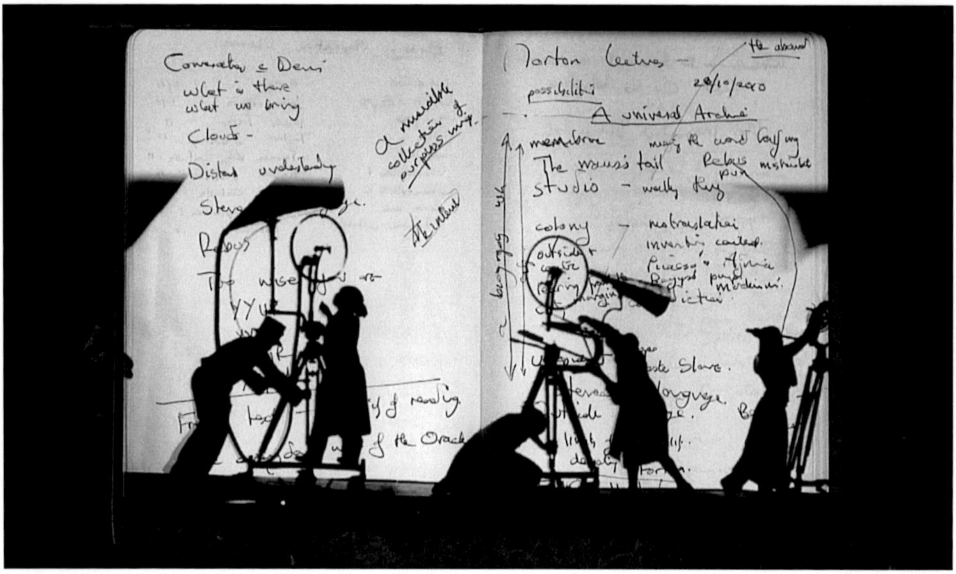

210

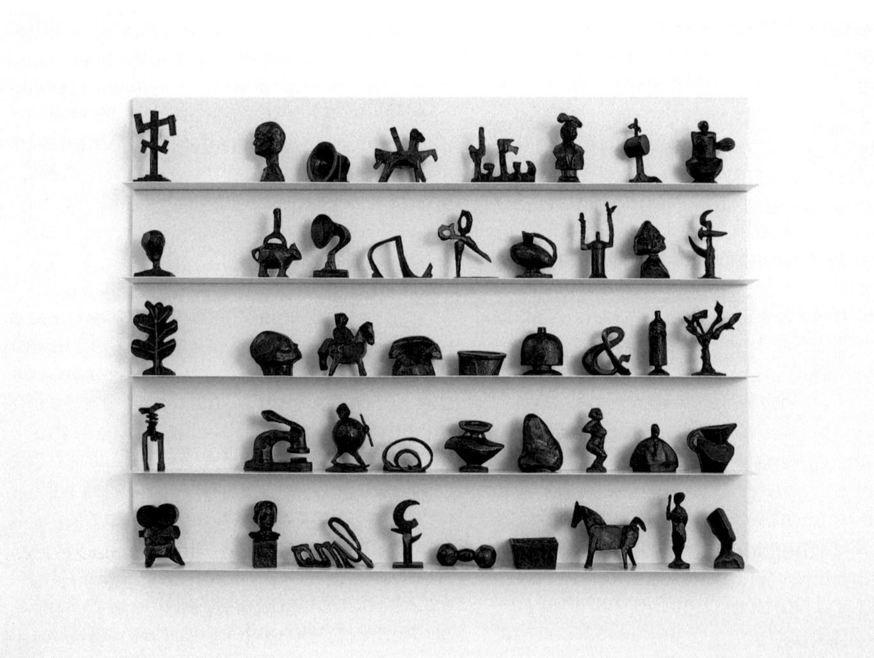

William Kentridge, Anti-Mercator, 2010–11
William Kentridge, Lexicon, Paragraph I, 2017

209

William Kentridge (Johannesburg, 1955)
Anti-Mercator, 2010–11
High-definition film transferred to video, b/w, sound, 9 min 45 sec, ed. 1/7
Acquisition, 2019. Inv. 2019-074

Born in Johannesburg, South Africa, William Kentridge was deeply marked by the country's political and social context. He studied political science and theatre before turning to drawing in the mid-1970s, eventually developing a body of work in charcoal that led to his first animated shorts. The drawings for his animations are always produced successively on the same sheet of paper, with the traces of previous erasures and alterations visible alongside the new drawings, reflecting Kentridge's stance on time and history as non-linear processes.

Anti-Mercator is one of the works Kentridge created in preparation for the installation *The Refusal of Time* at dOCUMENTA (13) in Kassel in 2012. It feeds into his research on the understanding of time and the measuring of space as tools of modernity and instruments of control and power. The title references Gerardus Mercator (1512–94), inventor of the map projection named after him and author of a chart that proved vital to navigators at a time when Europe was extending its territorial reach. The projection is still used to this day, though it distorts the size of various countries, particularly in Africa.

Kentridge's notebook fills the screen. The artist alternately leafs though it, draws in it, and writes sentences that refer to various conceptions of time and space, from Isaac Newton's linear time to Albert Einstein's theory of special relativity. A metronome keeps time, voices are heard, music lends the pictures rhythm, and Kentridge himself appears on the screen, walking at the front of his outsized notebook and then running as hard as he can across the pages as they are leafed backward. The film closes with a silhouetted marching band parading across the pages and a couple dancing as if to defy gravity and breathe fresh life into the present moment. [NS]

210

William Kentridge (Johannesburg, 1955)
Lexicon, Paragraph I, 2017
Bronze, 135 × 180 × 15 cm, ed. 7/8
Alice Pauli Donation, 2017. Inv. 2017-032

William Kentridge grew up in a South Africa marked by the apartheid regime (1948–91). Having studied theatre as well as the fine arts, but also political science and African studies, he has always produced work with a strong political character. Indeed, as he sees it, art is necessarily political.

He made his first animation film in 1989 (*Johannesburg, 2nd Greatest City after Paris*). This laid the foundations of his aesthetic, with drawing in charcoal, powdery material that records every trace yet is easily erased whereby the illusion of movement is given, not by the chronological succession of images, but by the evolution of a motif that is redrawn several times on the same sheet, and the importance of the sound track. Kentridge also makes prints, performances and sculptures; these media speak to each other through his work.

Lexicon, Paragraph I, like other series of small bronze sculptures, such as *Promenade II* (2002), reprises motifs and ideas from the artist's earlier works, which themselves originated in his notebooks. Here, for example, we find the nose from the opera *The Nose* premiered in 2010, a head from the frieze *Triumphs and Laments* (2016) and the recurring figure of the horse. These 'sculptural glyphs', as the artist calls them, or in other words, typographic characters, form a lexicon of 'Kentridgean' signs. Their aim is universal: self-reference combines with numerous memories and influences of different cultures and periods (Mexican ornaments and a Ghanaian head seen in museums, but also evocations of Pablo Picasso, Alberto Giacometti and Salvador Dalí). Each viewer can appropriate and interpret these signs as they wish and invent their own language. Although these bronze figures seem permanently fixed, in apparent contradiction with the ever evolving forms that Kentridge draws, movement reappears through the mental play of a multitude of possible combinations. [LSCH]

211

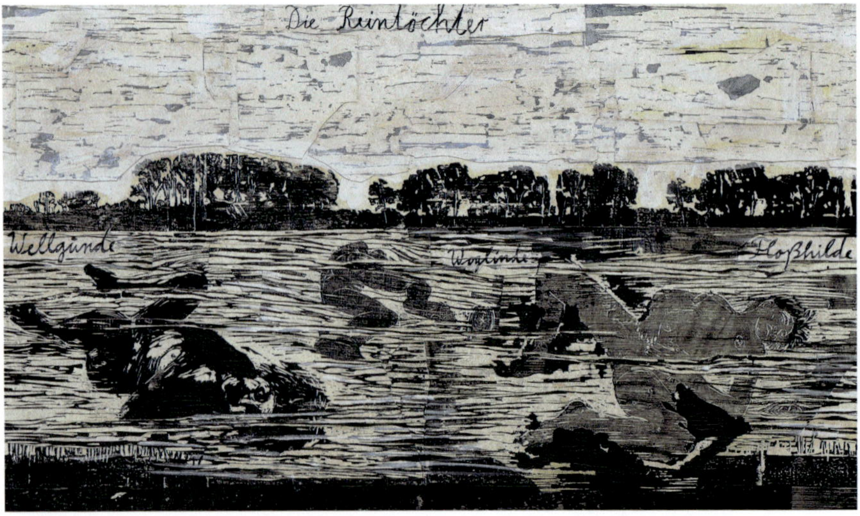

212

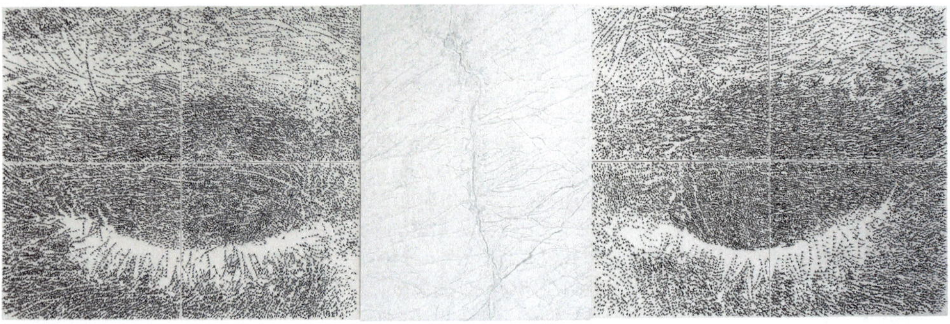

Anselm Kiefer, Die Rheintöchter, 1982–2013
Giuseppe Penone, A occhi chiusi, 2018

211

Anselm Kiefer (Donaueschingen, 1945)
Die Rheintöchter (*The Rhinemaldens*), 1982–2013
Collage of woodblock engraving, acrylic, and varnish on canvas, 190 × 330 cm
Alice Pauli Donation, 2016. Inv. 2017-004

This monumental work is part of a set of works on the Rhine, near Anselm Kiefer's childhood home, as a cultural symbol and a border. It refers particularly to the Nordic myth of the Daughters of the Rhine, tasked by their father with protecting the gold hidden in its bed. Kiefer's entire oeuvre explores the memory and history of his native Germany, bearing the traumatic traces of the Second World War. In this work, the artist refers to the *Nibelungenlied*, an epic poem dating from the early thirteenth century and rediscovered in the nineteenth, when it became the nation's founding myth and inspired Richard Wagner's *Der Ring des Nibelungen* (*Ring Cycle*, 1849–76).

Kiefer's composition is the work of over twenty years, its materiality reflecting the process of creation by hand. It is a collage of several black woodblock print fragments worked in with acrylic. The oblong format features the massive bodies of three water nymphs in the foreground, pushing the viewer back from the image. Wellgunde, Woglinde and Flosshilde, who is holding a candle, float on the water like logs swept along by the current, their benumbed bodies lying splayed wide. Yet their parted thighs and nudity are by no means lascivious. The work includes the punning words 'Die Reintöchter', 'rein' being German for 'pure'. Kiefer may consider them pure of political instrumentalisation or he may be referring to their innocence in the face of danger.

Kiefer's first woodblock engravings date from 1974. The Rhine became a theme in his woodblock work in the early 1980s, though he considered the technique to run counter to the river's very nature. The wood's resistance countered the fluidity of the water and the two-colour process was incapable of capturing its myriad hues. He used the radical process to recover the integrity of nature. [LSCH]

212

Giuseppe Penone (Garessio, 1947)
A occhi chiusi (*With Eyes Closed*), 2018
Carrare marble, acacia thorns, glass microspheres, acrylic on canvas, 200 × 630 cm
Alice Pauli Donation, 2018. Inv. 2018-149

Giuseppe Penone spent his early years in the countryside, giving him an inalienable sense of the importance of the bond between humans and nature and the often invisible ways in which they impact each other. This is the main theme of his art. *A occhi chiusi*, created half a century after his earliest works, is the perfect synthesis of his artistic career.

The central part of the grand triptych is made of a white marble plaque whose veins have been carved out. Penone lays bare the inner life of the marble, which resembles a vastly enlarged patch of human skin, evoking depth and yet at the same time the superficiality of skin. On either side of the plaque, he has drawn two huge closed eyes using acacia thorns. He shares the surrealist credo: with our eyes closed, our imagination – literally the faculty of picturing images – is greater than ever. The eyes here are shown as negatives, with white lashes and dark eyelids. Vision is thus doubly inverted, the closed eyes blinded, the light reversed, leading paradoxically to a limitless field of vision.

The thousands of acacia thorns, their tips pointing outwards, do not represent the artist's penetrating gaze as is the case for Alberto Giacometti's surrealist *Pointe à l'œil (Relations désagrégeantes)* (c. 1931–2, Paris, Centre Pompidou). Instead, they represent the almost infinite expanse of points of contact in our skin and nerve endings capable of registering touch. The body symbolised by the relief includes the mineral, animal, and plant kingdoms, a body in all its states, and an interface for connecting with the world. [BF]

1. Books on the Musée cantonal des Beaux-Arts de Lausanne collection

René Berger (ed.), *Promenade au Musée cantonal des Beaux-Arts*, Lausanne, Crédit suisse, 1970.

Erika Billeter (ed.), *Chefs-d'œuvre du Musée cantonal des Beaux-Arts, Lausanne. Regards sur 150 tableaux*, Lausanne, Musée cantonal des Beaux-Arts, 1989.

Erika Billeter (ed.), *Sculptures du Musée cantonal des Beaux-Arts Lausanne. Œuvres choisies*, Lausanne, Musée cantonal des Beaux-Arts, 1990.

Catherine Lepdor, Patrick Schaefer and Jörg Zutter, *La collection du Musée des Beaux-Arts, Lausanne*, Bern, Société d'histoire de l'art en Suisse, 1994 (coll. 'Guide des monuments suisses').

Catherine Lepdor and Jörg Zutter (eds.), *La collection du Dr Henri-Auguste Widmer au Musée cantonal des Beaux-Arts de Lausanne*, Lausanne, Musée cantonal des Beaux-Arts, Milan, Skira, 1998.

Catherine Lepdor, Patrick Schaefer and Jörg Zutter, *Musée cantonal des Beaux-Arts Lausanne*, Zurich, Institut suisse pour l'étude de l'art, Geneva, Banque Paribas (Suisse) S.A., 1998.

2. 'Les Cahiers du Musée des Beaux-Arts de Lausanne' Series

William Hauptman, *Charles Gleyre. La danse des Bacchantes*, 1995 (n. 1).

Catherine Lepdor, Patrick Schaefer and Jörg Zutter, *La genèse des formes. Œuvres sur papier de la collection*, 1995 (n. 2).

Anne Dary, Catherine Lepdor, Patrick Schaefer and Jörg Zutter, *Identités et affinités. Art suisse contemporain dans la collection du Musée des Beaux-Arts, Lausanne*, 1995 (n. 3).

Bettina Baumgärtel, Lucien Boissonnas, Laurent Golay, Pascal Griener, Myra Nan Rosenfeld, Marie-Dominique Sanchez and Dieter Ulrich, *Entre Rome et Paris. Œuvres inédites du XIV*[e] *au XIX*[e] *siècle*, 1996 (n. 4).

Jean-Paul Bouillon, Jura Brüschweiler, Rudolf Koella, Catherine Lepdor, Patrick Schaefer and Jörg Zutter, *De Vallotton à Dubuffet. Une collection en mouvement, acquisitions, dons, prêts*, 1996 (n. 5).

Catherine Lepdor, Didier Ottinger, Patrick Schaefer and Jörg Zutter, *Le Miroir vivant. René Magritte, Marcel Broodthaers, Bruce Nauman, Markus Raetz*, 1997 (n. 6).

Mauro Natale (ed.), Laurence Barghouth, Stéphane Cecconi, Sarah Clar-Boson, Sylvie Costa Paillet, Karin Défago et al., *Peintures et sculptures italiennes et espagnoles. Collections du Musée cantonal des Beaux-Arts de Lausanne*, 1998 (n. 7).

Jörg Zutter (ed.), Bernard Ceysson, *Un musée pour demain? L'art contemporain dans des collections privées vaudoises*, 1999 (n. 8).

Danielle Chaperon, Petra ten-Doesschate Chu, Catherine Lepdor, Paul Müller, Caroline Nicod and Jörg Zutter, *Le sommeil ou quand la raison s'absente*, 1999 (n. 9).

Christine Burckhardt-Seebass, Elizabeth Fischer, Ursula Karbacher, Catherine Lepdor and Corinne Walker, *Modes et tableaux. Œuvres de la collection et costumes de 1700 aux années folles*, 2000 (n. 10).

Dominique Radrizzani (ed.), Charlotte Contesse Barraud, Astrid Berglund, Julie Enckell et al., *L'attrait du trait. Dessins anciens et modernes de la collection*, 2001 (n. 11).

Catherine Lepdor, *Félix Vallotton. La vie recomposée*, 2002 (n. 12).

Ralf Beil (ed.), Corinne Bolle and Dominique Radrizzani, *Le monde selon François Dubois, peintre de la Saint-Barthélemy*, 2004 (n. 13).

Nicole Schweizer (ed.), Nathalie Bäschlin, Rachel Mader, *Interactions fictives. L'art vidéo dans les collections*, 2004 (n. 14).

Christine Giacomotti and Catherine Lepdor, *1906–2006. Cent ans d'expositions au Musée cantonal des Beaux-Arts de Lausanne*, 2007 (n. 15).

Frédéric Elsig, *Peintures des écoles du Nord (XVI*[e]*-XVIII*[e] *siècles). Collections du Musée des Beaux-Arts de Lausanne*, 2007 (n. 16).

Nicole Schweizer (ed.), Robert Ireland, Bernard Voïta, Yves Mettler, David Hominal, Anne-Julie Raccoursier, Jean Crotti, Elisabeth Llach, Pauline Boudry / Renate Lorenz and Luc Aubort, *9 = 10. Dix ans d'Accrochage [Vaud]*, 2012 (n. 17).

Frédéric Elsig (ed.), Angela Benza, Vincent Chenal, Geneviève Dutoit et al., *De la Renaissance au Romantisme. Peintures*

françaises et anglaises du Musée cantonal des Beaux-Arts de Lausanne, 2013 (n. 18).
Anne van de Sandt, *Les Frères Jacques et François Sablet. Collections du Musée cantonal des Beaux-Arts de Lausanne*, 2015 (n. 19).

3. Catalogues related to the Salons internationaux de galeries-pilotes

René Berger and Raymonde Moulin, *1er Salon international de galeries-pilotes: artistes et découvreurs de notre temps*, exh. cat. Lausanne, Musée cantonal des Beaux-Arts, 1963.
René Berger, *2e Salon international de galeries-pilotes: artistes et découvreurs de notre temps*, exh. cat. Lausanne, Musée cantonal des Beaux-Arts, 1966.
René Berger, *3e Salon international de galeries-pilotes: artistes et découvreurs de notre temps*, exh. cat. Lausanne, Musée cantonal des Beaux-Arts, Paris, Musée d'Art moderne de la Ville de Paris, 1970.
Yves Aupetitallot and Catherine Lepdor (eds.), *g.p. 1.2.3. Le Salon international de galeries-pilotes à Lausanne 1963 1966 1970 / The International Show of Pilot Galleries at Lausanne 1963 1966 1970*, exh. cat. Lausanne, Musée cantonal des Beaux-Arts, 2002.

4. Solo exhibition catalogues published since the 1980s

Bernard Wyder, *Jean Otth. Peintures au spray sur papier et sur toile de coton 1982–1984*, exh. cat. Lausanne, Musée cantonal des Beaux-Arts, 1983 (coll. 'Regard sur le présent', n. 5).
Marie Helène Cornips and Dieter Koepplin, *Martin Disler. Dessins 1968–1983 et le tableau monumental de 1982 'Ouverture d'une fosse commune,'* exh. cat. Lausanne, Musée cantonal des Beaux-Arts, Basel, Museum für Gegenwartskunst, 1983 (coll. 'Regard sur le présent', n. 6).
Erika Billeter, Jean-Pierre Cuzin, Maria Elisa Tittoni Monti and Anne van de Sandt, *Les frères Sablet (1775–1815). Peintures, dessins, gravures*, exh. cat. Lausanne, Musée cantonal des Beaux-Arts, Nantes, Musées départementaux de Loire-Atlantique, Rome, Musée de Rome, Palazzo Braschi, Rome, Edizioni Carte Segrete, 1985.
Erika Billeter and Silvie et Chérif Defraoui, *Silvie et Chérif Defraoui. 'Figures', 1981–1985*, exh. cat. Lausanne, Musée cantonal des Beaux-Arts, Villefranche-sur-Saône, Centre d'arts plastiques, 1985 (coll. 'Regard sur le présent', n. 7).
Erika Billeter and Friedhelm Mennekes, *Arnulf Rainer / Louis Soutter. Les doigts peignent / Die Finger malen*, exh. cat. Lausanne, Musée cantonal des Beaux-Arts, Francfort, Schirn Kunsthalle Frankfurt, Linz, Neue Galerie der Stadt Linz / Wolfgang-Gurlitt-Museum, 1986.
Luc Boissonnas, Enrico Castelnuovo, Pierre Chessex, Francis Haskell, Olivier Masson, Westby Percival Prescott and Lindsay Stainton, *Images of the Grand Tour. Louis Ducros 1748–1810*, exh. cat. London, The Iveaghe Bequest, Kenwood, Manchester, The Withworth Art Gallery, University of Manchester, Lausanne, Musée cantonal des Beaux-Arts, Geneva, Éditions du Tricorne, 1986
Bernard Wyder, *Anker. Chroniques intemporelles. Catalogue raisonné des œuvres d'Albert Anker au Musée cantonal des Beaux-Arts de Lausanne*, [Lausanne], [Musée cantonal des Beaux-Arts], [1987].
Erika Billeter, *Luciano Castelli. Images / Bilder 1872–1988*, exh. cat. Lausanne, Musée cantonal des Beaux-Arts, 1989.
Erika Billeter, Silvio Blatter and Peter Bürger, *Rolf Iseli*, exh. cat. Lausanne, Musée cantonal des Beaux-Arts, 1990.
Jérôme Baratelli and Marie-Claude Jequier, *Alain Huck. Autre chose encore*, exh. cat. Lausanne, Musée cantonal des Beaux-Arts, Lausanne, Placette, 1990.
Lesley K. Baier (ed.), Marina Ducrey, Rihard S. Field, Deborah L. Goodman et al., *Vallotton*, exh. cat. New Haven, Yale University Art Gallery, Houston, Museum of Fine Arts, Indianapolis, Indianapolis Museum of Arts, Amsterdam, Rijksmuseum Vincent Van Gogh, Lausanne, Musée cantonal des Beaux-Arts, New York/London/Paris, Abbeville Press, 1991.
Jörg Zutter (ed.), Franz Meyer and Jörg Zutter, *Bruce Nauman. Sculptures et installations, 1985–1990*, exh. cat.

Lausanne, Musée cantonal des Beaux-Arts, Brussels, Ludion, 1991.

Marie Luise Syring (ed.), Ralf Lauter, *Bill Viola. Unseen Images = nie gesehene Bilder = images jamais vues*, exh. cat. Düsseldorf, Kunsthalle, Stockholm Moderna Museet, Madrid, Museo Nacional Centro de Arte Reina Sofía, Lausanne, Musée cantonal des Beaux-Arts, Geneva, Saint-Gervais, Londres, Whitechapel Art Gallery, Düsseldorf, R. Meyer, 1992.

Jörg Zutter (ed.), *Balthus*, exh. cat. Lausanne, Musée cantonal des Beaux-Arts, Geneva, Skira, 1993.

Jörg Zutter and Raymond Farquet, *Christian Boltanski. Les Suisses morts: liste des Suisses morts dans le canton du Valais en 1991*, exh. cat. Lausanne, Musée cantonal des Beaux-Arts, Vevey, Éditions de l'Aire, 1993.

Jörg Zutter (ed.), Fernand Auberjonois, Oskar Bätschmann, Doris Jakubec, Claire de Ribaupierre et al., *René Auberjonois*, exh. cat. Lausanne, Musée cantonal des Beaux-Arts, Geneva, Skira, 1994.

Thomas de Kayser, *Thomas Huber. Arrêt sur l'image*, exh. cat. Lausanne, Musée cantonal des Beaux-Arts, Darmstadt, Jürgen Häusser, 1996.

Anic Zanzi, Danielle Zombath and Jörg Zutter, *Giovanni Giacometti*, exh. cat. Lausanne, Musée cantonal des Beaux-Arts, 1997.

Jörg Zutter (ed.), Pierre Chessex, Didier Prioul and Lindsay Stainton, *Abraham-Louis-Rodolphe Ducros: un peintre suisse en Italie*, exh. cat. Lausanne, Musée cantonal des Beaux-Arts, Québec, Musée du Québec, Milan, Skira, 1998.

Catherine Lepdor and Jörg Zutter (ed.), Nathalie Chollet Bel Hadj, Salome Maurer Gafner, Patrick Schaefer and Christophe Vögele, *Ernest Biéler, 1863–1948. Du réalisme à l'Art nouveau / Vom Realismus zum Jugendstil*, exh. cat. Lausanne, Musée cantonal des Beaux-Arts, Solothurn, Kunstmuseum Solothurn, Milan, Skira, 1999.

Jean-Paul Monery and Jörg Zutter (ed.), Dario Gamboni et Jean-Paul Monery, *Édouard Vuillard. La porte entrebâillée*, exh. cat. Lausanne, Musée cantonal des Beaux-Arts, Saint-Tropez, Musée de l'Annonciade, Milan, Skira, 2000.

Anne-Catherine Krüger, Catherine Lepdor and Gabriel P. Weisberg, *Louise Breslau. De l'impressionnisme aux années folles*, exh. cat. Lausanne, Musée cantonal des Beaux-Arts, Milan, Skira, Paris, Seuil, 2001.

Catherine Lepdor, Caroline Nicod, Doris van Drathen et al., *Leiko Ikemura. Les années lumière – Lichtjahre*, exh. cat. Lausanne, Musée cantonal des Beaux-Arts, Milan, Skira, 2001.

Hartwig Fischer (ed.), Hartwig Fischer, Heinz Holliger, Lucienne Peiry, Jean Starobinski and Michel Thévoz, *Louis Soutter 1871–1942*, exh. cat. Basel, Kunstmuseum, Lausanne, Musée cantonal des Beaux-Arts, Lausanne, Collection de l'Art Brut, Ostfildern, Hatje Cantz Verlag, 2002.

Lionel Bovier, Christophe Cherix, Paul Eli Ivey, Michel Gauthier et al., *Olivier Mosset. Arbeiten/Works 1966-2003*, exh. cat. Lausanne, Musée cantonal des Beaux-Arts, St. Gallen, Kunstmuseum St. Gallen, Santa Fe, SITE, Milan, 5 Continents Editions, 2003.

Ralf Beil (ed.), Thomas Groetz and F. Javier Panera Cuevas, *Albert Oehlen. Paintings/Pinturas 1980–2004. Selbstportrait mit 50millionenfacher Lichtgeschwindigkeit / Self-Portrait at 50 Million Times the Speed of Light / Autorretrato a una velocidad cincuenta millones de veces superior a la de la luz*, exh. cat. Lausanne, Musée cantonal des Beaux-Arts, Salamanca, Domus Artium 2002. Fundación Salamanca Ciudad de Cultura y Saberes, Nuremberg, Kunsthalle Nürnberg, Zurich, JRP Ringier, 2004.

Philippe Kaenel and Catherine Lepdor, *Eugène Burnand (1850–1921): peintre naturaliste*, exh. cat. Lausanne, Musée cantonal des Beaux-Arts, Milan, 5 Continents Editions, 2004.

Yves Aupetitallot (ed.), Ralf Beil and Catherine Macchi de Vilhena, *Didier Rittener*, exh. cat. Lausanne, Musée cantonal des Beaux-Arts, St. Gallen, Neue Kunst Halle St. Gallen, Zurich, JRP Ringier, 2005.

Paul-André Jaccard, *Alice Bailly. La fête étrange*, exh. cat. Lausanne, Musée cantonal des Beaux-Arts, Milan, 5 Continents Editions, 2005.

Florence Derieux (ed.), George Baker, Stuart Comer, Florence Derieux and Cerith Wyn Evans, *Tom Burr. Extrospective. Works 1994-2006*, exh. cat. Lausanne, Musée cantonal des Beaux-Arts, Zurich, JRP Ringier, 2006.

Catherine Lepdor (ed.), Marie Alamir, Thérèse Burollet, Patrick Shaw Cable et al., *Charles Gleyre. Le génie de l'invention*, exh. cat. Lausanne, Musée cantonal des Beaux-Arts, 2006.
David Hominal, Nicolas Pages and Philippe Pirotte, David Hominal. *You'll Never Walk Alone*, exh. cat. Lausanne, Musée cantonal des Beaux-Arts, 2007.
Nicole Schweizer (ed.), Georges Didi-Huberman, Griselda Pollock, Jacques Rancière, *Alfredo Jaar. The Politics of Images*, exh. cat. Lausanne, Musée cantonal des Beaux-Arts, Zurich, JRP Ringier, 2007.
Nicole Schweizer, *Anne-Julie Raccoursier*, exh. cat. Lausanne, Musée cantonal des Beaux-Arts, 2008.
Philippe Kaenel, in collaboration with Catherine Lepdor, *Steinlen, l'œil de la rue*, exh. cat. Lausanne, Musée cantonal des Beaux-Arts, Brussels, Musée communal d'Ixelles, Milan, 5 Continents Editions, 2008.
Nicole Schweizer (ed.), Nora Alter, Diedrich Diederichsen, Kobena Mercer, Catherine Quéloz et al., *Renée Green. Ongoing Becomings*, exh. cat. Lausanne, Musée cantonal des Beaux-Arts, Zurich, JRP Ringier, 2009.
Nicole Schweizer (ed.), Catherine Othenin-Girard, Hans Rudolf Reust and Nicole Schweizer, *Jean-Luc Manz. Peintures 1984-2010*, exh. cat. Lausanne, Musée cantonal des Beaux-Arts, Zurich, Edition Fink, 2010 (coll. 'Binding Sélection d'artistes', n. 35).
Whitney Chadwick, Doris von Drathen, Bernard Fibicher and Andreas Huyssen, *Nalini Malani. Splitting the Other. Retrospective 1992-2009*, exh. cat. Lausanne, Musée cantonal des Beaux-Arts, Ostfildern, Hatje Cantz Verlag, 2010.
Mathias Danbolt, Diedrich Diederichsen, Elizabeth Freeman, Denis Pernet, Marc Siegel and Andrea Thal, *Pauline Boudry & Renate Lorenz, Temporal Drag*, exh. cat. Lausanne, Musée cantonal des Beaux-Arts, Geneva, Centre d'art contemporain, Ostfildern, Hatje Cantz Verlag, 2011.
Catherine Lepdor (ed.), Marie-Ève Celio-Scheurer, Danielle Chaperon, Philippe Kaenel et al., *Eugène Grasset. L'art et l'ornement*, exh. cat. Lausanne, Musée cantonal des Beaux-Arts, Milan, 5 Continents Editions, 2011.
Catherine Lepdor, Sarah Lombardi Schlittler, Pascale Marini-Jeanneret, Céline Muzelle and Jacqueline Porret-Forel, *Aloïse. Le ricochet solaire*, exh. cat. Lausanne, Musée cantonal des Beaux-Arts, Lausanne, Collection de l'Art Brut, Chigny, Fondation Aloïse, Milan, 5 Continents Editions, 2012.
Bernard Fibicher (ed.), Bernard Fibicher, Catherine Lepdor, Camille Lévêque-Claudet and Éric de Chassey, *Peinture. Alex Katz & Félix Vallotton*, exh. cat. Lausanne, Musée cantonal des Beaux-Arts, Milan, 5 Continents Editions, 2013.
Nicole Schweizer (ed.), Amelia Barikin, Rebecca Lamarche-Vadel and Nadim Samman, *Julian Charrière. Future Fossil Spaces*, exh. cat. Lausanne, Musée cantonal des Beaux-Arts, Milan, Mousse Publishing, 2014.
Nicole Schweizer (ed.), Brigitte Derlon, Noémie Étienne, Monique Jeudy-Ballini and Kobena Mercer, *Kader Attia*, exh. cat. Lausanne, Musée cantonal des Beaux-Arts, Zurich, JRP Ringier, 2015.
Nicole Schweizer (ed.), *Yael Bartana*, Lausanne, Musée cantonal des Beaux-Arts, Zurich, JRP Ringier, 2017.

Musée cantonal des Beaux-Arts de Lausanne. Guide to the Collection

Museum Director:
Bernard Fibicher, Director

Editorial Coordinator:
Laurence Schmidlin, Curator, assisted by Camille de Alencastro, Assistant Curator

Authors:
Bernard Fibicher, Director [BF];
Catherine Lepdor, Chief Curator [CL];
Camille Lévêque-Claudet, Curator [CLC];
Laurence Schmidlin, Curator [LSCH];
Nicole Schweizer, Curator [NS];
Camille de Alencastro, Assistant Curator [CdA]; as well as Yves Guignard [YG] and Michel Thévoz [MTh]

Translators:
Charles Penwarden, Susan Pickford

Copy Editor:
Lisa Rosenblatt

Proofreader:
Charlotte Eckler
Nicole Schweizer

Graphic design:
Farner Schalcher, Zurich;
Simone Farner, Naima Schalcher

Photolithographer:
Datatype S.A., Lausanne

Printing and Binding:
DZA Druckerei zu Altenburg GmbH, Thuringia

Papers:
Invercote G, 280 g/m2 (cover)
Profimatt, 115 g/m2 (inside pages)

Cover:
Giuseppe Penone, *Luce e ombra*, 2011

Acknowledgements:
We wish to thank the artists and everyone who has been involved in the completion of this publication: Yves André, Thomas Ballot, Muriel Blancho, Célia Boldrini, Nathalie Boutin, Antoni Burzyński, Daniela Cadosch, Elizabeth Callinicos, Michael Chappuis, Edmond Charrière, Cyprien David, Kathy DeLap, Eleonora Di Erasmo, Antje Ehmann, Matthieu Gafsou, David Gagnebin-de Bons, Roman Grabner, Irene Grundel, Katharina Grünner, Caroline Guignard, Julien Gremaud, Nicola Hederich, Christine Humpl, Paul-André Jaccard, Mary Jane Jacob, Jean-Marie Jaccottet, Laurence Jaccottet, Monique Jacot, Heidi Joye, Annika Karpowski, Bettina Kubli, Sarah Landry, David Lemaire, Anja Lindner, Sarah Lombardi, Olivier Masson, Lindsay McGuire, Isabelle Mercier, Jean-David Mermod, Vincent Monod, Matt Moravec, Davide Nerini, Virginie Otth, Philémon Otth, Françoise Peter, Johan Pijnappel, Laure Poupard, Ronja Primke, Nicolas Raboud, Daniel Scheidegger, Katja Schöppe, Michael Schuster, Arno Stein, Alain Tarica, Penelope Truitt, Jacqueline Nicod-Urban, Matthias Urban, Danielle Wu, Gene Zazzaro, Alma Zorlak, Michaela Züge Bruton, as well as the MCBA team.

PLATEFORME 10
Musée cantonal des Beaux-Arts
Place de la Gare 16
1003 Lausanne
Switzerland

Verlag Scheidegger & Spiess
Niederdorfstrasse 54
8001 Zurich
Switzerland
www.scheidegger-spiess.ch

Scheidegger & Spiess is being supported by the Federal Office of Culture with a general subsidy for the years 2016–2020.

ISBN 978-3-85881-850-8

MUSÉE CANTONAL DES BEAUX-ARTS LAUSANNE

Scheidegger & Spiess